The Rites of Assent

Transformations in the Symbolic Construction of America

Sacvan Bercovitch

Routledge
NEW YORK • LONDON

Published in 1993 by

Routledge
An imprint of Routledge, Chapman and Hall, Inc.
29 West 35th Street
New York, NY 10001

Published in Great Britain by

Routledge
11 New Fetter Lane
London EC4P 4EE

Library of Congress Cataloging-in-Publication Data

Bercovitch, Sacvan.
    The rites of assent / Sacvan Bercovitch.
      p.   cm.
    Includes bibliographical references (p.   ) and index.
    ISBN 0-415-90014-X (HB).—ISBN 0-415-90015-8 (PB)
    1. American literature—History and criticism. 2. United States—
Civilization. I. Title.
    PS92.B45 1992
    810.9—dc20   92-19999
                                                                       CIP
ISBN 0-415-90014-X (HB)
ISBN 0-415-90015-8 (PB)

Contents

In Memory and Anticipation:
Bryna and Alexander,
Eytan and Sascha

Acknowledgments

This book began as a collection of essays and then turned into a sustained argument that runs more or less chronologically from colonial Puritanism to current literary debates. The chapters (as I now term them) bear many marks of the original essays, most flagrantly perhaps in the documentation, which I have decided not to update. In part, this is an effort to keep the endnotes to a minimum—i.e., only to works cited. In part, it is a decision not to burden the argument with extrinsic, largely decorative or self-serving post facto references. This has meant excluding reference to many valuable studies—from, say, Kenneth Silverman's biography of Cotton Mather to Martin Lipset's comparatist study of Canada and the United States and Carl J. Guarneri's history of American Fourierism—which were published after the relevant essays were completed.

The essays themselves, however, have all been substantially revised, some of them rewritten, and large sections have been added. For permission to use the original materials I would like to thank the following (in order of publication):

1. University of Wisconsin Press, for "Cotton Mather," in *Major Writers of Early American Literature*, ed. Everett Emerson (1972)
2. University of Massachusetts Press, for "How the Puritans Won the American Revolution," *Massachusetts Review*, XVII (1976), 597–630
3. Trustees of the University of Pennsylvania, for "The Typology of America's Mission," *American Quarterly*, XXX (1978), 135–155
4. University of New Mexico Press, for "The Rites of Assent: Rhetoric, Ritual, and the Ideology of American Consensus," in *The American Self: Myth, Ideology, and Popular Culture*, ed. Sam B. Girgus (1980)

5. University of Chicago Press, for "The Problem of Ideology in American Literary History," *Critical Inquiry*, XII (1986), 631–653
6. Willhelm Fink Verlag, München, for "How to Read Melville's *Pierre*," *Amerikastudien*, XXXI (1986), 31–49
7. The Johns Hopkins University Press, for "The A-Politics of Ambiguity in *The Scarlet Letter*," *New Literary History*, XIX (1988), 629–654
8. University of California Press, for "Hawthorne's A-Morality of Compromise," *Representations*, XXIV (1988), 1–27
9. Duke University Press, for "Emerson, Individualism, and the Ambiguities of Dissent," *South Atlantic Quarterly*, LXXXIX (1989), 624–662
10. Stanford University Press, for "The Ends of American Puritan Rhetoric," in *Rhetoricity: History, Theory, Practice*, ed. John Bender and David Wellbury (1991)

I owe special thanks to Gerald Graff, who had the idea for gathering these materials in the first place, and to other friends and colleagues who have commented on earlier versions of various parts of the manuscript: Daniel Aaron, Gila Bercovitch, Michael Blumenthal, Lawrence Buell, Wai-Chee Dimock, Philip Fisher, Eugene Goodheart, Stephen Greenblatt, Myra Jehlen, Michael Kramer, Bruce Kucklik, Frank Lentricchia, Christopher Looby, Barbara Packer, Carolyn Porter, Marc Shell, Werner Sollors, Wendy Steiner, Eric Sundquist, Brook Thomas, Priscilla Wald, and Donald Weber. I am grateful to the staff at the American Antiquarian Society and at the Woodrow Wilson International Center for Scholars, where I wrote and revised much of the manuscript, and to my graduate assistant, Margaret Reid. Above all, for sustained and sustaining understanding, patience, advice, and love, my deepest thanks, once again, to my son Eytan Bercovitch, and to my wife, Susan L. Mizruchi.

1
Introduction:
The Music of America

When I first came to the United States, I knew virtually nothing about America. This book represents a long and varied effort to come to terms with what I discovered. From the start the terms of discovery were interchangeably personal and professional. What began as a graduate student's research issued in a series of investigations that express both a developing sense of the culture and a certain process of acculturation. The story they tell begins with the Puritan vision of the New World; it ends, provisionally, with the dissensus within American literary studies; and as it proceeds, the explication of religious types opens into descriptions of national rituals, strategies of symbolic cohesion, and the paradoxes of Emersonian individualism, then and now. It might be read as a scholar's journey into the American Self. But its strengths, such as they are, lie in the sustained discrepancy between the journey's subject and object. It is a principle of socialization in the United States that the discovery of America is converted into a process of self-discovery, whereby America is simultaneously internalized, universalized (as a set of self-evident absolutes), and naturalized (as a diversity of representative social, credal, racial, and ethnic selves). In my case, the shock of discovery proved a continuing barrier to Americanization. What I called the reciprocity between the personal and the professional has hinged on my ability to channel my resistance to the culture into a way of interpreting it.

I attribute my immigrant naiveté to the peculiar insularity of my upbringing. I was nurtured in the rhetoric of denial. To begin with, I absorbed Canada's provincial attitudes toward "The States"—a provinciality deepened by the pressures of geographical proximity and economic dependence. Characteristically, this expressed itself through a mixture of hostility and amnesia, as

1

though we were living next door to an invisible giant, whose invisibility could be interpreted as non-existence. This interpretation was reflected in the virtual absence of America throughout my education, from elementary and high school, where U.S. history ended in 1776, to my fortuitous college training at the adult extension of the Montreal YMCA, where a few unavoidable U.S. authors were taught as part of a course on Commonwealth literature. I learned certain hard facts, of course, mainly pejorative, and I knew the landmarks from Wall Street to Hollywood; but the symbology that connected them—the American dream which elsewhere (I later discovered) was an open secret, a mystery accredited by the world—remained hidden from me, like the spirit in the letter of the uninitiate's text.

A more important influence was the Yiddishist–left-wing world of my parents. I recall it as an outpost barricaded from the threat of assimilation by radical politics and belles lettres, an immigrant enclave locked into a Romantic–Marxist utopianism long after its disillusionment with Stalin, and fortified by the alleged spiritual values of art in the face of utter cultural estrangement. It was there, far more than at school, that I learned the strategies of denial. Their object in this case was Canada. I cannot recall a single reference to national matters in serious conversation. Literary discussions ranged from Shalom Aleichem to Franz Kafka, with polemical excursions to Yiddish contemporaries published in the local newspaper, *Der Keneder Odler* ("The Canadian Eagle," a mixed metaphor, carrying cross-cultural ironies for me even then). Politics consisted in a conflict of imaginary options for world revolution, extending from Trotsky's lost cause to the visionary boundaries of anarchism. It seems appropriate that I should have graduated from high school not to college, but, for several years, to a socialist kibbutz in what used to be called the Arabian Desert.

The harvest of these experiences was an abiding suspicion of high rhetoric, especially as a blueprint of the future, and an abiding fascination with the redemptive promises of language, especially as a source of personal identity and social cohesion. Still, nothing in my background had prepared me for my encounter with a secular modern nation living in a dream. "I hear America singing," writes Whitman, and concludes: "The United States are themselves the greatest poem." So, too, Emerson: "America is a poem in our eyes." I arrived at a similar conclusion, but from a different perspective and to a different effect. My experience of the music

of America (as I came to think of it) was closer to the epiphany of
otherness recorded in Kafka's "Investigations of a Dog." The canine narrator of that story tells us that one day in his youth a
group of seven dogs appeared before him, suddenly, "out of some
place of darkness," to the accompaniment of "terrible" and rav-
ishing sounds:

> At that time I still knew hardly anything of the creative gift with
> which the canine race alone is endowed . . . for though music had
> [always] surrounded me . . . my elders had [never] drawn my attention
> to it. . . . [A]ll the more astonishing, then . . . were those seven
> musical artists to me. They did not speak, they did not sing, they
> remained generally silent, almost determinedly silent; but from the
> empty air they conjured music. Everything was music, the lifting
> and setting of their feet, certain turns of the head, their running and
> standing still, the positions they took up in relation to one another,
> the symmetrical patterns which they produced. . . . [M]y mind could
> attend to nothing but this blast of music which seemed to come
> from all sides, from the heights, from the deeps, from everywhere,
> surrounding the listener, overwhelming him. . . . I longed to . . . beg
> [the musicians] to enlighten me, to ask them what they were doing.
> . . . [Their music] was incomprehensible to me, and also quite defi-
> nitely beyond my capacities. . . . I rushed about, told my story, made
> accusations and investigations. . . . I was resolved to pursue [the
> problem] indefatigably until I solved it.

The pursuit unfolds as a series of ingenious inferences, deductions,
and explications extending to virtually every aspect of "dogdom,"
from the higher laws of "universal dog nature" to the specialized
issue of "soaring dogs" (how do they "remain for the most part
high up in the air, apparently doing nothing but simply resting
there?") and the still-controversial "rules of science" for getting
food: should you use "incantation" to "bring it down" or "water
the ground as much as you can"?[1] Nothing, it seems, escapes
observation, except the presence of human beings.

Kafka's story is a great parable of interpretation as mystification—facts marshalled endlessly to build up contexts whose effect, if not intent, is to conceal or explain away. It is also a great
parable of the limitations of cultural critique—*limitations*, not
just illusions, for in fact the story conveys a good deal about the
dog's world, in spite of the narrator's inability to transcend it; or

rather, as a function of his non-transcending condition. In this double sense, negative and ambiguous, Kafka's "investigations" apply directly to my own as an Americanist. The general parallels may be drawn out through a Chinese box of skewed interpretive positions: dog vis-à-vis human, Russian–Jewish immigrant vis-à-vis French Canadian Montreal, Canada vis-à-vis The States, and eventually "America," as I came to understand it, vis-à-vis the cultural norms and structures it represents.

These are not precise symmetries; but they point to certain common principles of exegesis. I begin with the negative implications. (1) To interpret is not to make sense of a mystery "out there." It is to discover otherness as mystery (something "overwhelming," "incomprehensible"), and then to explain the mystery as the wonders of an invisible world, a realm of meaningful "silence," resonant with universals. (2) To investigate those wonders is not to come to terms with the new or unexpected. It is to domesticate the unknown by transferring the agency of meaning from the mystery "out there" to realities we recognize, and so to invest the familiar—ourselves, or our kind—with the powers of a higher reality: "universal laws," the view of eternity, the canine principles of music. (3) To establish the laws and rules of that higher reality is not to break through the limitations we experience. It is to deny our conditions of dependency by translating those limitations into meta-structures of culture, history, and the mind. As for motives, we may infer from Kafka's parable that they are self-defensive or self-aggrandizing, and that in either case interpretation is a strategy for repressing the actual worlds around us which expresses itself through yearnings for a world elsewhere.

We might call this the hermeneutics of transcendence. The possibilities it offers for self-aggrandizement are not far to seek: one need only think of the manifold uses of "he" for God and/or humanity. But this is to interpret from the vantage point of dominance. From the dog's subordinate point of view, or the scholar's, to magnify the categories of our containment is to diminish our capacities for understanding.*

A negative prospect, as I said, especially since it is Kafka's donnée that we have no choice but to interpret. However, it is

---

*This is repression in a familiar psycho-cultural sense: interpretation as a strategy for concealing our subjection to a master discourse. Again, the advantages are not far to seek—among these, evading the facts of subordination in ways that allow for compensatory modes of control—but the sense of reassurance this brings comes at the expense of critical awareness.

complemented in the parable by the *enabling* ambiguities of limitation. As the title suggests, "Investigations of a Dog" points not only to the dog's attempts to describe Kafka's world, but, at the same time, to Kafka's attempts to describe dogdom. And the result, as I interpret it, is not a double impasse. It is a model of cross-cultural criticism. Its terms are reciprocity, as against dichotomy: not canine *or* human, but the contingencies of both, as revealed (in degree) through the re-cognition of limitation. We might call this the hermeneutics of non-transcendence. It may be said to reverse traditional comparativist methods by its emphasis on the historicity of archetypes and essences. Its aim is not to harmonize "apparent" differences (in the manner of pluralist consensus), but on the contrary to highlight conflicting appearances, so as to explore the substantive differences they imply. This entails the recognition of universals as culture-specific barriers to understanding; it is grounded in the faith that barriers, so specified, may become (within limits) avenues of discovery; and although it may take many shapes, as I hope this book demonstrates, its logic may be briefly stated. If dreams of transcendence are indices to the traps of culture, then inquiry into the trapping process may provide insight both into our own and into others' actual non-transcending condition. Such insight is problematic, provisional, and *nourished* by a frustrating sense of boundaries. It denies us access to apocalypse, but it helps make our surrounding worlds visible.

I would like to think that the investigations which follow show the benefits of this approach. For purposes of analysis, I review these thematically, not chronologically. My subject is the discovery of an other America, in the double sense of Kafka's parable: negatively, as cultural otherness, and ambiguously, as a set of cultural secrets, the other America hidden from view by interpretation. Emerson's American Scholar grows concentrically toward transcendence, in an expanding circle from nature to books to representative selfhood. My own unrepresentative (not to say eccentric) experience may be described as a series of increasingly particularized border-crossings: first, into America proper; then, into the interdisciplinary field of American Studies; and finally, into the special area of American literary scholarship.

I crossed into The States with a Canadian's commonsense view of the Americas: two continents, North and South, each of

them a mosaic of nations—which is to say, a variety of European
models of civilization—joined by the semi-tropical bush countries
of Central America. How could I *not* see "America" as a cultural
artifact? I knew that that sort of definition applied to all national
identities—except Canada, which by consensus was "a country
without a mythology."[2] But if Canada was an exception that
proved the rule, America was its antithesis, the example par excellence of collective fantasy. Consider the claims of Puritan origins.
By comparison, myths of other national beginnings were plausible
at least. The mists of antiquity cover the claims of Siegfried and
King Arthur and the exiled Trojan heroes who sired Virgil's Rome.
Scripture itself authorizes Joshua's claims to Canaan. But we
know that the Puritans did not found the United States. In fact,
we know that by 1690, sixty years after the Great Migration and
a century before independence, not even the colony of Massachusetts was Puritan. Nonetheless, the belief in America's Puritan
ur-fathers was evident everywhere three centuries later, at every
ritual occasion, from Thanksgiving Day to July Fourth, throughout the literature, from Harriet Beecher Stowe to Thomas Pynchon, and in every form of literature, including endless debates
about whether or not the Puritan legacy was a good thing.

My chapters on Cotton Mather and Jonathan Edwards started
out as investigations of what appeared to me a cultural secret. I
expected to discover the creation of a national past, the invention
of a Puritan tradition commensurate with the needs of a modern
republic. Instead, as I traced the act of creation back through the
nineteenth into the eighteenth and seventeenth centuries, I found
that its roots lay with the Puritans after all.* The tradition *had*
been made up, as suspected, but it was built out of historical
materials, selected for historical reasons. The fantasy of Puritan
origins had worked because these Puritans represented (among
other things) the movement toward modernity, because they associated that movement with their prospects in the New World, and

*What I found has sometimes given me pause: Puritanism as a venture in
utopia; a group of radical idealists whose insulated immigrant enclave was meant
to provide a specimen of good things to come; a latter-day Zion at the vanguard of
history, fired by a vision that fused nostalgia and progress, prophecy and political
action. The analogies to the rhetoric of my own past seem so striking it still
surprises me that they did not occur to me at once, and stop me in my tracks. I prefer
to think of it in retrospect as a happy coincidence of history and subjectivity—an
example of the non-transcendent process of scholarly intuition.

because they developed a rhetoric that joined both these aspects of their venture, cultural and territorial, in a vision that was simultaneously distinctive, expansive, spiritual, and secular. Their major legacy was neither religious nor institutional. The Puritans are not particularly responsible for the Calvinist strain in the United States, or for civil religion, or for any particular democratic forms, not even the town meeting. They did not invent guilt, or the Protestant work ethic, or individualism, or contract society. All of these were in varying degrees part of the New England Way, and together they might be said to express its movement into modernity. But the distinctive contribution, it seemed to me, lay in the realm of symbology. The Puritans provided their heirs, in New England first and then the United States, with a useful, flexible, durable, and compelling fantasy of American identity.

I mean "compelling" in a descriptive, not a celebratory, sense. My discovery pertained to the historicity of myth, and the secret it yielded applied as well to my Canadian geography of the New World: what I had considered to be my neutral, commonsense view of the territory out there as an extension of various European civilizations. To see America as myth was to historicize the Canadian identity—i.e., to see in it the contours of another, complementary myth. I refer to the dominant vision of Canada: a "loose scattering of enclaves or outposts of culture and civilization," protected from a "hostile bush-country" by the Royal Canadian Mounted Police.[3] The Mountie is a symbolic figure in this design, of course. But the design itself represents a distinctive national fantasy, which I now saw as a variation of the same myth of conquest that had shaped the growth of the United States.

"Canada" was the *colonial* version of the myth, a story told by invaders who claimed authority for conquest from abroad— from European royalty and civilizations centered in England and France. "America" was the indigenous *imperialist* inversion. It relocated the seat of empire from the Old World to the New; it reversed the very meaning of "newness" from its colonial status of dependency to a declaration not just of independence but of superiority; and in this new sense it sanctified the "empty continent" as itself constituting the natural-divine patent for conquest. Gradually, the imperial counterpart to the bush-country police became the frontiersman, living in harmony with nature and yet the harbinger of civilization, a paradox explicable by the fact that the frontier itself had been transformed from its colonial sense of "barrier" into an imperial summons to expand.*

The issue, then, was not a clash of opposites, Canadian facts versus American fantasies. It was a juxtaposition of myths, colonial vis-à-vis imperial, each of them a border-land of fantasy and fact. The colonial version had issued in "Canada," a country with a mythology elsewhere, systematically de-centered, and characterized, accordingly, by a rhetoric of absence: non-Indian, non-European, non-American, non-mythological. The other, imperial issue was America. As I followed its changing terms of identity (Puritan errand, national mission, manifest destiny, the dream), the windings of language turned out to be the matter of history. America, an act of symbolic appropriation, came alive to me as the twin dynamics of empire: on the one hand, a process of violence unparalleled (proportionately) by even the Spanish conquistadors, and sustained into the twentieth century by a rhetoric of holy war against everything un-American; on the other hand, an unleashing of creative energies—enterprise, speculation, community-building, personal initiative, industry, confidence, idealism, and hope—unsurpassed by any other modern nation.

It amounted to a demonstration from within of Walter Benjamin's thesis about barbarism and civilization. Polemicizing against the tradition of empathy in historical studies—which literary critics have inherited as the tradition of aesthetic appreciation†—Ben-

---

*The image of the "bush country" (as formulated by Margaret Atwood and Northrop Frye) links two other widely accepted, quintessentially colonial definitions of Canadian identity: the special conditions of geography and trade which, according to the classic Laurentian Thesis, shaped the course of Canada's development; and the concept of the "mosaic," which seems to me to show the English Protestant influence, as distinct from the monolithic Catholic versions of other colonial myths, from Mexico through Central and South America to Catholic Quebec.

†I expand upon this link later in the Introduction. Here it will suffice to quote Benjamin directly, since the affinities are obvious enough between the "cultural treasures" of the "victors" and the process of socialization (as we have come to understand it) embedded in the process of canon formation:

> To historians who wish to relive an era, Fustel de Coulanges recommends that they blot out everything they know about the later course of history. There is no better way of characterizing the method with which historical materialism has broken. It is a process of empathy whose origin is the indolence of the heart, *acedia*, which despairs of grasping and holding the genuine historical image as it flares up briefly. Among medieval theologians it was regarded as the root cause of sadness. Flaubert, who was

jamin presents "the triumphal procession" of "cultural treasures" through a contrast between "the great minds and talents who created them" and "the anonymous toil of their contemporaries. There is no document of civilization," he concludes, "which is not at the same time a document of barbarism." To some extent, my view of America is a cross-cultural variation of that outlook, with certain differences in emphasis and approach. Benjamin was seeking to historicize art's claims to transcendence, but he tended not so much to challenge those claims as to insist on a complicity of opposites: "great minds" and "anonymous toil," cultural treasures and the inhumanity of power. My approach was geared to the dynamics of complicity, which in this case called the opposition itself into question. What I discovered in America was the simultaneity of violence and culture formation. America, as its meanings gradually unfolded to me, was interchangeably a cultural treasure of barbarism, a barbaric dream documented by a procession of "great minds and talents," and an interpretive process through which the worlds out there had been triumphantly repressed—first, by myths of their inhabitants ("savage," "primitive") attended by facts of genocide; and then by symbols of the land ("virgin," "wilderness") attended by the creation of the United States as America.

So what began as English graduate studies in the United States became instead a trail into the myth and symbol thickets of American Studies. I encountered in its foundational documents a scholarly achievement commensurate with the cultural creation of

---

familiar with it, wrote: *"Peu de gens devineront combien il a fallu être triste pour ressusciter Carthage."* [Cf. Matthew Arnold's melancholy touchstones of Culture.] The nature of this sadness stands out more clearly if one asks with whom the adherents of historicism actually empathize. The answer is inevitable: with the victor. ... According to traditional practice, the spoils are carried along in the procession. They are called cultural treasures, and a historical materialist views them with cautious detachment.... He regards it as his task to brush history against the grain. ("Theses on the Philosophy of History," *Illuminations*, ed. Hannah Arendt, trans. Harry Zohn [New York, 1968], pp. 256–257).

Benjamin's contrast between empathic history and historical materialism applies in some measure to the contrast I suggest below between aesthetic and contextual criticism.

America: Perry Miller's intellectual construction of national origins out of the esoteric writings of forty Protestant sectarians; F.O. Matthiessen's aesthetic construction of a national literary tradition out of the masterpieces of five self-declared "isolatoes"; Frederick Jackson Turner's historical construction of the national character out of a frontier West that largely excluded its native inhabitants, not to speak of the nation's non-westering immigrants. In all of these monumental works, as well as in their successors, an extraordinary capacity to analyze intricacies of thought, emotion, and imagination seemed bound up with an extraordinary unwillingness to extend analysis beyond the intricacies themselves. The America they revealed appeared out of nowhere—"out of some place of darkness," or rather a *spirit* of place,* variously labelled "nature," the "New England mind," the "Jeffersonian '76," "pioneer democracy"—like the seven musical performers in Kafka's story.

I registered the anomaly as a cultural secret of academia. American Studies, as it had developed from the Forties through the Cold War decades, seemed a method designed *not* to explore its subject, somewhat as the dog's investigations, though conjured up by the music, are deliberately, exclusively, and astonishedly focussed elsewhere— on the wonders of canine artistry ("the lifting and setting of their feet, certain turns of the head . . . the position they took up in relation to one another, the symmetrical patterns which they produced"). The analytic tools of American Studies consisted of the same materials, the same patterns of thought and language, which Americanists had set out to investigate. This was empathic history with a vengeance. As in Kafka's story, analysis was the celebration of a mystery.

Nonetheless, their work had a compelling range and force, which I attributed to a daring act of transgression: the application of aesthetic criticism to what by tradition belonged to the province

*I adopt D.H. Lawrence's term deliberately, to suggest the limitations of even the most brilliant cross-cultural investigations. In this respect, *Studies in Classic American Literature* is itself a model subject for cultural study: a fascinating mixture of outsider's perspective, insider's mystifications (e.g., "spirit of place"), and common transatlantic myths, notably those rooted in Romanticism. Equally suggestive is Alexis de Tocqueville's *Democracy in America*, with its extraordinary mixture of French aristocratic "foreignness," rehashed American myths (ranging from Puritan origins to the "empty continent"), and common "modern" assumptions, notably those stemming from the Enlightenment.

of cognitive criticism. I refer to the familiar distinction between art and artifact, Kultur and culture, that reaches back through German Romanticism to the theological separation of sacred from secular. Theology, we know, had actually mandated separate methods of exegesis for that purpose: one method for unveiling the meanings of the Bible, proceeding from text to transcendent text; and another, profane method, an empirical approach suitable to ordinary books concerning the empirical truths of this world. The modern literary equivalent for that dichotomy, based on the sacralization of art, is the opposition between text and context. The latter is the arena of cognitive criticism, since "context" designates the world *pro-fana*, the "background" areas surrounding the temples of genius, a secondary reality illuminated by "secondary sources." Aesthetic criticism is designed to reveal the richness, the complexity, and the (unfathomable) depths of the "primary text" in its own "organic" terms. This so-called intrinsic method may draw on matters of context—psychology, sociology, philosophy, science—but only insofar as they serve the ends of appreciation. It may even reach outside of the strictly aesthetic to the realm of spirit (moral truths, universal values) provided that what it finds there is reincorporated, truth and beauty entwined, into the meta-contextual pleasures of the text.

American Studies seemed to have developed through a reverse strategy of incorporation. It drew methodically on contextual matters—it actively elicited cognitive analyses (of the American "mind," "heart," and "character")—but it required these to conform to the principles of aesthetic appreciation. If America was not literally a poem in these scholars' eyes, it was a literary canon that embodied the national promise. The Puritans had discovered America in the Bible; Jacksonians discovered the Bible in the Declaration of Independence and the Constitution; American Studies added to this *Biblia Americana* the national literary classics. It may even be said to have concentrated upon them as the key to it all, somewhat as Christian typologists had discovered the secrets of Holy Scripture, Old and New, in stories of Christ. What followed was a series of investigations of the country's "exceptional" nature that was as rich, as complex, and as interdisciplinary as America itself—a pluralist enterprise armed with the instruments both of aesthetic and of cognitive analysis, all bent on the appreciation of a unique cultural artifact. Aesthetic instruments had a privileged place here because it was as art, by modern consensus, that the spirit most fully revealed itself. But the instruments of cognitive analysis were no less important. It was their task to reconstitute history itself as American; and, as we might expect, they did so most appreciatively when they repressed the adverse facts of American history, or else, more empathically still, represented these as a violation of the nation's promise and original intent.

The music which thus came, in Kafka's words, "from all sides, from the heights, from the deep, from everywhere," sounded to me like ideology. I sometimes thought of it as Muzak, and I recognized in its strains a long series of scholarly ventures in culture formation, the nationalist project of modern literary history that had been baptized over a century before in the trinitarian faith of *Volksgeist*, World–Spirit, and the sanctity of art. One extreme application, or distortion, of this genre was the aesthetics of fascism. Another extreme was the humanist enterprise (mingling chauvinism, utopianism, and social critique) of Georg Gottfried Gervinus, Francesco De Sanctis, and Désiré Nisard. American Studies stood at the latter extreme, and no doubt it was the humanist difference which allowed me to appreciate the insight it embodied into the dynamics of culture. Without quite articulating it as a principle of analysis, American Studies taught by example, in practice, that rhetoric is not a surface coating, "mere metaphor," upon the deep structures of the real. It is substantially, fundamentally, what the real is, even (or especially) when the rhetoric serves to repress and deny. The dog's interpretations mask the rules of music, but they reveal the world he inhabits. Among other things, culture is how people interpret and what they believe.

A simple lesson, but it required time, observation, and participation to absorb. My outsider's view of American Studies was that its America was a barbaric context made text, empathically, by Americanists. My American experience persuaded me that the poem was in some important sense an accurate representation of the way things worked. America was more than an imperial wish-fulfillment dream brought to life in the assertion of nationhood. It was a way of imagining that expressed the mechanisms through which, in Elaine Scarry's terms, the made-up becomes the made-real. Like other modern nations, America was an imagined community. It was also a process of symbol making through which the norms and values of a modern culture were rationalized, spiritualized, and institutionalized—rendered the vehicle, as the American *Way*, both of conscience and of consensus.

The music of America still sounded to me like ideology, but it was ideology in a new key, requiring a blend of cognitive and appreciative analysis. Benjamin contrasts empathic understanding with historical materialism, an adversarial outlook of "cautious detachment" which, aware of the "origin" of culture, "cannot contemplate [its subject] without horror."[4] I sought a mode of mediation between horror and empathy. Accordingly, I turned to the more flexible, non-pejorative definitions of ideology available in anthropology: ideology as the web of ideas, practices, beliefs, and myths through which a society, any society, coheres and perpetuates itself. I hoped that ideological analysis, so conceived, would allow me both to exploit the insights of American Studies and to revise its outlook. American Studies had set out the interactions between symbol and fact, rhetoric and history, by synthesizing their different forms of discourse. I wanted to separate those forms in order to investigate the conditions of synthesis making. To that end, I hoped that ideological analysis would allow me to negotiate between the world and the word in such a way that the word, "America," might be contexualized, recovered for purposes of cognitive criticism, while the world of America might be apprehended in its fantastic textuality, as the development of an empowering and (within limits) genuinely liberating rhetoric and vision.

Necessarily, this set me at odds with the dominant concepts of ideology in the field. I thought of these as three models of the hermeneutics of denial: (1) *The consensus model*, adopted by the leading schools of literary and historical scholarship during the Cold War decades. This denied that America had any ideology at all, since ideology meant dogma, bigotry, and repression; whereas Americans were open-minded, inclusive, and eclectic. (2) *The old-fashioned Marxist model*, imported into academia during the Depression, and revived in the Sixties. This denied that ideology had any truth-value, since it was by definition false consciousness, the camera obscura of the ruling class. (3) *The multi-cultural model*, a medley of various indigenous themes, from the melting pot to the patchwork quilt, melded together or interlaced with various forms of neo-Marxism. This denied that America had an ideology, on the grounds that there were so many ideologies, all in flux: republicanism, agrarianism, free enterprise, consumerism, liberalism, working-class consciousness, corporate industrialism, and so on, to the point where it came to seem the other side of consensual open-endedness.

Against that background my concept of ideology was intended to insist on: (1) the ideological context of common-sense eclecticism; (2) the truth-value of ideology, as a key not to the cosmos but to culture, which mediates our access to cosmic truth; and (3) the de facto coherence of American culture, as for example in the ideological symmetries underlying the models of multi-culturalism and consensus. The symmetries seemed to me transparent in the relation I spoke of between the world and the word: the changing, conflictual, and yet continuously sustaining relation between the United States—in all its multifarious "realities" (pragmatic, agrarian, consumerist, etc.)—and the abstract, unifying meanings of America. Heterogeneity was not the antithesis to those abstractions; it was a function of hegemony. The open-ended inclusiveness of the United States was directly proportionate to America's capacity to incorporate *and exclude,* and more precisely to incorporate by exclusion. The culture seemed indefinite, infinitely processual, because as America it closed everything else out, as being Old World and/or not-yet-America. And vice versa: the process by which it closed out everything un-American was also the spur toward an ideal of *liberal* inclusiveness, a vision of *representative* openness that eroded traditional barriers of nationality, territory, language, and ethnicity, and eventually, perhaps, would erode even the barriers of race and gender—which is to say, would open the prospects of liberalism to women and blacks as it had to the Irish, the Jews, and the far-flung regions of Alaska and Hawaii.

I am describing a broad, deeply ingrained symbolic strategy; one need only think of the reciprocities between inclusive and exclusive representation in the concept of errand or of manifest destiny. But my concern here lay with a specific academic enterprise. It seemed to me that the process by which the United States had become America was nowhere more clearly displayed than in the bipolarities of American Studies: on the one hand, a multiculturalism (or experiential pluralism) that rendered invisible the structures of national cohesion; on the other hand, a consensual identity, "American," that by definition transcended the "ideological limits" of class, region, generation, and race (i.e., redefined

American identity, ideologically, as a process of transcending the boundaries of class, region, etc.). As this principle applied to American literary studies in particular, the relation between text and context opened into a cultural symbology: a configuration or tangle of patterns of expression common to all areas of society, including the aesthetic. So understood, "high literature" was neither an imitation of reality nor a Platonic (or Hegelian) ladder to a higher reality. It was a mediation between both, which I thought of in terms of ideological mimesis: a representation of the volatile relations between conceptual, imaginative, and social realities that was different from, often opposed to, and yet fundamentally reciprocal with the ways of the world in which it emerged. I intended my concept of ideological mimesis to convey not only literature's multi-valence, but its capacities (in degree, within limits) for autonomy. Nonetheless, I again found myself at odds with the dominant models of analysis in the field, in this case the field of literary studies. I think here in particular of the New Criticism, which through the Sixties and the Seventies still reigned in the area of textual analysis, and of oppositional criticism, which then as now comprised the most influential literary group in American Studies.

My objections to the New Critics antedated my discovery of America. They thrived on the invisibility of context, somewhat as Kafka's narrator's ingenuities depend on his disembodiment of the music; or as the mystery he marvels at of "soaring dogs," floating on air, depends on the invisibility of whatever or whoever is holding them up. My own reading had convinced me, on the contrary, that literary texts were deeply embedded in issues of context; that this embeddedment was a central source of creative, moral, and intellectual vitality; and that to deny that source of empowerment on principle, or by professional reflex, was a form of aesthetic minimalism which drained literature of its richest meanings. It was also to instate certain cultural values under the cloak of invisibility, as embodying the transcendent unities of the text. And finally, under the guise of reverence, it was to evade the most challenging questions posed by the trans-historical qualities of literature, which center on the relation (not the dichotomy) between "trans" and "historical." Criticism may aspire to judgments of eternity, but it takes place in history. As both Kafka and Benjamin remind us, the very forms of canonization are mediated by historical consciousness; we break through its limitations only in degree, and only by recognizing that we live in history, even if we live on literature.

But of course New Critics were ipso facto not Americanists. My direct engagement was with the oppositional critics. That term is a recent coinage, designating certain post-Marxist forms of cultural praxis. But in American Studies it has a far broader import. I have in mind the adversarial stance of Americanist literary critics from the very inception of the field: the school of subversion (as it has been called) that constitutes the mainstream tradition of American Studies from Vernon Parrington and Lewis Mumford through Matthiessen and Henry Nash Smith, and that has continued to provide many of its most distinguished figures. The principles of oppositionalism, so understood, center on an essentialist conflict between an always oppressive society and an always liberating literature—a sacred-secular library of America set against the ideologies in America of racism, imperialism, capitalism, and patriarchy. My objection to this particular text/context dichotomy was more complicated in application than that to the New Critics, but it was based on a similar premise. My reading of the classic American authors convinced me that they were imaginatively nourished by the culture, even when they were politically opposed to it. Melville's grandest No-in-thunder comes in an essay extolling America's destiny; and a similar dynamic (as I try to show in my essays on Hawthorne and Emerson) informs the cultural work of *The Scarlet Letter* and of "The American Scholar"; as it also underlies the multiple connections between subversion and representative selfhood in the adventures of George Harris, Ruth Hall, Huckleberry Finn, Frederic Henry, the Invisible Man, Oedipa Maas, and Rutherford Calhoun.*

---

*I am partly indebted for this (more or less random) list to a recent column by George F. Will, "Beyond the Literature of Protest," in the *Washington Post* of December 13, 1990 (p. A23):

> Rutherford Calhoun is one of those rapscallions who have enlivened American Literature [ever] since Huck Finn decided civilization made him itch and lit out for the territories. . . . Calhoun is black.
>
> So is his creator Charles Johnson, who teaches at the University of Washington, and has written . . . an emancipation proclamation for black writers. It is his novel "Middle Passage," the winner of the National Book Award. It is an example of triumphant individualism on the part of both Calhoun and Johnson.
>
> Johnson noted that he is the first black male to win the award since

In all cases, the complementarity of text and context reveals a cultural symbology which not only tolerates but elicits resistance as a staple of social revitalization. This is not to say that the literature is not adversarial in some sense. My disagreement with the oppositionalists lay not in particular interpretations of texts, but in their overall tendency toward allegory. I saw this as a sort of beatification of the subversive; as a denial against all historical evidence, from every field of art, of the continuously enriching reciprocity between dominant forms of art and forms of ideological domination; as a transfer of the powers of appreciative criticism to political agency; and as a confusion, accordingly, of literary analysis with social action. It was as though (in a mirror-inversion of Kafka's parable) to deconstruct the musicians' patterns of performance—or to uncover adversarial tendencies within the symmetries they enacted, or to discover different groups of performers (the music, so to speak, of Benjamin's repressed world of "anony-

---

Ralph Ellison won in 1953 for *Invisible Man*. Ellison's aim, says Johnson, was [the] creation of "a black American personality as complex, as multi-sided and synthetic as the American society that produced it. . . . Literature, he says . . . that is an extension of an ideology . . . lacks the power to change the reader's perceptions as the writer's perceptions change. . . . The novel is about—quietly about—patriotism."

"If," Calhoun muses, "this weird, upside-down caricature of a country called America, if this land of refugees and former indentured servants, religious heretics and half-breeds, whoresons and fugitives—this cauldron of mongrels from all points of the compass—was all I could right call *home*, then aye: I was of it. . . ."

Johnson anticipates in the 1990s a black fiction "of increasing intellectual and artistic generosity, one that enables us as a people—as a culture—to move from narrow complaint to broad celebration." I think he means celebration of the possibilities of American individualism. I know that his novel, and the award, are reasons for celebration.

A few notes may help situate Will's and Johnson's celebrations in relation to my own views. (1) Huckleberry Finn lights out for the territory in order to go "howling amongst the Indians" with Tom Sawyer, and he does so after a very long episode in which his "individualism," along with Tom's, is rather severely questioned. (2) Patriotism, even in its "quietest" manifestations, is not an example of thought freed of ideology, and neither, for that matter, is art. (3) Both Ellison's "synthetic" America and Calhoun's "upside-down caricature" of it are versions of a mainstream cultural ideal. (4) Will is wrong to identify Johnson's views specifically as a movement away from the Sixties: See, for example, Coretta Scott King, "King's Dream . . . is really the American Dream," *Atlanta Journal and Constitution*, January 5, 1986, p. 7.

mous toil")—were to threaten the entire world of music, and potentially to undermine the moral and social structures within which the musicians functioned.

This romance quest for the subversive seemed to me to have its roots in a venerable (though "dark" and often mystical) branch of hermeneutics, the esoteric tradition that bridges gnosticism, kabala, and the Romantic vision of Satan as the secret hero of *Paradise Lost*. And in turn that visionary fusion of politics and art recalled the radical aesthetics of my youth. Here again literature was invested with the spiritual values of protest, and literary criticism, by extension, raised to the status of revolutionary activity. But the national emphasis in this case—the focus, positive and negative, on the American-ness of American literature—called attention to a cultural difference in the very concept of radicalism. I refer to a broad tradition of political dissent inspired by the figural America. Its connection to literary oppositionalism, as this unfolded from the Vietnam years through the Reagan Eighties, was both theoretical and institutional. Briefly, the student rebels of one period became the academic authorities of the other. The continuities this transformation implies—beyond, or rather *within*, the profession of "generation gap," "rupture," and "politicization"—require me to return once more to my literal-metaphorical moment of border-crossing, this time into the suprising radical America of the Sixties.

It was not the radicalism that suprised me. Quite the contrary: I had expected to find the land of Sacco and Vanzetti an unincorporated America of class contradictions, residual resistance, and emergent struggle. And so it was. But the protest rendered invisible the cultural limitations which these conflicts implied. The sources of conflict persisted—indeed, according to the protesters they had deepened—but they were described in terms that reinforced this society's values and myths. The counter-culture swam into my view in a series of abstractions, two by two, like the procession of leviathans at the start of *Moby-Dick*, as the gates of Ishmael's wonder-world swing open: Freedom versus Tyranny, Opportunity versus Oppression, Progress versus Chaos; and midmost of them all, like a Janus-faced phantom in the air, America, real and ideal. The real faced toward doomsday. The ideal, facing the millennium, appeared sometimes in the form of national representatives (Jefferson, Lincoln), sometimes as representative texts (the Mayflower Compact, the federal Constitution), sometimes in cultural key words ("equal rights," "self-realization"), or else in the appositional symbology of pluralism ("heterogeneity," "nation of nations").

My commonsense response, recorded in my chapter on consensus, was "co-optation." What else could this Americanization of utopia be but some long-ripened generational rite of passage? In this culture, I concluded, the true conservatives were on the left; their characteristic strategy was to displace radical alternatives with an indigenous tradition of reform. Thus the alternative implicit in Nat Turner's revolt had been absorbed into the exemplary American protest embodied in *The Narrative of Frederick Douglass*; so, too, in the long run, were the alternatives offered by Paul Robeson and Malcolm X. The quintessentially liberal programs for change that linked Elizabeth Cady Stanton to Gloria Steinem encompassed, blurred, and eventually eliminated other feminist alternatives (those which did not focus on America), from the Grimké sisters to Emma Goldman and Angela Davis. It was the cultural work of Emerson and Emersonians, from (say) William James through Paul Goodman, to obviate socialist or communist alternatives to capitalism. This form of cultural work joined Jefferson to Thoreau and both to Martin Luther King, Jr., in an omnivorous oppositionalism that ingested all competing modes of radicalism—from the Fourierists to Herbert Marcuse and Noam Chomsky—in the course of redefining injustice as un-American, revolution as the legacy of '76, and inequities of class, race, and gender as disparities between the theory and the practice of American-ness.

These dissenters, it seemed clear, had miscalculated not just the power but the nature of rhetoric. They had thought to appropriate America as a trope of the spirit, and so to turn the national symbol, now freed of its base historical content, into a vehicle of moral and political renovation. In the event, however, the symbol had refigured the moral and political terms of renovation—had rendered freedom, opportunity, democracy, and radicalism itself part of the American Way.* But the results of their miscalcula-

* A century before, Southern leaders had learned that "America" could not be manipulated to mean the ideals of feudal hierarchy, because it already represented something else—a set of culture-specific ideals, among these representative individualism, pluralist democracy, and the rights of personal ascent. In the Sixties, as a century before, those ideals functioned through the denial of their cultural

tions, as I traced these back through the nineteen hundreds, had unexpected consequences. What I learned from that century-long lesson in co-optation altered my views both of American protest and of the radical outlook I had brought to it. The culture, I discovered, had indeed found ways of harnessing revolution for its own purposes; but the ways themselves were volatile, even (to a point) open-ended. They tended toward subversion even as they drew such tendencies into persistent, deeply conservative patterns of culture.

In short, the issue was not co-optation or dissent. It was varieties of co-optation, varieties of dissent, and above all varieties of co-optation/dissent. America was a symbolic *field*, continually influenced by extrinsic sources, and sometimes changing through those influences, but characteristically absorbing and adapting them to its own distinctive patterns. And in the course of adaptation, it was recurrently generating its own adversarial forms. The "alternative Americas" it spawned were (like the originating symbol) ideology and utopia combined. They opposed the system in ways that reaffirmed its ideals; but the process of reaffirmation constituted a radical tradition *of a certain kind*. Hence the ambiguities that linked Douglass to King, Thoreau to Goodman, Stanton to Steinem. In all these cases, dissent was demonstrably an appeal to, and through, the rhetoric and values of the dominant culture; and in every case, it issued in a fundamental challenge to the system: racism subverted in Douglass's story of a self-made man; patriarchy subverted through Stanton's revised version of the Declaration of Independence; the authority of government subverted by Thoreau's July Fourth experiment in self-reliance.

The theory of co-optation, like Benjamin's attack on empathic history, assumes a basic dichotomy between radicalism and re-

---

specificity; but of course there were certain adjustments now to meet new circumstances. First, "America" served to exclude the ideals of radical, rather than feudal, collectivism: it denied class identity as a century before it had denied racial hierarchy. Second, the protest leaders did not retreat into havens of un-American resistance, as had the Southern visionaries before them, from the inventors of the plantation myth to the literary Agrarians. Some radicals, of course, may be said to have seceded into the groves of academe (there is a telling emblem of cultural continuity in the movement from the Southern Agrarians at Yale in the Fifties to the neo-Marxists two or three decades later). But by and large this new generation of rebels did not need to secede because, unlike the Southern Agrarians, they had already identified their dissenting ideals with pluralist democracy, representative individualism, and the rights of personal ascent.

form, as though one *could* be for or against an entire culture; as though not to be against a culture fundamentally (whatever that means) was to be fundamentally part of it; and as though one could hope to effect social change by advocating ideas or programs that were alien to whatever held together the society at large—which is to say, to its strategies of cohesion. The radical/reformist reciprocities I discovered pointed me in a different direction. They called for a reconsideration of the entire structure of dichotomies by which I had found American protest wanting. The European forms of radicalism I had inherited were indeed opposed to that tradition, but they, too, I recognized, were couched in a rhetoric that expressed the cultures within which they had been generated. And they had given rise to forms of social action that were ambiguously liberating and/or restrictive, progressive and/or repressive, revolutionary and/or reformist.

The difference between the two traditions was not that of empirical analysis versus symbolic projection, activism versus aquiescence. It was an opposition between distinctive processes of culture formation, entailing, in each case, mixed forms of empirical (or detached) analysis and symbolic projection (or empathic understanding), and, as it happened, resulting in major differences both in modes of social cohesion and in prescriptions for social renovation. Insofar as this opposition, too, was a false one—insofar as (say) *Walden* resists *The Communist Manifesto* absolutely, denies altogether the theory of historical materialism, class identity, or the socialist state—it is because each rests on a hermeneutics of transcendence. Thoreau's appeal to self-reliance, like Karl Marx's to class struggle, implies a chiliastic solution ("the only true America," "the dictatorship of the proletariat"), built on apodictic either/or's: individualism or conformity, revolution or oppression. The result is not a contrast between true and false resistance to the barbarism of one's culture. It is a wholesale transfer of agency, as in Kafka's parable, from one's culture to the imputed higher laws of nature, history, and the mind.

What did seem to me distinctive in degree about the American instance was the cultural function of radicalism. It was a strategy of pluralism everywhere to compartmentalize dissent so as to absorb it, incrementally, *unus inter pares*, into a dominant liberal discourse. But American liberalism *privileged* dissent. In my chapter on early New England rhetoric, I suggest that one reason for the impact of the Puritans was their success in making a dissenting faith the cornerstone of community; elsewhere in this book, I trace the continuities in this regard through the rhetoric of American Revolution, the oppositionalism of Hester Prynne and Melville's Pierre, and the Emersonian re-vision of individualism as the mandate both for permanent resistance and for American identity—a transcendental license to have your dissent and to make it too.

This was the context as well of oppositional criticism as I encountered it in the late Sixties; and it remains the context of American literary studies in our time of dissensus. For although dissensus involves the disintegration of certain traditional structures of academic authority, nonetheless the *conditions* of dissensus do not transcend ideology. On the contrary: they are a purer expression of the liberal marketplace than the genteel modes they superseded, which offered at least some residual resistance to the pluralist incorporation of academia.* In an earlier, more innocent time, upstart ethnics could make their way into the humanities on the condition that they re-formed themselves (in dress, manner, accent, and moral outlook) as custodians of Arnoldian Culture, the preservers of literature as a transcendent "criticism of life,"

---

* The distinction sometimes made in this regard between multi-culturalism and cultural pluralism has the same symbolic function as other intrasectarian distinctions within American liberalism. It serves to exclude alternatives to the dominant culture by limiting the opposition to terms which are intrinsic to the patterns of dominance. It is not that the opposition is a false one; it is that the opposition expresses, on either side, solutions generated by the culture itself, so that the very act of setting these in opposition becomes at once a declaration of cultural self-sufficiency and a strategy for eliciting forms of reconciliation, compromise, and continuity. Hence the efficacy of such traditional American oppositions as self versus society, Jeffersonian versus Puritan values, Democratic versus Republican platforms, and liberal versus libertarian ideals. Characteristically, the tone of debate is apocalyptic, as in Arthur M. Schlesinger, Jr.'s recent attack on multi-culturalism in the name of pluralist integration. The new multi-culturalists, he argues, are conspiring to "disunite America"; whereas true Americans recognize that "'the United States has a common culture that is multicultural'," and that that common culture is the world's "best hope" (*The Disuniting of America: Reflections on a Multicultural Society* [Washington, D.C., 1991], pp. 81, 83). It would be easy to gather a host of similar claims from the other side. The issue is not national unity, but access to the spoils of culture on the part of previously excluded groups which have found in race, gender, and ethnicity a key to representative participation.

Schlesinger might have noted the analogy here to the transition from the Brahmin establishment to the "radicalism" of Jacksonian enterprise (*The Age of Jackson* [New York, 1945], p. 177 et passim). For once, genteel academia seems to be at the forefront of the process of Americanization.

meaning in their case the life of liberal capitalism. Their latter-day upstart heirs demand in effect that the humanities come down from that ivory tower, comply with the conditions of American free enterprise (equal opportunity, open competition, supply-and-demand specialization), and participate in the power structures of the state, including its structures of class, mass communication, and government.

This is not to disparage the work of oppositional critics, then or now.[†] They have raised important issues, exposed the constrictions of established theories and the injustice of established practices, and properly called attention to the pressures of history not only upon the literature we interpret but upon our categories of interpretation. In these and similar ways they have been right to call their criticism subversive. But subversive in what sense, and to what ends, and for whom?

My misgiving first expressed itself in my sense of wonder at the scope and intensity of their political claims. Particular questions of interpretation apart, why were these Americanists so intent on demonstrating the subversiveness of authors who for the most part had either openly endorsed the American Way, or else had lamented American corruption as the failure of New Eden? Or mutatis mutandis, why were they so intent on asserting the regenerative powers of literary studies (their own) that were not only inaccessible but unintelligible to society at large? I recall thinking in this regard of two Thurber cartoons, which might be considered examples by contrast of the advantages of cross-cultural perspective. One of these shows a copyist sitting before Rubens's *Rape of the Sabine Women* and carefully reproducing the flowers in a corner of the scene. The other cartoon shows a woman smiling like the Mona Lisa, while the perplexed man next to her asks: "What do you want to be enigmatic *for*, Monica?" What did these oppositionalists want Edith Wharton and William

---

†I should distinguish here between two kinds of oppositional criticism, one centered in the literature, the other in the criticism. In what follows, my critique of the first group of critics—we might call them authorial oppositionalists—is more elaborate, because they have predominated from the beginning of American Studies. The second group of critics—we might call these self-reflexive oppositionalists—represent a more recent development. They have come (in varying degrees) to acknowledge literature's cultural embeddedment, but they then proceed to transfer the source of opposition from aesthetics to praxis, from the object to the method of study.

Faulkner—or more strangely still, their recondite readings of Wharton or Faulkner—to be radical *for?*

For an America, I believe, that rendered invisible the interpreter's complicity in the culture. I do not mean complicity as a synonym for moral (or even clerical) treason. One may be complicitous simultaneously in various aspects of culture: those which help people rationalize their greed, those which help naturalize existing or emergent networks of power, and those which open the way to fundamental moral and social improvements. In this case, however, complicity involved a strikingly uncritical stance toward precisely these sorts of ambiguities. In allegorizing the powers of opposition—and in effect transcendentalizing the subversive—these critics seemed almost willfully oblivious to their own cultural function. It was as though their method had somehow recast oppositionalism itself in the image of America; as though, to recall Benjamin's thesis, they had found at the origins of the errand not the barbarism of civilized progress but the redemptive wholeness of utopia; or, in the terms of Kafka's parable, as though they had appropriated to their academic performances the radical potential of the symbology they opposed.

One sign of appropriation has been the alliance between radicalism and upward mobility in the profession at large—the rites of academia encoded in writings of dissent. A more telling symptom for my purposes is the cultural function of American Studies. Surely, it is no accident that, of all academic specialties, this field has been the most hospitable from the start to new waves of immigration from the other America into the profession. Nor is it by accident that, in spite of its very name, *American* Studies (as in *United* States) has gravitated toward a *denial* of cohesion; that this *rhetoric* of denial has presented itself in protests against exclusion (i.e., *for integration*); that the protest has taken the form of hyphenated ethnicity—Italian–American, Irish–American, and Jewish–American hand in hand with African–American, Asian–American, and Hispanic–American—and that the result has been an adversarial form of interpretation which roots subversion in institutions of culture. It makes for a paradox that could obtain, in the old immigrant myth, only in America: a school of subversion geared toward the harmony of political activism and the good life, and directed (under the aegis of American literary studies) toward a fusion of personal, professional, and national identity.

I have found in this institutionalization of dissent still another boundary demarcating the problematics of cross-cultural criticism.*

Toward the end of Kafka's "Investigations of a Dog," the narrator is granted a visionary consolation. As he lies alone, near death, utterly exhausted by a long series of frustrations, suddenly, he tells us,

> a beautiful creature . . . stood before me. . . . My senses . . . seemed to see or to hear something about him [of which he himself was unaware]. . . . I thought I saw that the hound was already singing without knowing it, nay, more, that the melody, separated from him, was floating in the air in accordance with its own laws, and, as though he had no part in it, was moving toward me, toward me alone.

I suppose that an analogy might be drawn with those ineffable moments of wonder that light up the republic of American letters: Whitman's vision of America singing, that turns out to be an epic "Song of Myself"; Phillis Wheatley's first sight of what she too called "the land of freedom's heaven-defended race"; the westward caravan at the start of *The Prairie*, face-to-face with Natty Bumppo, towering against the sunset; the uncut forests of Long Island at the end of *The Great Gatsby*, pandering in whispers to the last and greatest of human dreams; Perry Miller's vocational epiphany at the mouth of the Congo River, a calling (he reports) from the primal darkness to tell the story of a brave New World; and before even Miller's Puritans, the discoverer Columbus, as Emerson identifies him, and with him, at the beginning of *his* career, in the opening pages of *Nature*:

> this beauty of Nature which is seen and felt as beauty, is the least part. . . .
> The presence of a higher, namely, of the spiritual element is essen-

---

*I do not claim this as a neutral territory of analysis. As I hope my book demonstrates, cross-cultural criticism is not a form of cultural relativism. Non-transcendence is also a realm of ideals, however subject to contingency; of the real, however vulnerable to interpretation; and of radical agency, within the limits imposed by the social and rhetorical construction of radicalisms.

tial to its perfection. The high and divine beauty which can be loved without effeminacy, is that which is found in combination with the human will. Beauty is the mark God sets upon virtue. . . . When a noble act is done . . . are not these heroes entitled to add the beauty of the scene to the beauty of the deed? When the bark of Columbus nears the shore of America;— before it, the beach lined with savages, fleeing out of their huts of cane; the sea behind; and the purple mountains of the Indian Archipelago around, can we separate the man from the living picture? Does not the New World clothe his form with her palm-groves and savannahs as fit drapery?[5]

I offer this emblem of discovery as an *ultimum* of the rhetoric of transcendence—an interpretation of origins and ends that appropriates the mysteries of gender, nature, and the Oversoul to the culturally transparent "I." And it is worth remarking that Emerson's American Scholar fits well into its "living picture." He, too, stands at the rhetorical "shore of America": a "New World" which he claims by naming, as being his by visionary right, simultaneously his and not his, a hero's trophy of beauty, virtue, savagery, and representative selfhood. And the same is true of Emerson himself, standing in as the essential discoverer for Man Thinking and Columbus alike: "I do not make it; I arrive there, and behold what was there already. . . . And what a future it opens! . . . I am ready to die out of nature, and be born again into this new yet unapproachable America I have found in the West." That triumph of Culture is perhaps the richest instance in modern history of the dialectic Benjamin speaks of between barbarism and civilization. It is the fullest modern example of his argument against empathic history, as being the instrument of the victors:

> all rulers are the heirs of those who conquered before them. Hence, empathy with the victor invariably benefits the rulers. . . . Whoever has emerged victorious participates to this day in the triumphal procession in which the present rulers step over those who are lying prostrate. . . . According to traditional practice, the spoils are carried along in the procession. They are called cultural treasures.[6]

"The American Scholar" both mystifies the discourse of conquest and transfers its cultural spoils to the observer-interpreter (and those he represents). Even as he renders unto Caesar the things that are Caesar's, territory and inhabitants alike, Emerson also renders them transcendentally unto God. "I arrive there, and behold what was there already": Emerson raises the victors' *veni-vidi-vici*, as it were, into the music of the spheres by investing their noble act with the "presence of a higher, *namely*, of the spiritual element essential to its perfection." And he does so, like Columbus, draped in nature's purple, as the "savages" hasten in wonder toward his figural "bark," "fleeing out of their huts of cane," as once the Magi hastened from the East to witness the Nativity. Except that the drapery, for Columbus, was the "purple mountains of the Indian Archipelago"; in Emerson's case, the prospect extends indefinitely into and across the American interior, at once toward his own "inward mountains, with the tranquil eternal meadows spread at their base," and toward the Rockies of the "continental" West. And of course the "savages" are no longer visible in "The American Scholar." In their place, Emerson paints for us an awakening "our": "the sluggard intellect of this continent . . . look[ing] from under its iron lids" toward "the postponed expectation of the world . . . a new age, as the star in the constellation Harp, which now flames in our zenith . . . shall one day be the pole-star for a thousand years."[7]

My own America, if I may call it so, elicited a different sense of wonder. To put this in its proper prosaic terms, it elicited a critical method designed to illuminate the conflicts implicit in border-crossing, and to draw out their unresolved complementarities. I spoke of this method at the start as unrepresentative, thinking of the corporate American figured in Emerson's Scholar. But the contrast itself suggests another constituency: the other America hidden from view by that interpretation; or as I called it, appropriatively, the unincorporated country of my alien namesakes, Sacco and Vanzetti, a rhetorically United States of nonetheless mainly unresolved borders—between class and race, race and generation, generation and region, region and religion, religious and ethnic and national heritage—and a constantly shifting array of cultural crossings, including those between Jewish–Canadian marginality and Emersonian dissent.

In the concluding chapter, I urge the benefits of this perspective for American literary and cultural studies; and if anything they seem to me more pertinent now than ever, with the impending Americanization of what has been called, imprecisely, our postcapitalist world. I began this introduction directly after a talk I attended by a visiting Russian economist, Stanislav Shatalin.

It was a dramatic occasion, since Shatalin was then directing the marketplace transformation underway in the USSR; and it had an added personal edge (I fancied) for me alone, since he happened to come from the same region from which my parents had emigrated at about the time of his birth. "We have been wandering in the wilderness for forty years," was Shatalin's summary of the Communist experience; "the time of ideology is over, and the time for truth has arrived"—by which, he explained, he meant free enterprise, individualism, and liberal democracy.[8] As he proceeded to outline his 500-day truth plan, conjuring up transcendent things to come, I found my thoughts turning gradually elsewhere—drifting back, as though in accordance with a law of their own, to the process of my personal and professional discovery of New Canaan. I had had a different border-crossing experience, and I had a different, cross-cultural story to tell. The proper focus for this introduction, I realized, was the music of America.

2
The Ritual of Consensus

When I first encountered the ritual of American consensus, in the mid-1960s, it took the form of protest and despair: the Jewish anarchist Paul Goodman berating the country for abandoning its promise; the descendant of American slaves, Martin Luther King, Jr., denouncing injustice as a violation of the American Way; an interminable debate about national destiny, full of rage and faith, conservatives scavenging for un-Americans, New Left historians recalling the country to its sacred mission. The complaints on all sides amounted to an old refrain adapted to a New World prophecy: "When is our errand to be fulfilled? How long, O Lord, how long?" And on all sides the solutions joined celebration and lament in reaffirming the American dream.

I felt like Sancho Panza in a land of Don Quixotes. It was not just that the dream was a patent fiction. It was that the fiction involved an entire hermeneutic system. Mexico may have meant the land of gold, and Canada might be the Dominion of the North; but America was a venture in exegesis. You were supposed to discover it as a believer unveils scripture. America's meaning was implicit in its destiny, and its destiny was manifest to all who had the grace to discover its meaning. To a Canadian skeptic, a gentile in God's Country, it made for a breathtaking scene: a poly-ethnic, multi-racial, openly materialistic, self-consciously individualistic people knit together in the bonds of myth, voluntarily, with a force of belief unsurpassed by any other modern society.

This was not the homogeneity of which the "consensus historians" spoke. From George Bancroft through Louis Hartz, American exceptionalists had presented an image of a progressive middle-class uniformity. What I discovered was a corporate identity built on fragmentation and dissent: a hundred sects, factions, schools, and denominations, each aggressively different from the others, yet all celebrating the same mission. This *concordia discors* was not what census-takers would call a measure of society.

Indeed, its function was partly to mystify or mask social realities. Nonetheless it denoted something equally real: a coherent system of symbols, values, and beliefs, and a series of rituals designed to keep the system going. So, it seemed to me, the rhetoric of mission served through the Sixties. What was lost, apparently, in that endless debate about the meaning of America, was the fact that the debate itself was part of a long-ripened mode of socialization. And in trying to make sense of my discovery, I found myself back in the rhetoric of the antebellum North.* It was there the myth was established; there the rituals of God's country were constructed and sanctified.

My purpose here is to explore the nature of that American "consensus." I use the term *ritual*, accordingly, in its broadest sense, to mean the forms and strategies of cultural continuity. My major landmarks (derived from the ritual itself) are the Revolution and the Civil War; but part of the terrain is the long foreground to revolution. I assume, with many recent historians, that the Civil War was the result of a gradual consolidation of ideological forces, a process that reflected the steady if often turbulent growth of middle-class American culture. I assume, further, that the meaning of America was not God-given but man-made; that the men who made it were not prophets but spokesmen for a certain social order; and that the rhetoric of consensus, which helped sustain and mold the social order, originated in large measure in colonial New England. A long foreground, as I said, but crucial to an understanding of my subject, and so I begin with a brief account of New England's errand into free enterprise.

I trust that this view of the Puritan errand will not overstrain the worn links between Protestantism and the rise of capitalism. What I would suggest is simply that certain elements in Puritanism lent themselves powerfully to that conjunction, and precisely those elements came to the fore when the Massachusetts Bay emigrants, a group drawn mainly from the entrepreneurial and

---

*The question of Southern ideology lies outside my present concerns, but it may be pertinent to note that this did not yield a national identity. The institution of slavery gave the South a "peculiar" *regional* identity, but as a mode of cultural cohesion that identity was undermined by a commitment from the start to the tenets of free enterprise. This applies as well as to the ideals of the yeoman farmer and even (in practice and effect) to the plantation legend, where Cavalier norms and the cult of medievalism were contradicted by basic social, political, and economic realities, including the commercial role of the "gentleman planter."

professional middle classes (tradesmen, lawyers, artisans, clerics, and merchants), severed their ties with the feudal forms of Old England and set up a comparatively fluid society on the American strand—a society that devalued aristocracy, denounced beggary, and, despite its traditions of deference, opened up political and economic opportunities to a relatively broad spectrum of the population. All this has been amply documented. A recent *New Yorker* cartoon has one Puritan immigrant say to another, as they disembark from the *Mayflower*, "My immediate goal is freedom of religion, but my long-range plan is to get into real estate." No doubt Tocqueville had something like that in mind when he wrote, in a famous passage of 1835, that the "whole destiny of America is contained in the first Puritan who landed on these shores as that of the whole human race in the first man."[1]

Tocqueville was making the point by hyperbole, but the point itself is valid enough to suggest a general difference between New England and other modern communities. In Europe, capitalism evolved dialectically, through conflict with earlier and persisting ways of thought and belief. It was an emerging force in a complex cultural design. Basically, New England bypassed the conflict. This is by no means to say that conflict was avoided altogether. The first century of New England was a remarkable instance of rapid social change, involving widespread economic, political, and moral tensions. But by and large those were transitional stages in the growth of the dominant culture. They signified not a contest between an established and an evolving system, as in Europe, but a troubled period of maturation. There were overlays of earlier agrarian patterns of life, but these did not offer the obstacles to modernization that peasant culture did (say) in pre-Revolutionary France. There were vestiges of folk customs, and assertions of aristocratic privilege, but these found no soil in which to take root; they showed none of the stubborn and substantive resistance to bourgeois values that Keith Thomas has found among the lower classes—or Christopher Hill among the aristocracy—of seventeenth-century Britain. Conflict there was in Puritan New England, but no place or period better illustrates Eric Hobsbawm's dictum that "the value of studies of major aspects of society are inversely proportional to our concentration on brief moments of conflict."[2]

For in all major aspects, New England was an outpost of the modern world from the start. Capitalism came there, in Carl

Degler's phrase, "in the first ships"; or as Max Weber put it, "the spirit of capitalism . . . was present [there] before the capitalistic order," and "no medieval antecedents or complicating institutional heritage [intervened] to mitigate the impact of the Protestant Ethic on American economic development."[3] On the contrary: in their revolt against Old World antecedents, the Puritans brought with them a sense of purpose that facilitated the process of modernization in crucial ways. They were only one of many groups of immigrants, from Jamestown to Philadelphia, that brought the spirit of capitalism to the New World; but more than any others it was they who gave that spirit a distinctive New World identity—gave it a local habitation, the continental "wilderness"; a name, "American"; and an ideology, the New England Way, that would in time fuse both terms, in providing a distinctive rhetoric for the major free-enterprise culture of the modern world. New England evolved from its own origins into the American Way, because from the start the colony was knit together, rhetorically, by a cultural "errand" into the wilderness.

It is that ideological function of the errand I want to stress. Considered as theology, the Puritan errand was a radical troping of Christian tradition to fit the fantasies of a particular sect. Considered as ideology, it was a mode of consensus designed to fill the needs of a certain social order. Let me take a moment to explain the basic tenets of consensus in the Puritans' own terms. By errand they meant, first of all, *migration*—not simply from one place to another, but from a depraved Old World to a New Canaan. Properly speaking, they explained, the newness of their New World was prophetic: it signalled the long-awaited new heaven and new earth of the millennium. The desert land they were reclaiming had its past in Bible promises: America was there so that in due time they could make it blossom as the rose. In other words, they used the biblical myth of exodus and conquest to justify imperialism before the fact. The Puritans sometimes appear as isolationists, but basically they were as eager as any other group of emigrants for land and gain. The difference was that they managed more effectively to explain away their greed. Other peoples, they explained, had their land by "common providence"; *they* had it by prophecy and promise.[4] Others might stake their colonial claims on royal patents or racial superiority or missionary rights. For the Massachusetts Bay Puritans it was a matter not of claiming rights but of reclaiming ownership. The wilderness belonged to their errand before the errand belonged to them.

That was one tenet of their consensus: migration as a function of prophecy, and prophecy as an unlimited license to expand. A second tenet of consensus centered on the problem of discipline. For on the whole the Puritans were an unruly lot—a volatile group of dissenters, "militant, apocalyptic, radically particularistic." In effect, the emigrant leaders were confronting what was to become a focal issue of free-enterprise society: how to endorse individualism without promoting anarchy. They found a variety of solutions at hand: a doctrine of calling that linked private and public identity; a series of interlocking covenants that transformed congregational "polity from an instrument of rebellion to one of control"; a concept of preparation for grace that "generated both a respect for individual freedom and a need for external discipline." All these methods, as various scholars have shown, helped to "harness the turbulent force of [Puritan] individualism."[5] They found a common framework in the concept of representative selfhood.

The concept derived from what might be called the spiritual, as distinct from the prophetic, sense of the errand. I refer now to the concept of errand as pilgrimage. For each Puritan saint, the venture into the wilderness had an inward and private end. It was a journey of the soul to God, the believer's pilgrimage through the world's wilderness to redemption. In this sense, the Puritan venture was above all a matter of personal self-assertion. It built upon a series of free and voluntary commitments, and it made for a community grounded not in tradition or class status, but in private acts of will. Yet not merely private, for in a larger sense, as the Puritans never tired of saying, every one of those acts was part of a communal venture. To assert oneself in the right way, here in the American wilderness, was to embody the goals of New England. And let me say again that these goals were secular as well as sacred. The errand presupposed the actual flowering of the wilderness. It was a rare thing, the Puritans knew, for piety and prosperity to grow together; but New England was a rare place. Whatever furthered the errand hastened the kingdom. Every sign of an individual's success, moral or material, made New England's destiny visible.

As migration, then, the errand rationalized the expansive and acquisitive aspects of settlement. As pilgrimage, the errand provided for internal control by rooting personal identity in social enterprise. The third tenet of consensus spoke directly to the dynamics of the enterprise at large. By definition, the errand meant progress. It implied a teleology reaching from Genesis to the Apocalypse. As a community on an errand, New England was a movement from sacred past to sacred future, a shifting point somewhere between migration and millennium. Its institutions were geared not so much to maintain stability as to sustain process and growth. Problems of order were characteristically framed in such questions as "How far have we come?" and "Where are we headed?" Hierarchy remained, but it was increasingly subsumed in what amounted to a daring re-vision of social norms. The Old World ideal of society was vertical, a model of class harmony. Ideally, New England was a "way," a road into the future. Virtually all its rituals of control—its doctrines of calling and preparation, its covenants of church, state, and grace—were directed toward that ideal. They were rites of voluntarism designed at once to yoke the personal to the political and to spur the venture forward to completion. Even the legend of the fathers, as the Puritans construed this, was a summons onward. It was not enough for them to conform to the past; or rather, to conform in their case was to dedicate oneself to constant improvement. That is why their sermons rose to a pitch of indignation, a shrill insistence on the prospect of collapse, unmatched in the European pulpit. The Puritans' vision fed on the distance between fact and promise. Anxiety became their chief means of establishing control. The errand, after all, was by definition a state of *un*fulfillment, and only a sense of crisis, properly directed and controlled, could guarantee the outcome.

In short, the New England Way was not theocracy. It was the ideology of a new culture encased in outmoded, quasi-biblical forms. To the extent that the Puritans confused theocracy with ideology, their errand was no more than a tribal vision. Migration was defined by a certain locale, New England; pilgrimage expressed the outlook of a certain sect, nonseparating congregationalism; and progress was limited to an exclusive group, the visible saints and their offspring. But considered in its own terms, both symbolic and functional—considered, that is, as the ideology of a nascent free-enterprise culture—the errand was as boundless as the wilderness. For to the Puritans, congregationalism was not just another sect. It was the vanguard of the Protestant movement; and Protestantism was not just another creed, but the last stage of the worldwide work of redemption. So, it was, too, with their locale. The Puritans took possession first by imposing their own image on the land, and then by seeing themselves reflected back in the image they had imposed. The wilderness became their mirror of prophecy. What they saw in it alternated between "wilderness purity" and an Army of Christ advancing into a continental New Canaan. In either case, the identity it yielded pertained not just to a particular geographical region, but, primarily, to a chosen nation in progress—a New Israel whose constituency was as numerous, potentially, as the entire people of God, and potentially as vast as America.

It was that larger, American vision which the Puritans bequeathed to the culture. This was their legacy: a system of sacred-secular symbols (New Israel, American Jerusalem) for a people intent on progress; a set of rituals of anxiety that could at once encourage and control the energies of free enterprise; a rhetoric of mission so broad in its implications, and so specifically American in its application, that it could facilitate the transitions from Puritan to Yankee, and from errand to manifest destiny and the dream. That these transitions effected changes in rhetoric and ritual goes without saying. But the capacity to accommodate change is proof of *vitality*, in symbolic no less than in social systems; and through the eighteenth century the rhetoric of errand remained a major vehicle of social continuity. In the next three chapters, I discuss these continuities in some detail. Here I want briefly to note the changes, particularly during the Great Awakening and the French and Indian War, which expanded, deepened, and finally Americanized the rhetoric of consensus.

To begin with, the concept of representative selfhood took on a broad Anglo–American meaning. The Great Awakening opened the gates of New Canaan to any evangelical, North or South; and the French and Indian War opened them wider still, to include any loyal colonist, evangelical and non-evangelical. Between 1740 and 1760, the benefits of the errand as pilgrimage—the special sense of oneself as representing God's New Israel—were extended to every patriotic white Protestant American. Of course, this involved a general redefinition of the self. It also reflected a tendency of the age toward what we have come to term individualism. Eighteenth-century America offered brave new vistas for private

enterprise, provided higher incentives for self-assertion, and fortified self-interest with a new theological and philosophical rationale for self-love. To some extent, these liberal attitudes paral-
leled, or could be made to parallel, the tenets of Puritan ideology.
And most of them contributed in some way to loosen and enlarge
the concept of representative selfhood. But the concept itself, to
recall, was intended as a strategy of control. It was designed to
keep self-assertion within cultural bounds. So it was used, in
effect, by the leaders of the Great Awakening. Significantly, the
revivalist emphasis on the self issued in the first major rituals of
intercolonial unity. So also the spokesmen for the French and
Indian War appealed to conscience and self-interest, only to make
these synonymous with Protestant patriotism, and the Protestant
cause inseparable from the rising glory of America. Both in revival
and in war, representative selfhood bound the rights of personal
ascent to the rites of social assent.

In both cases, too, the terms of assent extended the meaning
of the Puritan migration. Indeed, the legend of the founding fathers
was virtually transformed during this period, from a tribal legend
to a legend of cultural origins. Transformation, however, did not
issue in substantive change. It involved a process of revision, not
replacement—a means of providing for continuity in change even
as it allowed for change through continuity. On the one hand, the
epic of the Puritan exodus became the common property of all
Anglo–American settlers. Long after the theocracy had failed, after
Puritanism itself had faded theologically, the heroes of 1630 were
being ritually invoked—not just in New England, but in Pennsylvania, New York, and the South—to unite colonial Americans in
their sense of heritage and purpose. On the other hand, the meaning of the Puritan exodus was adjusted to the conditions of a new
age. For revivalists, the Great Migration was a herald of the Great
Awakening, an image or type of the "blessed unions" of converts
that would soon knit together, as one city on a hill, the whole of
Anglo–America. For leaders of the French and Indian War, the
Puritan emigrants were heroes in the cause of liberty. Their mission was Protestantism and liberalism entwined. Freedom was
their motive. The promise of a New Eden of industry and free
trade was their sacred legacy.

These revisions of meaning had far-reaching consequences.
Eventually, they were to provide a civic base for religion and a
religious base for liberalism in America. And they could have such

broad effect only because the rhetorical and social implications of the New England Way expressed the tendencies of the dominant culture. Most dramatically, this applies to the eighteenth-century re-vision of the errand as progress. The crucial change here came with the revivalist doctrine of postmillennialism. Technically speaking, the Puritans were premillennialists. That is, they believed that the millennium was still to come, and accordingly they expected that their errand would terminate in the miracles of the apocalypse. Edwards and his followers had an idea better suited to the Enlightenment and the New Science. They envisioned a continual increase of moral, spiritual, and material goods in this world—an age of sacred-secular wonders within history. They inherited the hope of supernatural things to come, and they altered this to mean an indefinite course of human progress. The glories of the coming of the Lord, they explained, were to be the last act in the conquest of the New World wilderness. For the Edwardseans, those glories centered on revival and conversion. For the clergy of 1760, the millennial hope centered on the defeat of French Canada. Clothing imperialism as holy war, they described Catholic Quebec as the last bastion of evil. A golden age of peace and prosperity, they promised, would follow the Protestant American victory. In short, the errand for them was not just the way to the millennium. It was millennialism as the American Way.

In all this, the rhetoric of the errand contributed to the Revolution. And let me repeat that it expressed a developing ideological mode. During the Great Awakening, it helped both to elicit and to direct the energies of economic growth. During the French and Indian War, it was used both to mobilize the colonists for invasion and to fortify their civic institutions. That ritual of anxiety (as I have called it) the patriotic Whigs put to effective use—first, in their propaganda war against England, and then, even more conspicuously, in their struggle for internal control. The nature of that struggle is well known. The Revolution had inspired what the Whig leaders termed a dangerous upsurge of egalitarian demands. Antiauthoritarianism was abroad in the land, and the men of wealth and property who ran the republic had a great deal at stake in the status quo. They could not afford a breakdown of established forms of deference. They found the order they sought in the ideology of errand. Elsewhere, they pointed out, revolution was a threat to society. It meant hiatus, discord, the dysfunction of class structure. But revolution in America was a different matter. Here it meant the unfolding of a redemptive plan. It required progress through conformity, the ordained succession from one generation to the next. What the American Puritan fathers had begun, their sons were bound to complete—*bound* by covenant and precedent. The War of Independence signalled America's long-prepared-for, divinely *ordered* passage into nationhood.

In other words, the Whig leaders brought the violence of revolution under control by making revolution a controlling metaphor for national identity. In a sense this was simply the product of anticolonial struggle. The rhetoric that prepared the colonists for revolution provided their leaders with a vehicle of social control: the pattern has become so familiar as to seem a condition of modern nationalism. What distinguishes the American revolution within this pattern is the rhetorical mode it brought to fruition. When the patriot Whigs expanded the concept of the errand into an apologia for independence, they gave full and final sanction to the ideology of consensus. Once and for all, the errand took on a special, self-enclosed *American* form. Independence from England completed the separation of the New World from the Old. Henceforth, Americans could direct the process of migration toward its proper goal, the conquest of a continent. Independence became the norm for representative selfhood: independence of mind, independence of means, and these twin blessings, sacred and secular, the mirror of a rising nation—what could better demonstrate the bond of personal and social identity? Elsewhere, to be independent was to challenge society. In the United States, it was to be a model of consensus. Above all, independence gave a distinctive national shape to the idea of progress. The sacred origin was the Puritan migration; the telos was the Revolution. Drawing out the logic of the errand to a point undreamed of by their forebears, the patriot Whigs announced that the long-awaited apocalyptic moment had arrived on July 4, 1776.

It took another generation or so before all the details could be worked out—before Washington could be enshrined as savior, his apostles ranked, the Judas in their midst identified, and the Declaration of Independence adequately compared to the Sermon on the Mount. But the ritual plot, the narrative frame of the ideology of errand, had at last found its focus. With the revolution, the Puritan vision flowered into the myth of America. For the errand itself was rooted in biblical myth. However eccentric their interpretations, the Puritans had relied on the authority of scripture. No matter how flagrantly they distorted sacred history to justify their experience, they were appealing, finally, to Christian tradition. The Revolutionary Whigs took the justification, rather than the tradition behind it, as their authority. No matter how piously they invoked scripture they were appealing not to Christian tradition, but to the series of recent events through which they defined the American experience. Their symbology centered on the act of migration; their text was the progress from theocracy to republic; their source of prophecy was the pilgrimage of the representative American.

The story they told was broadcast through the land every July Fourth, the high holy day of American civil religion. A new era, so the story went, had begun with the discovery of the New World, and the Revolution confirmed it, as Christ had confirmed the new era of faith. In both cases, the event was at once definitive and heuristic. Christ had invoked the authority of the prophets, but it was His mission that verified their prophecies. Such too was the relation between Old and New Israel. As the patriot spokesmen put it, the Revolution "is indissolubly linked with the Redeemer's mission." It is "the wonder and the blessing of the world," the moment "from which the new order of things is to be reckoned," the epoch-making "accomplishment of all . . . the great events, designed from eternal ages" to "promote *the perfection and happiness of mankind.*" "Here, from the analogy of reason and providence, we can expect God's greatest works." With the Revolution, God has shown that "The UNITED STATES OF AMERICA are to be His vineyard"—"the principal Seat of [His] glorious kingdom"—wherein the promises of the past "are to be brought to harvest," for "the benefit of the whole world."[6]

What a harvest! The flight of Abraham, the desert wanderings of Israel, the revival of the church, its war of independence against Catholic Rome, and the march of civilization from Greece and Rome through Renaissance, Reformation, and Enlightenment: to all these the Revolution stood as fulfillment to promise. And as fulfillment, it obviated the need for any further American uprisings. In the cliché that George Bancroft made famous, it was a revolution to end revolutions. Revisions and cleansings there would have to be, but fundamentally the direction was set. Hereafter, the spirit of progress was the Spirit of Seventy-Six. And the converse was equally true. As the fulfillment of promises past, the Revolution was the guarantee of better things to come. "The American war [against England] is over," the Whig leaders explained in 1787; "but this is far from being the case with the American revolution. On the contrary, nothing but the first act of the great drama is closed." Now that we have "made good our fathers' covenant," the *magnalia Christi Americana* will continue, in the image of the Revolution "to the end of time."[7]

The leaders of Puritan New England had devised the errand to bring a group of potential revolutionaries under control. The patriot Whigs took control of the republic by translating the errand into the rhetoric of continuing revolution. In doing so, they set forth the one myth patterned specifically to the needs of liberal middle-class society. Protestantism may have given modern culture its ethic, but Puritanism gave it the myth of America. And no culture, let me add, ever stood more in need of a myth. From the seventeenth century on, modernism has meant a world where the self was cut loose in a marketplace of other independent selves; where no theory of government could offer a ready way to impose community; where the guiding philosophers were the masters of realpolitik—not Plato or Aristotle, but Bacon and Machiavelli; not Aquinas or Calvin, but Hobbes and Locke. The Constitution-makers had no substitute except nature's laws for the divine right of kings. "Neither Philosophy, nor Religion," they recognized, "nor Morality, nor Wisdom, nor Interest, will ever govern nations or parties, against their Vanity, their Pride, their Resentment or Revenge, or their Avarice and Ambition. Nothing but Force and Power and Strength can restrain them. . . . [Therefore,] power must be opposed to power, force to force, strength to strength, [and] interest to interest."[8] What they offered, accordingly, was a pragmatic federalism: division of powers, self-protective multiplicity. It was a model of modern statecraft, embracing the open competition of values (as of goods) and encouraging discrepant views to coexist in the same society even as they challenged each other's priorities. In effect, the Constitution-makers provided the first full-scale rationale for the forces of pluralism and secularization that shaped the postfeudal West.

It was not enough. Modern communities, as we have come to learn, have as much need for spiritual cohesion as did the communities of the past. The citizens of a republic, no less than the subjects of a monarchy or the members of a church-state, require some means of consecrating their way of life—a set of metaphysically (as well as naturally) self-evident truths; a moral framework within which a certain complex of attitudes, assumptions, and beliefs can be taken for granted as being not only proper but right; a superempirical authority to sustain the norms of personal and social selfhood. And those needs were particularly strong in the new republic. One has only to consider the traumatic effects of the break with monarchy, or Crèvecoeur's charges at the end of his *Letters from an American Farmer*, in a chapter rarely cited by Americanists, where he explains his preference for the "primitive" order of Indian society to the chaos of independence. The charges were reasonable enough. To all appearances, the country in the late 1770s *was*, as the Loyalists said, "anarchy set loose":[9] a nation without a past, a people of diverse customs, a territory without clear boundaries, an economy without a stable center—variously agrarian, urban, preindustrial, and in transition toward industrialism—and a free-enterprise system that was endangered by the very doctrine of self-interest it sought to encourage, and, if anything, endangered still more by the values of independence and revolt upon which the nation was founded.

One major reason for the Whigs' success was that the rhetoric of consensus filled the need for a communal myth. It gave the country a past and a future in sacred history, rendered its civic institutions a fulfillment of prophecy, elevated its so-called true inhabitants, the Anglo–Saxon Protestants who had immigrated within the past century or so, to the status of God's chosen, and declared the vast territories around them to be *their* promised land. Above all, it grounded the myth in a central symbol, "America," that joined the Hobbist and spiritual poles of the social order.* The effects of this fusion can hardly be overestimated. Translated into the terms of social anthropology, they imply the basic dynamics of the ritual process itself:

> At the ideological [or normative] pole . . . there is a cluster of meanings referring to moral values, principles of social organization, rules

---

*So considered, "America" (as a cultural symbol) bridges the antinomies that are often used by political scientists to distinguish between myth and ideology: sacred and secular, nostalgic and progressivist, millennial and utopian, prophetic and situational, holistic and particularistic, rational and irrational.

of social behavior, the ideals of corporate groups, in short all the obligatory elements in the social order. At the sensory [or oretic] pole . . . there are gross sensations, desires, and feelings. The norms, values, principles and rules at the ideological pole are abstract and remote and [so] . . . not sufficient to induce [a person] to action. It is only when he is emotionally agitated . . . that he will be moved to action. In the action situation of the ritual . . . the ritual symbol effects an interchange of qualities between the two poles of the symbol. Norms and values become saturated with emotion, while . . . basic emotions become ennobled through contact with social values. The irksomeness of moral constraint is transformed into the love of goodness. Ritual thus becomes a mechanism which periodically converts the obligatory into the desirable.[10]

This analysis probably applies in some degree to any cohesive culture. But its applicability to the new republic has special significance. Nowhere has constraint (social or moral) been more "irksome," potentially, than in the formative stages of free-enterprise capitalism; nowhere has "gross desire" more directly challenged the status quo; nowhere have desire and obligation stood more precariously opposed; and nowhere in the modern world were those threats more firmly converted into voluntary allegiance than in the formation of the United States. In a ritual procession of speeches and sermons that made oratory a high national art form, the spokesmen for the republic invested "America" with the double powers of materiality and the spirit. As the myth's dominant symbol, interchangeably sensory and ideological, "America" came to signify both self-gratification and the self-evident good, the most pragmatic of communities and the most abstract of ideals. Social organization, if *American*, was by definition noble. And to be noble in the *American* grain was ipso facto the practical way to get things done.

On that basis, the Federalist leaders channelled the volatile emotions of revolt into the structures of a (rhetorically) homogeneous nation. Their rituals of crisis proved a decisive moral mechanism in the war against excessive self-interest. Their invocations to continuing revolution effectually barred the influence of unsettling "foreign ideologies," particularly those of revolutionary France. Their summons to independence magnified the "pursuit of happiness" from a merely private enterprise into an enterprise that entailed not only the common good but the redemption of mankind. In virtually every area of life, the rhetoric of American consensus served to consecrate the practice and theory of democratic capitalism. Mediating between "gross feelings" and "remote abstraction," the felt rights of ascent and the imposed duties of assent, it gave contract the sanctity of covenant, free enterprise the halo of grace, progress the glory of millennium, and chauvinism the grandeur of typology. In sum, it wed modernism to the errand, conferred on both the blessings of continuing revolution, and certified the union with the Great Seal of the United States: *Annuit Coeptis, Novus Ordo Seclorum*—"God prospered this undertaking; it shall be the new order of the ages."

The union was a fruitful one. Its success is attested by the fact that the United States not only usurped American identity but retained its exclusive meaning. Elsewhere during this period, the Enlightenment rhetoric of "the people" proved to be a major obstacle for revolutionaries. The vagueness of Robespierre's appeal to "the people" forced him, in George Rudé's words, to fall "victim to his own ideals," trapped between the bourgeois who controlled the French Republic and the sansculottes he thought he represented. Similar ambiguities in Hidalgo's rhetoric undermined the 1810 revolution in Mexico. Preaching the parallels between the Gospels, Rousseau, and Adam Smith, Hidalgo had hoped to forge a coalition of Creoles and Indians against Spanish colonists. Instead, he incited a more basic conflict in which all the upper classes, alarmed at the threat to property rights, allied themselves against the dispossessed majority. The same conflicts worked to destroy Bolivar's dream of a South American Republic. Having made himself the Liberator of too many of "the people"— blacks, Indians, and mulattoes, as well as the aspiring middle class he came from—having succeeded too well, that is, with the liberal rhetoric of equality, Bolivar too, like Robespierre and Hidalgo, found himself betrayed by the realities of race and class conflict.[11]

The leaders of New Israel managed to sidestep those pitfalls. They could endorse universalism and yet exclude from it whatever then hindered their progress. The American was not (like the Frenchman or the Latin American) a member of "the people." He stood for a mission that was limitless in effect, because it was limited in fact to a "peculiar" nation. Thus (in the notorious paradox of the Declaration) he could denounce servitude and oppression while concerning himself least, if at all, with the most enslaved and inadequately represented groups in the land. Those groups were part of "the people," perhaps, but not the *chosen* people; they were in America, but not of it. I think here not only of moderates and conservatives, such as Adams and Hamilton, but of so-called radicals such as Tom Paine. If at first Paine "manipulated" the rhetoric of consensus, as some historians claim, eventually he became himself an instrument of the rhetoric, a missionary to Europe for the Constitution and the American Way. Thus in direct contrast to French radicals, who used "the language of the people" to stress class divisions, Paine appealed in that language for "social harmony" and the "spirit of reconciliation." The basis for his appeal throughout the 1790s was America— the one true "Republic in the world," a "veritable utopia" where "the poor are not oppressed, the rich are not privileged . . . government is just; and . . . there is nothing to engender riots and tumults"— a New Canaan charged "by the design of Heaven" with "the cause of all mankind."[12]

Paine was to change his mind, reluctantly, upon his return to New Canaan. But the consensus he espoused continued to gather strength during the Federalist period. Through the rituals of continuing revolution, the middle-class leaders of the republic recast the Declaration to read, "all propertied, white, Anglo–Saxon Protestant males are created equal." Through those rituals they confined the meaning of revolution to American progress, American progress to God's chosen, and God's chosen to people of their own kind. It is no accident that under Jefferson's administration, the Revolution issued in an increasing violation—for blacks and Indians—of life, liberty, and the pursuit of happiness. Nor is it by accident that so many of the electoral debates through the Jacksonian and antebellum periods turned on which party was the legitimate heir to the title of American Israel, and which candidate the true son of the Revolutionary fathers and Puritan forefathers. Nor is it by accident, finally, that while France and Latin America degenerated into factional pandemoniums, the United States generated a conformist spirit that foreign observers termed a "tyranny of the majority."

"A tyranny of the culture" would have been more precise. Nationalism served elsewhere during this period to unify modern communities, but it brought with it the archaic myths and mystiques of the communal past. This was the case in post-Revolutionary France, where the old pantheon of regal heroes remained intact—Charlemagne, Roland, Henry IV, the Sun King Louis

XIV—just as the term *aristocrat* retained its honorific meaning and *bourgeois* its pejorative meaning, despite the triumph of the middle class. This was also the case in nineteenth-century Germany, where nationalism helped equally to modernize the state and to conjure up an atavistic *Volksgeist*, fired by feudal legends and profound antilibertarian sentiments. A similar clash of interests attended the rise of Russian nationalism. Westernization and Pan-Slavism both contributed to that development, but the myth of Pan-Slavic destiny provided a wholly different basis for community from that offered by the progressivists, whether liberal, socialist, or communist.

The American rhetoric of consensus showed no such conflicts. Here, the ideals of community wholly supported the goals of free enterprise. Even when these ideals seemed to conflict, as between Jefferson and Adams, agrarian and entrepreneur, Jacksonians and bankers, even then the conflicts bespoke a systemic process of development. The process was not inevitable, of course, nor was the development teleological; but under the peculiar circumstances of the new republic—circumstances that included extraordinary resources of territory, economic abundance, and political leadership, as well as a burgeoning cultural symbology— the system that emerged expressed an increasing harmony between the ideological and experiential dimensions of modern liberal society (moral standards, principles of government, forms of desire, incentives to constraint). Here only, accordingly, of all new nations in 1800, the invocation of the past actually enhanced the values of of progress. Here only, of all the hopeful New World republics in 1820, the concept of independence fostered indigenous communal bonds. And here only, of all modernizing Western nations in 1840, the values of newness and of tradition were made to correspond. The Russian Church at this time denounced secular reform in the name of sacred history, peasant tradition, and the "Russian soul." French Romantics and German nationalists arrayed themselves against the Enlightenment.[13] But in the United States, all three movements, Christian, Deist, and Romantic, fused in the national symbol. By the mid-nineteenth century, America was the land of prophecy, reason, and nature entwined. Here as nowhere else, the very hope of improvement led social critics to reject the idea of alternative systems (not to mention class conflict) since improvement was the American Way, and "American," after all, was a consensual term. Ritually and ideologically, it embodied the promise of the New World, and therefore of the future at large.

It was a tyranny not of the majority but of a liberal-symbolic system of thought. The United States has never had what Tocqueville called a "universal middling standard," nor was it ever a nation of "similar participants in a uniform way of life," a people "all of the same estate," as Louis Hartz claimed. Rather, it was a culture bound by an extraordinary ideological hegemony. How else can we explain so many major writers bewailing the lack of history and diversity in the land? "I have never seen a people so much alike in my life, as the Americans," marvelled James Fenimore Cooper in 1828. He knew well enough about differences between whites and Indians or blacks, about differences between urban socialites, immigrant laborers, and rural gentry, and for that matter about the different customs in the North, South, and West. So, too, did Hawthorne when in 1860, on the eve of civil war, he described the United States as "a country where there is no shadow, no antiquity, no mystery, no picturesque and gloomy wrong, nor anything but a common-place prosperity, in broad and simple daylight."[14] It was not ignorance or insensitivity that led to these wry complaints. It was merely, astonishingly, that in terms of the myth such differences did not count. *Nation* meant *Americans, Americans* meant *the people,* and *the people* meant those who, thanks to the Revolution, enjoyed a *commonplace prosperity:* the simple sunny rewards of American middle-class life.

It is really beside the point to speak here of evasions or distortions of the facts. Those evasions or distortions express a fundamental truth about the culture. They reveal a dominant pattern of belief, reaching from Ben Franklin's Poor Richard to Horatio Alger's Ragged Dick. Of course, the pattern I speak of yields only one sort of truth. Seen from outside the consensus, mid-nineteenth-century America had a very different look. It was a stratified, conflicted society, rife with ethnic and class divisions. One of every five Americans was a black or an Indian; one of every eight whites was a recent immigrant; in the urban centers, where $1,000 a year was an average middle-class income, only 1 percent of the population earned over $800. During this so-called era of the common man, fewer than 2 percent of the rich were not born rich. Jacksonian democracy was a less egalitarian state than

Puritan theocracy. Consider these recent statistics: in 1670, when Samuel Danforth delivered his famous sermon on New England's errand, 5 percent of the saints owned one-quarter of the wealth. In 1770, when Franklin praised the colonies' "general Mediocrity of Fortune," 3 percent of the colonists owned one-third of the wealth. In the 1830s, when Tocqueville wrote his myth of egalitarian democracy, 1 percent of Americans owned almost half the wealth of America.[15]

Hence the importance of the *rhetoric* of consensus. It served then, as always, to blur such discrepancies. But in doing so, the rhetoric provides us with a map of social reality that is no less accurate in its way than any quantitative chart. It locates the sources of social revitalization and integration. It helps explain how the majority of people kept the faith despite their day-by-day experiences. It reminds us that although the concept of hegemony involves the dialectics of change, the directions of change are in turn crucially affected by the terms of hegemonic constraint. And in this case the effect was demonstrable in the way that the rhetoric of consensus molded what was to all appearances the most heterogeneous "people" in the world into the most monolithic of modern cultures.

For the fact is that what Cooper and Hawthorne said about the country may be found throughout the popular literature. Virtually every one of the hundreds of mid-nineteenth-century biographers of "great Americans" insisted that his subject was not someone unique, but the emblem of American enterprise: a self-reliant man who was therefore, paradoxically, a cultural pattern, the model of a rising nation. The same paradox of representation (self and community entwined, as in a secular incarnation) applied to the countless rags-to-riches stories. However humble their origins, these heroes were not members of the working class, nor were they, after their success, nouveau riche, and certainly they never became upper-class. They were rather, every fatherless son of them, aspiring, self-motivated (even when, like Whitman, they were inspired by Emerson), self-reliant (even when, like Alger's Sam Barker, they depended on employers), self-educated (even when, like Thoreau, they were Harvard graduates), mobile (even if they decided, like Hawthorne's Holgrave, to settle down), and independent. And independence, of course, signified not so much an economic state as a state of mind and being, an entire system of moral, political, and religious values. In short, the American hero could represent no particular set of interests because he represented the general good—which is to say, a cultural myth.

To be self-made in 1850 was more than to make one's own fortune; it was to embody a metaphysics. So it was, too, with the concept of "middle-class." Jacksonians invested that term—both in the singular and in its ubiquitous plural ("middle-classes")— with all the exuberant spiritual as well as material values of a thriving economy in an expanding capitalist nation. As European travellers were startled to learn, Americans regarded "middle-class" not as a relative position in the state but as an absolute state of mind. It meant not "bourgeois" but "aspiring"; not "ill-educated" but "self-taught"; not "unaristocratic" but "unshackled by tradition"; not "uprooted" but "authentic"; not "engaged in various occupations" but "mobile" and "adaptable." To be "middle-class" in the United States was to have a moral outlook, rather than a certain income; it displayed itself less in certain manners and mannerisms than in a set of virtues that opened into a program for self-perfection. Significantly, such European pejoratives as "parvenu" never took hold in this country. Here their equivalent was the *echt* Americanism, "self-made," a euphoric catchall that appropriated the feudal-religious rhetoric of "kingship" on behalf of middle-class individualism. The Revolutionary historian David Ramsay (himself a Virginia planter) boasted of Washington's "humble origins" and "middling circumstances," and pointed out that the War of Independence was won by "self-made, industrious men. These who, by their own exertions, had established or laid a foundation for establishing personal independence, [and so] were . . . most successfully employed in establishing that of their country." Half a century later, Emerson claimed that "all great men come out of the middle classes." Whitman poeticized that liberal golden mean as "the divine average"—"that law of average Identity . . . [which is] the divine law of the universal."[16]

By and large, it was a universal for men, but women found their own ways of joining the consensus. One way was through motherhood, reconceived in the middle-class terms of the cult of domesticity. As Catharine Beecher, the cult's high priestess, put it in 1841: "The shaping of the people" has been "committed mainly to the female hand." As mothers, she wrote, we mold the characters of our children; and as American mothers, we mold the character of those who are to continue the errand. We are therefore "agents in accomplishing the greatest work ever entrusted to human responsibility." Another way was militant feminism. We appeal to "principles cherished by all Americans," wrote Elizabeth Cady Stanton. The cause we fight for is no "foreign import." It is the "legacy of the Fathers," augmented now by "a new spirit of energy"—open competition, free labor, equal opportunity, and the sanctity of private property, especially the property of the self. That was 1848, the year of the first Paris Commune and the Communist Manifesto; the year also of the first Women's Rights Convention, at Seneca Falls, whose manifesto followed the form and phrases of the Declaration of Independence, and whose goal, in the words of Antoinette Brown, was to "remove the [last] stigma resting on this republic."[17]

Probably some of these feminists believed that they were merely *using* patriotism, manipulating the rhetoric of the republic for ulterior radical ends. But if so, they were miscalculating the relation of ends and means. In effect (as events proved), they were conforming to a ritual of consensus that defused all issues in debate by restricting the debate itself, symbolically *and substantively*, to the meaning of America. In this, the feminists were like most American radicals of the time. William Lloyd Garrison, for example, organized the American Anti-Slavery Society as "a renewal of the nation's founding principles" and of the "national ideal." Frederick Douglass based his demands for black liberation on America's "destiny," the "sacred meaning" of July Fourth, and "the genius of American institutions," which would one day, he hoped, transform the world (including "darkest Africa") in "all-pervading light." In that faith, Robert Rantoul defended his "left-wing programs" as expressing the "national errand" for "the renovation of mankind." With that prospect in view, Adin Ballou organized his "experiment in radical reform" at Hopedale. Like the transcendentalist founders of Brook Farm, he expected the venture in utopia to "provide 'types' for the millennium" in America. Similar examples abound in every area of the country. As a leading historian of the period has remarked, "the typical reformer, for all his uncompromising spirit, was no more alienated—no more truly rebellious—than the typical democrat. . . .

[He] might sound radical while nevertheless associating himself with the fundamental principles and underlying tendencies of America."[18]

Nothing more clearly attests to the continuing power of the myth than does the proliferation of "radical" manifestoes in antebellum America. For once the Revolution was secured, the rhetoric of consensus increasingly elicited social criticism. After all, what higher defense could one offer for middle-class society than an American Way that sui generis evoked the free competition of ideas? And what could make things safer for middle-class society than to define freedom in terms of the American Way? In mid-nineteenth-century Europe, the summons to "the people" exposed the pretense of unity; there, revolution bared the dynamics of historical change. In America at this time, the summons to dissent, because it was grounded in prescribed ritual forms, circumscribed the threat of basic social alternatives. It facilitated process in such a way as to enlist radicalism itself in the cause of institutional stability.

I do not mean by this to belittle the struggle of those reformers. Garrison, Rantoul, and Ballou paid a high personal price for their dissent. Douglass and Stanton claimed to be true Americans, and Thoreau called John Brown "the most American of us all,"[19] but to most of their neighbors they were three more in a long list of un-Americans, along with the other abolitionists, feminists, and utopians (not to mention such blatant outsiders as Chief Black Hawk, Rabbi Mayer Isaac Wise, and John England, the Catholic Bishop of Charleston, South Carolina). In this sense, the ritual meant consensus through negation: garden versus wilderness, chosen people versus the nations of the earth. One major characteristic of the period was its astonishing variety of official or self-appointed committees to keep America pure: "progressivists" for eradicating the Indians; "American Christians" for deporting the Catholics; "benevolent societies" for returning the blacks to Africa; "Young Americans" for banning European culture.

But in the long run exclusion was a strategy for absorption. Like the Puritan concept of errand, it was a way of saying "not yet" so that finally one could say "you, too." The conflict between garden and wilderness implied that what was wilderness now would one day be a greater New Canaan. So it was also in the case of the chosen people versus the world (including European culture); so also in the case of true versus false Americans. The

American consensus *could* absorb feminism, if feminism would lead into the middle-class American Way. Blacks and Indians could also learn to be True Americans, when in the fullness of time they would adopt the tenets of black and red capitalism. On that provision, Jews and even Catholics could eventually become sons and daughters of the Revolution. On those grounds, even such unlikely candidates for perfection as Alaska and Hawaii could be America.

All of these recent developments are implicit in the rhetoric of errand; and the implications help define what I called a cultural, as distinct from a national, mode of consensus. The biblical Hebrews were nationalists. Although they claimed their land by promise, Canaan itself was a country (like any other) with fixed boundaries; and though they called themselves a "peculiar people," their peculiarity was based (like any other people in their time) upon genealogy and a certain form of religion. Genealogy, boundaries, and a certain form of religion were precisely what American nationhood has *not* meant. American genealogy was simply the idea of mission brought up to date. As a community, New Israel was the heir of the ages; its representative citizen was independent, unbound by any public or personal ties, except the ties of culture that required him to be self-made. As for boundaries, political leaders dissolved that barrier to progress by reversing the meaning of frontier. Traditionally, a frontier was a border dividing one people from another. It implied differences between nations. In a sense, antebellum Americans recognized such differences— their frontier separated them from the Indians—but they could hardly accept the restriction as permanent. This was God's Country, was it not? So they effected a decisive shift in the meaning of frontier, from barrier to threshold. Even as they spoke of their frontier as a meeting ground between two civilizations, Christian and pagan, they redefined it, in an inversion characteristic of the myth-making imagination, to mean a *figural* outpost, the outskirts of the advancing kingdom of God.

The inversion has become so familiar by now as to seem an inevitable outgrowth of the Westward Movement. But the fact is that other immigrant groups responded in entirely different ways. I think here not only of the Spaniards, who had the whole run of the West from the Mississippi Valley to California, but primarily of the Anglo–Canadians, who had the same cultural heritage as the Americans, including a common set of dominant racial and religious traits (white Anglo–Saxon Protestant), a common liberal ideology, and a common commitment, virtually from the start, to the process of modernization. They also defined themselves in relation to the Western frontier, yet their definition issued in a decidedly un-American outlook. To Canadians, the frontier has always meant "antagonism," the clash of cultures, the "loneliness of a huge and thinly settled country," the problems of "carving out" a community "in the face of 'hostile' elements." The most widely accepted image of the Canadian West, "the bush country," derives directly from the commonsense meaning of frontier as barrier, dividing line, or state of separation. To be a Canadian pioneer in the nineteenth century was to be "surrounded with a physical or psychological 'frontier,' separated from . . . cultural sources"; it was to join for purposes of commerce and survival in "small and isolated communities: communities . . . that [were] compelled to feel a great respect for the law and order that [held] them together, yet confronted with a huge unthinking, menacing and formidable physical setting."[20] In short, the Canadians' errand was grounded in colonial history. Whether it denoted the Northland, the prairie, or the far West, their concept of frontier conveyed the conditions of imposing one culture upon another, or (as they sometimes reconceived this) of imposing culture upon nature—the contradictions inherent in the very notion of a *Canadian* wilderness.

The American rhetoric of frontier was designed precisely to obviate such contradictions. As Northrop Frye remarked, "Robert Frost's line, 'The land was ours before we were the land's . . .' does not apply to Canada." Nor does the Turner thesis, nor the idea of nature's nation or virgin land or American Adam—not because Canada had no vast tracts of uninhabited land, not because it lacked idealists or Edenic vistas, not because it could not offer immigrants the prospects of a fresh start, but because "Canada" was quintessentially a colonial identity. Like "Mexico," "Brazil," or "Argentina," it was a culture whose symbols of community were not only derived from but centered in Europe. And thus lacking an indigenous New World Vision, how could the Canadian frontiersman see, as his American counterpart did, that the "open territory" was "a holy text"? How could he draw the map of Alberta, as John Filson drew the map of Kentucky, in a series of prophecies, each "voicing a more sweeping vision of American glory"?[21] Even when Canadians transgressed boundaries, they retained the relativistic meaning of the term. The myth of America eliminated the very issue of transgression. From being a dividing line, "frontier" became a synonym for progress. And as New Israel progressed across the continent, the Westward Movement came to provide a sort of serial enactment of the ritual of consensus. It was a moving stage for the drama of exodus and conquest, a continuing act of self-vindication by a remnant of visible saints become a host of self-made entrepreneurs—a new chosen people that had broadened, in proportion to the broadening American landscape, to include all denominations of the American Protestant faith.

I refer here, of course, to the doctrine of multi-denominationalism, which became national policy after the Revolution. National, however, in that peculiar sense I mentioned: it revealed the absence in *this* nation of any traditional form of religion. Multi-denominationalism came clothed in the brightest rhetoric of the millennium, but it amounted to nothing more or less than a spiritual version of free enterprise. It issued in a religious identity that was as open-ended—as vague in scope and theological content—as was the concept of pilgrimage, migration, or progress. As the clergy kept insisting, the American churches were together carrying the Ark of Christ and the Constitution. Like standard-bearers of the twelve separate tribes of Israel, they all stood for one sacred-secular cause. It is not too much to say that the midcentury clerics turned the pulpit into a platform for the American Way. The great crusades of Lyman Beecher and Charles Grandison Finney brought "Gospel tidings" that "rugged individualism in business enterprise, laissez-faire in economic theory, [and] constitutional democracy in political thought" would "usher in the millennial morning." These were the tidings, too, of Francis Wayland in 1825, urging the parallels between piety, self-help, and the Second Coming; of Albert Barnes in 1832, explaining that "this land has been preserved [so] that there might be here furnished [through] . . . enterprise and liberty . . . the fairest civilization that the world has ever seen of pure Christianity"; of William Sprague in 1833, declaring that religion had made America the universal "model of social and civil renovation"; of Mark Hopkins in 1850, offering evidence for the approaching kingdom in the "liberty and rights of the individual"; of William Conant in 1858, explaining that "truly to be self-made" was to unite "the intensity of individual force with the majority of multitude and the spirit of Eternal

Love. . . . We certainly witness at present a revival of unprecedented power, in which *the people are the preachers* . . . in beautiful harmony with the nature of modern American existence."[22]

The nature of modern American existence: under that banner "the hope of Revival," as Perry Miller observed, "cut across denominations." In reply to all criticism, the "defense again and again insisted that [revivalism] was an *American* method." Thus "while the religious leaders were ostensibly talking about harmony among the churches, they were actually charting the way toward a homogeneous America." Through the various associations they founded—"The American Education Society (1815), The American Bible Society (1816), The American Sunday School Union (1824), The American Tract Society (1825), The American Home Missionary Society (1826)"—the revivalists "were not [just] preaching nationalism, they were enacting it." I would add to Miller's analysis that they were not just enacting nationalism, they were transforming it into cultural consensus. "The Spirit of the Lord," they declared, "was mightily at work," fusing "Protestantism and American patriotism, capitalist economics and Christian morality"; "free enterprise, bent upon the creation of a Christian commonwealth," was establishing "the millennium through the hallowing of America."[23] The Great Awakening has been called the last Calvinist offspring of the New England Way. The nineteenth-century revivals may be seen as the Frankenstein's monster of the Puritan errand. What they undertook, in effect, was a nationwide cooptation of the conversion experience—a wholesale reversal of spiritual *communitas* into a rite of socialization.

Naturally, none of this (including all the talk "about harmony among the churches") discouraged sectarian acrimony. Following the logic of pluralist consensus, the belief in a common cause elicited dissent and debate. The result was a *concordia discors* as deafening as the one I encountered in the 1960s—revivalists against Unitarians, premillennialists against postmillennialists, Methodists against Baptists, Calvinists against anti-Calvinists, Beecher against Finney, Wayland against Sprague against Hopkins against Conant—a thousand aggressively independent individuals and sects all saying the same thing. For if in some ways the American public order proved to be a more ambiguous text than even the Protestant Bible, the ambiguities it spawned, like those of the Bible, were self-enclosed: in all cases the true way was interpreted a priori by the meaning (like "middle-class," at once plural and singular) of America.

Let me illustrate how the clergy went about their business of interpretation by extracting one voice from the chorus. Philip Schaff was born in Switzerland, and educated in Stuttgart, Halle, and Berlin. He came to the United States in 1844, in his early twenties, to save immigrant Pennsylvania Lutherans from the dangers of Americanization. He stayed to join the consensus. Ten years later he explained why:

> When history shall have erected its central stage of action on the magnificent theatre of the new world, the extreme ends of the civilized world will be brought together in the achievements of modern science, the leveling influences of the press and public opinion, and the workings of the everlasting Gospel. Then . . . [will come] the millennium of righteousness. This . . . [is] the distinctive mission of the American nation, to represent a compact, well-defined and yet world-embracing. As the children of the sturdy Puritans, we are the nation of the future. . . . The first Adam was a type and prophecy of second Adam; the very name of Abraham pointed to Messianic blessings that should flow from . . . [our] seed upon nations of earth. . . .
>
> Such high views ought to humble us with a deep sense of our responsibility. . .[but] there are fearful tendencies in our national life. There is a false Americanism as well as a true one. I need only remind you of the wild and radical tendencies of our youth; the piratical schemes of our manifest-destinarians who would swallow in one meal, Cuba, all Central America, Mexico and Canada. . . . [Still, these various signs of degeneracy are] merely the wild oats of the young giant who will in due time learn better manners and settle down upon the sober discharge of his proper duties. God delivered us from greater dangers and will not forsake us until He has accomplished His purposes through our instrumentality.[24]

I have quoted this passage at length because it so vividly demonstrates what it meant to become acculturated into the antebellum North. Philip Schaff was one of the great church historians of his time, an immigrant deeply rooted in the traditions of European thought, and an outspoken opponent of some of the more outrageous forms of Americanism. Nonetheless, by 1854 he could not imagine a viable alternative to the American Way. The very terms of his denunciation—the sweeping opposition he asserts between true and false Americans—remind us how far the consensus reached, and how enveloping were its powers. It was a web spun out of scriptural myth and liberal ideology that allowed virtually no avenue of escape. Technology and religion, individualism and social progress, spiritual, political, and economic values—all the fragmented aspects of life and thought in this pluralistic society flowed into "America," the symbol of cultural consensus, and then, in a ritual balance of anxiety and reaggregation, flowed outward again to each independent unit of society. To celebrate the future was to criticize the present. To denounce American life was to endorse the national dream. Whether one felt "humble," "fearful," or "hopeful," the sense of crisis that attended those feelings affirmed a single, omnivorous mission. As an exponent of the errand, the Swiss-born, German-educated Philip Schaff had no more hesitation in calling the Puritans *his* fathers than did the "manifest-destinarians" he despised. Ten years later in fact he joined them in acclaiming the Civil War as the full and final proof of America's mission.

It would be easy to show the gathering force of this outlook through the 1850s. It would be easier still to document the persistent rhetoric of consensus, on the part of abolitionists and gradualists alike, on both sides of the Lincoln–Douglas debates (concerning "that great mission, that destiny which Providence has marked out for us"), and to some extent even on the part of Confederate leaders, such as the Virginia politicians who argued that not Lincoln's but *their* "America was God's beacon of light to the world," or the Mississippi and Alabama Evangelicals who read the "Apocalypse" of 1861 as "the ultimate sanctification in blood of the divine mission of the United States." But my point is not that the Civil War was inspired by a certain mode of rhetoric. It is that the rhetoric reflected and shaped a broad ideological movement which, for a variety of reasons, issued in civil war. In John Higham's summary account:

> ideology . . . links social action with fundamental beliefs, collective identity with the course of history. This combination of generality with directional thrust has enabled ideology to function as an important unifying force . . . in America [because here Puritanism] . . .

arrived not as a subversive or divisive force [as it was in England], but as a bedrock of order, purpose, and cohesion. . . . The Puritans had needed the discipline of ideology to . . . stave off fragmentation. Their descendants. . .put their ideological inheritance to expanded uses. What had been a discipline became also an incitement . . . [one that] offered Americans a collective task and a sustaining hope. . . . [With the Revolution,] Protestant ideology . . . attached itself to American nationalism. . .[and thereby] forged the strongest bonds that united the American people during the nineteenth century. . . . As the desire for ideological unity increased, slavery—a flat denial of the American ideology—became less and less tolerable. In that broad sense the Civil War, like the expansionism that preceded it, was the result of a general intensification of ideological forces.[25]

Ironically, then, what made conflict irrepressible was the irrepressible growth toward ideological unity. It is a fitting climax to what might be considered the major irony of colonial history, when the Puritans set out a rhetoric and ritual for a new culture, and so facilitated the growth from the New England to the American Way.

The movement toward consolidation permeated all levels of the culture. On the broadest scale, it issued in what Alan Trachtenberg calls "the incorporation of America"; it found its most dramatic expression, in the decade prior to the Civil War, in the American Renaissance. To see how indebted our classic writers were to the national symbol, how deeply engaged they were in the rhetoric of consensus, is to recognize the native grounds of American Romanticism. Both the American and the European Romantics presented themselves as isolatoes, prophets crying in the wilderness. But our classic writers were *American* prophets, at once lamenting a declension and celebrating a national dream. Directly or indirectly, their works formed part of the same ritual that enveloped (and transmuted) all forms of antebellum dissent. The European Romantics took a different course. Even for the nationalists and conservatives among them, "high literature" was (in Northrop Frye's words) "a conscious mythology: it create[d] an autonomous world" that stood apart from the "kind of mythology . . . produced by society." In this they were of course modern artists, representing a recent and far-reaching change in the relation between literature and society. Traditionally, "the same work could belong to both mythologies at once": literature in premodern societies was intrinsic to "the work of culture," and often designed to perpetuate existing social values. The European Romantics, on the contrary, tended toward a divisive, comparatist "play of the imagination."* Directly or indirectly, they express the separation of "high art" from "popular culture" that remains "a perspective of our own revolutionary age."[26]

It seems a paradox that in the United States—the land of the modern, a nation self-consciously founded on revolution, a culture committed to diversity and fragmentation—that here of all places the national myth should preempt the growth of "conscious mythology." But it is the sort of paradox upon which the entire mechanism of consensus was built. Precisely because the United States was the land of the modern, the symbol of America could subsume the "autonomous worlds" of Romantic (and post-Romantic) art. The same factors obtain here that I mentioned earlier with regard to American nationality. Modernization brought with it a distinctive set of free-enterprise ideals, but in Europe the old

---

*The development I speak of here is discussed from a somewhat different perspective by Raymond Williams. In *Culture and Society, 1780–1950* (New York, 1958), Williams traces the emergence and growth of a concept of culture that refers not to the integrated wholeness of a society, but, on the contrary, to a private wholeness, a spiritual and moral integrity embodied in certain privileged individuals, derived from the broad inheritance of the best of past civilizations, and often directly opposed to the values of modernization. "Culture" in this sense provided the grounds for dissent through the Romantic and Victorian periods. It emboldened "a certain number of *aliens*," in Matthew Arnold's words, to struggle against "the common tide of men's thoughts in a wealthy and industrial community," and inspired them to assert in its place "a general *humane* spirit," a "love of human perfection" that was grounded in one's "best self" as distinct from one's social identity, whether national, political, or economic (*Culture and Anarchy*, ed. I. Gregor [New York, 1969], pp. 169–76, et passim). The classic American writers did not perceive art or culture in quite this sense. Rather, they tended to associate the "best self" with a mythic American self, the "humane spirit" with the American "spirit of place," "human perfection" with the "true American Way," and culture itself with the mission of American democracy. None of them adopted the Romantic–Antinomian stand of Byron or Baudelaire against "the common tide." None of them envisioned, with Schiller, an "aesthetic state" beyond and apart from national ideals. And none of them challenged the political and economic *premises* of capitalism. As John Higham observes, "Even the troubled response to technology of an occasional Nathaniel Hawthorne or Herman Melville pales in comparison to the outrage of a Thomas Carlyle or a John Ruskin," and he attributes this, accurately I think, to the American "ideological cast of mind" ("Hanging Together: Divergent Unities in American History," *Journal of American History*, LXI [1974], 19–20).

ideals lingered, like deposed kings in exile, offering themselves at every opportunity as the solution to what appeared to be a world run out of control. Hence the power and profusion of "conscious mythologies." Ever since the Romantic period, high art has flourished through a symbolic play between cultural options—a sort of creative mediation between competing value systems which were still imaginatively (if not actually) available, and through which, therefore, the artist could offer a genuinely different perspective—whether radical, reactionary, or purely aesthetic—from that of the dominant culture.

None of our classic writers conceived of imaginative perspectives radically other than those implicit in the vision of America. Their works are characterized by an *unmediated* relation between the facts of American life and the ideals of liberal free enterprise. Confronted with the inadequacies of their society, they turned for solace and inspiration to its social ideals. It was not that they lacked radical energies, but that they had invested these in a vision which reinforced (because it emanated from) the values of their culture. Their quarrels with America took the form of intracultural dialogues—as in Thoreau's *Walden*, where "the only true America" beckons to us as a timeless image of the country's time-bound ideals (minimal government, extra-vagant economics, endless mobility, unlimited self-aggrandizement); or in Whitman's *Leaves of Grass*, which offers the highest Romantic tribute, the process of poetic self-creation, as text-proof of America's errand into the future. In these and other key instances, the autonomous act that might have posed fundamental alternatives, imaginative or actual, became instead a mimesis of cultural norms. The works of our classic writers show more clearly than any others I know how American radicalism could be turned into a force against any form of change that would decisively alter the norms, ideals, and structures of American culture. If (as I said) the nineteenth-century revivals were the Frankenstein's monster of Puritan rhetoric, then the American Renaissance was its aesthetic masterpiece, the creative *summum et ultimum* of a social myth designed to meet the exigencies of modern society in the New World.

I realize that in saying this I may offend just about everybody: those who see our classic writers as champions of the absolutes embodied in the American Way; those who dismiss them, quantitatively, as an unrepresentative elite; those who believe that as

artists they transcended their time and place; and especially perhaps those who seek in them a source of moral or political protest.
So I should at least point out, at the risk of stating the obvious,
that what I have said by no means reduces their achievement to
propaganda. Indeed, it may be no more than to speak of (say)
Chaucer's debt to "the medieval worldwiew"—except for two
things. First, Chaucer wrote openly from within his culture. Our
classic writers wore the Romantic mask of defiance. They have
been called the first modernists, and so they were—the traditional-
ists of modern society, doing the work of culture in terms appropriate to their culture, as individualists, isolatoes, and self-made
prophets. Second, Chaucer assumed a qualitative difference between temporal and spiritual ideals. He believed that Christianity
supported the forms of feudal England; but he believed, too, that
ultimately Christianity was not of this world. It was largely to
obviate the division between secular and sacred that the errand
was launched. The social myth (which the errand fostered) fused
eschatology and geography, nationhood and religion. When, therefore, our classic writers invested their ideals of art and the self in
the symbol of America, they were doing more than echoing cultural commonplaces. Elizabeth Stanton invested women's rights
in the concept of errand as progress. Philip Schaff rendered himself
the example of errand as migration. But American Romantics
enlisted the *pilgrimage* in that cause. I mean pilgrimage now in
its highest sense, as signifying the absolute claims of the spirit
within. Those claims inspired our classic writers to oppose the
status quo in many ways; but it also compelled them to speak
their opposition as keepers of the dream.*
    Damning or affirming, our classic antebellum writers offer
the most striking testimony we have to the power of American

---

*The testimony is perhaps clearest in the case of Emerson. No one made
larger claims than he did for the individual; no one has been more influential
upon the American literary tradition; no one was more centrally *the* American
Romantic; no one more passionately denounced injustice in America; and no one
more firmly upheld the metaphysics of the culture. When he felt himself exiled
for his religion, he remembered that America was bound to shape the religion of
the future; confronted with a "riot of mediocrities" in politics and art, he listened
all the more intently to his prophetic inner voice, revealing (through "the healthy
sentiment of the American people") "the promise of better times and of greater
men"; in the face of public discouragement and personal tragedy, he found solace
in recalling that "Asia, Africa, and Europe, [are] old, leprous, & wicked. . . . My
birthright in America [is] a preferable gift to the honours of any other nation

consensus. The many disparities they register between social and "ultimate" values were not to them intrinsic defects of the American Way. They were aberrations, like the backslidings of a de facto saint or the stiff-necked recalcitrance of a chosen people. Their denunciations were part of a ritual attempt to wake their countrymen up to the potential of their common culture. And, if anything, the ritual becomes more insistent in proportion to the writer's sense of despair. For of course the faith that magnified the culture into a cosmos carried with it an ominous prospect. If America failed, then the cosmos itself—the laws of history, nature, and the mind—had failed as well. Millennium or doomsday, American heaven or universal hell: it was the choice demanded by the rhetoric of consensus. Either way it served to obviate social alternatives, and on those grounds the leaders of American society, from Winthrop through Lincoln, have invoked the threat of doomsday, formulaically, as a rallying cry for cultural revitalization. In one form or another, they have always insisted that America is the last, best hope of mankind—meaning by *last* both telos (as in the Puritan sense of "latter days" or the Whig notion

---

that breathes upon Earth" ("The Fortune of the Republic" and "The Progress of Culture," in *Works*, ed. James Elliot Cabot [Boston, 1883], XI, 419; VIII, 221–222; "Wide World XIII" [1824], in vol. II of *Journals*, ed. William H. Gilman, Alfred R. Ferguson, and Merrell R. Davis [Cambridge, Mass., 1961], p. 218, and "Wide World 6" [1822], in vol. I of *Journals*, ed. Gilman, Ferguson, Davis, and George P. Clark [Cambridge, Mass., 1960], p. 127). "America" was always on some level a state of soul for Emerson. And on another level it was always a civic identity and a place. In this double (symbolic) function, it characterizes his early radical essays as well as his later conservatism: "There is always a reason, *in the man*, for his good or bad fortune, and so, in making money"; indeed, "money . . . is, in its effects and laws, as beautiful as roses. Property keeps the accounts of the world, and is always moral"; "The merchant has but one rule, *absorb and invest*: he is to be capitalist. . . . Well, the man must be capitalist. Will he spend his income, or will he invest?" ("Wealth" and "The Nominalist and the Realist," in *Essays and Lectures*, ed. Joel Porte [Library of America: New York, 1983], pp. 997, 578, 1010). F. O. Matthiessen felt that it was "staggeringly innocent" on Emerson's part to "commit himself to such remarks" (*American Renaissance* [New York, 1941], p. 4). If so, it was the same staggering innocence that allowed multitudes of Americans to believe that the principles of their culture were the laws of God, reason, and nature. As the *Schenectady Reflector* reported, following a lecture by Emerson in December 1852: "Those who went to hear Transcendentalism came away astonished to find that they had understood, admired, and most heartily approved."

This is not to reduce Emerson to a liberal apologist. It is to say that his radicalism cannot be understood outside of his conservatism. I discuss this paradox in a later chapter.

of a revolution to end revolutions) and final choice, one last chance to redeem humanity. Both versions carried the same message. *Last* plus consensus (i.e., the United States as "America") meant *best*; *last* minus consensus (i.e., the United States as just one more nation in the Americas, like Mexico, Argentina, or Brazil) meant catastrophe. The point was not to offer alternatives but to induce a state of anxiety, an apocalyptic urgency, that would enforce compliance. And generally, through the nineteenth century, the American middle class responded by embracing the covenant.

Those who did not join in hope conformed in desperation. Thus the Populist Ignatius Donnelly, confronted with what he thought were the consequences of America's "betrayal of promise" ("utter social destruction," "world cataclysm"), found a way out of "perpetual nihilism" by rededicating himself to the "unfathomed reservoir of virtue . . . within all Americans." Edward Bellamy made the same sort of Pascal's wager on the side of America. "*Let us bear in mind,*" he cautioned his militant followers, "*that if it be a failure, it will be a final failure. There can be no more new worlds to be discovered*"; and on that premise he summoned them (along with all other "true nationalists") "forward to the American Jerusalem." The young Whitman was even more direct in his reasoning. On November 24, 1846, as the left-wing republican editor of *The Brooklyn Daily Eagle*, he reminded his readers that

> The time will surely come—that holy millennium of liberty—when the "Victory of endurance born" shall lift the masses. . . and make them achieve something of that destiny which we may suppose God intends eligible for mankind. And this problem is to be worked out through the people, territory, and government of the United States. If it should fail! O, dark were the hour and dreary beyond description the horror of such a failure—which we anticipate not at all!

When he did dare to anticipate it, decades later, Whitman promptly recoiled from the horror into what remains the most impassioned paean in the literature to the nation's "Democratic Vistas." The excesses of business and technology, he explained, the greed of politicians and "this almost maniacal appetite for wealth prevalent in the United States," all these were "parts of amelioration and progress, indispensably needed to prepare" for

America's "assur'd" and "unparallel'd success." The very "darkness of the hour" cast figural shadows, intimating "imperial destinies, dazzling as the sun."[27]

Most major writers did not enlist so readily in the party of hope. A few, like Henry Adams, grimly settled for the doomsday option. Others, like Mark Twain, seem to have slid into it, against their will and with unresolved ambivalence. Still others, like Melville, vacillated between options ("the political Messiah has come in *us*"; "Columbus ended earth's romance"). But by and large our classic writers found the prospect of final failure too painful to sustain. Here as elsewhere, Emerson's reaction is representative; it constitutes a major testament to the doomsday trap of the rhetoric of consensus, the double bind of best and/or last. Having alternated often and long between euphoria and despair, Emerson finally opted outright for the culture. "My estimate of America," he confided in his journals, "is all or nothing." Beyond America, *nothing*: it was the errand internalized, and made an avatar of the Self. And since Emerson refused to abandon hope, since for him the Self was center and circumference of the spirit, he gave *all* to America. "They [who] complain about the flatness of American life," he decided, "have no perception of its destiny. They are not Americans." They cannot see that America is "a garden of plenty,... a magazine of power.... Here is man in the Garden of Eden; here, the Genesis and the Exodus," and here is to be the Revelation.[28]

In that spirit, Emerson greeted the Armageddon of the Republic. He had been slow to endorse abolitionism. He continued to believe in the inferiority of the blacks (as well as of the Chinese, the Irish, and the Indians); and he had recently defended states' rights. But he had no qualms about the war. By 1860 he was the oracle of an ideology fully matured, a ritual of crisis and control that had virtually assumed a dynamic of its own. America, he declared, in an oration delivered in Cleveland, Ohio, was in covenant with the future—it was consecrated, that is, to progress, unity, and the middle class—and the South was not. Hence, once again, Americans had to rally to the task of fulfilling God's will. The fathers had provided the pattern and set the direction. It was time for the sons to complete their work. When the South would conform, it too could join the errand toward the American City of God. Meanwhile, Emerson concluded, destiny left the

North no alternative: "We must realize our rhetoric and our rituals."[29]

A century later, when I discovered "America," the rhetoric and rituals were still being realized, this time under the auspices of a third set of fathers, among them Lincoln and Emerson. The process was accompanied, then as before, by threats of fragmentation and collapse, together with funereal forecasts about the passing of the myth; and then as before the ritual of consensus rose to the challenge. The rhetoric of the late Sixties was distinctive in many particulars; it may be said to have propelled important social and moral changes; and in these distinctive, oppositional ways it was bounded *and nourished* by the strategies of cultural revitalization from which it arose. I think now not only of the strategies I have traced in this chapter—from the colonial through the antebellum period—but, more directly, of those that followed, from the Gilded Age into our own time: the strategies through which late-nineteenth-century radicals recast socialism in "the framework of progressive liberalism" (Dorothy Ross); which effectually prevented even the muckrakers of that era from challenging "the premises . . . of progress in its American guise" (Rush Welter); which led Frederick Douglass, on "Colored People's Day" in 1893, to renounce all basic alternatives to the system ("There is no Negro problem. The problem is whether the American People have . . . patriotism enough to live up to their own Constitution"); which made "the radical social critic" William Dean Howells center his hopes for utopia upon his own "home, the true, the original, the real America" (Alan Trachtenberg); which "inspired" the labor leaders of the Gilded Age, and their New Deal counterparts half a century later, to define unionization as the "Good Old American Way" ("we mean no conflict with legitimate enterprise, no antagonism to necessary capital"); and which allowed American Stalinists through the Forties and Fifties to enroll "Washington, Jefferson, and Franklin . . . posthumously in the popular front, under the slogan 'Communism is twentieth-century Americanism'" (Edmund Morgan).[30]

There were times during the protests of the Vietnam decade when those strategies seemed rather strained, thread-worn. "Myth is a type of speech chosen by history," Roland Barthes has remarked; "it is human history which converts reality into speech, and it alone rules the life and death of mythical languages";[31] and for a certain unruly period in the late Sixties and early Seventies, history appeared to be making dangerous incursions upon the rhetorical frontiers of "America." I thought I discerned a cultural schizophrenia that had intensified ever since the Civil War, like a widening fissure in the house of consensus. That house had been built upon the rejection of limits; its cornerstone was the perceived perils of Gog and Magog; it had expanded through its special structural capacities to accommodate process and change; but it could not survive the reduction of "America" to the level of common sense. What if, under the pressures of history, the errand should come to rest, where it began, in the realm of the imagination? What if this country were to be re-cognized for what it was, not a beacon to mankind, as Winthrop announced in his *Arbella* address of 1630; not the political Messiah annually proclaimed through the mid-nineteenth-century in July Fourth addresses—not even (in Studs Terkel's reformulation) a covenanted people robbed by un-American predators of their sacred trust—but simply *goy b'goyim*, just one more nation in the wilderness of this world? What would happen, in short, if "America" were severed once and for all from the United States?

Nothing much, from an outsider's point of view: only a fresh, non-apocalyptic sense of the exigencies of industrial capitalism; a certain modesty about the claims of nationality; a more mundane distinction between the Old World and the New, as denoting metaphors of geography, rather than the progress of humanity; a more traditional sense of "frontiers," as signifying limits and barriers rather than new territories to conquer; a relativistic assessment of the prospects and constraints of liberal democracy (the benefits of open competiton, for example, or the abuses of representative individualism), none of these heaven-ordained either as a sign of national election or as an augury of doom.

But that (to repeat) was an outsider's perspective. Considered from within the culture, the de-mythification of "America" meant everything. It would dissipate the very core of personal and communal identity. It would undo this society's controlling metaphors and narratives, its long-ripened strategies of cohesion, assimilation, and crisis control. To imagine a liberal United States without "America" was like imagining feudal Europe without the myths of aristocracy and kingship. It seemed a contradiction in terms. So indeed, it proved in the next two decades. I think, for example, of the Civil Rights movement, as emblemized in Martin Luther King, Jr.'s classic oration on the dream. Or again, I think of the student protest movement. In a detailed retrospective survey, the sociologist Paul Sniderman concluded that what really united those variously "alienated radicals" was their "utter incapacity" to "conceive of an alternative ascendant polity, in this world or any other," to the American Way. The question he had asked had the naive "objectivity" one might expect from an "outside observer" (in this case, a Jewish Canadian immigrant): "how close does it [the American Way] come to fitting your idea of what the best possible form of goverment should be?" The replies he received, from even the most "politically embittered," persuaded him that "the choice" he had set out to explore

> —whether there are a great many alienated or hardly any—is a false choice. . . . The idea of another promised land, one that might surpass the promise of America itself, has never taken hold. . . . Even in the years of bitter discord which this study records [the late Sixties], in an area of the country [Berkeley, California] where nearly every form of political disillusion and rejection wins a substantial measure of symbolic support. . .the idea of America remains the idea of promise.[32]

In April, 1980, the year that Sniderman completed *A Question of Loyalty*, a new "Citizen's Party" was launched in Cleveland, Ohio. According to the laconic *New York Times* reporter, it marked the "birth" of "the latest in a historic series of left-wing progeny." His report is worth citing as a state-of-myth address in the aftermath of the turbulent Sixties:

> Some 275 delegates represented 30 states at the founding of what they call a "second party" rather than a third, on the frequently stated contention that the Republicans and Democrats and their prospective candidates were one indistinguishable mass.
> Delegates included old radicals of the Socialist era, young environmentalists, ardent feminists and labor union activists; almost everyone was a "ist" of some kind. . . . Speaker after speaker emphasized how different the Citizens Party convention would be from those of the major parties. . . .
> Keynoting the convention . . . Studs Terkel, the Chicago writer, predicted that the new party would "reclaim the American dream

from the predators who've stolen it—that's what this meeting is all about."[33]

Bridging as it does an era of protest and the Reagan Eighties, this adversarial reclamation of the dream may stand as an exemplary instance of the cultural-symbolic processes I have been discussing and for their continuing efficacy in our times.

3
The Ends of Puritan Rhetoric

Thinking back in spring 1692 to "the antiquities of New England," Cotton Mather came upon a crucial connection, as he saw it, between the voyage of Columbus two centuries before and the Puritans' Great Migration. Considered together, the founding of the Massachusetts Bay Colony and the landing at San Salvador held the key to a great design. To begin with, Columbus's voyage was one of three shaping events of the modern age, all of which occurred in rapid succession at the turn of the sixteenth century: (1) *"the Resurrection of Literature,"* which had been made possible by the invention of the printing press (1456), and which in turn made the Bible accessible for the first time to the entire community of believers; (2) the discovery of America, which opened a New World, hitherto shrouded in "heathen darkness," to the light of the Gospel; and (3) the Protestant Reformation, which signalled the dawn of a new era "after the long night of Catholic persecution." And all these three beginnings— respectively textual, geographical, and spiritual—pointed forward to something grander still: the imminent renovation of all things in "a new heaven and a new earth." A new beginning, then, and a newly urgent sense of an ending; and intermediate between these, at once linking them in time and confirming the overall design, like an apocalyptic play within a play, was the story of New England. That, too, had its providential beginnings, culminating in 1630 when the fleet under the *Arbella* set sail for British North America. Mather describes the journey in language appropriate to its momentous spiritual-geographical-textual significance:

> the *Church* of our Lord Jesus Christ, well compared unto a *Ship,* is now *victoriously* sailing round the Globe . . . [carrying] some thousands of *Reformers* into the Retirements of an *American Desart,* on purpose that . . . He might there, *To* them first, and then *By* them, give a *Specimen* of many Good Things, which He would have His

68

Churches elsewhere aspire and arise unto. . . . [This is] the HISTORY
OF A NEW-ENGLISH ISRAEL . . . to anticipate the state of the *New
Jerusalem*.[1]

By the 1690s all this was commonplace. Mather's recognition
was a summing-up of local tradition, the re-cognition of a long-
nurtured view of the colony's origin and mission. One reason for
its persistence was the power of the vision itself. Another reason
was that on some basic level it told the truth. I mean not only the
truth as rhetoric, the growth of New England as the Puritans
perceived it, but historical truth, as the facts bore out their perception: history as rhetoric and fact entwined, inseparably the event
interpreted and the interpretation become event; the dialectic
between what forces itself into our view and the view by which
we force it to conform to our habits of perception. So understood,
Mather's formulaic recognition is interchangeably the past seen
under the aspect of prophecy and prophecy redefined through what
historians now consider to be three central factors in the making
of the modern world: the invention of the printing press, the
discovery of America, and the growth of Protestantism.

Of the three, the invention of the printing press, along with
"the resurrection of literature," is perhaps the clearest example of
the historical process I referred to. Gutenberg's galaxy, as Marshall
McLuhan termed it, has particular relevance to the New England
colonists because of their extraordinary reliance on texts. Like all
Puritans, they were a self-declared people of the Book. In these
latter days, wrote the English martyrologist John Foxe, "the Lord
began to work for His church not with the sword . . . but with
printing. . . . How many printing presses there be in the world, so
many block-houses there be against the high castle of St. Angelo,
so that the pope must either abolish . . . printing or printing at
length will root him out."[2] That faith the colonists shared with
their Calvinist brethren everywhere, but it held a special, heightened meaning for them. In leaving Europe, they had turned to the
Book to discover their new identity as emigrants—had invented
the meaning of their community *ex verbo*, by the word—and,
increasingly through the seventeenth century, they kept asserting
that identity to a bemused or indifferent world, expanding, modifying, and revising it in a procession of sermons, exhortations, and
declarations, histories and hagiographies, covenants and controversies, statements and restatements of purpose, a sustained pro-

cess of rhetorical self-definition unsurpassed by any other community of its kind. That mode of identity the Puritans bequeathed to the nation which was to usurp the symbol of America for itself. Not accidentally, it was the New England theocrats who first used the name "American" to refer to European immigrants, rather than (like other emigrants) to the continent's native inhabitants. The legacy of the Puritan vision, as the first-begotten offspring of the printing press, was a rationale, a technique, and (in the material sense of the word) a *process* whereby a community could constitute itself by publication, declare itself a nation by verbal fiat, define its past, present, and future by proclamation, and justify its definition in histories, like Mather's *Magnalia Christi Americana* (1692–1702), which in one form or another translated geography into Christianography.

I mean Christianography in a far broader sense than Mather intended. The publications through which the republic established itself were political rather than theological, they appealed to reason, they celebrated civic virtues, and they addressed "a large, new class of readers, Franklin's middling class," which they "came increasingly to treat . . . as the very definition of the American."[3] But the same conditions applied *in kind* to Puritan New England. The transition from colony to province was not a process of secularization. It was an expanding sacred-secular process of textual self-identification from the *Arbella* covenant through Timothy Dwight's epic of the Revolution, *The Conquest of Canaan*. A distinguishing feature of this development was the confluence in the eighteenth century of three moral-political traditions that were to become the basis of American "civil religion" and that all depended upon the dissemination of the printed word: colonial Puritanism (especially in its revivalist transformation), civic humanism, and libertarian ideology. Significantly, the two best-sellers of 1776 were Samuel Sherwood's sermon, *The Church's Flight into the Wilderness*, which politicizes the metaphor of sacred history, and Tom Paine's *Common Sense*, which heralds the American republic as New Israel.

In this sense, Mather's concept of Christianography may be said to apply after all. And the application extends as well to the two other germinal events to which he refers: the discovery of America and the growth of Protestantism. The Puritan vision was the offspring of both, in what amounted to the century's most unlikely union of rhetorical forms. The discovery of America was preeminently a secular venture, a process of exploration and appropriation empowered by what scholars have come to call the forces of modernization: capitalist enterprise, state nationalism, the expansion of Western forms of culture throughout the world. So considered, "America" meant the triumph of European colonialism. It was an act of naming that doubly certified the invaders' control of the continent: it meant not only conquest by violence, but control by symbol and trope. "America" denoted far more than the Italian entrepreneur, Amerigo Vespucci, whose falsified sightings, once published, claimed the terra incognita for the Spanish throne. "America" entitled a carnival of European fantasies. It meant the fabled land of gold, the enchanted Isles of the West, springs of eternal youth, and "lubberlands" of ease and plenty. It verified theories of "natural man" and "the state of nature." It promised opportunities for realizing utopia, for unlimited riches and mass conversions, for the return to pastoral arcadia, for implementing schemes for moral and social perfection. Columbus thought that it had been the actual site of Eden. Later explorers and settlers, translating the myths of biblical geography into the landmarks of Renaissance geo-mythology—spoke of America as a second Eden, inhabited by pagan primitives (or perhaps the ten lost Hebrew tribes) awaiting the advent of Civilization and the Gospel Truth.

History and rhetoric—which is to say, conquest by arms and conquest by the word: the discovery of America is the modern instance par excellence of how these two kinds of violence are entwined; how metaphor becomes fact, and fact, metaphor; how the realms of power and myth can be reciprocally sustaining; and how that reciprocity can encompass widely disparate outlooks. The same thing may be said about the rise of Protestantism, though from a wholly different perspective. Protestantism was in its inception a spiritual movement. It began as a protest against the worldliness of the Roman Catholic Church—specifically, against the Catholic emphasis on temporal authority (as in the papacy), geographic locale (the Holy Roman Empire), and mercenary practices, from the selling of indulgences to political alliances. According to the early Reformers, Catholicism had set itself as mediator between God and His people, whereas Christianity demanded a direct relation between the believer and Christ, the one true Mediator, as He manifested Himself in the believer's soul, and as He was manifest for all to see in the Bible (in the Old

Testament, proleptically, as well as the New). *Sola fides* and *sola scriptura*, the primacy of personal faith and the supreme authority of Scripture: upon these twin principles Protestantism was established. But once established it, too, like every other venture in transcending human limitations, found itself entangled in the web of history and rhetoric.

Scholars have described that entanglement from various angles, including virtually every concept associated with the discovery of America: capitalist enterprise, nationalism, and the expansion of Western forms of culture. Indeed, in this case as in others, the very impulse toward transcendence may be traced to the needs of a certain historic moment and the logic of particular rhetorical modes. For my present purpose, I limit myself to one aspect of the process: the Protestant view of history. For in spite of their emphasis on the individual (*sola fides*) the Protestants identified themselves collectively, as a church or association of churches, in opposition to Roman Catholicism. And through their emphasis on the Bible (*sola scriptura*), they identified themselves temporally, as part of the gradual progress of God's people, from the chosen Israelites to the New Christian Israel to the "latter-day" Israel that would usher in the millennium. The main text for that divine plan, the Book of Revelation, spoke in figures or types of an "elect nation" which in the "last days" would defeat "Antichrist, the Beast of Rome," and so prepare the way for the Second Coming. That became the framework of Martin Luther's view of the Protestant mission. For a time he identified Germany as the elect nation, and although he later abandoned that particular dream, he and the other founding Reformers retained the basic tenets of his historiography. Protestantism, they declared, was the true church; Catholicism, the Antichrist; and the conflict between these, the central action of this final period of time, attended by all the long-awaited "signs and wonders" (political and natural as well as ecclesiastical) of the apocalypse.

After its initial spiritual protest, then, Protestantism returned to history with a vengeance. But it was a special kind of history, sacred as distinct from secular. It was the story not of mankind but of God's "peculiar people," the covenanted saints who constituted the real subject of the unfolding drama of redemption. Basically, that is, Protestant rhetoric retained its traditional Christian roots—remained grounded in the belief that Christ's kingdom was not of this world—and so could break free, if necessary, of any national specificity. Thus Luther could reject the concept of national calling without qualifying his vision of universal progress. Thus, too, English Protestants of the late sixteenth century could abandon their revision of Luther's concept—their chauvinist rhetoric of *England* as elect nation—without in any way modifying their allegiance to the Reformation. It should be added that the rhetoric itself remained a force in the development of modern nationalisms. It would surface again in England under the Puritan Commonwealth and later in the imperial claims of Victoria's "British Israel." In Germany it informs Hegel's encomia to the Prussian State, and (in our century) the millennialist Sturm und Drang of the Third Reich. But in all cases the concept of national mission retains the imprint of its universalist origins. Prussia's decline did no basic damage to Hegelians' faith in the progress of the World-Spirit. Milton could abandon the dreams of Cromwell's Revolution—as the English Romantics later turned from *their* political millenarianism—without forgoing his faith that a universal New Jerusalem would one day renovate England's green and pleasant land.

The immigrant Puritans of 1630 shared this ambiguous nationalist-universalist outlook. Broadly speaking, they represented one of three Puritan groups of the time. The largest, most eclectic of these were the Presbyterians, who sought to purify the country at large to a state worthy of its special calling. The smallest of the three groups, the Separatists, took the opposite course. They purified their faith to the point where they refused allegiance to any institutional authority, including that of the English Protestant church, whether Anglican or Presbyterian. Instead, they hoped to join the progress of the "universal invisible church" in small congregations, modelled after the first Christian communities. Some remained in England, others fled persecution to Amsterdam, and then, in the case of the Plymouth Pilgrims, to the New World. The Massachusetts Bay immigrants sought a "middle way" between these extremes. In doing so, they meant not to compromise but to perfect. They set out to combine what seemed to them in each case a partial gesture at reformation, in church and in state. Accordingly, they proclaimed their "purified church-state" a model for all Christendom. They were congregationalists in a "federal" or "national" covenant; a community of "visible saints" gathered for a venture in history; de facto Separatists who insisted not only on their vital connection to English Protestantism, but (through this) on their central role in the worldwide struggle against Antichrist.

The European connection thus opened to the far broader connection, through New England's mission, between the Old World and the New. And that connection in turn opened up the meaning (again, mediated by the concept of New England's mission) of the New World as America. It seems a logical sequence in retrospect, but it was neither natural nor inevitable. The Puritan vision was not brought to New England aboard the *Arbella*, nor was it a flower of the New World wilderness. Rather, it was the product of certain unforeseen historical exigencies and certain possibilities for interpretation inherent in Puritan rhetoric.

The immigrants of the 1630s do not seem to have had a distinct vision of the continent at large. Their focus was on the Reformation already under way: New England was to be a "model of Christian charity" for Protestants abroad, "a city [set] upon a hill" as a beacon to Europe. These phrases come from John Winthrop's justly famous lay sermon aboard the *Arbella*, and when he added that "the eyes of all people are upon us" he was thinking mainly of the peoples of England, Germany, Holland, and other Protestant countries. His vision was transatlantic, rather than American; it tended toward the universalist aspect of the emigrants' ambiguously nationalist-universalist outlook. By placing New England at the apex of history, Winthrop was admitting its dependency on the Old World. It was not enough to set up "a Specimen" of New Jerusalem; *their* eyes had to be on it, and their hearts and minds ready to follow. So it was that Cromwell's Revolution lured back a considerable number of immigrants. So it was, too, that after the failure of the English Puritan Commonwealth—and with it the waning of apocalyptic fervor throughout Protestant Europe—New Englanders found themselves trapped in an embarrassing paradox. They had declared themselves the advance guard of the Reformation, committed themselves to a worldwide mission, and invested their credentials of authority in scriptural prophecy. In 1660, the vision was intact, the community prospering, and their authority still dominant; but to all appearances history had betrayed them. They were a beacon unheeded by the world, a city on a hill that no one noticed, or noticed only to scorn. In Perry Miller's words, they "were left alone with America."[4]

Not entirely alone, however; for the rhetoric they carried with them offered a ready means of compensation. It allowed them by scriptural precedent to *consecrate* their "outcast," "exiled," "wilderness condition." If they could not compel the Old World to yield to their vision, they could interpret the New in their own image. That interpretation was implicit from the start. I said before that Winthrop emphasized the universalist aspect of the Protestant outlook, but the "national" or "federal" aspect—the sense of the importance of *this* people in *this* locale—was there as well. New England was to be an example for others by providing a model in its own right. From his opening reference to the immigrants as "Christian Tribes" to his concluding comparison of himself with Moses, exhorting Israel into Canaan, Winthrop was subtly redefining the immigrants' identity. Genealogically, of course, they were *English* Puritans, but as a *New* English community, he implied, they were a new chosen people, all "knit . . . into one body . . . in Christ" and together commissioned by "the God of Israel" to secure a new promised land, there to progress toward a better state in "wisdom, power, goodness, and truth than formerly" existed.[5]

Progress and *New Canaan*: these terms, though relatively muted in Winthrop's address, were nonetheless organic to his vision. They became increasingly prominent as the first generation leaders consolidated the enterprise and defended its claims against an increasingly indifferent or hostile world. Gradually, in promotional tracts, apologias for the church-state, and evangelical treatises, in sermons on Indian conversion and the saint's preparation for salvation, in exegeses on Bible prophecy, proof-texts of the millennium, histories of the Good Old Way, and polemics against sectarians at home and opponents abroad, from antinomians to Anglicans, the colonists drew out the implications of their New England Way.

In doing so, they laid the ground for the great rhetorical shift that once and for all resolved the paradox of vanguard isolation. Having been left alone with America, the second- and third-generation Puritans felt free to incorporate Renaissance geo-mythology, as it suited their purposes, into their own vision. Explicitly and implicitly, they adapted the European images of America (land of gold, second paradise, utopia, primitivism as moral regeneration) to fit the Protestant view of progress. And having thus taken possession of the rhetoric of America, they proceeded one crucial step further. Reorienting their vision from a transatlantic to a transcontinental direction, they situated the Protestant apocalypse—or what amounted to the same thing, the Protestant road to the apocalypse—in the New World.

We can hardly overestimate the importance of that astonishing Westward leap of the imagination. It was an achievement comparable in its way to the two great rhetorical shifts on which it built: the Hebrews' redefinition (by verbal fiat) of Canaan—territory, name, "antiquities" and all—as *their* country; and the imperialism of the *figura* or type, whereby the church fathers declared that the Old Testament, the story of Israel in its entirety, from Adam through Abraham and David to the Messiah, heir of David, really belonged to Christ.

The Hebrews' triumph was nationalist, the self-assertion of a scattered community in exile. The triumph of early Christianity was universalist, the self-assertion of marginal, multi-national groups of believers. The nationalist-universalist vision of New England arose out of similar circumstances. Having been left behind by Europe, the Puritans proceeded to recapture Europe for themselves, rhetorically, as part of all that was not America—the benighted "Old World," awaiting its redemption by the mighty works of Christ in America. Confronted with the uncertain meaning of their locale, the Puritans discovered the New World in Scripture—not literally (in the way Columbus discovered it), as the lost Eden, but figurally (in the way the church fathers discovered Noah in Moses and both in Jesus), as the second paradise foreseen by all the prophets. New Canaan was not a metaphor for them, as it was for other colonists. It was the New World reserved from eternity for God's latter-day elect nation, which He would gather as choice grain from the chaff of Europe/Babylon/Egypt, so that (to recall Cotton Mather's phrase) "He might there, *To* them first, and then *By* them, give a Specimen of many Good Things" to come. In short, driven back by history upon the resources of language, the second- and third-generation New Englanders united geography, textuality, and the spirit into something genuinely new and (as it turned out) enormously compelling, a cultural symbology centered on the vision of America.

Their achievement warrants a brief historical digression. When the early Christians adapted the Old Testament to their purposes, they spiritualized its sacred places. The holy land became for them the kingdom of heaven; its milk and honey, sustenance for the redeemed soul. With the growth of the church, however, the emphasis on sacred place reappeared. Medieval Catholicism found its own equivalents for Canaan—the Papal Seat, the Holy Roman Empire—which churchmen Judaically invested with sweeping spiritual authority. So at least the Protestant Reformers charged. Directing their protest precisely against this mode of sacralization—this granting of holy significance to temporal, worldly places—they demanded an unmediated relation between man and God. In sum, they rejected sacred place for an exclusive concern with sacred time, the interior realm of the spirit and last things. Eventually they came to value institutions more highly, but they never revoked their anathema against sacred place. Until the Second Coming, they maintained, the only Canaan in this world was the kingdom within, accessible only by a radical inward turning of the will from self to Christ, from secular to sacred time.

The immigrant Puritans, as Puritans, were extremists in this cause. No Protestant sect insisted more adamantly than they did on the unmediated relation between man and God. But they were also extremists, we have seen, in another, antithetical cause. As immigrants, they declared the New World another promised land, counterpart of Canaan of old but greater, because closer to the millennium, and they documented their claim with scriptural prophecies as befit a chosen people.* "Know [that] this is the place," wrote their first historian, Edward Johnson, "where the Lord will create a new Heaven, and a new Earth."[6] For him and his fellow exiles, the meaning of *place*, the actual, terrestrial new continent before them, lay in the prophetic figures of Psalms, Ezekiel, Isaiah, Revelation. In effect, the New England Puritans

---

*It is worth noting the historical irony this involves. Because the Puritans were sectarians, a group self-reconstituted according to certain general principles and beliefs, they could enlarge their identity to universalist proportions. Because European Protestant movements sought common cause with all segments of a nationally defined people, they had to limit their identity to a particular secular history—to base their "federal" claims on territorially specific antiquities, the legends and chronicles of a particular "race." Not Luther's Germany, not Foxe's England, or Cromwell's, could find exemption from this process. Political expediency and common sense together compelled European Protestants to ground their rhetoric of "national election" in the national past. The New England Puritans felt no such scruples. On the contrary: it was politically expedient for them to transcend their English ties, and it seemed to them common sense to locate the meaning of America's past not in its native antiquities but in the promises of scripture.

delivered sacred place back to Protestantism with a vengeance, in the form of America.

It would be hard to overestimate the importance of their legacy to Protestant America. Let me note just one of its aspects: the relation (within the Puritans' federal covenant) between the colony's progress and the saint's journey to God. The saint's journey, by all tradition, involves the conflict between sacred and profane, which in turn entails the qualitative differentiation between sacred and secular place. Eden is forever the garden of our innocence through our willing suspension of geography. Jerusalem is the "holy city" insofar as we dissociate it from the cities of the earth. Sacred meaning is fixed, impervious to the vicissitudes of the profane; and part of that meaning is progressive, leading upward from Eden to New Jerusalem.* The Protestant Reformers, we have seen, confined their concept of progress to sacred time—to the individual believer, and by extension, to the universal invisible church, the totality of believers in all countries and ages. This remained their legacy to European Protestants through the nineteenth century. Thus the nationalist Hegel, who reformulated sacred history as the dialectics of the World-Spirit, found his chief metaphor for progress in the self-perfecting consciousness. And thus Marx and his followers inverted Hegel's World-Spirit into the dialectics of international class struggle. Even for the chauvinists among them, *national* progress could serve the cause only by coincidence, by a happy temporary conjunction of essentially dif-

---

*This progressivism is based on two principles, both relevant to the fantastic rhetorical inversion I am describing. First, the sacred defines itself in radical conflict against the profane. Its very meaning therefore presupposes both the persistence of the profane and a persisting state of conflict. The holiness of the "holy land" depends on other lands *not* being holy; the chosenness of the chosen people implies their continuing difference from the *goyim*, the profane "nations of the earth." Second, sacred history means the gradual conquest of the profane by the sacred. The believer cultivates the inner wilderness in prescribed stages of spiritual growth; the church as a whole wins the world back from Satan in a series of increasingly terrifying and triumphant wars of the Lord. Continuous conflict, then, and gradual fulfillment become mutually sustaining concepts. Hence the powerful visionary dynamic behind the Puritan concept of errand—the ongoing, endlessly processual, continental, and eventually international and universalist scope of that concept. Having invested the meanings of sacred progress, personal and federal, in *their* "holy commonwealth," they redefined the commonwealth itself as holiness in process, and explained that process through a continuing opposition to the profanities "out there"—from local "heretics" and Indian "Canaanites" to the "vast wilderness" before them, waiting to be reclaimed.

ferent goals. Both Hegel and Marx may be said to have secularized sacred history, but each in his way endorsed the Protestant rejection of sacred place for sacred time.

The legacy of the Puritan conflation of sacred and secular may be stated, retrospectively, in the boldest terms: only in America did nationalism come to carry with it the Christian meaning of the sacred. Only "America," of all national designations, took on the combined force of eschatology and chauvinism. Many forms of nationalism have laid claim to a world-redeeming promise; many Christian sects have sought, in open or secret heresy, to find the sacred in the profane; and many European Protestants have linked the soul's journey and the way to wealth. But only the "American Way," of all modern symbologies, has managed to circumvent the contradictions inherent in these approaches. Of all symbols of identity, only "American" has succeeded in uniting nationality and universality, civic and spiritual selfhood, sacred and secular history, the country's past and paradise to be, in a single transcendent ideal.

I do not say that the Puritans did all this. But they established a visionary framework within which that symbology could evolve and develop. The decisive moment came in the 1660s and 1670s when a series of crises threatened to put an end to their enterprise altogether. First, the Restoration of King Charles endangered not only the colonial charter but the Puritan rule. Next, the apparent decline of religion among the immigrants' children—what the clergy bewailed as the "degeneracy of the rising generation"— forced important modifications in the New England Way. In the course of the debate and turmoil, the last of the immigrant leaders died, and anxieties of succession became a main theme of pulpit and press. Then, in the mid-1670s, the several Indian nations in the region allied to reclaim their land, in a sudden attack that threatened to decimate New England from Stockbridge to Boston.

The literary result of these "Wars of the Lord" (as the ministry termed all the various events) was the first native flowering of New England mythology, through the first English-language genre developed in the New World, the American Puritan jeremiad. The immigrants had imported the jeremiad as an immemorial mode of lament over the corrupt ways of the world. Their heirs transformed it into a vehicle of social continuity and control. The lament continued, but here it served to celebrate the trials of a people in covenant. Here as nowhere else, the clergy explained,

God's afflictions were like a "refining fire," intended to purify and strengthen, or like the punishment meted out by a loving father, the token of His special care. "God's Controversy with New England," wrote the poet Michael Wigglesworth in 1662, *ensured* the colony's success. In the words of the Reverend Dimmesdale in *The Scarlet Letter*, it signalled "a high and glorious destiny for this newly chosen people of the Lord."[7]

Dimmesdale is an immigrant minister, of course, here delivering the election-day sermon of 1649. This was not inaccurate on Hawthorne's part: there were ample first-generation foreshadowings of the American Puritan jeremiad, from John Cotton's *God's Promise to His Plantations* (1630) through Edward Johnson's *Wonder-Working Providence of Sion's Savior in New England* (1649–54). But as a distinctive New World genre the jeremiad was essentially a ritual of continuity through generational rededication. It required a set of *local* precedents, a pride of tribal heroes to whom the community could look back in reverence, and from whom, therefore, it could inherit its mission. The immigrants had imported the rhetoric; their children and grandchildren supplied the antiquities needed to make the rhetoric American. They enshrined their forebears in scriptural types, re-cognized them as giants of a golden age, like Virgil's legendary Trojans entering upon the future site of Rome. Winthrop could compare himself to Moses only by implication; Cotton had only the story of the pre-American Israel to illustrate the terms of "God's promise to His New World plantations." The next generations felt neither of these restrictions, personal or historical. They could sanctify Winthrop as the New England Moses—or as the American Nehemiah (after the prophet who rebuilt the walls of Jerusalem)—and Cotton, as the American Abraham, Joshua, and John the Divine combined. These and other immigrant leaders they canonized as founding fathers, translated their Atlantic crossing as the Great Migration, antitype of the Hebrew exodus, and consecrated their church-state as a venture that, *because* it fulfilled Old World prophecy, was wholly an event of this New World. It led by promise from New England *then* to New England as it *would be*, when the "American desert" would reveal itself to all people as the "Theopolis Americana, the Holy City, the streets whereof are pure gold."[8] It was a mission into America, by the American Israel, for America first and then the world.

So it was that the second- and third-generation colonists completed the founders' errand into rhetoric: they grounded the Puritan vision in history. What they achieved has become something so familiar by now, so much a matter of cultural reflex, that it is difficult to convey its sheer audacity and sweep. Only once afterward was there anything at all comparable to it in the culture. That was the consecration of the "nation's founding fathers" by the generation following the Revolution—a myth that relegated the colonial immigrants, by figural rite, to the role of *ur*-fathers, as Noah was to Moses and both were to Jesus—and undoubtedly the rhetoric of this second founding was much indebted to that of the first.

The Puritans made three lasting contributions to the American Way. First, they justified the New World in its own right. Other colonists and explorers brought utopian dreams to the New World, but in doing so they claimed the land (New Spain, New France, Nova Scotia) as European Christians, by virtue of the superiority of Christian European culture. In short, they justified their invasion of America through European concepts of progress. The Puritans denied the very fact of invasion by investing *America* with the meaning of progress and then identifying themselves as the people peculiarly destined to bring that meaning to life. "Other peoples," John Cotton pointed out in 1630, "have their land by providence; we have it by promise."[9] The next generation of New Englanders drew out the full import of his distinction. They were not claiming America by conquest, they explained; they were reclaiming what by promise belonged to them, as the Israelites had once reclaimed Canaan, or (in spiritual terms) as the church had reclaimed the name of Israel.

By that literal-prophetic act of reclamation the Puritans raised the New World into the realm of *figura*. America for them was neither an outpost nor a backwater of Europe. Nor was it simply an open stage for Europeans to experiment on with models of church-state, or quick ways to get rich, or schemes for social and moral perfection. All of these things might well happen in the New World, but only because the continent itself had a unique meaning, involving a special kind of teleology—an identity *in progress*, not so much defined by the past as directed toward the future. Beginning with New England, continuing into the wilderness, and culminating as the New World Jerusalem, America, they announced, was nothing less than what scripture prophetically termed "the ends of the earth"—meaning, geographically, the end of exploration; historically, the "end-time" in the grand design of providence; and hermeneutically, the end point of prophecy itself. From all three perspectives, America was *"pulcherrima inter mulieres,* the youngest and loveliest of Christ's brides,"[10] the last, best hope of mankind, whether mankind knew it or not.

That vision of the New World was the harvest of the Renaissance rhetoric of discovery. It marked the Puritans' first contribution to American identity; and the second was inextricably bound up with it. I refer to the corporate ideal through which they resolved the ambiguities of their nationalist-universalist venture. For as their opponents were quick to point out, this self-proclaimed latter-day Israel was unlike any other community, sacred or secular. It was not limited by genealogy, as was Israel of old. Nor was it circumscribed by territory, tradition, and custom, as was modern England or Germany. Nor was it a wandering congregation of Christians seeking a haven in the world's wilderness, as were the Plymouth Pilgrims or the Pennsylvania Quakers. And yet the Puritans insisted on incorporating all of these aspects, tribal, territorial, personal, and spiritual. Their key to incorporation, I have suggested, was the Protestant concept of national election. But the concept itself was by definition uncharted. It signified an entity that had never before existed: a "latter-day" community designed for (and confined to) the "end-time." That lack of specificity, that absence of precedent or principle of delimitation, left the colonists open to attack from all quarters. But the same conceptual vagueness that made them vulnerable to historical analysis also freed them, rhetorically, to unite what tradition and common sense had declared fundamentally separate: a community gathered together voluntarily, by spiritual commitment, and a community defined by locale, local origins, and territorial errand.

In retrospect, we can see how these ambiguities were latent in the idea of national election, inherent in the Reformers' sense of the historicity of their spiritual protest. But *as* ambiguities they presented a problem to European Protestant nationalists. Elect nationhood was a textual abstraction. Its concept of "nationhood" differed from any historically formed nationality, and it actually conflicted with the then dominant pre-Reformation, even pre-Christian bonds of community. The Reformers tried to solve the problem by a *rhetorical* ambiguity. They spoke of the covenant of national election as being interchangeably national or *federal*, and the federal alternative suggests its distinctively Protestant character. Federal identity carried national implications, but mainly in the loose sense of a community of belief. It defined a "people" neither in the genealogical terms of Israel nor in the linguistic-geographical-antiquarian terms of other secular peoples, although in some sense it combined both aspects, credal and secular, in a new figural concept of nationality. The concept itself, however, remained vague, visionary. Fundamentally, federal identity was a wild seed of the Reformation, a by-blow of regional pride and apocalyptic hope that never found a stable home in the Old World. Despite its reappearance in various guises of chauvinism, it remained a suspect and disputed foster child in the ancient European family of nations and city-states, wandering uneasily from Luther's Germany to Calvin's Geneva to John Foxe's England—an identity in search of a community—until, in the Westward course of empire, it found a home in Puritan New England.

For as Cotton Mather might have put it, the dream of national election was heaven-sent for the Massachusetts Bay colonists. As nonseparating congregationalists they had effectually de-historicized their venture. Their effort at intellectual synthesis ("visible saints," "church-state") deprived them of their concrete connections with the past—all their English antiquities, except those inscribed in Protestant historiography—just as the past they invented for America deprived the continent's native inhabitants of *their* past, all their indigenous antiquities except those inscribed in the Christian-progressive view of history. The Puritans were a community in search of an identity commensurate with their New World mission. When they adopted the rhetoric of federalism as their "peculiar" social bond, the covenant of national election flowered, and the elect nation of Jeremiah, Isaiah, and John the Divine became incarnate in the first wholly Protestant contribution to modern nationalism, the American Israel.

What I am suggesting is that the federal covenant became for the colonial Puritans a quasi-national, proto-cultural mode of identity. Their federal selfhood was at once exclusive and unlimited, regional and teleological. It was designed to replace, or redefine, the secular facts of the past with a visionary history of the future. I call that design "proto-cultural" because the vision it entailed was geared toward general principles and values—rather than toward distinguishing communal traits (heredity, locale, customs, language)—and because these general principles and values expressed the institutions and expressive forms of a certain emergent way of life. As I noted in the last chapter, the Puritans' federal "contract" or "compact," the binding tenets of their "company in covenant," were part and parcel of the nascent capitalist modes that Christopher Hill has shown to have been dominant in seventeenth-century English Puritanism, and that applied still more directly (because relatively unimpeded by residual feudal forms) to the society established by the Massachusetts Bay Company, Incorporated. The society itself was not nationalist, though it clothed itself in the metaphors of Israel, and it was not theocratic, though it claimed to be God's special instrument, the vehicle of Christ's latter-day *magnalia*. Or rather, it was both nationalist and universalist *in potentia*: a group of sectarians whose rhetoric of independence declared them to be a "peculiar people"; a New World community which defined its purpose and locale in abstractions that fused the dynamics of modernization with the tropes of sacred history.

These hybrid enclosed-and-expansive qualities the Puritans invested in the symbol of America. The genealogy of "the American," understood as a distinctive national-cultural identity, leads back to "the city upon a hill" announced by John Winthrop, "the *American* Nehemiah," to the "Christian *Tribes*" under his command, in "their Passage" to New Israel. A century later, in 1710, Cotton Mather elaborated that image as the *Theopolis Americana*, the "Holy City" that was to be at once the harvest of New England's mission and yet, paradoxically, "not something *new*, but the *Unveiling*, to the light of a *New Day* of all *Revealed Truth* . . . through His *peculiar people*, unto a *Renovated Earth*." A century later, Jefferson restated that universalist-exclusivist vision in the language of liberal common sense. The Declaration of Independence, he explained in 1825, was an attempt

> Not to find out new principles, or new arguments never before thought of, not merely to say things which had never been said before; but to place before mankind the common sense of the subject, in terms so plain and firm as to command their assent. . . . Neither aiming at originality of principle or sentiment, nor yet copied from any particular and previous writing. It was intended to be an expression of the American mind.[11]

"Common sense" here is universal, rational, and natural, even (in the philosophic sense) empirical. But the ideology it embodies of "the American mind" compels assent to a *special* federal identity. That ideological reciprocity between inclusion and exclusion, both *in extremis*, explains how the Declaration could be canonized (by 1825) as the Book of Genesis in "the Bible of the Free." It explains the consecration of the Constitution's "We, the people" into what Representative Robert Winthrop in 1846 termed "the universal Yankee nation." "We are the only great people of the civilized world that is a pure democracy," wrote Henry James in 1878 (in perhaps the most infamous year of Gilded Age Reconstruction), "and we are the only great people that is exclusively commercial. . . . In respect to the United States the European imagination is *motionless*." He later immortalized that cultural commonplace in the protagonist of *The American*.[12]

My point is not that "America" is Puritan. It is that the Puritans contributed in a central way to what was to become the American symbology. They called themselves New Englanders, colonials, and (for a short time) Puritans; but they also invented themselves, through their federal covenant, as God's people in America, meaning by this a community in process, and therefore released from the usual national restrictions of genealogy, territory, and tradition. As their leaders kept reminding them at every covenant-renewal ceremony, they were "a nation born in a day," according to biblical prophecy, for the express purpose of making "the desert blossom as the rose." Nationally considered, that is, they were a "Way," an errand, a corporate body defined (in opposition to Old World "motionlessness") by the preposition *into*: into the future as into the wilderness. Thus the terms of their voluntary sacred-social contract merged the principles of *sola fides* and *sola scriptura*, the inward spiritual road to salvation and the communal road in time and space to the millennium. Thus, too, the ritual I mentioned of generational rededication focussed on the past in order to elicit the anxieties of progress. To recognize the meaning of New England, as Samuel Danforth explained in his great election-day address of 1670, was to understand the colony *now* in terms of its cause and end, in relation to its New World antiquities and to the New World Jerusalem, of which those antiquities were a specimen. Inevitably, this was to realize (through an inward sight of sin) how far they had fallen, and at the same time to realize (through prophetic insight) how far they must rise to make themselves worthy of their errand. And that double sense of short-coming implied its own remedy: an *act* both personal and public, through which the inward turning to the spirit issued in a social commitment to progress.[13]

It has been argued that the rhetorical assertions of the immigrants betray feelings of nostalgia and guilt. If so, it may be said of their successors that they managed to redirect whatever was negative about such feelings into a positive anxiety about the future. Turning nostalgia into a commemoration of the fathers' pristine wilderness, and guilt into an incentive toward what still remained to be done, their rituals celebrate a federal identity expanding, in a moveable symbolic-territorial feast, from regional myth to continental prophecy.

Danforth's *Brief Recognition of New England's Errand into the Wilderness* is characteristic in this regard. It echoes and is echoed in turn by a long procession of exhortations, which together constitute a triumph of what may properly be called the *American* Puritan imagination. To some extent the addresses persisted in their own right, as a literary genre, through intertextual connections from one ritual occasion to the next—on fast and thanksgiving days, days of humiliation, election days, and days of covenant renewal. But above all they persisted for functional reasons, as an organic expression of the community. They were the *cultural* issue of a venture dedicated to the proposition that prophecy is history antedated, and history, postdated prophecy. They represented a community in crisis and therefore using crisis as a strategy of social revitalization; a settlement in peril and therefore drawing strength from adversity, transition, and flux; a company in covenant deprived by history of their identity and therefore using their self-declared newness to create a vision of America that reconceived history at large (including that of the Old World) as hinging on *their* failure or success.

The legacy of this ritual mode may be traced through virtually every major event in the culture, from the Great Awakening through the Revolution and the Westward Movement to the Civil War, and from that "Armageddon" to the Cold War, the Star Wars, and the New World Order of *our* latter days. At every point, the rituals of generational rededication build on the distance in terms of "errand" or its equivalents ("manifest destiny," "continuing revolution," "new frontiers"). And at every point, the errand is defined as the special obligation of the "Israel of our time," federally covenanted as "the nation of futurity" to be "the heir of the ages" and "the haven for God's outcasts and exiles"—"a new breed of humans called an American," destined "to begin the world over again" and "to build a land here that will be for all mankind a shining city on a hill."[14]

These phrases come from a variety of Americans, as distant in time from each other as John Adams and Ronald Reagan, and as different in mind and imagination as Herman Melville and the manifest destinarian John O'Sullivan. My purpose in running their words together is not to blur the differences. On the contrary, it is to highlight the disparate uses to which the Puritan vision has lent itself. In particular now, I think of its legacy to our literary tradition: the internalized, ideal America that inspired Emerson and his heirs; "the only true America," as Thoreau called it, which the country's major authors have recurrently drawn upon (or withdrawn into) as an alternative to the dominant American Way. "Not America," was the way W. E. B. Du Bois put it, "but what America might be—the Real America." In the words of Langston Hughes:

> America never was America
> to me
> And yet I swear this oath—America
> will be.

It is a paradox of, by, and for the culture that Hughes should have titled his poem, nostalgically, "Let America Be America Again."[15]

That alternative America, as it has been called, is the third aspect I referred to of the Puritan legacy, and it has its roots in the last phase of the development of the New England Puritan vision. By the spring of 1692, when Cotton Mather started on his *Magnalia Christi Americana*, the church-state was defunct, and in his view New England had tragically abandoned its calling. The *Magnalia* self-consciously affirms the vision *in spite of* history. As "the HISTORY OF A NEW-ENGLISH ISRAEL . . . to anticipate the state of the *New Jerusalem*," it reconstitutes the entire errand, from its antiquities in the Great Migration to its fulfillment in the millennium, as rhetoric.[16] I describe the process of that defiant, poignant, and far-reaching transvaluation of fact into trope in my next chapter. Let me note here that it stands as the logical end of the Puritan vision. The second-generation colonists had turned to rhetoric to compensate for the betrayal of the Old World. Mather took their strategy one step further: he transformed the rhetoric into compensation for history's betrayal of the New World. For him, too, "New England" was a conjunction of geography, Scripture, and the spirit; he, too, created his symbology out of the rhetoric of discovery, the authority of the word, and the primacy of personal faith. But his ends were not to clothe local history in myth. They were to preserve the myth from history. These were the ends also of many of his later works, through *Terra Beata* (1726), as well as the works of other Old Guard visionaries—all of which might have been titled, like Samuel Sewall's tract of 1697, *Phaenomena Quaedam Apocalyptica, or A Description of the New Heavens as It Makes to Those Who Stand Upon the New Earth.*

This procession of anachronistic visionary tracts would seem to be an apt finale to what I termed the apocalyptic play within a play of the history of "New–English Israel." "Elect nation," "New World," "wilderness," "New Canaan," "latter-day Israel": all the foundations of the New England Way were figures of speech. Conceived in rhetoric, they sprang to life for a season, a nation born *ex verbo* in a day; and we might have expected—by the laws of narrative closure, or of poetic justice—that they would return in due time to the realm of rhetoric. But the fact is that the Puritan vision survived the demise of the church-state. Like Hawthorne's anachronistic Gray Champion, it returned as an agent of social cohesion at every stage of cultural transition—including, ironically, the transition from Puritan colony to Yankee province. The fact is, too, that New England retained its mythic status as the origin of American identity long after the region had lost its national importance, just as the telos it claimed to prefigure remained (in one form or another) inherent in the cloud-capped American dream. And the fact is, finally, that the strategy of Mather's *Magnalia*, his determination to make "history" of *his Theopolis Americana*—to bring interpretation to life, whether it lived anywhere else or not—became a ritual mode of our literary tradition. What distinguishes our classic writers in this respect is what distinguished the latter-day New England Puritans from *their* European contemporaries and predecessors: they did not abandon the vision even when they were persuaded that the country had. Of course, they re-cognized the vision in their own terms (as the "open territories," or the Great Desert/Garden of the West); they made the spirit consonant with Romantic consciousness; and they reconceived the text as a vaguer expression, at once more general and more subjective, of the principle of *sola scriptura*.

But here as elsewhere re-cognition suggests the way a vision persists; it attests to the process of imaginative continuity *through* social and conceptual revision. Intrinsic to that process, from the Romantic period onward, was the spiritual use of geography as *American* nature, the geographic specificity of consciousness as *American* self-realization, and the figural use of scripture as pre-text of *America's* promise. That symbology our classic writers never disavowed. However universalist their outlook, however fixed they were on transcendence and the self, they invested the meaning of those concepts in the same federal vision. In their optative moods, they spoke as unacknowledged representatives of America. In their despairing moods they interpreted the betrayal of the vision as the betrayal of all human aspirations—inverted millennium into doomsday, and mankind's best hope into its last. From either perspective (or both), their aesthetic achievement speaks directly to the profoundly historical ends of Puritan rhetoric. The vision of New England was the child of Protestantism, Renaissance exploration, and the printing press. But America, both as the single most potent cultural symbol of the modern world and as the symbolic center of the nation's literary tradition, was the discovery of colonial New England.

4
Cotton Mather and the
Vision of America

I: Images for Myself: Cotton Mather in his Diaries (1724)

Increase Mather died in August 1723, rich in years and honors, widely mourned as the foremost American Puritan of the age. Several months later his eldest, best-known, and most devoted son, now de facto heir to the theocratic dynasty, took stock of his own life and works. He had early and eagerly accepted the greatness to which he had been born, had assiduously prepared himself for the high destiny which his very name blazoned forth, proclaiming as it did his preeminence among the remnant that God had sifted two generations before and directed under the aegis of his grandfathers, Richard Mather and John Cotton, to establish a specimen of New Jerusalem in the Western wilderness. At the age of twenty-two—five years after his victorious debut in the family pulpit, and already acknowledged "an Excellent Preacher, a great Writer, next in Fame" to Increase alone—he had secured divine assurance of his calling. From the Throne of Christ, his face shining like the noonday sun over Damascus, an angel had brought him special prophecies of the mighty deeds which he, Cotton Mather, should do not only in America but the world over to usher in the millennium. It was reserved for him, he learned, as he humbled himself in the dust of his study floor, to fulfill the messianic vision of Ezekiel 31: "*Behold hee was a Cedar in Lebanon, exalted above all the Trees of the Field, because of the Multitude of Waters when hee shott forth. Thus was hee fair in his Greatness in the Length of his Branches for his Root was by the great Waters. Nor was any Tree in the Garden of God like unto him in his Beauty.*"[1]

Cotton Mather had subsequently received many visits and messages from his "particular angel." And he had often reminded himself of that "strange and memorable" prophecy. He had invoked it two years later when the citizens of Boston selected him their spokesman against the royalist-Anglican Governor Andros. Soon after he had cited the text to preface the book with which he hoped to rescue Massachusetts from its witchcraft enchantments. He had called it to mind in 1689, when, considering the hermeneutic through which he was preparing to expound New England's errand, he found "the Types, like the Waters in Ezekiel's *Vision, Growing and Rising still.*" He had developed the image into a central theme of his paean to Harvard College (the introduction to Book IV of the *Magnalia*), where he was then serving as its youngest overseer and where at fifteen, as its youngest graduate, he had heard President Chauncey declaim his peerless ancestry and prospects. He had returned to it throughout the first quarter of the eighteenth century, in his efforts to sustain the Good Old Way at home and to further the Reformation abroad: in his defense of the Half-Way Covenant (*A Tree Planted by the Rivers of Water*), his missionary ventures in providing *Another Tongue* for the heathen Indians or a *Temple Opening* for frontier settlements, his political *Observanda* and *Icono-clastes* against Catholicism, his descriptions of *Baptismal Piety*, the proper *Resort of Piety*, and the country's *Shaking Dispensations*. The "Emblem of the *Goodly Cedar*" had become a standard for his daily self-appraisals, whether at prayer ("*Lord*, Let me be Fruitful"), or in moments of despondency ("My Barrenness! My Barrenness!," how long "has this unprofitable tree been Standing in the Field of the Lord!"), or in token of public recognition, as when he commemorated his honorary D.D. with a signet ring bearing a tree and the legend *Glascua Rigavit*, "the University of Glasgow has watered it." His son Samuel tells us that "The Cast of his Eye upon this, constantly provoked him to pray, O GOD, *make me a very fruitful tree.*" He was summarily to urge Samuel from his deathbed on February 13, 1728, to "Remember only that one word *Fructuosus.*"[2]

Now on the ides of March 1724, at the age of sixty-one, in the fortieth year of his pastorate at Boston's North Church (whose direction he was assuming at last), Cotton Mather confided to his diaries the fruits of his long labors. It is surely one of the grimmest accounts of lost expectations in American letters. What had he not done to promote God's Kingdom, both in the Old World and the New! Setting aside the more than four hundred books he had published while shepherding the colony's largest congregation, his good deeds spread across every sphere of society, like branches of towering cedar over all the garden within its reach. He had devised projects to aid sailors and "the poor *Negro's*," had worked tirelessly for Harvard's improvement, had distributed alms to the needy (well above the required one-seventh of his income), had established societies to advance piety and to strengthen civic authority, had given generously of his time to the distressed and the errant, had written treatises "for the Profit and Honor of the *female Sex*," had dispensed tracts, hundreds of them, to his neighbors and acquaintances, had tendered support of all kinds to his parents and children and destitute relatives. "AND YETT"—at each point, with a relentless self-lacerating tough-mindedness that rivals Henry Adams's *Education*—Mather recorded the disastrous reversals:

> AND YETT, there is not a Man so cursed, among the *Sailors*. . . .
>
> AND YETT, some, on purpose to affront me, call their *Negro's* by the Name of Cotton Mather. . . .
>
> AND YETT, where is the Man, whom the *female Sex* have spitt more of their Venom at?. . .
>
> AND YETT, where is the Man, who has been tormented with such monstrous *Relatives*?. . .
>
> AND YETT, how little *Comfort* have I seen in my *Children*? . . .
>
> AND YETT, the Discountenance I have almost perpetually received from the *Government*! . . .
>
> AND YETT, the *Colledge* forever putts all possible Marks of Disesteem upon me. . . .
>
> AND YETT, my *Company* is little sought for. . . .
>
> AND YETT, I see no man for whom all are so lothe to do *good Offices*. . . .
>
> AND YETT, I have had *Books* written against me. . . .
>
> AND YETT, I am a very *poor Man*. . . .
>
> AND YETT, Every Body points at me, as by far the most afflicted Minister in all *New England*. And many look on me as the *greatest Sinner* because the *greatest Sufferer*.[3]

Undoubtedly, Mather's complaint tends toward melodrama. Set as it is alongside his chronicle of accomplishments, it conveys an unsavory egotism, a mixture of self-pity and self-congratulation which has repelled most readers of his diaries. And indeed these character traits, or their equivalents—spiritual rigidity, narrow and reactionary dogmatism, a lust for affliction wedded to a petty and pompous complacency—form the core of the stereotype through which he has come to represent Puritanism in the popular mind: a stereotype promulgated by his contemporary enemies, embellished by nineteenth-century historians, and reaffirmed in our time by influential scholars and critics. Like most stereotypes, this one expresses a measure of truth; like all stereotypes it is essentially misleading.

In the first place, it obscures the fact that Mather's charges are accurate in substance. If he sometimes exaggerates, he also understates. Regarding his achievements, he omits mention, *inter alia*, of his crucial part in the founding of Yale, his mastery of the Iroquois language (in addition to the six others he already knew) so as to help evangelize the Bay Indians, the scientific investigations which earned him membership in Britain's famed Royal Society and acclaim in our time as the first significant figure in American medicine, his considerable contribution to the persecuted Huguenots and to German Pietist charities. More striking yet is his restraint in enumerating his most painful setbacks. We know from other sources that during 1724 he not only abandoned hope of the Harvard presidency—which the College Corporation then offered to three obviously less qualified candidates—but resigned himself to leaving his "Biblia Americana" unpublished, the massive twenty-year compendium of scripture commentary which he treasured as his masterpiece and for which he had solicited subscribers with increasing desperation for some three decades. We know, further, that in the same year he found himself threatened with imprisonment for debts incurred by his wife's former husband, and that Lydia Lee Mather herself was, if not insane, decidedly psychopathic. He had been happily married twice before. All evidence indicates that he was a devoted father and husband, "agreably temper'd with a various mixture of Wit and Chearfulness,"[4] in an age of paternal severity disposed toward persuasion or compromise, careful to instruct his daughters as well as his sons, deeply affected by the succession of illnesses that by 1724 had proved fatal to twelve of his fifteen children. His silence about Lydia on this occasion reveals something of his forbearance toward her in the face of public shame and private distress. Similarly, the absence of explicit grievances against his son Increase may be taken as testimony (elsewhere made abundantly clear) of his patience and readiness to forgive, his abiding faith in the young man despite the persistent anxieties he caused him. We can hardly blame what resentment we do feel in the muted contrast between his own lifelong sacrifices for his father—whom he had honored always and thrice eulogized in biography—and the intractable prodigality of his favorite child. Later that year he learned that "Cressy" too was dead, drowned in a storm at sea.

The genuine pathos that informs Mather's statement suggests another, more serious limitation in the stereotype. When we juxtapose his disappointments with his unremitting sense of mission, the recurrent "AND YETT" takes on a distinctive purity and force. It comes to signify—beyond its cry of private indignation—a representative gesture of defiance, the righteous anger of a Jeremiah against the betrayal of the promise he alone now still embodies.

Of course, Cotton Mather was not a sackcloth prophet in the wilderness. His biographers have justly portrayed him as a contradictory figure, at once a "primitive Puritan in a Boston that was becoming Yankee" and the most cosmopolitan of Yankees, champion of the New Science, fashionable in dress and decorum, stylistically at times a model of Augustan refinement. Like Henry Adams, that primitive Yankee in a Boston hurling into the twentieth century, he functioned as a sort of customshouse through which the latest European notions entered the country, from plant hybridization and Newtonian optics to Milton's theory of unrhymed verse. But (again like Adams) he was a casualty of change. Intellectually, he was not so much transitional as schizophrenic, a dispossessed leader caught between two eras, one dead, the other beyond his moral and emotional comprehension. For in his basic convictions Mather belonged entirely to the former era. His very sophistication seems to have hardened his allegiance to the past; in effect, it sharpened the shocks of reality that impelled him inward, toward the shelter of the imagination. The more he discovered how thoroughly his education had failed him—the further he drifted (to paraphrase *The Education of Henry Adams*) into the supersensual chaos of the Age of Reason—the closer his identification grew with the vanished theocracy which for him enshrined the true meaning of the country. It is this commitment, this visionary's No-in-thunder to the way of the world, which adds, I think, a redeeming suprapersonal dimension to Mather's outrage. More largely, it is this self-concept which welds the fragmentary entries in his "Testimony," as he referred to his voluminous diaries—along with his constant revisions and later insertions—into a spiritual autobiography of remarkable coherence and extraordinary cultural import.[5]

Mather's stubbornly archaic moral idealism pervades every aspect of his self-portrait. It accounts for his astounding naiveté, his inability not only to cope with but to grasp the meaning of new social and ideological trends: the reasons, for example, for the clergy's loss of political influence after the Andros revolt, or (in theological matters) for the rise of Stoddardism, or again, on a more intimate level, for the depletion of his flock and his ostracism from the councils of government. It underlies his courage in defense of certain old friends (like the discredited Sir William Phips) and under public attack, as when he pioneered the use of inoculation despite violent general resistance, issuing in at least one attempt on his life. Indeed, it helps explain why he should have been so much a prey for attack: why he should have stood as scapegoat for the witchcraft debacle when his conduct then was at worst representative and in sum notably moderate; why he should have become an exemplum of bigotry although, at "the Hazard of much Repro[a]ch," he repeatedly condemned persecution for civil or religious dissent.

Finally, his emotional commitment explains the curiously static character of his thought. The diaries exasperate even the sympathetic reader by their unflagging intellectual monotony. Notwithstanding Mather's international correspondence, varied concerns, and prolific reading, notwithstanding also the series of crises (diplomatic, theological, and scientific) that marks his career, his outlook remains virtually unaltered. Nor does this impression misrepresent his attainments. His sermon of 1724 that set out his plan for benevolent societies he had delivered verbatim forty-five years earlier, at the age of sixteen. The same didactic and hermeneutic strains run throughout the corpus of his work. His interest in medicine, which led him to undertake the widest-ranging colonial inquiry into the subject, derives from his earliest adolescence. The obsessions of his last years—with the spectre of death, with his professed slothfulness and much-lamented "ambitious Affectation of Praeheminencies"—abound in his first manuscripts.[6] The persecution itself which he detailed at sixty-one he decries so often previously that it seems part of a self-styled course of martyrdom.

His development lies in the realm of the imagination. It consists simply, astonishingly, in his capacity to transform public defeat into private triumph by recourse to metaphor and myth. If, as we are told, we can glean so little from the diaries of concrete historic value, that in a sense is precisely their intent. They trace the growth of a prophet's mind in opposition to a recalcitrant world. The mystical rapture with which they open returns time and again ("glorious," "incredible," "triumphant, weeping," ultimately "inexpressible") to raise the author with a "Supernatural and Immediate *Efficacy*" into "an high, a sweet, an heavenly" plane of *"Joy unspeakable and full of Glory"*; it returns after every adversity carrying "wondrous Assurances" of "a rich Compensation for all the Sorrows, which are appointed for me." In this reciprocity between humiliation and triumph, Ezekiel's vision (which, significantly, Mather seems to have experienced later than he claims) may be seen as the centerpiece in a long procession of epiphanies through which he gradually discerns, or unveils, the nature of his calling. He offers, in short, not a self-examination but a cosmic self-affirmation—in the Calvinist meaning of the word, a "justification" of his life. His reflections on periods of public distress picture him an epic hero in "a dismal Emblem of Hell." "This Assault of the *evil Angels* upon the Country," he concludes at one point, "was intended as a particular Defiance, unto *my* poor Endeavors"; a subsequent analysis demonstrates that "Extraordinary Things were done for me, that cannot be related. I will only say, the Angels of Heaven are at work for me."[7] Within this mythopoetic framework, the diaries present with gathering confidence a procession of biblical figures or types which all but submerge the actual man within the metaphorical—specifically, within the dual image of John the Baptist and Christ, alternately (and in the end simultaneously) messenger of the New Day and Man of Sorrows, the greatest of sufferers misjudged as the greatest of sinners.

Through the image of John, Mather sought to recover the social role that history denied him. As he conceived of the parallels between the Baptist and himself, the prophetic or progressivist meaning of the relation absorbed the literal. The parallels bespoke not just a mission to "prophesy Christ," but, more largely, a progression of seers (Daniel, the Baptist, the author of Revelation) leading forward from the Bible to Cotton Mather, climactically, as witness for the millennium at hand. The basis for his conception lay at the roots of New World Puritanism. As I argued in the preceding chapters, millennial anticipations had played a central part in the Massachusetts Bay Colony venture. They were a key source of the vitality which had wrought the New Canaan out of the howling American desert. In his famous definition of *New-England's Errand into the Wilderness,* Samuel Danforth described the Baptist as a forerunner not only of the Incarnation but, implicitly, of the Second Coming and compared his wilderness mission in the latter regard with that of the theocracy. Other ministers before and after Danforth announced the good news with the same visionary enthusiasm. When *"John* the *Baptist* arose like a bright and shining light," Jesus appeared to him "at the end of the Jewish world *in the end of the world* [i.e., the wilderness]" as a "partial fulfillment" of "the last and great day"; accordingly, another light shone forth more clearly to reveal Christ when the Reformation dawned after the long night of the "Roman Antichrist"; to bring that light to its full brilliancy was "the end of our coming hither" across the Atlantic—and now, considering our accomplishments, "you may conclude that the Sun will quickly arise upon the world" and "New Jerusalem come down from heaven" to the American strand.[8]

These declarations come from first- and second-generation ministers. By the time Cotton Mather had grown to manhood the energies they expressed had largely dissipated, or at any rate had radically changed. No one knew that better than he; but he could retain the source itself—"the Cause of God and his People in *New-England* according to its *divine Originall* and *Native beautie"*— in compensation for the authority that by all right, he believed, heavenly as well as human, he ought to have inherited. Had not God called him, Cotton Mather, "as a John, to bee an Herald of the Lord's Kingdome now approaching"? Did he not "feel the Lord Jesus Christ most sensibly carrying on, the Interests of His Kingdom, in [his] Soul, continually," and so directing him, "as poor and as vile" as he was, to "become a *Remembrancer* unto the Lord, for no less than whole *Peoples,* Nations and Kingdomes"? He especially liked to contemplate the prospect on the Sabbath. Since the Lord's Day was "a Peculiar Type of the Blessed *Millennium,"* it invited his researches into the prophecies concerning "the Great *Sabbatism,"* his prayers for their swift fulfillment, and his preparations for "being eminently *serviceable* in the *mighty Changes."* Together, these activities inspired him to assume an oracular political clairvoyance, to declare himself at once interpreter, personification, guide, and forecaster of the corporate future. In the death of England's King Charles II he read the beginning of "the *Resurrection of* [the] *Witnesses*"; religious turmoil in Europe meant variously "a wondrous *Revolution*" in Scotland and Ireland, an end-time convulsion in France, and a "glorious Reformation" in the Spanish Indies; the civic instability of late-seventeenth-century Massachusetts pointed to the collapse of the Ottoman Empire and the imminent conversion of the Jews.[9]

Such prognostication was by no means unusual. Indeed, it had become something of a Reformation pastime ever since Luther had announced the *clavis Apocalyptica*, the key to the secrets of the Book of Revelation, in the equation of Roman Catholicism with the whore of Babylon. What distinguishes Mather is the intense responsibility he takes for the shape of things to come. To judge by the diaries, it is *his* tears that will liberate France, *his* "Prayers and Pains" that will shortly enlighten the Jewish nation, *his* "Goods Devised" that will ready the colony for the Second Coming. It is, comprehensively, in *him* that we are to locate the burgeoning "*Manifestations* of what the Lord is *going to do in the Earth.*" European Puritans studied the prophecies for either personal or political reasons, either as an independent scholarly undertaking or (like New England's founders) as part of their adherence to a collective enterprise. In Cotton Mather, particularly after 1690, both motives are joined and transmuted. The "great Revolutions expected in the Dayes approaching" become for him a substitute for a manageable political context. The "Consuming of the Ten Kingdomes"—and all the other doomsday cataclysms that he predicted in 1724 would "suddenly come upon us"—constitutes an ambiguous retribution-reward meted out to the backsliding New Israelites from whom he willfully divorced himself *and* whom he was directing into the *Theopolis Americana*. I have "made Sacrifices of all, even my dearest Enjoyments," he wrote at several different moments during that bleak time, and so "I went to the Lord; and cried unto Him that the Ministry of His holy ANGELS might be allowed unto me, that the holy ANGELS may make their Descent, and the Kingdome of the Heavens come on." Refusing to resign himself merely to a proud isolation, glorying in the "sacrificing Stroke" that bespoke his solitary midnight watch, Mather established within the apocalyptic imagination itself his mastery over the forces of history. In a more literal and immediate sense than the most sanguine Romantic would dare lay claim to, Mather believed his special capacity for vision and insight rendered him the unacknowledged legislator of his world.[10]

In his private afflictions Mather cast himself in the image of a suffering Savior. No image is more familiar to Christian tradition; the diaries stand out among Puritan journals, however, for their insistence on the *imitatio Christi* and in personal literature generally for their conscious, diversified, and transparently compensatory application of the concept. If we can trust Mather's "Paterna"—his manuscript autobiography, composed mainly of diary extracts chosen to edify his sons (first Cressy and then Samuel)—the application dates from his childhood. "When I was about seven or eight years old," he writes, "I rebuked my play mates for their wicked *words* and *ways*; and sometimes I suffered from them, the persecution of not only *Scoffs* but *Blows* also for my Rebukes, which when somebody told your Grandfather, I remember he seemed very *glad*, yea, almost proud of my Affronts."[11] The anecdote has provoked a number of caricatures of the preacher as a young prig; it remains valuable nonetheless as the first recorded instance of a dominant pattern of Mather's thought. No doubt he did not mean to associate his father with God, as the logic of his rhetoric here suggests.* But the explicit fusion of

Certainly such conjecture should not be pressed too far; but the implicit association is pervasive enough to warrant comment. It may be fairly discerned in his eulogies to the abused but forgiving saint ("These are my Brethren, they and I have the same Father"*), in the recurrent tree-imagery of his trinitarian discourses ("God the *Father* as the Sacred *Root*, Christ as a *Trunk* issuing from it, [and] the Holy *Spirit* as a *Sap* running thro' it"), and even (considering the biographical parallels) in his references to "*the Glorious Pattern of the Blessed Jesus, Readily and Cheerfully Submitting to take the Cup, which His Father had given Him.*" "It is impossible," he wrote, "that the SON should be without the FATHER, or the FATHER without the SON, or both without the HOLY SPIRIT." We ought to recall in this connection his numerous private expressions on the subject—his reiterated urgency to embrace "the Spirit of Adoption in the *Abba, Father*" and to penetrate "the Sweet Mystery of Going to God as my Father, and crying *Abba, Father*"—as well as his excessive zeal against Arianism, and his strange attraction to it in moments of despair. When he was a young man he recorded a "little Accident" that he believed emblemized his "own Transactions with Heaven": his son displeased Increase one day, and Cotton Mather, as father-become-son, pleaded "as an Advocate for the Child [become mankind] in his Infirmity. So the Child was presently received into Favour with my Father; my Father look'd on him with a pleased Aspect, and bestow'd aggreable Illuminations upon him." In his old age he customarily referred to Increase as "Adoni Avi," "my Lord, my father." (Quotations are from *Diary for the Year 1712*, pp. 82–83; *Serious Thoughts in*

himself and Jesus recurs with growing frequency and amplitude: in Jesus' persecution and temptations, in His ministry, habits of prayer, and behavior toward kinsmen, even in His relations with His consort, the church, and above all in His resignation to the scoffs and blows of the wicked. When Mather's congregation dwindles (like "the Withdrawal of the Disciples"), when during the inoculation crisis Mather sees, with Christ, only malice for his efforts to heal the diseased, when in 1724 he finds himself (like "the Sheep before the Shearers" and "the Stone, which the Builders have refused") deserted by his wife and rejected by Harvard,

---

Dying Times [Boston, 1691?], p. 12; *Unum Necessarium* [Boston, 1693], p. 25; *The Duty of Children Whose Parents have Pray'd for Them* [Boston, 1703, bound with Increase Mather, *The Duty of Parents to Pray for their Children* [Boston, 1719], p. 28; *Diary*, I, 583.)

As we might expect, these sentiments carry a deep ambivalence. It lies beyond the scope of this chapter to trace Mather's complex, shifting attitude toward his father, but it seems pertinent to suggest the personal implications of his obsessive use of the filial bond for subject and simile. On the one hand, we can doubt neither his abiding respect and affection (which he summarized in his funeral eulogy and embodied in his lengthy and very readable *Paternator* [1724]), nor his marked temperamental affinities to Increase (their diaries resemble one another in their millenialism, their mystical assurances, their laments over spiritual barrenness, and their hypersensitivity to persecution). On the other hand, we know that the relationship must have entailed severe emotional strains, not least of which lay in its incalculable cost to Mather's political ambitions. The strains appear even in the polemics which espouse his parent's quarrels, such as *Political Fables* (1692), where he plays Orpheus to his father's Mercury, the "divine harpist" obliged to protect the "not much concerned" celestial messenger. Most vividly, they are manifest in his contradictory thematic or metaphorical applications. Although, for example, he often invokes his parentage to justify himself, he constantly asserts the superiority, in elect families, of son to father: "*Young People* are more fit than *Old*," they radiate a "*Double Glory*" and the Lord "will do more for [them] than ever He did for their elders," since the "*Covenant-Mercy* of God, oftentimes the *further* it Rolls, the *bigger* it grows." Or again, he seems too much to protest his concern with his "dying parent," not only because of his insistence on the image, but, more strikingly, because of his many allusions to *Vatermord*. "Disobedient Children," he thunders at the unconverted, "You kill your parents; you are *Murderers of your Parents*"; and on several occasions he refers to the story of Croesus's "Dumb Son, who tho' he never spoke before; yet seeing a man go to kill his Father, his Agonies made him shriek, *O don't kill my Father!*" The relationship was of course further complicated by Mather's intense feelings for his own first and favorite son, whom he named Increase, after his father. Quotations are from *The Fisher-Mans Calling* (Boston, 1712), p. 6; *Paternalia* (Boston, 1715), p. 26; *The Duty of Children*, pp. 68, 88; *A Family Well-Ordered* (Boston, 1699), pp. 27–28; *The Wayes and Joyes of Early Piety* (Boston, 1712), pp. 53–54; and *The Present State of New-England* (Boston, 1690), p. 45.

he wears the affronts with jubilant thanksgiving: "A conformity to Him in Sufferings, Injuries, Reproaches from a malignant world, makes me, even to rejoice in those Humiliations"; by forcing "me [to] entirely submit unto the Will of GOD," it makes all but inevitable "those Things, wherein Satan will be marvellously bruised under my Feet." If it also made martyrdom inevitable, as he felt throughout the last decade of his life, he could only rejoice the more. "I behold myself nailed unto a *Cross*. My spirit is reconciled unto this condition; 'tis welcome to me, in regard of the glorious Designs which my SAVIOUR has, in ordering such a Conformity unto Himself." Thus in 1717; seven years later he was still luxuriating in that "incomparable Satisfaction. And I am willing," he added, drawing perhaps upon his boyhood memory for the crowning analogy, "that my Crucifixion should go on, [so] that I should be made a Spectacle which the glorious GOD will with Delight look down upon."[12]

Mather supplemented this beatific conformity with an assortment of scriptural precedents (Jeremiah and Isaiah in the Old Testament, Paul and Stephen in the New); he augmented it through a variety of typological guises. In different scenes during his agon, his lifelong combat with the Devil, he appears an obedient Adam or a defiant Elijah, a persevering or an assertive Job, another Samson combating the conspiring Philistines abroad, or, ill in bed, a shorn Samson awaiting a renewal of strength to "vex the Dragon." This therapeutic-exegetical technique forms a structural principle of the diaries. His early identification with Moses enabled him to overcome the most severe trauma of his youth, the stammer which almost foreclosed his clerical vocation. As he noted in his initial entry (March 12, 1681, one month after his eighteenth birthday), Moses had not heeded God's promise that He would "*bee with his Mouth*. And now, because I would not so sin, therefore I trust in thee! Thou dost send mee forth, as thou didst *Moses*, and thou wilt bee with my Mouth." When the stammer persisted he took courage by recalling how "Moses complained that the Infirmitie of his *Utterance* continued, after his Entrance upon his Ministry." Mather sought sustenance from the comparison over and again, until, confident at last in God's promise to *him*, feeling that he (unlike Moses) would "*speak* with Fruitfulness," he could hymn his vow "to make my *Tongue / A Tree of Life*." At sixty-one he was relying on the same approach to gird himself against adversity. Faced in 1723 with the possibility

102 / Rites of Assent

of arrest, he remembered that "*Joseph* was a Type of our admirable JESUS, in this among other Things, that the very Methods which their Enemies took to defeat the Purposes of Heaven concerning them, did but help to fulfill those very Purposes." And in the autumn of that year, his elaborate, moving threnody over his "poor beloved Absalom"—"Ah! My son *Increase!* My Son! My Son! My Head is Waters, and my Eyes are a Fountain of Tears! I am overwhelmed!"—came not as a spontaneous outburst of grief but as the finale of a figural drama he had long engaged in, mentally, as director and main actor, in an effort to bring under control the most traumatic personal frustration of his old age.[13]

From Moses to David the diversity of types highlights the Christ-image which unifies Mather's presentation of his private life. To some extent this image conflicts with that of millennial herald. One is essentially self-contained, the other sweeps the protagonist into the dynamic, futuristic, all-encompassing movement of history. What links the two is their common basis in the outlook that prompted the Great Migration, the joint personal/social eschatology that flourished for a generation or two as the New England Way. It may be valid, therefore, to speak of Cotton Mather as representing in extremis the thrust and tensions of American Puritanism—if we recognize that his representative attributes take the form of wish fulfillment. They blend and reinforce one another not, as his grandfathers had planned, in a community of saints on a historic errand, a church-state where the stages of inner preparation reflect the settlement's actual progress, but in a process of self-definition designed to create a distinctively self-contained *figure*, the embodiment of things past and to come, paradoxically insulated from the present and symbolic of his culture. Broadly considered, the figure evokes a number of earlier heroic models, such as the postexilic Hebrew seer. Most directly and pointedly, its counterpart appears in the isolatoes who through the nineteenth century shaped the nation's literary tradition: the "keepers of the dream," who, unlike their European counterparts—whether Puritan (like Milton) or Romantic (like Blake and Wordsworth, Hölderlin and Schelling)—*refused* to substitute an apocalypse of the mind for a disappointed historic expectation, and whose epic-autobiographies, accordingly, transform personal failure into social ideal. "Once History inhabits a crazy house," wrote Norman Mailer in *Armies of the Night*, "egotism may be the last tool left to History."[14]

I discuss the different implications of these continuities in later chapters (on Melville and Emerson). Here let me simply recall the recurrent crises of national identity, and the recurrent emergence of Jeremiahs seeking to set in order the crazy house of history and finding instead "rich compensation" for an untoward political reality in an egotism transformed into a self-contained, all-encompassing, exemplary American self. In this tradition Mather deserves a place of honor both as a colonial Puritan and as a man of letters. "The Cross is a dry sort of wood," he once remarked in recording a Lord's-Day epiphany; "but yett it proves a *fruitful Tree*."[15] However deceived he was in his mystical assurances, whatever our ad hominem judgment of his "Martyrdom," his diaries—and his major published writings, each of them in some form an extension of the diaries— vindicate his trust in rhetoric, vision, and the imagination.

II. Images of Myself: Cotton Mather in His Writings (1683–1700)

Few Puritans more loudly decried the bosom serpent of egotism than did Cotton Mather; none more clearly exemplified it. Explicitly or implicitly, he projects himself everywhere in his writings. In the most direct compensatory sense, he does so by using literature as a means of personal redress. He tells us that he composed his discussions of the family to bless his own, his essays on the riches of Christ to repay his benefactors, his tracts on morality to convert his enemies, his funeral discourses to console himself for the loss of child, wife, or friend. More often, his self-projection serves to magnify some intimate problem into a tenet of the system he is defending. His first sermons expound texts on "the noble faculty of speech" from Psalms and the life of Moses. Subsequent sermons establish a continuing parallel between personal concern and public exhortation. At the appropriate point in the chronology of his affairs, Mather speculates about the nature of angels, the holiness of the children of saints and their filial responsibilities, how properly to "take arms against adversity" or, in other cases, to resign oneself to it (in accordance with *The Religion of the Cross*), the advantages of a successful marriage or the temptations of bachelorhood and widowhood, the dangers of vanity, the mutability of earthly goods—envisaged in revealing particulars of fire, illness, debt, or the loss of a son at sea—and, finally, the solacements of *A Good Old Age* and *Death Approaching*, including prospects of heavenly discourse with the heroes of the Bible.[16]

It would be easy from this vantage point, and not entirely inaccurate, to see in Mather's enormous literary productivity a compulsive and omnivorous self-involvement. But here as in the diaries, the clue to his *creative* energy lies in his persistent stress upon the images through which he forged his identification with Puritan New England. Thematically considered, conformity to Christ and the hastening apocalypse delineate his main areas of concern. The *imitatio Dei* forms the basis of his practical theology. His millennial politics, he tells us, follow from "the signalizing Advantage the *John Baptist* had, in an Opportunitie, to tell [his countrymen], *what they are to do.*" Mather himself took the opportunity at every public ceremony—before the local artillery company, at times of thanksgiving and humiliation, from the election-day desk—speaking through the phrases of Ezekiel, drawing upon Isaiah to justify his chiliastic "med[d]lings," turning to a variety of predecessors (Moses, Jeremiah, Daniel, John the Divine, the angels at the Incarnation) to prove that the "long line of *Inter-Sabbatical Time*" is coming to a close. "Le Coeur du Sage," he wrote at the head of his prophetic summons to France, "connoist le temps."[17]

In his most ambitious works he invokes both these images of himself and builds his argument upon the tension generated by their dual perspective. One such example is *The Wonders of the Invisible World* (1693), his once-notorious assessment of the Massachusetts witch scare, recently defended as a cautionary, level-headed effort at reconciliation. The defense unquestionably improves upon the former view: like his father, Cotton Mather tried to curb the use of "spectral evidence" which lay at the heart of the crisis. But the book itself is as far from sweet reasonableness as it is from self-serving hysteria. Its purpose rests in its impassioned affirmation of the colonial cause. As it portrays the descent of Satan and his legions, all details of court procedure are subsumed in what becomes, like Milton's *Paradise Regained*, a brief epic of eschatological tribulation. The preface presents the author as an amalgam of suffering servant and seer, a saint subjected to "buffetings from Evil Spirits" and a prophet whose fortitude and foresight "countermine the whole PLOT of the Devil." The narrative transfers these terms to the settlement at large. "The Errand of our Fathers into these Ends of the Earth," Mather explains, fulfilled "the Promise of old made unto our Blessed Jesus, *That he should have the Utmost parts of the Earth for his Possession.*" What wonder, then, "that never were more *Satanical Devices* used for the Unsetling of any People under the Sun." Those devices, from the outbreak of heresy in the 1630s to King Philip's War in 1675, had hitherto collapsed, and the inevitable finale was hastening: "Wherefore the Devil is now making one Attempt more upon us," "a thing, prodigious, beyond the Wonders of former Ages," a war "so *Critical*, that if we get well through, we shall soon Enjoy *Halcyon Days* with all the *Vultures* of Hell *Trodden under our Feet.*"[18]

In accordance with this prospect, Mather turns for his text on witchcraft not to the Hebrew law (as in Exod. 22:18) but to the Book of Revelation: "*the Devil is come down unto you, having great Wrath; because he knoweth, that he hath but a short time.*" His application pictures the settlers as another David, "*afflicted from youth,*" and as a second Job, his dwelling "hurricano'd" and his wife inciting him to curse God, pleading with his friends for compassion: "*Have pity upon me, for the Wrath of the Devil has been turned upon me.*" Here, however, the wrath has a much farther-reaching significance, "such an one as is indeed Unparallelable." Recalling the Baptist's times, Mather notes "That just before our Lords *First Coming*, there were most observable Outrages committed by the Devil upon the Children of Men." Surely, therefore, the present "unusual Range of the Devil among us, a little before the *Second Coming*" means that *we* shall deliver "the last stroke." Did not Israel go "further in the *two last* years of their Journey *Canaan-ward*, than they did in 38 years before"? Drawing together the Apocalyptic time schedule, the progress of the Reformation, God's miraculous protection of His American vineyard, the political and natural occurrences abroad—in short, all of history—Mather proclaims

Good News for the *Israel* of God, and particularly for His *New-English Israel*. The Devil was never more let *Loose* than in our Days; and it proves the *Thousand Years* is not very *Far Off*. SHORTLY didst thou say, Dearest Lord! O Gladsome word! I may Sigh over *this* Wilderness, as *Moses* did over *his, We are consumed by thine Anger,* [yet] if God have a Purpose to make here a Seat for any of *Those*

Glorious Things, which are spoken of Thee, O Thou City of God; then even thou, *O New-England,* art within a very little while of Better Dayes than ever yet have Dawn'd upon thee. Our *Lord Jesus Christ shall have the uttermost parts of the Earth for his Possession,* the *last* [shall] be the *first,* and the *Sun of Righteousness* come to shine *Brightest,* in Climates which it rose *Latest* upon![19]

Thus, as Jonathan Edwards was to render Northampton half a century later, Salem village becomes the setting for the climactic drama in the story of redemption. "*The Walls of the whole World are broken down!*" Mather exults. "The very *Devils* are broke in upon us, to seduce the *Souls,* torment the *Bodies,* sully the *Credits,* and consume the *Estates* of our Neighbours, as if the *Invisible World* were becoming *Incarnate.*" When he considers the specifics of the situation he urges restraint. Many of the accused, he fears, are innocent. As in "a *Blind Mans Buffet,*" encircled by "the *Tydogs of the Pit,*" terrified by "*the Fires that are upon us,*" we are "hotly, and madly, mauling one another in the *dark.*" But in the main it is the invasion from the Pit that seizes his imagination. In the fires of diabolism, consuming alike the virtuous and the possessed, he sees the conflagration from which, phoenix-like, will arise a new heavens and a new earth. And he highlights the link between affliction and resurrection by conflating the American wilderness and the wilderness of Christ's agon. This fusion of secular and apocalyptic perspectives is the key to his narrative structure. It reveals Salem as a model of New England, each of the "Bewitched" a representative of the suffering community, every untoward act symbolic of the entire "snare," and New England itself, summarily, an emblem of the invisible universal church. Mather's introductory discourse on the "Enchantments Encountered" ends with a prayer to the Savior in His anguish; the last section ("The Devil Discovered") concludes with a lengthy comparison of each of the three temptations with the Devil's present wiles. What more, Mather asks, need be said of the tidings which all this "Hints unto us?"[20] At the dawn of the Christian era the Tempter was repulsed and the Eden of the redeemed soul raised in the wilderness; some seventeen hundred years later the full meaning of that victory is to be made manifest in the antitypical Eden, New Jerusalem, shining like the meridian sun from the uttermost ends of the earth.

Mather's actual Salem experiences were altogether different.

Reaction against the trials had already set in (as he tacitly concedes at several points in the book) and was beginning to erode not only his family's dynastic claims but the theocracy's very foundations. By 1700 the counter-offensive came to focus upon him in particular. Why he should have thus been made bête noire of the entire episode remains a matter of conjecture. Even after we acknowledge his excessive zeal, it seems undeniable that most of the accusations were at best tangential to his stand on the trials themselves. Mather's critics assailed him because he upheld the authority of the court (although he dissented from its more reprehensible tactics and decisions); because *Wonders* paraded an approving preface by Lieutenant Governor William Stoughton (with Hathorne the sternest of the "hanging judges"); because Mather had too confidently trumpeted his cure, four years earlier, of a "possessed" Boston girl and then, by methods some considered suspect, tried to repeat his success at Salem (though it is worth noting that the cure itself anticipated the psychosomatic treatment of hysteria); because he authored the official, collectively formulated clerical position on the proceedings; because he was later reluctant to recant, and, when he did, persisted nonetheless in his apocalyptic interpretation; and fundamentally, perhaps, because he was the youngest, least experienced, and hence most vulnerable of the old-guard spokesmen involved in what came to be considered the triple misfortune of the 1690s: the Salem trials, the new colonial charter, and the appointment of Sir William Phips as governor.

Whatever importance we assign these factors individually, in general Mather had good reason, I think, to complain of persecution. In any event, as the reaction turned more and more into a vendetta against *him*, his writings increasingly strike up an antiphonal movement, reminiscent of the diaries, between prophet and people. We can follow its rising counterpoint through his various treatments of witchcraft, from *Memorable Providences* (1689), his rather straightforward tale of the Goodwin children of Boston, to *Triumphs over Troubles* (1701), his reply to Robert Calef's slanderous satire-denunciation of 1700, *More Wonders of the Invisible World*. For instance, in *Wonders* Mather likens the colony to Joseph importuned by Potiphar's wife (Satan's instrument) and to a martyr at the stake who had the Book of Revelation thrown at him "by his Bloody Persecutors"; in *Triumphs* he transfers the figures from history to biography. Taking his text from Joseph's response to his adversaries ("*ye thought evil against me*; But God meant it unto Good"), he compares the Mathers to the martyr Constantine cast into a dungcart. By a "*Strange and Fierce Assault*, All the Rage of Satan against the Holy Churches of the Lord falls upon us," he exclaims—meaning now his father and himself in *opposition* to the colony—and yet we will prove instead to "be a precious Odour to God."[21]

This is by no means to say that the Salem experience reversed Mather's convictions. Insofar as he deals only with the witches— outside the circle of private recriminations, so to speak—his outlook retains its former unity. What he learned in essence solidified the role for which, I have suggested, he had been preparing from childhood. He entered into the witchcraft debate in 1688 in his mid-twenties, with public honors thick upon him. He emerged from it, less than a decade later, something of a political exile (in his own eyes the victim of "Contempt, & Cruel Mockings"), but determined to uphold in his writings the "Utopia that was NEW-ENGLAND," to *use* his isolation as a means of revealing himself foremost among "those *Watchmen* that God hath sett upon ye *Walls of Jerusalem, which never hold their peace, and give Him no Rest, until He make Jerusalem a praise in the earth.*"[22] The basis of this development lies in the aesthetic formula through which, in the diaries, he resolved his identity crisis: the interchangeability, and mutually sustaining import, of the images of Christ and the Baptist. The passion which his new-found assurance elicited suggests itself in sheer quantity of publication: seventy-nine titles between 1692 and 1700. At best, it is embodied in the most forceful political sermons of the age, worthy precursors of a national genre that culminates in Whitman's *Democratic Vistas* (1871).

Some of these sermons devolve upon witchcraft; others deal with parallel disturbances: Indian battles, natural disasters, threats of invasion. In each case the strategy builds upon the same model. All the temptations or injuries recapitulate those of Christ (Satan "would *run* us over the most amazing Precipice in the World"); every encounter assumes epic proportions ("Our *Air* has an *Army* of Devils in it," with "marvellous *Energy*" to "*Crack* and *Craze* the Soul"); in every circumstance the lesson for the individual as for the community is that God's American remnant must "travel through the valley of Baca, that is of weeping, unto their everlasting happiness."[23] Together, these elements constitute a view of history which absorbs even the traditional doom-clauses of the federal covenant within a profoundly optimistic framework, an absolute against which this world's temporal evils cannot prevail.

The framework had been established long before. It was intrinsic to the rhetoric of John Cotton and Richard Mather, with its interlinking of the providential and the predetermined; it was embellished and elaborated by their colleagues and successors. What their grandson more than any other colonial Puritan contributed was an emphasis upon the mythical. Scholars have traced the evolution of seventeenth-century New England thought as a process of compromise and disintegration, step by stubborn step, under the exigencies of what was becoming the modern world. Only in the realm of the imagination could the idea remain intact. Mather's misfortune became his most formidable asset. It not only stimulated but, in self-protection, *compelled* him to draw upon the metaphorical. Of course he was also temperamentally suited for the task. His first published sermon, *The Call of the Gospel* (1686), is rich in figural expression and fired with the significance of "this Wilderness, that like *Gideon's* fleece, enjoys these Dewes of Heaven when the rest of the world is dry"; his first political *Declaration* (1689), expands the issues at hand—the abuses of authority during the Andros regime—to incorporate the "horrid *Popish Plot*" against Protestantism, and sees in matters like taxation without representation (as certain Americans were to do a century later) a conspiracy instigated "by the great *Scarlet Whore*." He could not repress this sense of drama even in the little almanac he issued in 1683 ("*for the year of the Worlds Creation 5632*") and supplemented with a disquisition on time and eternity.[24]

The authorial stance he created for himself in the next decade brought these tendencies to full flower. "If *this* world will deny me," he wrote, he could "appeal to the *other*" as a prophet-leader bearing the cross of New England's sacred Old Principles. It was in effect an appeal to the legendary past and future, a method (not unlike Whitman's) of establishing his connection with the present by dissolving and then reconstituting it in accordance with his self-concept. That the new generation was sinful he could not but admit: God's "Ax is laid unto the Roots of the Trees"; His "*Knife ha's been cutting and Pruning of us*"; "*Every thing looks Black.*" But it was a narrow literalist view that despaired at such setbacks. As Mather understood these, they opened out into a magnificent overarching plan, one that not only justified *him*, but (in doing so) pronounced the colonists the long-typed-out New Israel. His public addresses transform what his private writings tell us were a "vicious Body of mockers" into a beleaguered but "Precious *People* of God," a "people which may say before the Lord, as they in Isa. 63:19. Lord *We are thine*," the blessed remnant of which "it was said Rev. 18:20. *Rejoice over her, thou Heaven.*" A veritable "cloud of witnesses," Mather claims, attests to his position, including the fact of the colony's supernatural growth into a second Paradise. How, then, can any "true" New Englander not "*Venture his all, for this Afflicted people of God*?" How can he fail to "say as the Martyr once, *Alas That I have but one Life to loose! 'Tis Immanuels Land* that we Venture for."[25]

Politically considered, Mather's grandiloquence is an expression of sheer delusion. Considered as literary strategy, it serves brilliantly to bring his materials under control. First, it inverts the facts of declension into symptoms of a grand design. Second, it conjures up an ideal audience through which Mather can seize the present, after all, for his view of history. For though the younger generation (he admits) in many ways stands inferior to the moral giants who "laid the Foundation of our *Heaven* and our *Earth*," nonetheless, as these children of the saints appear in his pages, they show themselves worthy of their inheritance. The founders' goal depended on continuity from father to son, in the manner of the Hebrew Exodus, and, on a mystic plane, of the scheme of redemption. In celebrating past and future, therefore, Mather is obliged to include his own times; and he does so, as always, through rhetoric and vision. We are now, he argues, in these closing years of the seventeenth century, like our ancestors "a *People* which have proportionately more of God among them than any part of mankind beside." In particular, "the youth in this country are very sharp and early ripe in their capacities, above most in the world," so that it seems likely "our little New England may soon produce them that shall be commanders of the greatest glories." In general,

> He that looks upon these Colonies, will see them filled with precious and Holy Churches. He will see a great Instance of the Protestant Religion, in its purest, and fullest Reformation, maintained, by the Children which are the product and Off-spring of that Choice Grain, which God sifted [from] Three Nations, to bring into this Wilderness;

and he must have his Eyes not open *if he do not make that Exclama-
tion,* How Goodly are thy Tents, O New-England, *and thy Taberna-
cles,* O thou American Israel![26]

In this context, Mather finds solace in God's very displeasure.
We are not the first to suffer thus, he points out. "Endless" punish-
ments were meted out to our forebears, "Awakening and Horrible
Calamities" which anywhere else would have brought a speedy
ruin to the enterprise. Our punishment is so harsh, then and now,
because the Lord, Who loves us *"above the rest of mankind,"* will
not let us fail. He has pledged as much in chastising His elect;
"for us," reversals are an "inspiriting" sign, "a token of divine
affection." In short, the substance of federal condemnation—the
lament itself over promises forsaken—becomes for Mather a vehicle of affirmation. God's "corrective" rod demonstrates the unbro-
ken, unbreakable tie between generations. And hence it presages
a far greater fulfillment. Had not Daniel, for one, foretold that
*"There shall be a Time of Trouble, and at that Time thy People
shall be delivered"*? Granting then that the colony had regressed
from its original luster, supposing even that evil had spread like a
cancer beyond human control—what of it? God has also revealed
to us that His end-time mercy would *gratuitously* redeem his
chosen. "Hee'l [sic] then give Peace to His unsanctified [but justi-
fied] people, and make this Peace to be the means of Sanctifying
them. *Not for your sakes,"* as He had declared in Isaiah and Revelation, *"but for my Holy Names sake!"* The "contrary and Terrible
Appearance of Things" was no more than that—appearance; reality lay in Scripture and in things to come. "So, then, the Blacker
you see the *Troubles* of the Age to grow, the sooner and the surer
may be the *Peace* which we are hoping for." What seems "a dismal
Tragedy" is really a prothalamium, Christ's preparation for the
marriage of heaven and earth. All humanity ought to be concerned
in the event, but we especially: "'Tis the prerogative of *New-
England* above all the countries of the world."[27]

On the strength of that prerogative, Mather salutes the Sun
of Righteousness dawning from behind the clouds of wrath, the
American City of God emerging through the mists of history, and
(in what surely required the most audacious leap of the imagination) Christ's New England host standing, as it were beyond the
pews of hostile faces, *"terrible as an Army with Banners"* at the
very threshold of the millennium. *"O what has God wrought?,"*

Mather exclaimed in 1689 and again in the year following. "My brethren, we shall very quickly see those *glorious things which are spoken of* [the] *City of God*"; "I now speak to some Hundreds, who are like to live unto the Day, when mankind shall no more be Inebriated with the *Cup of Abominations* in the Hand of the old Romish *Whore*"; "I am verily perswaded, A great part of this Assembly may live to see those Blowes given to the *man of Sin.*" In 1696, in his sermon *Things for a Distressed People to Think upon*, his fervor rose to a higher pitch still:

> The *number of years*, for the Church to Ly under its Desolations, is very near to its Accomplishment, and the bigger part of this Assembly, may in the course of Nature, Live to see it: There stand those within these Walls this Day, That shall see, *Glorious Things done for* [the] *City of God*! An *Age of Miracles* is now *Dawning* upon us. My Fathers, and Brethren of this *New-English Israel*, you are concerned [in this] more than any men Living.[28]

Here again Mather's confidence reflects the outlook of early New England, and again with the same crucial difference. In the first decades, the mingling of secular and sacred views of history flowed logically from a profoundly social outlook, one which embraced church and state, individual purity and collective mission; which yoked together (under the uneasy label of "nonseparating congregationalism") the glory of Separatism and the grandeur of national election. Accordingly, what gives dramatic force to the literature of the emigrants is the tension it expresses. We sense that their relentless quest for coherence entails a deep insecurity, not of purpose but of adjusting means to ends within a recalcitrant day-by-day reality. What gives dramatic force to Cotton Mather's work is, on the contrary, the resolution or relaxation of tension. This absence of conflict, I believe, accounts for his much-noted indifference to theory, his focus on synthesis and interpretation as opposed to theology proper. In any event, it explains the facility with which he shifts from one level to another, from prophecy to history, from texts on the saint's wayfaring and warfaring to admonitions about details of behavior. "We have seen a *great* REVOLUTION," he writes in *Eleutheria*, "and we are e're long to see a *greater*"; and then, almost without transition, he connects the latter with daily principles of conduct. He begins *The Duty of Children* by proclaiming that the final triumph of the church is at hand; he continues with a historical parallel (reserved by European Puritans for solely secular purposes) but magnifies it into "a Figure and Shadow" of the imminent fall of Antichrist; and only when this framework has been established does he address himself to his main theme, the necessity of conversion.[29]

The finest sermon-length illustration of these shifts of perspective is *A Midnight Cry* (1692). The subtitle speaks of the *"peculiar things* [occurring] *in THIS TIME for our AWAKENING,"* the dedication then defines the preacher's office as "that of a WATCHMAN," the text (from Rom. 13:11) announces: "now is our SALVATION nearer." Each capitalized word deliberately carries the many-layered implications noted above (temporal and atemporal, personal and communal), as does the title itself, which exhorts both reformation and regeneration through the doomsday parable of the ten virgins (Matt. 25). The sermon brings these disparate areas together by what can only be called the sheer arrogance of its controlling metaphors. It opens by linking justification and sanctification implicitly through the negative metaphor of sleep: the *"Moral Sleep"* of the quiescent reason, the *"Spiritual Sleep"* of the soul (when it lies unresponsive to its principle of grace), and the *"Corporal Sleeping"* which delays good works. On all levels, the sinners are avoiding the same ultimate question. Or more accurately, they have committed themselves, on every level, to the same dread choice. To sleep is finally to die, not to be; and their not-being at *this time* foreshadows a terrifying consummation, reveals them to be hanging by a "Rotten Thread over the Mouth of that heated *Furnace* from whence the smoke of Torment ascends for ever." Mather invokes this Calvinist sight of sin, however, as a watchman's ruse, the more dramatically to prelude the "Ravishments" of *waking*. As he proceeds, his picture of declension fades into an altogether different prospect for New England. The colonists appear, as of old, in the aura of the suffering servant: Samson amidst the Philistines, Daniel in the lion's den, Joseph in prison, Jacob wrestling the angel. Their wakening terrors, Mather assures his auditors, herald their *salvation*. And he invites them in *this time* to rouse their sluggard intellect from the long sleep of linear time.[30]

The vista of glory he opens thus molds history itself to the terms of his midnight watch. It enables Mather to cope with time's complexities and contrarieties by relegating them to the realm of not-being. Having "measured the *Last Hours*," he sounds the great final alarum in the world's "heavy Ears, *Behold, the Bridegroom comes! THE TIME OF THE END*, seems just going to lay its Arrest upon us. May we now *Awake* unto it, KNOWING THE TIME!" To the hypocrite, the unconverted, and the transgressor alike, he reiterates the same eschatological challenge: "In what condition would we desire to be found, if we were sure that within a very little while our Lord should come to take his *Kingdome?*" Well, precisely that condition is "to be *Now* Endeavored; and I say *NOW*, with an emphasis." The cosmic revolution we are engaged in (for already "we are got into the *Dawn* of the Day") suggests the stakes we face, and, specifically, teaches us in *this time* how "to walk in [its] *Light.*" To drive home his point, Mather proposes in conclusion that the congregation join in a renewal of covenant, a "voted" declaration by those under the covenant of grace, that they bind themselves to the laws of the community.[31] This proto-revivalist procedure had begun with the Half-Way Covenant (or earlier), and had become something of an institution after the Indian massacres of 1675, when the clergy began calling on their flocks to rededicate themselves to the Good Old Way. But in *A Midnight Cry* it serves not (as before) to admonish, but to celebrate; joyfully to reassert the relation between the bonds of works and of grace and to advance the marriage of heaven and earth as a paradigmatic course of action for the settlers.

The once thorny question, "What is to be done?"—"*What shall we do?*"—raises no real problem here. "*Labour to be found in such Wayes,*" Mather counsels, "*as the State of PEACE now advancing upon the world, would oblige us unto. Awake,* out of this unbecoming *Sleep*" so that "the *Father of Lights* [may give] you some *Light* of those *Prophecies*" together with "*a large measure of Grace in [y]our Souls.*" Thereafter the road ahead is irresistibly clear. As Christ will then, so we may now drive the Devil from our land. Like the saints then, so now we can "assay to do every Thing in the whole of both our Callings": each man by his continual inward query, "Am I in a Fit *State to appear before the Judgment Seat,*" and the whole of New England by a unanimously positive response to its watchman's demand: "Suppose that before to morrow Morning, the Lord Jesus Christ were to become visible, and make the Sky to rattle, the Mountains to tremble, the Hills and Rocks to melt; could we *Rejoyce?*"[32] In sum, *waking* for the settlers means, individually, living in the present as though they were already in the future, and collectively, restructuring experience in light of the church-state-to-be, prefigured by the Great Migration.

Thus if Mather could not reconcile history with myth, he could sunder them as Christ had sundered the dead world from the life of faith. And if the apodictic turned out to be nothing more than imaginative assertion, that served his purpose well enough. "History," wrote Henry James in *The American Scene*, "is never, in any rich sense, the immediate crudity of what 'happens,' but the much finer complexity of what we read into it." Mather's reading allowed him not only to relegate "what happens" to ephemera, but to recreate New England in his own likeness. Through the dual image of righteous affliction and messianic mission he managed, under the aspect of the imagination, to preserve *his* New England against both the crudity and the complexity of contemporary events. His reading of history allowed him, furthermore, to bind his social role inextricably with his literary calling. Most broadly, it led him to develop a rhetorical form which continued to inspire the watchmen of God's Country long after Puritanism gave way to new and alien modes of thought. It may be found in Thoreau, for example, who substituted for the "list of failures" he recorded in a draft of *Walden* his famous proposal "to wake my neighbors up," or in Walt Whitman, who, sensing that "the Almighty had spread before this nation charts of imperial destinies, dazzling as the sun, culminating time," sensing too "the people's crudeness, vice, caprices," offered his "prophetic vision" (in which speaker and subject merge) as guarantee of the rising glory of America.[33]

Whitman's vision leads back through Barlow's *Columbiad* (1807) to Edwards's *Thoughts on the Revival* (1742). It is explicit in the self-justifying strategies of Mather's *Midnight Cry*, as the sermon graduates from the opening jeremiad toward the peroration: toward Mather's summons to a national greatness which (in Melville's phrase) "was predestinated" at creation, and, simultaneously, to a revival of the soul whereby "the suddenly awakened sleeper" (in the words of Emerson and Margaret Fuller) "is instantly apprised not what part of dead time, but what state of life and growth is now arrived and arriving." "I affirm," Mather concludes, "that all the *Peace* of *New* England," and of each one of her inhabitants, "*lies* in her *going forth* to meet *this Blessed*

Reformation. Awake, Awake, put on thy Strength, O New-English *Zion, and put on thy Beautiful Garments, O* American *Jerusalem.*"[34]

III: The Eschatology of Service: Cotton Mather's Essays to Do Good (1700–28)

It would be inaccurate to read Mather's shifts of perspective as a slackening of Puritan principles. Much less should we read them as a covert capitulation to Arminianism or as a conscious transition from piety to moralism. Undoubtedly, they were so adapted later in the eighteenth century, but we ought not to burden the author with the sins of his readers. He held adamantly to Orthodox Calvinism, the system erected by the master's Swiss, Dutch, and English disciples, which, despite basic modifications, built upon the notions of man's depravity and impotency. A year before his death, Mather denounced the Arminians as vigorously as had his grandfathers. Deism he regarded as a front organization for the atheist conspiracy. With the earlier Puritans, he respected the intellect as a dignified but decisively limited faculty. Like his father, he supported the Half-Way Covenant because he believed it carried forward the theocracy's original design. When he directed the saints' unconverted heirs to will themselves to heaven, he was articulating what he considered, with good reason, to be a theory indigenous to the New England Way. Virtually every major first-generation theoretician (as Increase argued impressively in 1675) had assumed that church-membership tests reliably segregated the sheep from the goats, and that, for the most part, the line of election ran "through the loins of godly parents."[35] Virtually all of them believed that the spiritual seed passed genetically from father to son. By this logic (a consequence or extension of the doctrines of preparation, visible sainthood, and the distinctive New England Puritan view of history), the unconverted but baptized children were saved in all ways but one, their unthawed wills, just as their once repentant but backsliding parents were already redeemed, though in need of corrective affliction, and just as the colonial errand, which by God's time was long since accomplished, demanded their present services.

To that unique community, and not to the world at large, Mather thundered the duty actively to seek after salvation. For them alone he stressed social responsibilities in sermons on *Free-Grace Maintained* (1706) and *The Salvation of the Soul* (1720); only before an American Puritan congregation did he claim that baptism indicates that God "has *Prae-ingaged* these Children for Himself." What elsewhere would be flat self-contradiction, what had in fact been denounced abroad as well-nigh heretical presumption, became a paradox of faith in the pulpit of Boston's North Church: "it is *Grace*, pure *Grace* that helps us; *God is* with *you, while you are* with *Him*"; or again: "there is a COVENANT OF GRACE; And by our *Consent* unto this most gracious *Covenant*, we are to *make choice* of the Great GOD for *Our God*, and [thereby] *make sure* of His being so"; or once again, at the close of a covenant-renewal ceremony: "Let us Request for, and Rely on, the Aids of Grace for a *Self-Reformation*" *and* for "all the [outward] Designs of *Reformation; the Land mourns and fades because we have broken the everlasting Covenant.* Wherefor if we would be recovered," one and all, now and eternally, "'tis the *Covenant* that must Recover us, the *Covenant of Grace*, which is Brought unto us all as have been Admitted unto any [!] *Ecclesiastical Priviledges among us.*"[36]

Mather's approach varies not so much in thought as in expression from that of his forebears: in the confident, easy sweep of his language. Yet here too the variance betokens a qualitative distinction. Transferred to the domain of letters, the struggle for a Holy Commonwealth issues in the foregone triumph of the absolute over the temporal. By means wholly of rhetoric Mather subdued reality in his political sermons and accredited himself as prophet-watchman; by those means elsewhere, especially after 1700, he integrated that role with his functions as pastor. Forced back from the political arena, he absorbed himself in the possibilities for public awakening provided in his vocation. Increasingly he turned to the "watchfulness in particulars" which led Samuel to say that "the Ambition and Character of my Father's life was Serviceableness,"[37] and Ben Franklin to acknowledge Mather as an inspiration for his own way to wealth, benevolence, and moral self-improvement. This tendency also underlies the familiar charge that Mather launched the national success ethos, with its unsavory alliance of grace and cash, and the popular definition of the Puritan as an inveterate meddler, driven by the fear, as Mencken put it, that someone, somewhere, might be enjoying himself. Whatever justification these charges may have in Mencken's

America, they belie the character of Mather's writings. In the first place, insofar as doing good expresses an immemorial Christian attitude (reinforced anew by the Reformation), Mather's preoccupation reveals him as a conservative rather than an innovator. He modelled his views, as he takes pains to point out, upon scores of earlier authorities, and in this sense his sermons on serviceableness stand with his political sermons as an effort to recover the theocratic ideal. "We live in faith in our vocations," said John Cotton, "in that faith, in serving God, serves men, and in serving men, serves God." Secondly, judged from a practical standpoint, Mather's well-doing is genuinely well-meant. When we read of him as "a Man of *Whim* and *Credulity*," dangerously eager "to make Experiments on his Neighbours," we should remember that those phrases originated during the smallpox epidemic with the opponents of immunization. His own words suggest at least a different motivation: "*They have lived longest in the World, who have done the most Good in the World*; whatever contributes unto the *Welfare of Mankind*, and a *Relief* of their *Miseries*, is to *Glorify* God." His pastoral advice follows his precept. In sermon and treatise he urges the practice (not merely the profession) of charity, denounces the slave trade, and extols the benefits of ecumenism. He instructs parents to look to their own ways before mending those of their children, and to discipline, when necessary, by example rather than brute authority. So, too, he would have teachers attend to "not only the *brains*, but also the *souls*" of their pupils, supplementing instruction with tutorials designed to bolster the student with "*expectations and encouragements*." He applies similar strictures to the relations between master and servant, ruler and subject, minister and layman, lawyer and client, physician and patient.[38]

Bonifacius (1710) is Mather's classic formulation of the nature and meaning of these "essays to do good." At some level, predictably, he intended the book as an advertisement for himself. His exhortations about rising to an "*afflatus* that will conquer *temptations*," about being such "a son that the best surname for the glad father would be, *the father of such an one*," about responding with Christ's meekness to "vile INGRATITUDE from Communities as well as *individuals*"—these and many other imperatives (buttressed by quotations from his previous writings) unmistakably mirror his most private aspirations. Most telling of all in this respect is the tree image which grows into the controlling metaphor of the work. According to its preface, "to *plant trees of righteousness* is the hope of the book now before us"; its first section argues that "we begin to bring forth *good fruit* by lamenting our own *unfruitfulness*"; the next section explains how "to live fruitfully" for others; subsequent sections make the obligations specific: ministers must seek "pardon for *unfruitfulness,*" the prosperous must remember that "gathering the fruit relieves the tree," the educated must share their learning like "a *tree that brings forth fruit.*" In every instance, the delegated function becomes the means of replanting oneself, in unity with all men, within "*the garden of God,*" like the Second Adam "abound[ing] in the fruits of *well-doing.*"[39]

The harvest, Mather promises, will yield blessings both in this world and in the next. In light of current criticism, it needs to be reemphasized that the promise does not mark a departure from orthodoxy. It was standard fare in the early colonial churches, intrinsic to the rationale for corporate calling and for preparation for salvation. Like his forebears, Mather circumscribed the discussion by positing first that sanctification is not a means to redemption ("*Woe unto us if it were!*"), and then by limiting it effectually to the visible saints. "Though we are *justified,* yet good works are demanded of us to *justify* our *faith,*" he puns; the agency of free grace compels us (in time) and, simultaneously, disposes us (from eternity) to the outward forms of Christianity. To be sure, the staggering difference between the principle and its local application—and the problematic distinction in the latter context between the virtues and vices of wealth—required delicate exposition to the world at large; his predecessors had tread warily in the realm of theory. Like them, Mather sought to hedge his position with traditional denunciations: "Riches are a Fine, Gay, speckled Bird; but it is a Bird in the *Bush*"; he who "*has nothing but Gold and Silver in his mouth*" is a fish swimming into "*the Nets of Perdition.*" But because he knew that prosperity might follow the labor of the covenanted (in the New Israel above all other lands), he set his sights upon its positive implications; and because he could not resolve the tension between dogma and practice, between a flourishing New England as it should be and as it was, he turned as usual to rhetoric in order to dissolve it. With an easy fluency which has shocked later theologians, he elaborated on the metaphor that the righteous are the trustees of God's world, on the parable of the bread thrown upon the waters, and on the prophecies concerning the blessed remnant. In these terms he measured the distance between the saintly rich and those who rise by fraud, and, affirming the correspondence between God's temporal and spiritual aid, he urged parents never to "*Concern themselves more to get the World than Grace for their Children,*" since "if God giveth them Grace, Earthly blessings shall never fail."[40]

In *Bonifacius* Mather incorporates these various explanations into an imaginatively more heightened and more comprehensive approach, one which absorbs the transitory, at all levels, into the eschatological. As he develops his argument, every good work becomes magnified into a momentous demonstration of "the *judgment to come.*" When he states that "the more *good* any man does, the more he really *lives,*" he means "life" as an emblem of eternity, wherein "the only *wisdom* of man" lies in his union with God. When he terms "GOOD DEVICES the most *reasonable religion,*" he does so to persuade the reader to embrace them "with *rapture,* as enabling him directly to answer the great END of his being." On these foundations he proposes beneficence as a bridge between the visible and the invisible. "To do *good,* is a thing that brings its own *recompense,*" he writes; it stands of itself as "your powerful, and perpetual vindication." It must begin, like conversion, in the soul-struggle to "be perfected in the image of God." Subsequently, of its own accord it leads outward to others; but its essential motive, "the *greatest* and *highest* of its glories," remains first and last atemporal. Thus morality seeks no worldly remuneration (in fact, "your conformity unto Him, yet *lacks one thing*" if you are not "*despised and rejected of men*"); thus also it may be said to win heaven ("the more you consider the *command* in what you do, the more assurance you have" of redemption); and thus, finally, the elect may find material recompense. As the saint in solitude prepares himself for Life by meditating upon death, so conversely the well-doer, by eschewing the glories of the earth, shows himself worthy of the earthly blessings vouchsafed to certain servants of the Lord.[41]

Even on a practical level Mather's notions merit respect. They signify a wholesome if chimerical reaction against the "*Private Spirit*" he had long lamented, an effort to impose some spiritual cohesion upon a community that he believed was disintegrating under the "liberating" ruthlessness of enlightened self-interest. Appropriately, one of the key terms in *Bonifacius* is *relatedness*.

The section on "Home and Neighbourhood," for example, re-minds us that not only family members but *"Neighbours* stand *related* unto one another," and that in both spheres the relation-ship entails duties: "reliev[ing] the afflicted with all agreeable kindnesses," assisting the destitute with gifts or loans (the latter "to be repaid not at a certain day," but when the borrower "should find himself able to repay it, without inconvenience"). Emanating from the center of one's concern for his soul, such circles of relat-edness, as Mather conceived them, would widen progressively to envelop the whole body social. His most ambitious conception centered on "reforming societies." None of his projects has come under sharper attack, and none more unjustly. His intent was neither repression nor prurience but the desire to curb expediency by attaching the mean to an ideal—without, however, discarding the notion of the mean: he asked for temperance, not prohibition, and taught his "sodalities" (the prototypical graduate seminars he inaugurated) "rather *Socratically than Dogmatically,*" aware that "what is now most in vogue may anon be refuted like its Predeces-sors." If he required zeal of his "Societies of Young Men Associ-ated," he sought to temper excess through compassion and discre-tion. What he envisioned at most was a "blessed concord" of visible saints, "bound up in one *bundle of love,*" "charitably watchful over one another" and rejoicing in *"opportunities to do good."*[42]

His scheme had immediate precedents in Augustan England. More important for him, certainly, was the parallel it offered with the bonds of church-covenant which knit together, "as one man with one soul," the citizens on a hill. To the degree that we grant him the validity of the parallel, *Bonifacius* stands, Janus-faced, as a crucial document in the continuity of the culture. Hopelessly nostalgic from one perspective, it looks forward from another not only to Franklin's "Clubs for Mutual Improvement" but to Edwards's "Blessed Unions." Its connection with the Great Awak-ening, indeed, appears to be the more basic of the two. I refer to *Bonifacius*'s consuming eschatological thrust, personal and social, its emphasis alike upon conversion and upon groups animated by "the wondrous force of *united prayers,*" with "the *savor* on them of the saints" of old, seeking to revivify a dead land by doing that only, in Edwards's words, which added to "the glory of God or the good of men."[43] Above all, I refer to the book's pervasive millennial expectations. That Mather never abandoned those expectations is evident everywhere in his published and unpublished works; and if after 1700 he had little or no following at home he found support abroad. Through his enormous European correspondence, to which he increasingly gave his energies, he aligned himself with the millenarians in Scotland. In 1709 he came into contact with August Hermann Francke and German Pietism, whose influence was extending through many regions of Europe, including England and Scotland, and whose missions had reached across the Atlantic to the East Indian Islands.

The impact of Franckean Pietism upon colonial thought is as broad as it is diverse. It may be gleaned in different ways from Samuel Mather's *Vita Franckii* (1733) and from Edwards's tribute in his *History of the Work of Redemption* to Francke's leading role in the events which led to the Revival. Cotton Mather was especially affected by Francke as a kindred spirit whose efforts (unlike his own) met with "amazing" success. To further their "Marvellous Effects" he contributed to Pietist enterprises at Halle and advocated their emulation in America. He had himself urged similar enterprises often before. Now, however, he felt emboldened by a gathering international movement, one that based its social beneficence on the same chiliastic vision as that which informed the Great Migration (though for the Franckeans this meant a *spiritual* migration from local corruption). Like Edwards, Mather carefully insisted on the priority in all this of the New World theocracy; the American church, he pointed out, as the last and most beloved of Christ's brides, deserved the "Honour of making the *First*, Right, Fair, and Genuine *Beginning*."* But

* The argument about the historical priority of New England in the Pietistic scheme for "these latter days" was crucial to Mather because it allowed him at once to embrace German Pietism and to fit it into the framework of New England historiography. Thus he feels obliged even in his flowery epistles to Francke and Boehm to affirm that "There is not a place in which true Christianity is more cultivated than here in New England," and to note that "*American Puritanism* is so much of a Peece with the *Frederican Pietism*" that his *Magnalia* would prove "serviceable to [your] glorious *Intentions*." Indeed, he introduced Francke to the "true *American Pietism*" in 1710 as a system which embodied the "Principles and Practices of [our] Immanuelan People" (adding privately that, "admirable" as they are, the German "Professors are not without their Errours"). And in reprinting Francke's resumé of the Pietist missionary triumphs, he points out that those undertakings followed the lead of the emigrants: of John Eliot in particular ("no One is wronged if it be confessed, that our ELIOT shone as the *Moon among the Lesser Stars*"), and in general of the theocracy's "Pure MAXIMS of the *Everlasting Gospel*," harbinger of the "*Mighty Showers* to be expected in the *Latter Days*." The relations between German Pietism and American thought merit close study,

Mather was eager to express his gratitude and solidarity. He did so most notably by assimilating the Pietists' techniques and terminology: their integration of homiletic "uniting maxims," for instance, with the neo-Joachite "Everlasting Gospel," their emphasis on the "prophecy of Joel" in conjunction with the emergent "Age of the Holy Spirit," and, in general, their shifting sense of the apocalypse, from the premillenarianism of the New England planters toward something approaching the postmillenarianism that characterizes American thought from the Great Awakening onward—toward a view, that is, which sees the millennium *within* history rather than as the result of a cataclysmic, supernatural break with history.[44]

The shift was not a radical one. As I argue in some detail in the next chapter, the postmillenialist view of New England's mission was consonant with the emigrants' gradualistic-typological outlook. In both cases, the church-state served as fulfillment of the Old Testament Jerusalem *and* as forerunner of the Jerusalem-to-be. What German Pietism offered Mather was the potential for a renewed activism within a broad intellectual-spiritual Zeitgeist. It was too late in life, too far into the Yankee apostasy, for Mather to reawaken his political ambitions. (Though he continued to interfere in public affairs, he recognized that he would never command the authority he once dreamed of, and exercised momentarily two decades before, in his father's absence.) But he could transfer the momentum of Pietism's burgeoning success into literary summons and "Goods Devised." "I am dismissed from any expectation of much encouragement," he confessed in 1717 to an English correspondent. "And the truth is, I have dismissed and even divorced myself in a great measure from every party, but one which is now going to be formed."[45] Yet that party of the future, *already* combining as it did the best of the past and the present (the New England Way and the Franckean revival) provided encouragement enough.

Its impact upon his schemes for doing good appears in his revived enthusiasm for local reform, particularly in the ministry and in education.* It is evident, too, in his reanimated call for

not only in their direct manifestations (e.g., Mather and Edwards) but in their later indirect influences—through the writings of Schiller, for example—in the nineteenth century. Quotations are from CM, *Diary*, II, 411, 23, 193; and Benz, "Ecumenical Relations," pp. 179, 185, 187 (quoting Mather).

* *Manuductio ad Ministerium* (1726), his chief contribution in this area, owes much of its pungent forcefulness to that enthusiasm. Fundamentally, like all his

missionary endeavors, to awaken not only the Indians but the Jews. Through the 1690s he had made several gestures, as another "Evangelical Elias," toward bringing about the restitution of Israel. A ten-year silence on the issue followed. When he then returned to it, his new-found fervor, he explained, stemmed from the "Tokens for Good" at Halle, and the "miraculous" conversion of several Jewish children in Berlin.[46] He set forth his convictions in 1718 in *Faith Encouraged*, an expanded version of the Berlin miracle, and, most dramatically, in *Psalterium Americanum*, whose preface and commentary magnify the enterprise of translation into a concerted missionary service, preparatory to the Marriage of the Lamb with His first-and-still-beloved spouse at the altar of the apocalypse.

Of course, Mather stresses that the Psalms also pertain to every *spiritual* Israelite. Insofar as they continuously invoke Christ, they remind every Christian reader "here of the Character of those who are to be admitted [into] the *Messiah*['s] glorious Kingdom." And insofar as they contain the "*Key of David*" to "the *Mysteries* of the *Great Salvation*," they illuminate the contours of Christian history, from the church's persecution under Antichrist to its victory on the fields of Gog and Magog. But beyond such private aids, they may also provoke the reader to a sublime serviceableness, one that concerns the mightiest of the end-time events. Nowhere, Mather exults, is the progress of the Jews more vividly depicted than in the Psalter. Indeed, "the Design of the PROPHETIC SPIRIT in the PSALMS all along has been to describe the Sufferings" and "predict the Recovery of the *Jewish Nation*." What nobler service, therefore, could a second John the Baptist aspire to, what surer means for making way for the City of God, than to render their meaning intelligible? What time could be more suit-

---

books, it is a personal testament, at once the product of his pastoral experience, an apologia for his style, a paean to the persecuted Christ-like servant, and compensation for his failure to attain the Harvard presidency. But the sublimating process is undergirded by the appeal to an immediate historic thrust: specifically to the curriculum in use at Halle; generally, to the "new type of ministerial leadership," admittedly modelled upon Francke's *Manuductio*, which would control "the lives of the people through pietism." The appeal begins with the familiar do-good eschatology (subordinating all studies, actions, and intentions "to An UNION with GOD"); it proceeds through the maxims of Pietism—seconded by a "dear Brother of mine, a Professor in the *Frederician* University"—which raises the well-doing minister into the "State of Paradise." The book's running title is *The Angels Preparing to Sound the Trumpets*.

able than the present, when "the condition of the *Jewish Nation* is like to be"—by that very nation—"more considered than in the former Ages"? What place, finally, could be more advantageous for the task than the New World, since the Psalms specifically hold out "Hopes for *Americans*," predicting (Ps. 18:43) that after "Our Saviour had seen and known *Asians, Africans, Europeans*," He would turn, at the close of history, to the unknown continent at the world's fabled fourth corner? Taking all this into account, "the PSALMS put into the hands of the *Jews* with so Entertaining a *Commentary* thereupon, may be a powerful and perswasive Engine" for guiding them into "the Grand Revolution which concludes our Bible."[47]

To that end Mather gears the whole machinery of translation and commentary, recasting the Psalter into a divine comedy of the wandering House of Israel. Substantiating his figural readings by way of rabbinical opinions (his most frequently used source), he expands the poetry into a prophetic story of decline, fall, and recovery: the destruction of Jerusalem, followed by Babylonian captivity; the Hebrews' stiff-necked disobedience, culminating in their rejection of Christ; and their subsequent persecution, preservation and "happy Restoration." Threading the narrative is the theme of National Conversion. Over one-third of the Psalms (by Mather's account) center on this concept. The focus alternates, that is, between temporal advance and absolute revelation, in what becomes a counterpoint of human action and divine will, promise and fulfillment. The process itself takes several forms. Sometimes it shapes the meaning of an individual set of verses, as in Psalm 69, which is said to relate the sufferings of Christ and the Jews. More often it evolves by juxtaposition, so that the Jews' songs of praise upon their rejuvenation (Psalms 96 and 97) seem to flow logically into the cosmic jubilee at the Second Coming (Psalm 98).[48]

Characteristically, the process unfolds in separable series or blocks of poems, all built around the same theme, though following one another with rising intensity. Thus Psalms 125 through 136 describe successively the grounds of Israel's perseverance, its retrospective lament for sins past, and its thankful devotions to the Lord of its salvation. The next series (137–50) opens by recapitulating the sorrows of the dispersed Jews, then recounts their prayers for help, announces their redemption, and ends in an extended encomium to the New Jerusalem. In every case the movement proceeds from the urgency for conversion; and through the book as a whole the reiterated miracles to be wrought "when *Israel* shall be returned from Exile" broaden to include the well-doer, beneficent societies, and, in the "transcendent efficacy" of the end-time wedding ritual, "the supreme and final true PIETY" whose signs have already appeared:

> DOUBTLESS, *the Day approaches* wherein the *Kingdom of GOD* will appear in brighter displays than the World has ever yet been Enlightened withal. There are certain MAXIMS of PIETY wherein all Good Men are *United.* GOD will bring *His People to receive one another* upon these Generous MAXIMS. An admirable *Peace* and *Joy* will arise from the operations of the *Holy Spirit;* and *Joels* Prophecy will be accomplished. ANGELS shall *Fly thro' Heaven*, having the *Everlasting Gospel.* That cry *Babylon is fallen* will ensue upon it; and wondrous *Changes* upon the World [reflecting in grander form the accomplishments of New England] will turn an horrid and howling *Wilderness* into a *Paradise.*[49]

The strains of *Psalterium Americanum* thus lead back to *Bonifacius*, as do most other aspects of Mather's pietism. Written in the first flush of his contact with Halle, *Bonifacius* unites his earlier concepts of doing good with the possibilities newly opened by the Franckean revival. His proposals here for missionary undertakings extol those of the Pietists—they should "animate us, to imitate them"—and affirm New England's superiority in this respect by a detailed summary of the work "*formerly done* for the Christianizing of our *Indians.*" Now, he promises, our missions will extend much further. The Holy Spirit will clear our path, as it did in the infancy of Christendom, with irresistible influences which will "cause whole *nations* to be *born at once*" and "render this world like a *watered garden.*" A century before, the Bay emigrants had carried those influences to a new continent; the children of that exodus are to amplify the joyful sound to all peoples. As for the Hebrews, Mather would seem here to summon them primarily by the example of the reborn New World garden (as Increase did in 1669, in *The Mystery of Israel's Salvation*, and Edward Johnson in 1654, in *Wonder-Working Providence*). Hence the importance he places on rabbinical commentaries: partly it is to prod the colonists to "outdo *Judaism*"; mainly it is to remind his readers of the way of living which the rabbis foretell for "the *generation wherein the Messiah comes*," the perfect serviceableness which will characterize that "*illustrious state of the Church of God, which is to be expected, in the conversion of the Jews*."[50]

This millennial way of living, Mather tells us, most fully expresses the spirit of his essays to do good. It also serves most lucidly to explain his position as precursor of Franklin and Edwards. The rags-to-riches stories he recounts, in a number of biographies as well as in *Bonifacius*, become "charming examples" of godliness chiefly in terms of his pietistic eschatology. It is a distinction which separates him from the conventional Protestant apologists for laissez-faire; and it is a distinction which applies, in different ways, to the spirit of the Great Awakening, and, later, to the concept of national mission. For well-doing (in Mather's vision), beyond the material benefits it brought, beyond its excellence per se, beyond even its value as a private passport to heaven, carried forward the standard of the Everlasting Gospel. The chosen heirs of the uttermost parts of the earth could hardly consider their redemption merely as single, separate persons; assuredly, too, their "relatedness," under the ascending sun of the Holy Spirit, would never stop short at secular goals. "In engaging as many others as we can, to join with us," *Bonifacius* insists, we are "promoting His Kingdom among the children of men." The "*springs of usefulness*" we dig open by each act, "having once begun to run, will spread into *streams*, which no *human foresight* can comprehend."[51]

"Throw a stone into the stream, and the circles that propagate themselves are the beautiful type of all influence": this is Emerson's vision of the relation between divinity, self, and society. It might serve as motto for Mather's vision of doing good. Each "proposal" realized, he writes, "like a *stone* falling on a *pool*," will cause "one *circle* (and *service*) to produce another, until they extend" ad infinitum. So our magistrates will enact solely those laws by which "the reign of holiness may be advanced"; so our universities, charged with "*collegia pietatis*, like those of our excellent *Franckius*," will accomplish "*wonders in the world*"; so our societies, "discoursing on the Mysteries wherein His *Will* shall *be done on Earth as it is in Heaven*," will by that "blessed symptom be together associated in the *Heavenly City*"; and so we will reconstitute ourselves, what once we were, what God wishes us to be again, a serviceable light to the world, a knot of saints associated whose *"works of the day* fall in with the designs of *Divine Providence."*[52]

In this perspective, as in subsequent American millenarianism, secular employment contrasts as unequivocally with the work of the day as does the house built upon sand with the spreading circles upon the waters of the spirit. The one stands self-contained, trapped in the limits of space and time; the other swells *sui generis* into an image of the entire human-divine order, expanding by a dynamic of its own from the personal sphere to the "federal" and the universal. By that dynamic, too, the work of the day comes (as in Emerson, Thoreau, and Edwards) to image the order of nature. "Serious and shining *Piety,*" Mather writes in *Bonifacius,* "will glorify the *God of Nature.* Nothing so *unnatural* as to be *irreligious."* He notes that the concept derives from Thomas Browne's *Religio Medici* (1643). Its larger context is the "natural theology" which developed in the seventeenth century, the belief that creation, as the New Science revealed it in all its majestic, intricate symmetry, embodied God's goodness and wisdom. Mather was the first American actively to espouse the belief, in league with European religious scientists and scientifically minded clerics: William Derham, for example, author of *Physico-Theology* (1713), and Halle's Philip Spener, and of course Sir Isaac Newton, physicist and chiliast (as he was popularized in Richard Bentley's *Confutation of Atheism* [1693]). In *Bonifacius* Mather projects as part of this tradition his own *Angel of Bethesda,* designed to "instruct people how to improve in agreeable points of piety; and at the same time, inform them of the most experimental, natural, specific *remedies* for diseases." He might already have included his *Wonderful Works of God* (1690), his eloquent *Winter-Meditations* (1693), and perhaps the "Declamations on Natural Philosophy" he delivered as a student at Harvard.[53] His most important undertaking of this kind, begun within a few months of *Bonifacius,* was published a decade later as *The Christian Philosopher: A Collection of the Best Discoveries in Nature, With Religious Improvements.*

In his scientific pursuits, Cotton Mather (again like Thoreau, Edwards, and Franklin) was an avid dilettante, with an encyclopaedic range of interests and a predisposition toward the experimental and the pragmatic. His manuscript "Curiosa Americana," together with his communications to the Royal Society, reveals an amusing credulity. As historians of the subject have recognized, these writings also display a "striking ability to select, from the maze of 'natural philosophy,' those discoveries and problems which were eventually to prove of major importance." *The Christian Philosopher* unites this ability with his still more striking ingenuity in extracting "religious improvements" from the selections, drawing upon the discoveries and problems to erect a monument to the God of his fathers. The discoveries celebrate the reaches of the human mind; the problems teach us not to try to exceed our grasp. They show that our "reason is too feeble, too narrow a thing to comprehend the infinite," and leave us "so transcended" that we will not "cavil, but adore . . . mysteries altogether beyond [human] penetration."[54] The interaction between the two strains, resembling the theocracy's blend of mysticism and rationalism, conveys Mather's purpose. As in *Bonifacius*, he was not so much adapting Puritanism to the Enlightenment as trying to dam up the excesses of the latter by recourse to orthodoxy: in effect, updating the Ptolemaic providential-natural theology that ran from Augustine's *Confessions* through John Cotton's *Briefe Exposition upon Ecclesiastes*. And as in *Bonifacius*, his contributions to the humanitarian-scientific outlook of Franklin forms the lesser aspect of his legacy. In its quality of imagination at least, *The Christian Philosopher* belongs to a different national tradition—meta-scientific and at some level counter-rationalistic—which includes Edwards's *Images or Shadows of Divine Things* and Emerson's *Nature*.

This is not to deny *The Christian Philosopher* its transitional importance in the transformation of the earlier cosmology. Unquestionably, it is a crucial expression in the New World of the configuration of Puritanism, Pietism, and science which has been identified as a mainstream of American thought. Unquestionably, too, Edwards's epistemology, insofar as it derived from either Berkeley or Locke, is as difficult to reconcile with Mather's "spiritualizations" as it is with Emerson's transcendentalism. The similarity between the three writers hinges on the fact that their subordination of science proper to divinity resulted in comparable symbolic modes. In part, the comparison appears in the terms of natural theology: in certain common sources, for example, such as Thomas Browne; or in the effort to restrain the "tide of materialism" stirred up by the New Science; or in the "feeling akin to the poet's" which their passages evoke; or in the anachronistic "inconsistencies" which insinuate themselves into their technical expositions (Edwards's strangely medieval notes, Mather's obstinate belief in special providences). But such parallels may be found in scores of European works. What distinguishes *The Christian Philosopher*, and what seems specifically to relate it to later American works, is the confluence of personal and social eschatology, transferred now to the mind of the awakened observer of Nature. "The whole *World*," writes Mather, "is a temple of God," where "Every thing about me preach[es] unto me" concerning "the grand end of [man's] being," the "evangelical spirit of Charity," and "the blessedness of the future state."[55] This threefold pattern, integrating salvation, serviceableness, and history *with reference to America*, may be seen as part of Mather's legacy to the culture. It serves to define the method of *The Christian Philosopher*.

Mather's fundamental assumption here is a Christian commonplace: the correspondence between the Book of Nature and the Book of God. "We will now for a while read in the *Former* of these *Books*," he explains, "'twill help us in reading in the latter." But of course he means equally that (in Edwards's words) "the Book of Scripture is the interpreter of the Book of Nature," and he organizes his material in accordance with Genesis 1, proceeding from light to the celestial bodies to the elements to the forms of life on earth, and concluding, in the longest section, with man. Hermeneutically, the creation story conveys his meaning on all three levels. Its literalistic aptness allows him to set the progress of science within the biblical framework. On a figural plane, the first seven days shadow forth the seven ages of man, so that the natural wonders he records bespeak the impending Judgment Day and the millennial Sabbatism to follow, when "our Saviour may feast his chosen people with exhibitions of all these creatures, in their various natures." Anagogically, the mystery of Creation, like the mystery of the Scriptures, stands revealed in the Incarnation; all things refer ultimately to Christ. From the magnet to the laws of gravity they constitute a "shadow" of His parturient love. The human cognitive process follows this paradigm in that it recreates the individual in harmony with the cosmos. The principles of plant growth or of light are bare statistics "unto him that has no Faculty to discern *spiritually*." Granted that agency of inner renewal, we find the light to be correlative to our own reason, our capacity (in Christ) to overcome the powers of darkness. Through that agency, we discern in the plants' physical structure "the analogy between their states and ours" and, spiritually, in their revival in the spring an emblem of the resurrection and "of the recovery which the church will one day see from a winter of adversity."[56]

Right perception, then, reconciles us with Creation, with history, and with our Redeemer. And in so doing it unites each of us in ourselves, individually, as paragons of Nature and of the Bible: the human being as "a machine of a most astonishing workmanship," which is also "the most exquisite figure for a holy temple"; a "*Microcosm*" that also represents "the highest link in the golden chain, whereby heaven is joined to earth." "*Opera Creationis externae habent in se Imaginem Creationis internae,*" Mather declares, anticipating Emerson's "every appearance in nature corresponds to some state of mind." Our inner and outer worlds are synonymous: "he [that] speaks to man, speaks to every creature"; the Me and the Not-Me reflect one another through their common generative divinity. But beyond both, for Mather (unlike Emerson), circumscribing and delimiting their linked analogies, stand the Scriptures and ecclesiastical authority. As though he divined the subjectivism potential in his outlook, Mather requires the observer to uncover meaning rather than invent it, to gauge the spiritualizing faculty by an objective hierarchy of values which lies beyond human understanding and yet communicates itself to the individual through concrete, restrictive obligations: the maxims of piety that "the whole creation of God would mind us of," the good works that result from his homage to the sun as "an image of the divine goodness," the services that a man will render when he can feel toward his neighbor the "law of attraction, whereby all the parts of matter embrace one another."[57]

The Christian Philosopher fails in this attempt to bridge science and Pietism. Its inadequacies have been discussed from either scientific or theological standpoints. They seem to me most glaring in the haphazard proliferation of literary modes. Allegory and analogy, sacred and secular similitude, *figura* and trope follow indiscriminately from one another, often within the same context. Some such confusion appears in every Bible culture, but here it tends conspicuously toward chaos. It issues palpably in a dissolution of external controls, in contrast to medieval Catholicism with its boggling excess of imposed categories. The result is a kind of democratic blur of traditionally distinct forms: a universal levelling which (unintentionally) discards the differences between wit, metaphor, and hermeneutic, and invokes moral authority equally through the notion that faith is a telescope to the heavenly world, that ornithology provides a norm of filial devotion, and that typology highlights the botanical curiosa of a well-tended garden. It is this collapse of rhetorical distinctions, I believe, that most clearly marks the cultural significance of the book. For one thing, it offers an interesting perspective on the failure of natural theology and, more broadly still, on the aesthetic revolution implicit in Reformed thought, which set the individual in relation to God, the literal fact in relation to its cosmic significance, without an officially sanctioned intermediary network of meaning, and so opened the road to modern symbolism. In particular, it serves—precisely in its levelling of symbolic dimensions, as reality is ingested and "improved" in the microcosmic imagination—to highlight the beginnings of a movement which has been seen to continue through Edwards's Berkeleyan idealism to mid-nineteenth-century American Romanticism. The continuity here should not obscure the many differences between Mather and later writers. But neither should the differences discourage us from tracing the lines of development, especially perhaps through the affinity Mather draws, in the metaphor of Creation, between Nature, the symbolic observer, and the exemplary American, the book's autobiographical-suprapersonal protagonist who explores himself in exploring the world, and for whom, as for Emerson's Poet, the world-self "is a temple whose walls are covered with [theological] emblems, [aesthetic] pictures and [moral] commandments of the Deity."[58]

It is true that *The Christian Philosopher* does not have a pronounced American setting. It does not, as Thoreau does in "Walking," apply the individual's spiritual rebirth in Nature to the "true tendencies" of the renovated, or renovating, wilderness. Its historiographic implications emerge in context of related undertakings, as those in Emerson's *Nature* may be discerned in "The American Scholar," and as those in Edwards's *Images or Shadows* reveal themselves by way of *Thoughts on the Revival* and *The History of the Work of Redemption*. Probably the relevant texts in this particular connection are the passages (in *Bonifacius* and elsewhere) dealing with American Pietism, and the manuscript "Biblia Americana," which Mather advertised in a concluding appendix to *Bonifacius*, and within which he intended to incorporate *The Christian Philosopher*. As the advertisement describes the organization of "Biblia Americana," the sixth and central section deals with *"Natural Philosophy*, called in to serve *Scriptural Religion*." Here *"the best thoughts of our times"* on science combine with those concerning the three *"grand revolutions*, the *making*, and the *drowning*, and the *burning* of the *world*." Surrounding this section are a history of Jerusalem (until its present and wretched condition, in which it waits *the set time to come on*"), the saga of Israel, concluding with its imminent recovery, a discussion of types and prophecies—all of which (except those pertaining to the chiliad) "have had their most punctual *accomplishment"*—and an exhortation on the advantages of *"experimental piety*." The entire configuration explains Mather's emphasis on "Americana"; his last proud words apply with equal force to *Bonifacius* and *The Christian Philosopher*: "All done By the blessing of CHRIST on the Labors of an *American*."[59]

IV: New England Epic: Cotton Mather's *Magnalia Christi Americana*

From an American perspective *The Christian Philosopher* is a germinal symbolic work. To what degree Mather may be called a literary artist, in this or any of his major writings, is a matter of emphasis and definition. Certainly, he would consider himself an artist (if at all) only in the strictest didactic terms. Yet his lifelong concern with belles-lettres betrays a commitment to the aesthetic that exceeds the usual Puritan clerical confines. His chapter on poetics in *Manuductio*, the first large-scale New World critique of the subject, demonstrates not only a wide knowledge of literature but a salient liberality of taste. Notwithstanding his warnings against the "pagans," he recommends Horace's *Ars Poetica* enthusiastically and quotes everywhere from "the beauties" of Greek and Latin poetry, as well as from contemporaries like Herbert and, the first American to do so, the poet Milton. His own verse rarely rises above the mediocre, but he wrote a great deal of it, from his initial publication (1683) to the hymns he composed to cheer his last days. Indeed, his service to the New England psalmody was a considerable one. In addition to his lost *Songs of the Redeemed*, he adapted hymns from Isaac Watts, wrote a treatise on melodies, commented astutely on the formal defects of the Bay Psalm Book, and, in the preface to his own *Psalterium*, offered a careful exploration of the possibilities of language that pioneered prosodic theory in the colonies.[60]

If these interests do not themselves prove artistic intent, they point to a more persuasive fact: Mather's sophisticated sense of style. His sensitivity to form is manifest in his diverse, adroit use of rhetorical effects in his sermons; critics have yet to do justice to his astonishing range of technique, his ear for good phrasing, his flare for the dramatic, and his sense of rhythm. Most significant in this respect is his choice of the baroque as a vehicle for content and self-expression. While he pays due homage to the plain style, he also praises the "piercing eloquence" of embellished prose: the oratory that captivates with "a *silken line* and a *golden hook*," the writing that dazzles by its "easie fluency bespangled with glittering figures." "Every man will have his own *Style*," he notes, "which will distinguish him as much as his *Gate*," and at its most ambitious, when he wished to reach the widest audience, his prose is distinctively, almost belligerently ornate—the "Massy *Way*" which he compares to a marble monument, a "great musical harmony," or a Byzantine "*Cloth of Gold*" adorned with jewels and "*choice flowers.*"[61]

He did not mean these analogies to suggest a standard for his own work. Overburdened with duties and overzealous to communicate his every thought, he could hardly permit himself to strive for anything like formal perfection. (He regularly apologizes for the haste with which he wrote.) Unduly anxious, furthermore, as an American, to prove himself before his European peers, his allusions, citations, and verbal ingenuities sometimes wax almost grossly ostentatious. And self-consciously alienated from his American contemporaries, he often tends toward hyperbole. Yet insofar as his analogies to art bespeak a concern with the interaction of manner and substance, they imply an important aesthetic rationale for his "massy" style. His grandfathers had advocated simplicity of language to combat the "florid and carnal" Anglicans. But their outlook itself was far from simple, and the discrepancy was made painfully evident after the Restoration, when the plain style came under attack from the proponents of a still starker purity: the Moderns who denigrated book-learning, the Hobbists who scorned elocution, the "*Coffee-House* Blades" who cultivated an urbane, conversational wit, the enthusiasts who spoke directly from the heart, the Deists who demanded a sparse scientific exactness. The Puritan world-outlook stood antithetically opposed to each of these tendencies of the new era. Eschewing uninformed "prophecying," it placed a virtually scholastic primacy upon erudition. In acknowledgment of human imperfection, it encouraged eloquence as a wholesome psychological aid to the reason ("fit bait to catch the will and affections").[62] Its view of providence invested each human and natural phenomenon with symbolic import. Its system of logic required arguments adduced from every branch of intellectual endeavor. Its mode of scriptural interpretations was founded upon the premise of interlinking congruities in sacred, fabulous, and secular history.

When, therefore, Mather took upon himself the mantle of his forebears he chose in the same instant his style, his subject, and his intellectual gait. His display of learning, culled from his prodigious "Quotidiana" (the notebooks in which he recorded memorabilia from his reading), his fondness for puns and anagrams, for esoteric authorities and digressive anecdotes—all his "multiplied references to other and former concerns" are bent toward one end, the affirmation of a cosmology rooted in the concept of the unity of knowledge.[63] They constitute, that is, variations upon a central *rhetorical*—not pedantic, nor even pedagogic—strategy. As logical argument they are arbitrary (even superfluous), as moral instruction excessive, as history unreliable, or hazy, or blatantly provincial. Their value lies in their cumulative imaginative impact. They are meant to convince by indirection and participation: by bringing readers face-to-face with the vast tradition that culminated in the New England theocracy, and, through that encounter, by engaging them in a fluid but coherent universal design. It was a design that incorporated nature, as in *The Christian Philosopher*, and moral eschatology, as in *Bonifacius*. It is most amply embodied in Mather's largest and greatest book, which he labored over from 1693 to 1697 (the pivotal period in his literary development) and published in 1702 under the title of *Magnalia Christi Americana*—"the mighty acts of Christ in America"—or, *The Ecclesiastical History of New England*.

Mather intended the *Magnalia*'s very "massiness" to repudiate the outlook of the age. He expected contempt and he received it. From the start "a *Supercilious* Generation" ridiculed the immense work— packed with narratives, sermons, church decrees, and biographies—as "a mighty chaos," flung together huge and undigested. For Mather it amounted to nothing less than a confirmation of his role. He anticipated the hostility by introducing himself over and again as the isolated artist. At one point he adopts the persona of Orpheus, "whose song might [Christ-like] draw his disciples from perdition"; but mainly he emphasizes the bleakness of his position. Scoffers, he cries, dismay him no more than they did Virgil when he "read his *Bucolicks* reproached and his *Aeneid* travestied." Like the poet Antomachus he continues his declamation though "the assembled auditory all left in the midst of his reading." Like the sculptor Policletus he will persevere in the face of calumny: "let the impotent cavils nibble at the *statues* which we have erected; the statues will out-live [them] all." His "recompense, which will abundantly swallow up all discouragements," lies in the work itself, simultaneously in its manner and substance, as it did for David, who "built a House of God in his psalms."[64]

Mather underscores these comparisons by likening the composition of the book to the process of artistic creation, in music and portraiture, sculpture and theater. Especially he parallels his task with that of the epic poets: du Bartas, Tasso, Blackmore, Homer, and, most extensively, Virgil and Milton. From *Paradise Lost*, where he found his supreme example of the Puritan literary imagination, Mather quotes at length, "taking the colours of Milton to describe our story"; and he alludes throughout to the *Aeneid*, in which he saw the pagan counterpart to his own undertaking. For though he never says so explicitly, and though of course he was also writing in the tradition of ecclesiastical history, the *Magnalia* itself bears out what these numerous references suggest, that its author *intended* to celebrate a great legend in epic form. He conflates theology, history, and "poesy," drawing the lives of Adam and Aeneas into the "typical pattern" of the American church-state, and lifting his story into a heroic world in which, as Hawthorne pointed out, "true events and real personages move before the reader, with the dreamy aspect which they wore in Cotton Mather's singular mind."[65]

The epic form was eminently appropriate to his designs. Its vision grew naturally from that of his jeremiads (several of which he incorporates into the work). The *Magnalia*, says Mather, describing as it does the colonial venture from its pristine origins to the last conflict with Antichrist, is "an history . . . to anticipate the state of the New-Jerusalem." As such it integrates the native rhetoric of the New England political sermon with the universal thrust of Protestant ecclesiastical history, and so attempts—what the *Aeneid* did for Rome—to establish an inviolable corporate identity for America. In more personal terms, the epic form provided Mather with the widest scope for his role as solitary watchman and as the afflicted well-doer. He suspected by 1693, and knew by 1697, that the colony had strayed beyond recall, that "hardly any but my Father, and myself," as he complains in his diaries, "appear in Defence of our invaded *Churches.*" He had also learned from his Salem experience to accept the burden of the legacy. When, sporadically, he turns in the *Magnalia* to the world about him, it is to reject it for the world of his creation. With the "stones they throw at this book," he declares proudly, "I will build my self a monument. Whether New-Engand may *live* [in fact] any where else or no, it must *live* [in letter and spirit] in our History!"[66]

Accordingly, he starts with an elevated invocation of his muse and theme, emphasizing his chosen literary convention by pointed allusions to the *Aeneid.* Assisted by Christ, not Clio, he sings in "all conscience of Truth" rather than in a *furor poesis,* and glorifies not a fabled hero but a covenanted community directed by Divine Providence to the ends of the earth. His church history, that is, parallels but surpasses Virgil's poem—as the founding of New England antitypes the founding of Rome, as the Puritan emigrants resemble but excel the Trojan exiles (not only as pious men but as seafarers and conquerors of hostile heathen tribes), and as the millennium toward which the Reformation is moving will immeasurably outshine the Augustan *Pax Romana.* Within this framework, the opening lines combine every aspect of colonial historiography as it had evolved from John Cotton through Increase Mather: the renunciation of Europe, the brilliant achievements that irradiated the heathen darkness, and the wonders yet in store for the American strand. But where his forebears had at least confronted the dichotomy between anticipation and actuality, Mather transforms both into myth. America, he explains, remained so long under Satan's exclusive dominion so that the Lord might more awesomely reveal His power when, "in the fulness of time," He undertook the renovation of the church, carrying a chosen number of His "faithful servants unto an American desart," in order to establish there a preview of the thousand-year reign of the saints.[67]

The issue of that "Great Migration" was another "*golden Age.*" "There are golden Candlesticks (more than twice seven times seven!) in the midst of this 'outer darkness,'" Mather exults;

"unto the upright children of Abraham [i.e., the elect], here hath arisen *light in darkness.*" The image, which looks back to Eden and forward to the millennium, stands as a comprehensive symbol of his enterprise. He refers to it throughout the narrative, from the theocracy's "small beginnings," when "there were [but] *seven* Churches, all of them golden candlesticks," to its most recent triumphs, which announce "a time of wondrous *light.*" The candlestick as *figura* envelops the church-state, as it were, in a configuration relating the Hebrews, the primitive church, the city on a hill, and the Old–New Jerusalem of the redeemed remnant. And its seven branches, emblem of the *Magnalia's* sevenfold division, outline the seven stages of mankind's development from Creation to the Sabbatism ("within the last few sevens of years nearer to accomplishment"), sound the seven trumpet blasts that bring down the walls of Jericho, stronghold of Satan, and foreshadow the seven end-time trumpets that are to announce the consummation of the New World mission. [68]

Mather's style provides a fitting Cloth of Gold for his epic theme. His pedantry and rhetorical devices (pun and paradox, repetition of key words, the metaphorizing of proper names) function here not only to convey the Puritan outlook, but to adjust historic substance to aesthetic vision. The plethora of learned citations, for example, in Hebrew, Greek, and Latin, present themselves as choice moments of truth, fragmentary revelations of God's will, reordered in accordance with the nature of the Holy Commonwealth. As they are infused into a given action, they tend to draw it out of its immediate context into a realm of universal relevance which (for the author) mingles the best insight and experience of all peoples. Cumulatively, they provide a kind of Matherian anthology of epiphanies, whose purpose is to erode historic lines while establishing a past for the country, rendering New England at once a timeless ideal and the heir of the ages.

The *Magnalia's* New England, then, transcends material boundaries. Its past is shaped by the imagination and its future is anticipated in prophecy. And more intensely than in most of Mather's works, the present is charged with apocalyptic energy. If *Wonders of the Invisible World* is Mather's brief epic, the *Magnalia's* action (which subsumes the witchcraft episode within other, larger events) stands equal but opposite to the action of *Paradise Lost;* it precisely inverts Satan's anti-heroic errand. Mather begins the narrative in the Old World inferno, seen under the aspect of the Exodus motif. As he describes Europe in the first three books, it is an extension of Egypt, Babylon, and pagan Rome. Flying its deprivations, the emigrants, like the Hebrews or early Christians escaping their persecutors, shut behind them the gates of a lost world. The terrors of the Atlantic (another River of Lethe) reveal the emigrants' unprecedented courage and faith, while their deliverances surpass the miracles that carried the Israelites through the Red Sea or Aeneas through the supernatural Mediterranean. Finally, their progress in the New World, reversing as it does Satan's conquest of earth (and so rendering the continent in this sense an ensign for the world), is conveyed through the overriding metaphor of the Garden of God.

Though Mather devotes some space to the Puritans' early hardships, primarily he stresses how quickly they converted the barren strand into a greater Canaan. The triumph of Milton's Satan all at once lays waste the world; the New Englanders complete the first stage of their calling when the wilderness, as in dream or legend, springs suddenly into full bloom. Mather presents the metamorphosis through variations on the image of the plantation as the Tree of God; he amplifies the rich Edenic echoes of the image in his "History of Harvard College" (Book IV). Established by the emigrants and continued by their sons, the college becomes a "fit emblem" of both fructification and fruition. The *Magnalia* personifies the harmony between generations through the lives of ten graduates (the number of perfection), all *"cedars"* of filiopietism, who "had their whole growth in the soyl of New England." So "the *root* gives verdure to the *branches* and the flourishing *branches* again commend the root," in an organic process which proves that the theocracy supersedes the holy communities of the past. "Where God had before planted his church," the harvest had withered and lay desolate upon the hard ground, "overgrown with thorns and nettles." But in New England "the proverb 'that vinegar is the son of wine' and 'that the son of heroes are trespassers' has been contradicted." Here as nowhere else the paternal "vine [that took] deep root and filled the land" has borne abounding filial "clusters of *rich grapes*."[69] Having set before us the founding of the colony (Book I), the magistrates' achievements (Book II), and the superior attainments of the divines (Book III), Mather now displays the lines of continuity in the theocracy—the perpetuation of the New England Paradise—in assurance of the Paradise to come.

He affirms this development most graphically by his biographies. Mather's biographical emphasis places the *Magnalia* in the mainstream of Protestant ecclesiastical history through Foxe's *Book of Martyrs*; it diverges in its special thematic interweaving of hagiography and historiography. Obviously drawing upon the parallel between these genres and his own role as representative conscience of New England, Mather discovered in the motifs of Exodus and Garden a cogent method of integration. Of course, these motifs were in themselves entirely traditional, a staple of the vocabulary of spiritual pilgrimage. Mather's impressive contribution was to make the pilgrimage a persistent reflection of New England at large, and vice versa: to gather both into the same literary ambience, so that one may support and be realized through the other. The epic of the soul in the *Magnalia* lends credence to the social epic, and the social epic substantiates the daily private works by which justification is made manifest. The morphology of conversion (in the biographies) and the flourishing of the church-state (in the narrative) become alternate perspectives on the ongoing work of redemption.

This union of the personal and the communal expresses various tenets of American Puritan thought. I discussed this earlier with regard to the concept of preparation; I would now add to this their concept of migration and settlement. The New England colonists described their collective experience as immigrants—flight from a corrupt old world, sea-crossing, and "wilderness-condition"—in terms of the saint's pilgrimage to God. In effect, they collapsed the traditional Christian distinctions between history and allegory, secular analogy and sacred trope, biography and social narrative. They sought support in this from two sources: first, the inherently ambiguous vocabulary of grace, whereby Christ antitypes the elect both individually and collectively; and second, their own "peculiar" dual allegiance, as schismatics, both to congregationalism and to the concept of national election. Were they not, they argued, as visible saints one man in the body of Christ? And did not sacred history concern the whole story of mankind, thus applying as surely to their terrestrial calling as it did to the soul's journey to God? Nonetheless, so long as they wrestled with the untoward facts of backsliding, they could never quite discard the possibility of error. Beneath the aggressive optimism of their rhetoric, the first- and second-generation ministers convey an unmistakable disquietude. In the course of the century,

however, as expectation and reality veered farther apart, the orthodoxy came more and more to rely on rhetoric; but even the third
generation acknowledged that the parallels between the allegory
of saint's life and the story of their New Canaan might be provisional, perhaps misleading. Cotton Mather followed this pattern.
He makes abundant reference to the dangers of decline and fall.
But he *also* insists on the visionary correspondence between the
saint's life and the progress of New England society. And by and
large, in the *Magnalia*, it is the visionary element that dominates.
In the epic world where *his* New England "lived," Mather felt free
to collapse tradition, invention, dream, and reality into metaphors
that made the errand impervious to history.

He had laid the foundations for this strategy in the diaries and
in such sermons as *A Midnight Cry*, with its shifting personal/
social perspectives. He was to magnify it, interestingly but unsuc-
cessfully, in *The Christian Philosopher*. In its more focussed application in the *Magnalia*, it gave him an important means of control
over his material. Perhaps the most striking of its effects appears
in his reversals of context. Not infrequently, the biographies stress
public issues, whereas the narrative builds on images of the journey of the soul. For example, Mather minimizes the conversion
experience (traditionally a central focus of hagiography) and places
the emphasis instead on the saint's conversion to Puritanism,
his (sometimes her) subsequent persecution, and the decision to
migrate. Conversely, but with similar intent, Mather often represents the theocracy as the archetypal Christian. Thus his descriptions of the Atlantic crossing abound in allusions to baptism
which lend an eschatological dimension to the contrast between
the New World and the Old. Thus too his narrative of the settlers'
privations, probations, and perseverance render them, allegori-
cally, a Pilgrim entering upon the New Life, venturing "into the
wilderness to a sacrifice unto the Lord," finding the world "well
stocked everywhere with the thorns of vexations," and radiating
through all trials the image of Christ.[70]

Mather uses this technique elsewhere, but it is especially
effective in the *Magnalia*. The Christ-figure in *Wonders* transparently reveals the author's attempt to impose *himself* upon the
events. Mather makes the same attempt here, of course, and on a
far more comprehensive scale. But he also objectifies his self-
projection in portraits of "exemplary *Actors*," all attesting to the
author's dynastic rights (either indirectly, as loyal theocrats, or

directly, as his regal Cotton and Mather forebears), most of them in varying degrees reflections of John the Baptist and the suffering servant, and each of them compared, further, to hosts of modern, classical, and scriptural figures. These "biographical parallels," set at the start and end of the Life—generally an emphatically "American" Life—invest the subject with a magnitude and diversity which, as in the diaries, seem to spring from the subject himself, and by implication from his "American-ness." In sum, they reveal him a representative man: representative of the pagan virtues (though superior to them), representative of the godliness of the Old Testament Israelites (but building upon their precedent), and above all representative of a culture that incorporates the past even as it presages the future. On all these levels, each of Mather's subjects comes to embody, and hence to justify, New England's "special appointment." John Mitchel, writes Mather, "was a circle, whereof the circumference took in all New-England"; and again: "I shall now invite my readers to behold the 'wonders' of New England, in one Thomas Hooker"; and once more: "the New-English principles and practices are found in the character of our celebrated [John] Eliot."[71] This approach to biography, which extols the individual not as an exceptional being but as an exceptional community, a circle encompassing the country's wonders, principles, and practices, may be seen to have certain broad cultural affinities to Emerson's notion of representative man and Whitman's personalism. In any case, it allows Mather to redeploy hagiography, martyrology, and ecclesiastical history for his own epic purposes.

In narrower structural terms, it allows him to establish the proper tone of jubilation for the fifth book, "The Acts and Monuments" of New England. Mather organizes the documents thematically rather than chronologically. He opens in 1680 with the "Confession of Faith," the orthodoxy's lament for a wayward people, which he interprets as a general thanksgiving for half a century of "*rest* and *growth*." He then turns to the Cambridge Platform (1648)—by 1690 the defunct Magna Charta of the theocracy—explaining that "the churches have cheerfully embraced it, practised it, and been prospered in it, unto this very day." And upon the basis of this imagined "vigorous unanimity" he proceeds to the church decrees of the second generation. The Half-Way Covenant (1660), which scholars have designated the locus classicus of colonial decline, for Mather bears out the expectations of "*our seers*" and seals the bond between fathers and sons. There then follows (in Mather's account) a festive parade of synods that with undeviating faithfulness to first principles guides the plantation to "an exactest *unity*" in which all controversy is resolved "unto the general joy." The New World garden, displayed hitherto in its physical lushness and godly inhabitants, appears now in its brightest spiritual splendor—the whole of time encompassed within its mythical-green glow—against the background of an ecclesiastical harmony that Mather likens to the music of the spheres.[72]

Mather's theocracy may be said to flower *against* the backdrop of history; but it never quite becomes (what he sometimes calls it) a sanctuary. To the end the natural perils of the New World mar New England's prosperity, and neither its "guard of angels" nor its "wall of fire" can keep it safe from heretics, Indians, and witches. Milton's epic concludes with paradise lost; Christ's mighty acts in America form the road to the New Jerusalem. The theocracy, like the saint, advances by overcoming a series of obstacles that grow progressively more formidable, more cataclysmic. Our topmost glory, Mather reiterates over and again, lies in our direst test, one in which the legions of hell will gather from every corner of the universe for "a furious but a fruitless attempt" upon the children of light. He orders the *Magnalia*'s last sections accordingly. It begins (Book VI) with minor skirmishes—vignettes of suffering and regeneration at sea, on the settlements, in the relations between father and son—so structured as to recapitulate the colony's progress. How far the latter had gone toward ending the Devil's long reign Mather dramatizes in thirteen scenes of witchcraft, unified implicitly by analogy to Christ's exorcizing of the demons (apocalyptically interpreted) and explicitly by typological association with Christ's wilderness temptation. He expands upon this "most particular prefiguration for us" in the battles against the heretics, proceeding with a swelling note of victory from Roger Williams through the more dangerous antinomians to the Quakers, who constitute all "the *vomit* cast out in the by-past ages" now "lick'd up again for a *new digestion*." Their banishment, therefore, together with the expulsion of the witches, shows the "heirs of salvation" literally "treading Satan underfoot."[73] Moreover, it exhibits the unabated doctrinal solidarity, civil power, and clerical wisdom which girds the theocracy for its most arduous and most splendid task, the Indian wars.

For several reasons, these battles provide the right conclusion to Mather's epic. First, they serve to round out his parallel with the *Aeneid* (as he emphasizes by entitling the section "ARMA VIROSQUE CANO"). Secondly, they had not yet reached a decisive end, as had the heresies and witchcraft, and so imply the settlers' continuing ascendancy over the forces of evil. Thirdly, because the Indians, again unlike the heretics and witches, were indigenous to America, their destruction could better symbolize the near completion of the Puritan mission. Most important, the Indian conflicts afforded a fitting finale to the *Magnalia*'s dominant Exodus-Garden motif. As "Wars of the Lord" against primitive tribes, they enforce the resemblance between Christ's American army and the wandering Hebrews. And as prelude to total victory, they reveal the crucial distance between New England's destination and the Good Land won by the earlier, biblical, "erratick church of Israel." Elsewhere Mather had urged, and had himself participated in, the "civilizing and Christianizing of the savages." Here, following the logic of his vision, he identifies them with the Canaanite peoples conquered by Joshua (not only as parallel but as genealogical fact). And he goes further than this: Joshua, he explains, is Jesus; the Indian king is the Old Serpent; and the theocracy is Christ's "*true* Church." In short, the struggle to dispossess America's native inhabitants is the struggle not simply for territory (as in the *Aeneid* or the Old Testament) but for a renovated earth. Having secured its temporal Canaan, the New Israel, as Mather unveils its full meaning in this seventh book of the *Magnalia*, stands at the van of mankind, engaged in a fatal enterprise against all "the *devils* and the *damned*."[74]

In terms of metaphor, the enterprise allows Mather to fuse the temporally distinct (because sequential) concepts of Exodus and Garden into an aesthetic absolute which in his epic *is* New England. In terms of Puritan historiography the enterprise terminates the *magnalia* that God had worked in America even before the *Arbella* arrived, when He decimated the Indians by pestilence to prepare the land for His particular people. In the view of redemptive history, as Mather intimates by citing *Paradise Lost*, it brings to the verge of completion the cosmic combat initiated by the war in Heaven. As it was to be seen in a later, secular American perspective, the enterprise prepared for the rhetoric of manifest destiny that framed the Westward Movement. Mather sketches the outcome for us in phrases that illuminate both the rhetoric and its consequences. He had begun his general introduction with the Ark of God en route to the New World, changing geography into "*Christiano-graphy*"; throughout the narrative he had hinted at the proximity of the millennium. Now, as his epic draws to a close, he sets the church-state directly within the halo of "THINGS TO COME." Quoting from his own and others' sermons, he announces "a REVOLUTION AND A REFORMATION at the very door, which will be more wonderful than any yet seen from the beginning of the world"—and, he adds, my "*fancies* and *juggles* have their foundations laid in *realities*."[75] He means, of course, to refer us to the realities of scripture and the colonial past: to the juggles of Revelation, to the prophetic fancies still to materialize, and to the types which saw a partial realization in the Great Migration. What his achievement reveals is the self-contained coherence of his vision. Built as a monument against history, the *Magnalia* survives as a testament to its author's ability to incorporate New England, the world, and time itself within the symbol-making imagination.

As such, it remains, for all its many flaws, an essential part of American letters. As epic, it differs from the *Aeneid* and *Paradise Lost* in a way which may be said to begin a distinctive national mode, through *Leaves of Grass* into our own time. Latium and Eden come to us from an irrevocable past; Mather's New England, like Whitman's "fervid and tremendous IDEA" of the United States, is a golden age which remains perpetually near, even "at the very door," requiring one last great act in order to realize itself. It is (to quote Whitman again) "a passageway to something, rather than a thing concluded," its hodgepodge of allusions trying to establish an American past commensurate with America's "infinite" (and indefinite) future, its disparate metaphors of Garden and Exodus entwined in the country's perennial quest for fulfillment, and its apparent structural chaos controlled by a dream which looks always beyond the present.[76] As historiography, the *Magnalia*'s definition of the dream (capping a half-century of similar formulations) may be traced in all its basic elements, such as the contrast between old Babylon and New Israel, or the divine scheme behind the continent's "discovery," in the exuberant national eschatology that runs from the Revolution through the Civil War. Finally, Mather's rhetorical strategies, bespeaking as they do a fundamental cultural polarity between prophet and people, presage those of a long line of American Jeremiahs; while in their aesthetic implications, as a symbolic method which fuses objective and subjective, plural and singular, internalizing history as a defense against time, they may be seen to have found their highest creative expression in the American Renaissance.

This is not to say that Cotton Mather's significance consists in his adumbration of later writers. It consists in his resolution of a profoundly cultural dilemma in a way that was dictated by his cultural allegiances and by the dilemma itself. As it turned out, this was also the way Puritanism came most fully to be absorbed in the national consciousness: as image and metaphor, as mythico-historiography, and, paradigmatically, as the dream of an ideal personal-corporate identity which perpetuates itself—in different forms corresponding to the vocabularies of different cultural moments—as an apocalyptic wakefulness destined to overcome the sleep of time, a fusion of Exodus and Garden embodied simultaneously in the ever-new nation and its representative men. In this ironic-prophetic sense, Mather's resolution may stand as the literary summa of the New England Way. When, shortly after his death, his son Samuel (following family tradition) wrote his father's biography, he recalled that "while [Cotton] was yet young, he bid fair to be great, for he *believed* he should be so; he expected it; and therefore he *bore and did many things.*"[77] In this conviction at least, Mather was not altogether deceived. Out of his failure and his faith he wrought a number of works which have prospered, in the realm of the American imagination, better than he expected or believed.

5
The Typology of Mission, from Edwards to Independence

The Puritans invented the sacred history of New England; the eighteenth-century clergy helped establish the concept of America's mission. I spoke of this development earlier in general rhetorical and conceptual terms. In this chapter I elaborate specifically upon what I take to be its central aspect, the problem of civil millennialism.

The problem I refer to centers on the often-noted differences in outlook between the seventeenth- and the eighteenth-century colonists. The Puritan millennialists saw their errand into the wilderness as part of the final stage of history. In doing so, they distorted traditional forms of exegesis, but they were careful to justify themselves by recourse to scripture. They always rooted their interpretations (however strained) in biblical texts, and they appealed to (even as they departed from) a common tradition of Reformed hermeneutics. Their Yankee heirs felt relatively free of such constraints. During the Enlightenment, the meaning of Protestant identity became increasingly vague; typology took on the hazy significance of image and symbol; what passed for the divine plan lost its strict grounding in scripture; providence itself was shaken loose from its religious framework to become part of the belief in human progress. The eighteenth-century clergy took advantage of this movement to shift the focus of figural authority, from Bible history to the American experience. In effect, they substituted a regional for a biblical past, consecrated the American present as a movement from promise to fulfillment, and translated fulfillment, from its meaning within the closed system of sacred history, into a metaphor for limitless secular improvement.

These transformations have been described as a process of secularization. It would be more accurate to speak of a process of adaptation, revision, and extension within a certain secular-sacred outlook. The Puritan clergy had effectually blurred traditional distinctions between the world and the kingdom. Their rhetoric issued in a mode of ambiguity that obviated or eroded the conflict of heavenly and earthly time. "Canaan" was a spiritual state for them, as it was for other Christians; but it was also (in another, but not conflicting sense) *their* country. By "church-state" they meant a separation of powers in the belief that in their American Canaan, as nowhere else, the ecclesiastical and the civic order had been made to correspond. And in the course of time the correspondence yielded the secular basis of multi-denominational religion and the sacral view of economic free enterprise. Both of these developments were rooted in the heterodox tenets established a century before: the moral distinctions between the Old World and the New (as between Egypt and Canaan), the reciprocity of material and spiritual blessings, the concept of a new chosen people whose special calling entailed special trials, and above all a mythic view of history that extended New England's past into an approaching apocalypse, one that required a last great act, one more climactic pouring out of the spirit, in order to realize itself.

Scholars have frequently traced the influence of millennialism in American history back to the Edwardsean revivals, because of what they assumed to be a fundamental shift in New England theology. Technically speaking, the seventeenth-century colonists (like most Protestants of their time) were premillennialists. That is, they believed that the descent of New Jerusalem would be preceded and attended by a series of cataclysmic divine judgments and followed by a universal change in all things. Jonathan Edwards, on the contrary, was a postmillennialist; he posited a final golden age *within* history, and thereby freed humanity, so to speak, to participate in the revolutions of the apocalypse. Students of the Great Awakening have used this distinction to make Edwards out to be a radically innovative historian, the first New World spokesman for an optimistic view of human progress.

The distinction is a questionable one. Historians of religion have long recognized that pre- and postmillennialism may coincide in the same movement, sometimes in the same thinker. In the last chapter I argued that this was the case with Cotton Mather; scholars have attributed a version of postmillennialism to other latter-day theocrats as well (Samuel Sewall, Joseph Morgan). I would go further and connect that outlook to an earlier generation of Puritans who made the doctrine of the chiliad almost canonical in their church-state. Chiliasm is the dream of a second earthly paradise; the belief (drawn principally from the Book of Revelation) that at the end of history, but before the final "dissolution of all things," the saints will reign on earth in a terrestrial New Jerusalem for a thousand years, "hence called *the Millennium.*" What links this doctrine to the Edwardsean idea of secular-divine progress is not just its this-worldly emphasis. It is the combination of that worldliness with New England's distinctive typology of errand. According to the Puritans, the chiliad would be qualitatively different from all preceding historical periods, but it was not therefore unprecedented. On the contrary: it was intrinsic to a design made up of a long series of interlinked quantitative transformations, each of them (like the descent of New Jerusalem) preordained. As William Hubbard put it in an election-day sermon of 1676: "The flourishing beauty of . . . heavenly grace which did so strangely metamorphose the visage of the face of things at first in the world . . . was the verdant lustre . . . that turned [our] rough and barren wilderness . . . into a fruitful Carmel or fragrant Sharon"; and New Jerusalem, in turn, would bring that lustre to a "more brilliant glow."[1]

"Metamorphose" is the precise word. It speaks to the *process* that Hubbard outlines (and that by his time was a staple of New England pulpit rhetoric)—the spiral of fulfillment, from Eden to Canaan to New Canaan in America to New Eden. It implies (what Mather makes explicit in *Theopolis Americana,* for example, and Sewall in *Phaenomena Quaedam Apocalyptica*) an ambiguously pre/post *American* millennialism. For although all of these Puritans believed that the end-time would involve a drastic overturning, that too was for them a "metamorphosis": a change *in* this world, and most dramatically in their New World. Their errand led not from earth to heaven (as did the pilgrimage of the first Plymouth settlers), but from lesser to greater glories on the American strand. As they conceived it, New Jerusalem would come to complete their venture, not to abolish it. The apocalyptic wonders were for them part of the serial latter-day *magnalia Christi Americana.* And the millennium itself, by extension, was part of the country's history, a sort of final blossoming of their wilderness. They spoke of it, accordingly, as both their motive and their goal. New Jerusalem was of course all too distant from the New England church-state. But in the eye of prophecy, it was already present for them, as the harvest is implicit in the planting, the glorified in the justified saint, and the antitype in the *figura*. "Though there be in special one grand accomplishment of Scripture Prophecies," said William Adams on a fast-day in 1678, "yet there hath been a glorious accomplishment of it already," albeit a "partile accomplishment . . . wherein those . . . promises are fulfilled in their measure and degree." That was the message, too, of James Allen and Increase Mather, among many others: in transforming the American wilderness, God was providing through their church-state "a type and emblem of New Jerusalem," "A *First Fruits* of that which shall in due time be accomplished in the world throughout." As the theocracy foreshadowed New Jerusalem, so New Jerusalem would be the Good Old Way metamorphosed, enlarged, and perfected—written large in letters "of *Pure Gold*."[2]

We might well term this faith the Puritan version of what has come to be called civil millennialism, and appropriately enough Edwards claimed direct descent in this matter from his New England forebears. In 1744, complaining about the "slanderous" charges of Charles Chauncy, the leading spokesman for the Old Light orthodoxy, Edwards denied that he had "often said [as Chauncy said he had] that the millennium was already begun." The revivals, Edwards insisted, were no more than "forerunners of those glorious times." Even at the peak of his enthusiasm, during the harvests of 1739–41, he had stated (following "the First Fathers of New England") "that there would be . . . many changes, revivings and intermissions, and returns of dark clouds and threatening appearances, before . . . Christ's kingdom shall be everywhere established." Was that not, Edwards demanded (with good reason), just what Thomas Shepard had said in *The Parable of the Ten Virgins* (1636)—along with "all the fathers" (John Davenport, John Cotton, Richard Mather, and others)—concerning the prospects in store for New England?[3]

No doubt such assertions of filiopietism were a source of Edwards's appeal. The New Lights revolted not (as some have said) against paternal authority, but against a generation they thought had betrayed the founding fathers. No doubt, too, Edwards exaggerated his bonds with the past, much as the latter-day Puritans had exaggerated theirs with the theocracy, and as nineteenth-century evangelicals were to exaggerate their loyalty to Edwards. That sense of continuity, however, was itself part of the myth; the very discrepancy between assertion and fact attests to the persistence of Puritan rhetoric.

This does not quite explain the discrepancy away, and I will return to it later. First, let me trace the development suggested by Edwards's assertion of continuity. In contrast to European chiliasts, the Puritans and Edwardseans alike concerned themselves far less with the final event than with the unfolding of the design. For both groups "the time" was always at hand, but somehow that was of secondary interest. The real issue was the *figural* meaning of the present, which is to say the union now, at this nick of time, of history and prophecy. What distinguishes Edwards's approach is the greater consistency of its logic. The Puritans' concept of errand, for all its internal coherence, is marred (from the standpoint of historic process) by its official premillennialism. Their sense of continual progress, leading upward from Eden to New Canaan, is undermined and to an extent contradicted by its reliance on an entirely extraterrestrial agency—some superhuman "shattering of the order of nature." Edwards, by changing the scenario for this last act of the errand, welded the whole progression into an organic human-divine whole. That was his contribution. In cultural terms, it had enormous import for the course of American millennialism. But as a view of history, it simply drew out the implications of the outlook developed a century before. "Though there has been a glorious fulfillment of . . . prophecies already," Edwards wrote in 1740, describing the chiliad in phrases that make the legacy unmistakable, "other times are only forerunners and preparatories to this," as the exodus of Israel from Babylon "typified" the Reformation and the Great Migration. And what the Great Migration meant *now* seemed to him gloriously visible. Christ, he announced, will have "the heathen for his inheritance," a "nation shall be born in a day," and Protestant America, climactically, will become another, greater Mountain of Holiness, "Beautiful as *Tirzah*, comely as *Jerusalem*, and terrible as an Army with Banners"—"*Put on thy beautiful garments,* O America, *the holy city!*"[4]

Edwards's conviction that sacred history was reaching its apex in the New World makes his case against Chauncy—his declaration of "faithfulness to the Puritan fathers" (in regard to millennialism)—undeniable. Without forgetting his very considerable borrowings from European thinkers it seems safe to say that, during the Great Awakening at least, Edwards adopted wholesale the Puritan vision of the New World. For him as for his forebears, the discovery of America was not just an event in secular history, the opening of new territories to European Christians. Edwards, too, discovered America hermeneutically, in scripture, specifically in the apocalyptic text of Isa. 66:19. And like his forebears from Samuel Danforth through Cotton Mather, he proceeded to celebrate the golden age of the first planters as the millennial dawn. Given these premises, his view of the Awakening was a foregone conclusion. English millennialists such as Moses Lowman helped him decide on particular apocalyptic dates; German Pietists such as August Hermann Francke and English evangelists such as George Whitefield heightened his sense of expectancy. But in the main Edwards's concept of the Northampton Millennium— including not only his account of things past and present, but also his forecasts of things to come (vast increases in population, ecumenism in faith, great piety, true liberty, general prosperity, and an expansion of scientific, moral, and religious knowledge)— derived from Puritan New England.

Especially revealing is Edwards's emphasis on trial. The familiar contrast between the Puritans' "cosmic despair" and the revivalists' "high cosmic optimism" simplifies the attitudes of both groups. As the earlier group had found a way out of despair, so conversely the eighteenth-century Calvinists found ample opportunity to remind their audiences of the dangers before them— the cataclysms, the "most violent struggle," and the "mighty opposition" which would precede the overthrow of Satan's kingdom. In these latter days, they explained, darkness and affliction were always to be expected. Like the Puritan Jeremiahs, the Edwardseans fused threat and promise in making probation their overriding metaphor for the times. If it seemed that God was about to forsake this land, and to bring awful judgments upon it, then there was cause to rejoice. It was precisely through such a time of testing that Christ's American saints could (as it were) assert their right to make New England a "heaven upon earth." There are numerous parallels for such statements in seventeenth-century sermons— most strikingly, perhaps, in the federal covenant-renewal ceremonies established during King Philip's War (1675–76). In both the federal covenant-renewals and the revivalist concerts of prayer, the clergy linked personal salvation and the progress of the work of redemption with a special American enterprise. And in both cases the ritual was based on the Israelites' covenant-renewals under Joshua and Nehemiah. Then, God had led His people from captivity to Canaan; now God was calling upon His people in New England to complete the liberation of the church. According to

Cotton Mather, that call had first been answered by the Great Migration, with the Puritan "Ark of Christ" "*victoriously* sailing round the *globe*." Exactly a century later, in 1792 (during the tricentennial of Columbus's voyage), commenting on the Revolutionary "period of trial" then underway in the United States, David Austin confirmed the promise in his "Advertisement" to Edwards's *History of the Work of Redemption*:

> Though to the eye of unbelief, the Ark may seem, now, to be involved in tempestuous weather, and soon to be foundered through the probable failure of borrowed strength; yet, to the joy of the passengers there are those, who, looking through the mists of human or internal jars, do hail the approach of MILLENNIAL DAY! On the Ocean of the Millennium [our] . . . Ark shall safely and uninterruptedly sail.[5]

Austin was speaking directly to the fate of revivalism in the eighteenth century. His scorn for the sceptic's "unbelief" reminds us that ever since 1742 a growing number of Enlightenment liberals had been heaping contempt upon "enthusiasts" like himself. But the liberals failed to persuade. Austin's optimism, his sense of the apocalyptic "joy" aboard the American ship of state, recalls the continuing vitality of Edwardsean revivalism. And revivalism remained vital to the culture, I would suggest, because Edwards neither broke with the Puritans nor aligned himself with them, but molded their federal myth to fit the needs of his own times. From the perspective I have been advancing, his contribution was to make revivalism a force toward independence by making it part of the evolving typology of America's mission.

This is of course a partial perspective on Edwards's achievement. It reveals the provincialism of his nurture, the capacity of a brilliant philosophic mind to be carried by cultural afflatus into an astonishing arrogance, on behalf of his region, his creed, and his society. But his rationale for American civil millennialism is no less important for those limitations. The arrogance it expressed was not his own, after all, but that of his culture. It reflected the beliefs through which provincialism became nationalism, and nationalism, in this case, a form of universalism.

Edwards's postmillennial outlook drew out the proto-cultural tendencies of the New England Way. He inherited the concept of a new chosen people, and he enlarged its constituency from saintly

New England theocrats to newborn American saints. In fact if not in theory, theocracy had meant tribalism, the literal and direct continuity from elect father to (presumably) elect son. Revivalist conversion opened the ranks of the American army of Christ to every white Protestant believer. Whereas the Puritan rituals of federal covenant called the children of New England to their filial obligations, the Edwardsean concerts of prayer sought to awaken all prospective American saints, North and South, to the state of their souls, the shortcomings of their society, and the destiny of their New World Canaan.

In effect, Edwards expanded the Puritans' sectarian genetics of salvation into a genealogy of the latter-day American church. The second- and third-generation clergy had extolled the immigrants as founding fathers, but they limited the legend perforce to the story of New England. Edwards freed the errand from the confines of regional theocracy. He rendered the legend of the founding fathers the common property of all New World evangelicals, and thus opened the prospect for expanding the Puritan past into a *figura* of the American Way. This accounts for the impression that many scholars have had of the relatively high optimism in the revivalist sermons. The Puritans also described their mission in terms of "Christ's mighty deeds in America." But they were committed to a regionally defined, doctrinally exclusive way of life; and for all their self-assurance they never quite managed to reconcile the restrictive and expansive tendencies of their thought. Edwards may be said to have resolved the problem. His view of history, like his evangelicalism, was couched in terms of continuous and indefinite enlargement. He could afford to adopt a post-millennial view because he required no supernatural event to bridge the gap between an "enclosed garden" and the country at large, or between an outmoded past and a world-redemptive future. The New England Way was for him above all a shadow or type of the "union of love" that would knit together, as one city on a hill, all of Protestant America.

For if Edwards abandoned the Puritan belief in theocracy, he nonetheless retained the Puritan vision of personal/communal exceptionalism. He differed from English revivalists, we know, including Whitefield, by his emphasis on corporate mission. Edwards attacked the Separates for their spiritual pride, and the colonial Establishment for its lax method of church admission. The "middle way" he espoused was, like John Cotton's, an ambiguous union of extremes: it aspired simultaneously to absolute purity and to a full involvement in this world. In America, Edwards insisted, "the holy community must serve as a type of New Jerusalem" and hence as an earthly "instrument for bringing it into being." The Separates argued (as Roger Williams had against Cotton) that typologically there was a "plain Difference between the World and the Church." Edwards replied (as Cotton had to Williams) that the story of America was intrinsic to sacred history. The aim of the American church, as "a type of New Jerusalem," was not merely "the salvation of individuals, but of society," since the society, *in this case*, was by definition engaged in "the forwarding of the Work of Redemption."[6]

I invoke the parallel now to stress the *change* from 1640 to 1740. We have often been told that Edwards's position in the culture was a transitional one. Undoubtedly it was, if we add that the transition marked not so much the end of an old order as the unfolding of a new stage of growth in colonial society. According to Perry Miller, Edwards was a modernist in spite of himself—the first American to recast Puritanism into "the idiom of empirical psychology"—and thus a central figure in the movement toward the values of liberal free enterprise. There is a good deal of evidence for this view; but even more to support the case for Edwards the traditionalist—the orthodox Calvinist who sought passionately to curb the threat of modernism by all means at his disposal, including the ideal of Christic selfhood. In direct opposition to Locke, he maintained that true individuation was not a self-interested, empirical process but a public and spiritual commitment. Regeneration for him depended on conformity through grace to "a principle of oneness that is manifested . . . as identical multiple units of generic counsciousness."[7]

What brings together these two sides of Edwards's thought, at least during the period of the Awakening, was his effort to link regeneration to the destiny of the New World. American Protestants, in his view, had a special role to play in God's plans. For them above other peoples, conversion, rebirth, and "generic counsciousness" were manifested typologically, through the correspondence (which Edwards's never tired of explaining) between personal fulfillment and social harmony. The result, however unintended, was that he went further than his predecessors in adjusting the Puritan vision to the norms of his age. Historians of American religion have observed that Edwards's "ethics were prudent and flexible applications of the early Puritan tradition to the settled life of mid-eighteenth-century Massachusetts," that his chief followers "tended to espouse a . . . radically egalitarian, libertarian, and fraternal view of . . . social and political life," and that his theology proved flexible enough for them to "empower the theory of a nation."[8] Edwards should not be burdened with all the sins of his disciples, of course; but in this case we cannot entirely dissociate his thought from theirs. By implication, it seems clear, his long labor to wed Calvin and Locke issued in the union of eschatology and self-interest under the canopy of American progress.

So understood, Edwards's postmillennialism was indeed a major advance upon the Puritan vision. By opening the future to human control, he adapted the belief in process to the needs of an enterprise that had grown beyond the limits of a particular region or religious sect. The Bay theocrats had joined secular to sacred history, and posited a continual increase of material/spiritual blessings. Edwards made the spiral of redemption synonymous with the advance of mankind. In doing so, we are told, he "provided an exit from the harsh confines of Calvinism [that he himself] expounded and paved the way for . . . new Arminian theologies of belief in the free will and moral strivings." The historical ironies this involved may be more strongly stated. Edwards sanctified a worldliness he would have despised and lent support to an ideology that openly and proudly linked American striving with scripture prophecy, economic reform with the work of the spirit, and libertarian ideals with the approach of New Jerusalem. Thus his use of commercial imagery and his secular homiletics ("persons ought not to neglect the business of their personal callings") became a mainstay of Yankee pietism. Thus his figural view of economics (the increase in colonial trade "is a type and forerunner" of the time when the whole world "shall be supplied with spiritual treasures from America") reappears in countless promotional tracts. And thus the Awakening he inspired, according to social historians, encouraged "worldly ambition and resistance to [conservative forms of] social authority"—a middle-class upsurge that resulted in territorial expansion, "increased economic opportunities," a "multitude of new traders who called for currency issues," and a rising demand for democratic self-government, all of this sustained and augmented by the sense that it reflected some grand providential design*—in Edwards's words, "the rising of a New Heaven and a New Earth in the New World."[9]

Edwardsean revivalism was only one factor in this development. My argument is not that it caused the Revolution but that it helped provide a framework within which the Puritan outlook could be harnessed to the conditions of a new age. Its impact appears, for example, in the revision of the concepts of Adamic naturalism and *translatio imperii*, "the Westward course of empire." Traditionally, the return to nature meant a static condition (whether pastoral or utopian); whereas the "Westward course of empire" implied a cyclical view of history, the recurrent rise and fall of civilizations. In Enlightenment America, these conflicting views were absorbed into a wholly progressive outlook, and transformed into alternative modes of cultural affirmation. When colonial writers sang of a New World paradise, they were not thinking of Adam's garden. They envisioned the new end-time Eden, where a gathering of new Adams would complete God's grand design. Far from being nostalgic or primitivistic, their paradise was to be the result of a series of reformations in history, and therefore a fulfillment of social as well as spiritual norms. And if by other standards "Eden," "paradise," and "God's design," as they repeatedly used these terms, were merely metaphors for secular achievements, for Americans they also served as reminders that *here* the secular was infused with teleological significance.

*Let me repeat that, here as elsewhere, the effect was something very different from the intent. Undoubtedly, Edwards differed in many ways from Revolutionary Calvinists such as Abraham Keteltas, who "welcomed to the cause of God anyone who would take up the sword against the anti-christ of British tyranny." The revivalists were addressing "bands of pious saints" in the hope of "promoting the kingdom," whereas the radical Whigs were mobilizing citizens for political ends. (Nathan O. Hatch, "The Origins of Civil Millennialism in America: New England Clergymen, War with France, and the Revolution," *William and Mary Quarterly*, XXXI [1974], 409). Nonetheless, a common pattern may be discerned. The striking cultural fact is that civic oppression took the form of Antichrist, while at the same time the crusade to "drive back the forces of darkness" assumed such specifically *American* implications that ministers like Keteltas could see "American society as the model upon which the millennial kingdom would be based," and vaunt republicanism as "the cause of . . . heaven against hell" (Keteltas, *God Arising and Pleading His People's Cause* [Newburyport, Mass., 1777], p. 30).

The same teleology was imposed upon the classical concept of *translatio imperii*. Edwards (following the Puritans) had recast this into a variation of Daniel's apocalyptic scheme of the Four Empires, and by and large it was the Puritan–Edwardsean version that the eighteenth-century colonists adopted, transferring their proof-text as they did so from scripture to the story of America. The Westward star of empire meant much more to them than the movement of civilization from East to West. It signalled the complete fulfillment of the prophecies. It was the morning star heralding the triumphant sun/Son that (in Edwards's words) would "rise in the west, contrary to the course of [the] world." And this holds true for everything that *empire, West,* and *fulfillment* evoked in eighteenth-century America. Libertarianism was not just a better way of life, but "the long-promised glory"; the prospects of free trade and open competition called to mind the "beauties of IMMANUEL'S LAND"; Westward expansion promised the endless bounty of "the kingdom of the latter days." It was not just a matter of attaining innocence, more land and wealth, the refinements of high culture. These were tangible proof of something greater. Elsewhere, such advances might make (temporarily) for a good society. In the New World, as a mid-century English traveller marvelled, the "course of empire" entailed a new "idea, strange as it was visionary," that at some approaching "destined moment . . . America is to give law to the rest of the world."[10] Not only the Edwardseans were responsible for that strange, visionary idea. But they did sanction the union it entailed of sacred history, local progress, and spiritual self-fulfillment, and so helped establish the terms in which Yankee Americans could usurp the types of scripture for explicitly national ends.

In the long view, the Great Awakening succeeded in making the evangelical mode central to the culture. In an immediate sense, its concept of mission fed into the rhetoric of the French and Indian War. The result was a triumph equally for English foreign policy and for American millennialism. Extending the old techniques to accommodate commercial and territorial aspirations—clothing imperialism as holy war—the mid-eighteenth-century clergy summoned the colonists to an Anglo–Protestant errand into the Catholic wilderness. The French were "the offspring of that *Scarlet Whore*"; French Canada "the North American Babylon"; and the invasion itself a "grand decisive conflict between the Lamb and beast," preview of Armageddon. From the siege of Louisbourg (1745) to the Peace of Paris (1763), all of New England, as religious historians have shown, was gripped in "millennial optimism." Liberals and revivalists from Massachusetts to Virginia, including Edwards's old antagonist Charles Chauncy, joined in chorus. The downfall of French Canada, they predicted, would bring a "most signal revolution in the civil and religious state of things in this world"; victory meant nothing less than "the accomplishment of the scripture-prophecies relative to the Millennial State."[11]

Significantly, Edwards himself adopted essentially the same view of the war. From his wilderness exile at Stockbridge he exulted in every hopeful scrap of news. His "Account of Events Probably Fulfilling the Sixth Vial"—fulfilling, that is, the last of the prophecies before those concerning the advent of New Jerusalem—includes reports culled from a host of local newspapers in Boston and New York. No item was too petty, too flagrantly secular or self-seeking, to contribute to his calculations. The capture of French ships, statistics of New England's "trade and acquisitions," signs of commercial, military, and moral decline in France, political "distress" in French Canada, the (piratical) seizure of French stores of gold, provisions, merchandise, and armaments—every fact that touched upon the war was pregnant for him with prophetic meaning, as much an image or shadow of things to come as was any fact of scripture. "The late wonderful works of God in America," Edwards wrote after the battle of Cape Breton, were hastening the completion of the divine plan. They bespoke "an extraordinary spirit of prayer given the people of God in New England, with respect to this undertaking, more than any public affair within my remembrance." Clearly, "the Most High has made his hand manifest, in a most apparent and marvelous manner . . . it being perhaps a dispensation of providence, the most remarkable in its kind, that has been in many ages . . . and a great argument . . . that we live in an age, wherein divine wonders are to be expected."[12]

Edwards's enthusiasm about the French and Indian War is a striking testament to the continuities between revivalist and civil millennialism. But the war contributed in its own right toward broadening the scope of the rhetoric. The revivalists had enlarged the errand to include the visible saints not only of Massachusetts but of all the English colonies. The established clergy from 1745 to 1763 went further still. In mobilizing the "patriotic inhabitants of Protestant America," they associated "our Sion" with "our Colonies" in a wholly secular sense. The basis of their plea was not only religion but specifically the civic traditions of Anglo–America—not only Protestantism, that is, but English libertarianism. To some extent, this issued in a heightened sense of loyalty to "the mother country." Britain was the source of colonial liberties, and the writings of this decade continually celebrate that legacy. But they also speak over and again of *America* and *Americans*, and increasingly they extol "the founding fathers, who left England" in order to enjoy "the blessings of freedom" in a "New Canaan of *Liberty*."[13]

A Canaan of Liberty! The phrase offers a convenient index to the growth of the myth. The Puritans had justified the errand by reference to the Israelite exodus. Eighteenth-century Americans justified both the Israelites and the Puritans by reference to their own progress. And having done so, they invoked the example of the Bay emigrants in order to inspire their countrymen to still greater deeds. "Liberty was the noble errand of our fathers across the Atlantic"; they "set the seas and skies, Monsters and savages, Tyrants and Devils at Defyance, for the sake of liberty." So adapted and revised, the legend of the Puritan founders belonged unequivocally to all white Protestant colonists. As "the children of *Israel* [were] led out of *Egypt*," thundered Theodorus Frelinghuysen of New York in 1754, "So [were] our Ancestors brought over from Europe to this land." And as "God Almighty [gave] them the Land of the Heathen," so now He intends to give French Canada to the forces of Protestant America.[14]

The message was repeated steadily through the war years, and it was accompanied, as of old, by the figural rhetoric of probation. During the last, critical stage of the conflict, the ministers tended to mute their threats. But no sooner was peace declared than they resumed the lament in full force. The battles just past, they warned, did not resolve the issue. Far from it: the real crisis had only begun. Like the revivalists, they saw evidence wherever they looked of degeneracy, and the thunder of their moral complaint continued into the Revolutionary era. Popery, corruption, delicacies and luxuries abounding, rampant lust, gaming, idleness, and intemperance—all the "enormities" enumerated by the Synod of 1679 and the sermons of 1740 returned in the orations of the 1760s and 1770s. The cause was independence now, not British–American Protestantism; the social ideal a republic, not an Enlightened monarchy. And of course the enemy assumed another, subtler, and more perfidious form. The English King, rather than the French, was now the instrument of the Scarlet Whore; England rather than French Canada was the modern Babylon; the danger within came from European fashions and royal agents rather than from Indians, Jesuits, or heretics.

And yet the rhetoric, while dramatically enlarged in its applications, has essentially the same structure. Never did the voice of Jeremiah sound more loudly in the land than in the springtime of the republic. It may be the "Will of Heaven," wrote John Adams on the eve of independence, that "Americans shall suffer Calamities still more wasting and Distresses yet more dreadful. . . . The Furnace of Affliction produces Refinement, in States as well as Individuals." That was July 3, 1776. Not long before, he had heard a minister predicting that God would "come with a vengeance" upon the land—and "the whole prophecy," Adams told his wife, "filled and swelled the bosom of every hearer." He knew that in saying this he was not instructing but confirming Abigail in her faith. She herself had comforted him often enough about the ambiguities of God's wrath with His chosen. Both of them realized that, by "the intention of Heaven," it was *through* "all the gloom," by *means of* "blood and treason," that the nation's "deliverance [would] be wrought out . . . as it was for the children of Israel." Declension, doubt, political and economic reversal—as they detailed the afflictions of God's Country it all amounted once again to the "day of Israel's trials." Both of them could endorse the promise, emblazoned in rough print on a Vermont Thanksgiving broadside, that "God would yet make us glad, according to the Days wherein we have been afflicted, and the Time in which we have seen Evil."[15]

The Vermont broadside is characteristic of a host of civic as well as clerical writings—treatises, orations, pamphlets—which, having detailed every local iniquity, sound an urgent summons for covenant-renewal and concert of prayer. And as Gordon Wood has observed, it was a summons that generated millennial frenzy out of the very process of self-doubt. Increasingly during the 1760s and early 1770s, patriot leaders drew on the image of a "chosen band, removed from the depravations . . . of Europe," going forth to receive "the heathen . . . for an inheritance and these uttermost parts of the earth [for] a possession." Increasingly, they invoked what they construed to be the libertarian legacy of the Puritan founders. And increasingly, they spoke of the emerging conflict for independence in apocalyptic terms. When in 1774 Thomas Jefferson revived the fast-day ritual, he noted with some surprise that "the effect of the day thro' the whole colony was like the shock of electricity, arousing every man & placing him erect." He learned the lesson well enough to return to those rhetorical devices on other important public occasions, from his exhortations during the Revolutionary era to his Second Inaugural Address. Tom Paine must have learned the same lesson, to judge by his otherwise startling recourse to that language in *Common Sense.* I refer to his use of biblical precedents, to his emphasis on providence, and above all to the figural blueprint he presents for American exceptionalism, with due emphasis on the landmarks of early New England Christianography: a fallen Old World (harboring a Romish Antichrist), an Egyptian England (in bondage to a "hardened, sullen-tempered Pharaoh"), and a New Canaan charged "by the design of Heaven" with "the cause of all mankind."[16]

No doubt these Enlightenment heroes capitalized on the work of the "black regiment," that "numerous, learned and respectable body," as the Revolutionary historian David Ramsay described the New England clergy, "who had a great ascendancy over the minds of their hearers. They connected religion and patriotism, and in their sermons and prayers represented the cause of America as the cause of heaven." To varying degrees, most of the leading Revolutionaries—not only the clerics but such disparate political thinkers as Washington, Hamilton, Sam Adams, David Humphreys, and Elias Boudinot—responded in similar fashion. Their appeals for unity, sounded from military camp, scholar's study, and political platform, affirm the same typology of mission: the Hebrew exodus, New England's errand, America's destiny. Athens and Rome offered various practical incentives or warnings for the republic. But as before, sacred history provided the controlling metaphors. It need not surprise us that the first proposals for the Seal of the United States, submitted by Franklin and Jefferson, featured Moses leading the chosen people; nor that the symbol adopted instead was widely interpreted in just this way. "If any should be disposed to ask," said Edwards's disciple David Austin, "what has become of the eagle, on whose wings the persecuted woman [Rev. 12:14] was borne in to the American wilderness, may it not be answered, that she hath taken her station upon the Civil Seal of United States?" So indeed it was answered (to no one's surprise) by Samuel Sherwood on the eve of revolution. Invoking the same text from Revelation, Sherwood proceeded to link this to the corresponding commemorative and proleptic passages in the Old Testament: "Ye have seen what I did unto the Egyptians, and how I bare you upon eagles' wings. . . . Now therefore . . . ye shall be unto me . . . an holy nation" (Exod. 19:4–6), and "shall mount up with wings as eagles" (Isa. 40:31). Then, making explicit the figural import of all three texts, Sherwood announced to his election-day audience of May 1776:

> When that God, to whom the earth belongs, and the fulness thereof, brought his church into this wilderness, as on eagles' wings by his kind protecting providence, he gave this good land to her, to be her own lot and inheritance forever. He planted her as a pleasant and choice vine; and drove out the Heathan before her. He has tenderly nourished and cherished her in her infant state, and protected her amidst innumerable dangers. . . . God has, in this American quarter of the globe, provided for the woman and her seed. . . . He has wrought out a very glorious deliverance for them, and set them free from the cruel rod of tyranny and oppression . . . leading them to the good land of Canaan, which he gave them for an everlasting inheritance.[17]

The Church's Flight into the Wilderness was the most popular and inflammatory sermon of 1776, the clerical counterpart of Tom Paine's Common Sense, and no less representative than Common Sense of what was to become the dominant culture of the new nation. The figural outlook it sets forth is a striking example of an expanding cultural symbology. Almost a century and a half before, in the spring of 1630, John Cotton had chosen the same texts (from Exodus, Isaiah, and Revelation) to instruct the Arbella passengers about their venture into the New World. But whereas God's Promise to His Plantation uses the authority of tradition (the standard view of the eagle as Christ) to justify the venture, Sherwood takes that justification, rather than the tradition behind it, as his authority. Ultimately, he appeals not to church tradition, and not even to the Bible, but to the American experience; and in doing so he virtually reverses the hermeneutic process—turns figuralism inside-out. Sherwood's authority is the country's progress, his text the Puritan past, his exegetical framework the prophecies of America's future. Hence the ease with which he interprets the eagle as the Puritan spirit of liberty, *figura* of the Spirit of Seventy-Six. The radical Whigs, he is saying, are the children of promise, as Joshua was the heir to Moses: it is all one grand spiral of fulfillment from theocracy to democracy. Though he includes the Reformation and forecasts the millennium, as Cotton does, Sherwood describes the main redemptive events in terms of the growth of colonial society. The sacred point of origin is the Puritan settlement; its climax, the impending War of Independence.

The second- and third-generation Puritans had posited a figural unfolding from the Great Migration toward new heavens and new earth, but their pre-millennial view precluded a secular process of fulfillment. Edwards had opened the way for identifying American progress with the work of redemption, but the Great Awakening was only one more landmark in the unfolding drama of the New World. The development of the Anglo-American colonies, as Edwards conceived this, stretched indefinitely into the age of the spirit. For Sherwood and his compatriots, the concept of mission took on a distinct, self-enclosed American form. Drawing out the logic of their forebears to a conclusion undreamed of by Winthrop, Mather, or Edwards, they announced that the long-promised, eagerly awaited apocalyptic moment had arrived with the American Revolution. The patriot Whigs, "acting for the benefit of the whole world and of future ages," were sounding the same clarion call "as that of the heavenly host that announced the birth of the Savior." The Revolution, they explained, marked the full and final "accomplishment of the *magnalia Dei*—the great events . . . designed from eternal ages to be displayed in these ends of the earth . . . to the end of time"; the "independence of the United States of America is not only a marked epoch in the course of time, but it is indeed the end from which the new order of things is to be reckoned. It is the dividing point in the history of mankind; it is the moment of the political regeneration of the world." Appropriately, the July Fourth tradition began with an oration of 1778 (delivered in Charlestown, South Carolina) which defined "the Revolution as the beginning of a new age in human history."[18]

We can trace the development of this figural scheme through the patriotic addresses of the Revolutionary and Federalist periods—Nicholas Street's *The American States Acting Over the Part of the Children of Israel in the Wilderness* (New Haven, 1777), Samuel Langdon's *The Republic of the Israelites an Example to* the United States (Exeter, N.H., 1788), Abiel Abbot's *Traits of Resemblance in the People the United States of America to Ancient Israel* (Haverhill, Mass., 1799). In all of these state-of-the-federal-covenant messages, and countless others like them, such terms as "acting over," "example," and "resemblance" denote a biblical figuralism thrice removed. For the Puritans the errand carried forward the biblical exodus; for Edwards, the revival brought to fruition the Puritan errand; for the Whig preachers, the Revolution unveiled the meaning of exodus, errand, and revival. The flight of Noah, the wanderings of Abraham, the desert march of Israel, the formation of the early church, the revolt of Luther and Calvin against Rome: to all this the Revolution stood as antitype. Like the Incarnation, it marked a qualitative change in the spiral of human history. A new era had begun with the discovery of the New World, and the Revolution confirmed it, as Christ had confirmed the new era of faith. In doing so, He had invoked the authority of scripture, but it was His mission that defined and explicated the prophecies. Such too was the relation between Old and New Israel. Now that the Americans had fulfilled the covenant, their *magnalia Dei* would continue, in the image of the Revolution, "to the end of time."

It would be another generation or so before the typology of America's mission could be fully rendered—before Washington could be enshrined as savior, his mighty deeds expounded, his apostles ranked, the Judas in their midst identified, the Declaration of Independence compared to the Sermon on the Mount, the sacred places and objects (Bunker Hill, Valley Forge, the Liberty Bell) properly consecrated. It would take several decades for the Constitution to be duly ordained (in Emerson's words) as "the best thing in human possession" next to the New Testament, and for the Revolution to be "indissolubly linked" (as John Quincy Adams put it) with "the birthday . . . of the Savior," as being the social, moral, and political correlative of "the Reedeemer's mission on earth" and thus "the first irrevocable pledge of the fulfillment of the prophecies, announced directly from Heaven." But the pattern was well established by the end of the eighteenth century. And fittingly enough, a key figure in its establishment was Edwards's grandson, Timothy Dwight, a leading member of the black regiment, signer of the Declaration of Independence, Enlightenment intellectual, Connecticut wit, libertarian, Calvinist, and patriot Whig. "This great continent," Dwight exclaimed, "is soon to be filled with the praise, and piety, of the Millennium; *here*, is the stem of that wonderful tree whose topmost boughs will reach the heavens."

> The period is now on the wing in which "the knowledge of the LORD shall fill the earth as waters fill the sea." . . . Another sun, rolling around the great Centurial year will, not improbably, have scarcely finished his progress, when he shall see the Jew "reingrafted into the olive, from which he was broken off." . . . Think of the manner in which God *bare* your fathers in this land *on eagles wings*. Recall[l] their numerous deliverances. . . . A work, thus begun, and thus carried out, is its own proof, that it will not be relinquished.[19]

Dwight expressed these hopes most fully in his epic poem, *The Conquest of Canaan*, which builds on constant crises and "trials" (backsliding, treachery, holy war) toward a celebration of the New World republic—America, the second "blissful Eden bright," "by heaven design'd." Dwight's hero is Joshua; his subject, the battle for the biblical Canaan. But the action itself, he makes clear, is part of a grand process culminating in the Revolution. The Israelite leader serves by comparison (as harbinger of a "greater dispensation") to reveal Washington as the Christlike "Benefactor to Mankind," directing a "*more* fateful conflict" on "*new* Canaan's promised shores." Ultimately, that is, Israel's conquest of Canaan finds its vindication, its epic-heroic quality, in what it tells us of America's mission.

> To nobler bliss yon western world shall rise,
> Unlike all former realms. . . .
>
> . . . .
>
> Here union'd choice shall form a rule divine;
> Here countless lands in one great system join;
> The sway of Law unbroke, unrivall'd grow.

Some twenty years later, Washington's successor to the role of the American Joshua, John Adams, contemplated the meaning of that more fateful conflict. He decided, in a justly famous passage, that the motives behind the Revolution "ought to be traced back for Two Hundred Years, and sought in the history of the Country from the first Plantations. . . . This produced, in 1760 and 1761, AN AWAKENING and a REVIVAL of American Principles and

Feelings, with an Enthusiasm which went on increasing till in 1775 it burst out in open violence."[20] Adams's use of the Great Migration as precursor of the War of Independence is a significant testament to the secular-sacred typology developed through the eighteenth century. Significantly, too, his key terms remind us, whether by intention or not, of the Northampton millennium: *enthusiasm, awakening, revival.*

6
Continuing Revolution: George Bancroft and the Myth of Process

It is as if the ambiguity is not in the text but in us, as we struggle in our natures—our consciences with our . . . self-interests—just as the Founding Fathers struggled . . . providing us with a mirror of ourselves to go on shining, shining back at us through the ages, as the circumstances of our lives change . . . and our young republic becomes a plated armory of ideological warfare: a mirror for us to see who we are and who we would like to be.

E. L. Doctorow, "A Citizen Reads the Constitution,"
The Nation, CCXLIV (February 21, 1987), 216–17.

Philadelphia, July 4—President Ford came here from Valley Forge to recall that first Fourth of July as "the beginning of a continuing adventure," unfinished, unfulfilled, but still . . . "the most successful realization of humanity's universal hope. The world may or may not follow, but we lead because our whole history says we must."

New York Times, July 5, 1976

And verily, yours is the best and happiest land under the sun. But not wholly because you in your wisdom decreed it; your origin and your geography necessitated it. Nor, in their germ, are all your blessings to be ascribed to the noble sires of yore who fought in your behalf, sovereign kings! Your nation enjoyed no little independence before your declaration declared it. Your ancient pilgrims fathered your liberty. . . .

Melville, *Mardi*

So we beat on, boats against the current, borne back ceaselessly into the past.

Fitzgerald, *The Great Gatsby*

The American Revolution plays a curious role in American classic literature. Like Beckett's Godot, it is at once omnipresent and conspicuously absent. All contemporaneous accounts suggest that the Spirit of Seventy-Six was the muse of the American Renaissance. Bronson Alcott tells us that Thoreau acted as though he were the sole signer of the Declaration of Independence and a revolution in himself. Emerson's followers, taking their cue from the Master, hailed his essays as the vindication of the Revolutionary War. Young America's call for intellectual liberation deliberately echoed the call to arms against the British, and Whitman responded with a revolutionary poetics whose origins he located in the events that shaped the republic. For as Melville put it (in a review of Hawthorne), America was bound to carry the Revolution into literature and all the arts. Melville himself returned obsessively to the theme of revolution, or of revolution repressed, as did Hawthorne, Cooper, and Poe. Yet no more than a handful of their writings—a few stories and minor novels—can be said to deal with the American Revolution, and even these do so obliquely, if not evasively.

The forgotten popular writers of the time responded avidly (in romances, poems, plays, and epics) to the clamor for literature about the Revolution. Those writers through whom the American imagination has been defined remained silent on the subject, or at most ambivalent. Consider the canonized "representative Americans": the hero of Franklin's *Autobiography*, whose exemplary rise to power and fame conspicuously excludes the War of Independence; or Irving's Rip Van Winkle, who sleeps through the birth of the nation, and awakens to find things much as they were before; or Crèvecoeur's American Farmer, who derides the Revolution, in brief but vivid sketches, as democracy in riot, the snake in New Eden. Consider, above all, the Revolutionary figures in canonical American fiction: Cooper's Spy, the lonely, unacknowledged hero of a world gone mad; Melville's mock-heroic Israel Potter, who languishes away the Revolution in English captivity; Hawthorne's Robin Molineux, for whom independence takes the form of a witches' Sabbath. America's classic writers have given us splendid national heroes representing a variety of historical periods, including those of war and national upheaval. But none, apparently, found the Revolution fit matter for his highest themes. The great harvest of American literature—the self-styled American literary revolution—yielded no "Lilacs" for Washington, no *Pathfinder* at Valley Forge, no *Red Badge of Cour-*

age for the patriot cause, no Yoknapatawpha County for mourning Loyalists, not even a sentimental Whig's *Farewell to Arms*.

We could write off this anomaly to temperament or chance, were it not for a striking parallel in the culture at large. I refer to the uneasy association in the United States of revolution with America. Americans honor their Revolution as the shaping influence in their history, yet they shrink from accepting revolution as a defining American characteristic; or more typically, they accept it by contrasting the American Revolution with other modern revolutions. It is as though the term "American" altered the very meaning of revolution, while the term "revolution" conferred some special honorific status on the meaning of America. Again, the classic writers illustrate the ambivalence. To be American is for them ipso facto to be radical—to turn against the past, to defy the status quo and become an agent of change—and at the same time to be radical *as an American* is to transmute the revolutionary impulse in some basic sense: by spiritualizing it (as in *Walden*), by diffusing or deflecting it (as in *Leaves of Grass*), or more generally by accommodating it to the culture (as in *The Scarlet Letter*). In every case, the work of art resolves a conflict of values by redefining the conflict in terms of national self-fulfillment. Directly or indirectly, that is, the writer converts revolution into the service of culture.

I refer to long-term effect, of course, rather than to intention or even to immediate impact. Often enough, the service to culture I speak of has been rendered posthumously, through a slow process of absorption. But that process, I would argue, follows from, rather than belies, the substance of the work. In every case, the defiant act that might have posed alternatives to the system becomes instead a force for change within established patterns of life and belief. Whether these writers focus, like Thoreau, upon the individual, or like Hawthorne upon history—whether they denounce society, as Melville does, or like Emerson waver between praise and blame, or like Whitman simply ingest society, good and bad, into the self—the radical energies they celebrate serve in complex, contradictory, volatile but nonetheless compelling ways to *sustain* the culture.

This paradoxical effect recalls the troubled mood of the American Revolution. Historians of the period have shown that the overthrow of colonial power set loose a libertarian spirit which terrified moderate and propertied democrats. That terror underlies the entire literature. It surfaces in nervous satires of an egalitarian world turned upside down; in gothic novels and tales of violated taboos (parricide, incest, idolatry); and explicitly in the Federalist jeremiads I mentioned in the last chapter, warning against the people's inherent violence and denouncing a long series of local insurrections, from the Whiskey Rebellion to the Anti-Rent Wars, most of which had invoked the slogans and symbols of the American Revolution. I need not dwell on the fear of democracy which these writings convey or how deeply this affected the theory of representative government. Clearly, the first aim of legislators after 1776 was to curb popular demands. They were bent on defusing an explosive conflict within the system: between the minority in power (the leading merchants, lawyers, and landholders)—and the majority they represented, now newly-emboldened by military success, and by the rhetoric of independence, to challenge established norms of control. To quote a leading authority on the subject, the Constitution, which rescued the republic from "confusion and disorder" expressed "a beautiful but ambiguous ideal," one that served to mediate (rather than to meet) the call for self-determination, to curtail (without crushing) the surge of democratic individualism, and to insist on equality before the law while instituting a minority "rule of the best," drawn from the propertied and educated classes.[1]

In retrospect, we can see how appropriate that ideal was for modern liberal society. It was beautiful, we might say, *because* of its ambiguities. It managed both to advocate liberty and to protect property, to inspire "the people" at large and to mold their "universal rights" to the demands of a free-enterprise economy. Still, the ambiguities proved a shaky foundation for a new social structure. Like most ambiguities, they had a tendency to recoil upon themselves. If they allowed for flexibility and manipulation, they also served to highlight contradiction. Even as they encouraged compromise, they nourished radical dissent by calling attention to the principles that were being compromised. Alarmed at the "rage for innovation" that swept the infant Republic, David Ramsay ended his patriotic *History of the American Revolution* by summoning all "friends of order" to extirpate "the vicious principles and habits which have taken deep root during the late convulsions." The substitution of "convulsions" for "revolution" speaks for itself;

and its meaning grew more ominous after the French Revolution. If prior to 1790 (according to those in power) the unpropertied "rabble" seemed hell-bent on usurping due authority, what would they *not* do under the intoxication of Jacobin excess? Republican leaders, recognizing the link between pre- and post-Revolutionary unrest, warned sternly that "mob action, [though] necessary in monarchies, has no place in America." But the Spirit of Seventy-Six lingered, and by 1815, a host of clerical, literary, and civic "friends of order" had arrayed themselves against the threat. "Revolution," as they now employed the term, conjured up "corruption," "anarchy," "atheism." Retooling the old anti-colonialist rhetoric to defend the status quo, the aging firebrand Sam Adams turned his oratorical cannons against the "unbounded" "Ambition and Avarice" of King Mob. Timothy Dwight's epic previews of New Canaan darkened into visions of "unclean," "impious," and "ignorant" masses infected by the "poison" of revolutionary "licentiousness"—a "contagion of liberty" become license.[2] As we might expect, the lament grew increasingly shrill in the Jacksonian era, with the expansion of cities, technology, transportation—all the elements, in fact, of a flourishing capitalist economy—which certain established groups within that economy misconstrued as a collapse of order.

Misconstrued is too strong a word. Basically, these Jeremiahs seem to have understood that the challenge came from within the system and to have used their denunciations to keep things in hand. In any case, they refused to surrender either the Republic or the Revolution to the Jacksonians. Instead, following an old native tradition, they turned their anxieties about history into an affirmation of the ideal. Far from disavowing the "revolutionary spirit" of the times, they sought to redirect it (by threat and lamentation) toward *their* vision of the American Revolution. In effect, they joined the leading Jacksonians in an effort to safeguard the future through a mythical reconstruction of the past.

It may be worth recalling the events that prompted their effort. In 1826, with the death of Jefferson and John Adams, the Revolution passed officially into the possession of a new generation. It was an uneasy succession. According to anti-Jacksonians, especially after they had witnessed the revolutions of 1830 in France, Belgium, and Poland, and then two years later suffered an unprecedented electoral defeat, the difference between generations was nothing short of sinister: on one side, the newly-consecrated fathers of the Revolution (Washington, Franklin, Jefferson, Adams); on the other side King Andrew, the tyrant-demagogue, classical symptom of the breakdown of democracy. Theirs was the minority opinion, of course. Jacksonians defended their president as the heir of Washington and Jefferson. My point is that both parties, each from its own perspective, proposed the same rhetorical solution. They redefined the meaning of the Revolution by tracing it back to what they claimed were the true origins of the country. By general consensus, at least so far as New England's influence reached, independence was not the spoils of violence, but the harvest of Puritanism. It was not some sudden turbulent challenge to the system, provoking frustrations that threatened, in their issue, to sweep away all local (along with foreign) agencies of control, but the most remarkable in a series of uprisings that began with the migration to Massachusetts Bay.

In this view, the very concept of uprising set America apart from other countries. Uprising in France meant the unleashing of discordant national elements, the clash between mutually exclusive French interests and ideologies. Uprising in America meant the progress through revolution of "the people" at large. It stood for a consensus that rose above religious, social, economic, or sectional divisions, and that revealed itself, with increasing clarity and purity, in struggle against an oppressive Old World. In the early nineteenth century, the Spanish American colonies undertook a similar struggle, but they followed the French model of revolution: the uprising of New against Old World Spaniards brought to light tangled antagonisms of race and class, and if anything independence deepened the sense of internal conflict. The American Revolution, according to Jacksonians and anti-Jacksonians alike, proved that American identity erased all such distinctions. It was simply, comprehensively, the flowering of the spirit that first arose in Puritan New England. From this perspective Emerson argued in 1835, at the Concord bicentennial, that the national future was secure in spite of Jacksonian barbarity. From this perspective in 1834, George Bancroft began his great defense of Jacksonian democracy as American destiny made manifest.

Bancroft's *History of the United States* was almost instantly acclaimed as definitive—Emerson himself pronounced it a noble work, nobly done—and it retained its authority throughout the antebellum period as *the* source for the matter of America. But in fact it is neither a history (in any ordinary sense of the word) nor about the United States. Rather, it is an epic of the development from colony to nation, demonstrating through that development God's unfolding design for the New World, culminating in 1776 in the revolution to end revolutions that was born aboard the *Mayflower* and *Arbella*.

Bancroft's outlook has direct precedents in the patriot historians of the preceding generation. They, too, regarded the Revolution as a moral and spiritual (as well as political) culmination; they too claimed that independence was an extension of indigenous rights, rather than a break from the past; and they too looked back to the seventeenth century (in old and New England) as the ideological seeding-time of the Republic. Bancroft differs from them in his ability to reconstitute the facts as legend. He was just far enough removed from the Revolution to mythicize its major figures and events. He was responsive enough to the crisis of his times to perceive the basic cultural ties between the Revolution and the Jacksonian era. And he was rooted deeply enough in New England tradition to seize upon the Puritan errand as the underlying theme, the élan vital, of that continuity. The Revolutionary historians, who inherited the same tradition, used Puritan imagery as a metaphoric device to justify the War of Independence; it was part of their moral and legal self-vindication. They show us how ideology arises out of social conflict. Bancroft shows us how ideology becomes invested with the power of myth. Taking the vindication for granted, he identifies the American Revolution as the link between what for him (and many of his contemporaries) were the two quintessential moments in the story of America—the twin legends of the country's founding fathers—the Great Migration and the War of Independence. His purpose is to reveal in that sacred movement the paradigmatic cultural event, the symbolic drama of American nationhood.

Bancroft's *History of the United States* canonized the distinctive figures, events, and stories that constitute the myth of *American* revolution. Its underlying premise might be termed either a secular version of sacred history or a sacral version of human progress: Bancroft assumes that God is working behind and through history, guiding mankind step-by-step toward perfection. Revolution functions here as a vehicle of providence. It takes the form of a mighty, spontaneous turning forward, both regenerative and organic, confirming the prophecies of scripture as well as the laws of nature and history. So understood, revolution is diametrically opposed to rebellion. Revolution fulfills the divine will. Rebellion is a primal act of disobedience, as Lucifer's was, or Adam's. Rebels seek to negate, thwart, and destroy; revolutionaries are agents of the predetermined course of progress.

This distinction has a long background in religious and intellectual history. As Bancroft inherited the term, "revolution" had two entirely different meanings. In the secular tradition from Aristotle through the Italian Renaissance, it meant the violent overthrow of government. "Revolution" bespoke discord, contradiction, and discontinuity, and, so understood, it lent itself both to progressive and to cyclical views of history. For radicals, it proved that people could change their fate—that indeed, they might found a paradise of reason by overthrowing the institutions of the past. No doubt Mirabeau envisioned something like this when (according to legend) he replied to Louis XVI's "Ceci est une révolte," "Non, sire, c'est une révolution." For conservatives revolution proved the tragic consequences of the Fall. It demonstrated the recurrent human failure to perfect society, and they found its moral emblem in the treacherous, repetitive wheel of fortune. *Eadem, sed aliter* was Schopenhauer's comment on the French Revolution: the rhetoric of progress through revolution brings back the same old evils in new guise.

In opposition to this tradition, the religious meaning of revolution posited a gradual, preordained movement toward redemption. As such it pertained both to the individual believer and to humanity in general, and on both levels it was emphatically (if sometimes obliquely or ironically) progressive. Individually, each believer had the promise of heaven, through what Augustine termed the *revolutio* of the soul toward God. Collectively, humanity was advancing toward New Jerusalem in accordance with God's promises, through a series of revolutionary upheavals. Thus the Anglican Thomas Hooker spoke of the revolution of Jesus Christ against the Hebraic Law; thus Reformers spoke of the revolution of the true church against Papal Antichrist, the Beast of Rome; and thus English Puritans anticipated the worldwide revolutions that would inaugurate the millennium. The New England Puritans, we have seen, applied this millennial-revolutionary outlook directly to their errand, and they bequeathed that American teleology to Edwards, the mid-eighteenth-century Awakening, and the leading patriot ministers of the War of Independence.

Liberty, democracy, and nationhood, *conceived as worldly goods,* became spiritual goals in Revolutionary rhetoric. On this premise, the Reverend Samuel Sherwood in 1776 justified the overthrow of British power as a foreshadowing of the end-time revolutions. On the same premise, sixty years later, John Quincy Adams, former president of the United States, reviewed the American Revolution as part of "the progress of the gospel dispensations":

> Is it not that, in the chain of human events, the birth-day of the nation is indissolubly linked with the birth-day of the Savior?... Is it not that the Declaration of Independence first organized the social compact on the foundation of the Redeemer's mission upon earth? That it laid the corner stone of human government upon the first irrevocable pledge of the fulfillment of the prophecies, announced directly from Heaven at the birth of the Savior and predicted by the greatest of the Hebrew prophets six hundred years before?[3]

From this sacred-secular standpoint, Bancroft contrasts the American Revolution with the European "rebellions" of 1642, 1789, and 1830. And as though to make the legacy clear, he patterns his concept of progress upon the biblical exodus. In Europe, one tyranny succeeds another. In America a people is summoned to lead mankind, it rises up against its oppressors, and in the conflicts that ensue it forges its corporate identity. By that principle, Bancroft establishes America's revolutionary ancestry: not England, France, or Germany, but Israel, the apostolic church, and the Reformation. Each one of these civic-religious movements represents a revolution in itself; but unlike the repetitive cycles of *Fortuna,* each revolution is linked to the others in a spiral of ascent. Quoting Jonathan Edwards, whom he acclaims (accurately enough) his great precursor as historian, Bancroft compares that spiral to the wheels of a chariot in motion. All revolutions tend harmoniously toward the same end, and every revolution brings us closer to our destination. And like Edwards, he declares the settlement of New England to be the prime mover in the last and best of human revolutions. Representing Protestantism as well as the Anglo–Saxon race, at once re-enacting the drama of Exodus and carrying it toward completion, the New England planters, Bancroft tells us, rescued from the Old World the truths that would renew humanity. Winthrop's charter was "a summons from

Heaven" to "the happy destiny [of] preparing for . . . representative government."[4]

As Bancroft develops this theme, his revolutionary genealogy dramatically reverses the Loyalists' rankling child-parent metaphor. The Enlightenment radicals of an earlier time had defended their separation from England by recourse to Locke's contractual theory: the father-king's betrayal of trust justified the children's disobedience. Bancroft shifts the grounds of defense from abstract contractual theory to an indigenous federal identity. If the war for independence, he writes, had really breached the Fifth Commandment, then it would have been rebellion and thus indefensible. But in fact it demonstrated the children's *obedience*. The fathers were not English. They were *New* English, the English-speaking founders of a new kind of community, and what they initiated the Revolutionary sons fulfilled. The Pilgrim compact foreshadowed the Declaration of Independence; the Constitution realized the intentions of the *Arbella* covenant; what theocracy *truly* meant was representative democracy.

That fabled genealogy of American Revolution was (to repeat) Bancroft's inheritance from an earlier generation. His contribution was to make it the basis of a full-scale narrative of "America" as the United States. In doing so, he consolidated the myth of a new set of fathers; represented the Revolutionary leaders as a model of consensus; explained the moral necessity of their uprising; and (looking from Winthrop to Washington) illustrated the unprecedented pace of "national" progress. His narrative gave substance to the rhetoric of an American "people," providing as it did a substitute for what European nationalists were then terming "folk culture." And it served to project the movement from colony to republic forward to the transition from Jeffersonian fathers to Jacksonian sons.

Struggle as unity, continuity as progress: Bancroft's myth casts a soft, haloed glow over the events of 1776. It was not so much the War of Independence that mattered, he insinuates—not that alarming eruption of popular violence so much as the process that engendered it, enveloped it, and directed it toward higher ends. I do not mean to say that he minimizes the struggles and tensions of revolution. On the contrary: he increases these by extending the Revolution back through the eighteenth and seventeenth centuries, and forward into the nineteenth. Formally and conceptually, his overriding emphasis on process is the major tenet of Bancroft's approach. To that end, he consciously, pointedly inverts the biblical motifs of exodus and preordained progress. His *History*—published serially, incrementally, from 1834 through 1850; then expanded (revised to accommodate new facts and new times) annually from 1856 through 1874; and subsequently reissued with "improvements" for various official occasions (such as the 1876 Centennial)—may be seen as the historiographic model of process for the two great literary epics of antebellum America, *Moby-Dick* and *Leaves of Grass*. Bancroft's story, like theirs, invokes the Bible for uniquely American purposes. And in his case as in theirs, though far more explicitly and graphically, the American difference turns upon a shift in focus, from the scriptural process of fulfillment to the modern process of fulfillment.

The distinction is a crucial one. I have been suggesting that the concept of continuing revolution builds on the Puritans' arrogation to "America" of the Bible's mythic patterns, Christian and Judaic. The Christic pattern is personal, spiritual, and universal; the Judaic pattern is national, historical, and geographical; and Bancroft's *History*, like Mather's *Magnalia*, combines both of these in a progressivist national (or federal) New World drama, enacted through a procession of representative Americans. Each life in itself is a complete *revolutio* of the spirit (Mather's imitation of Christ transformed into a mirror of independence); and together they constitute a continuing revolution from colonial to national to continental identity. It makes for a compelling adaptation of Puritan figuralism to Jacksonian needs; but the terms of adaptation involve a basic change in structure and technique. I refer to the narrative and thematic shift I just mentioned. Fulfillment is guaranteed in the Judaic and Christian myths because it is inscribed in the Bible. The telos is already accomplished, as it were—as firmly secured as the miracles of the past. The end-time Zion is no less real than Joshua's rights to Canaan; the Second Coming is inseparable from the Resurrection. But "America" is *not* in the Bible. Its telos had to be inferred, step by embattled step, from the progress of Americans.

"America" is not in the Bible: that simple fact carried enormous complications for the prophets of New Israel. One solution was to *force* the new continent into scripture. "AMERICA is *legible* in these Promises" was the biblical guarantee proffered by colonial figuralists such as Cotton Mather and Jonathan Edwards.

But that sort of allegorizing was itself problematic—a symptom of the fragility of their new federal identity—and in any case it was no longer available to Bancroft. The Jacksonian "nation of futurity" depended for narrative resolution on *historical* continuity. Its futurity had to be demonstrated through serial re-enactments of exodus across the continent. The land had to prove its promise from one frontier (and frontiersman) to another, and from one generation to the next. These challenges elicited extraordinary energies of rhetorical invention, from the Puritan doctrine of *visible* sainthood to Jacksonian images of *manifest* destiny. But they left the American myth, by comparison with its Judaic and Christian precursors, peculiarly vulnerable to history. To modernize the Chosen People and God's Country meant opening those concepts to precisely the uncertainty of things to come which the Bible precludes.* Surely, that is why Jacksonian politicians boasted so often about their openness to the future; why the classic writers (Melville, Whitman) aspired to "gospelize the world anew";[5] why the leading painters located the Books of Exodus and Revelation in their Westering landscapes; why certain sects went so far as literally to find the Holy Scriptures in America, as Joseph Smith did in the caves of upstate New York—a brand-new Bible for Americans now, about America past and to come.

The two major cultural projects to secure the future came in the 1830s, during the unsettling period that followed the deaths of Jefferson and Adams and the election of Andrew Jackson. One of these projects was Emerson's revision of the theory of individualism, which he first outlined (in "The American Scholar") as a continuing biography, unfolding from year to year, of the representative national self. The other, complementary project was Bancroft's epic of nationhood. In both cases, the solution to the prob-

*I am referring here to the dangers of common sense, the threat of demythification, which I spoke of in the last chapter, and not to the failure of the dream. In fact, it is worth repeating that the long effort I describe below to create scripture ex nihilo is not at odds with but complementary to the tradition of the doomsday jeremiad—that endless cautionary lament about the ever-imminent apocalyptic "fall of America," which has served in its grim way to *confirm* the belief in a divine plan. Both modes are inherent in the myth; but behind both, I am suggesting, lies an anxiety about the openness of the story of America, and a corresponding effort to make openness itself, ritualized as "process," into a form of control. In later chapters I argue that Hawthorne's *The Scarlet Letter* is the aesthetic flowering of this aspect of the American symbology, and Melville's *Pierre* its most incisive and sweeping critique.

lem of the future was to make telos a function of process. Emerson located that sacred-secular function in the dynamics of self-reliance. Bancroft narrated it as the continuing revolution of the United States. He supported his claims for American destiny by biblical precedents and metaphors, but his "high argument" centers on the country's ongoing struggles.

As Bancroft envisions it, the Revolution opens into an indefinitely self-renewing rite of passage. His hero is a people in transition, advancing generation by generation through severe trials of character toward a consummation that remains forever beyond the next frontier, requiring always still another generational rededication, yet one more test of character and faith, in order to realize itself. There is something in this of the Whig view of history, but Bancroft (unlike, say, Macaulay) makes *revolution*, not evolution, the principle of "organic growth," moral, political, and economic. And there is something here, too, of the Sturm und Drang of Romantic Striving, but it is emphatically not the Promethean self-assertion of the European Romantics. Prometheus, like Cain, Satan, and other Romantic heroes, was a rebel, defiant of providence and the paternal gods. Bancroft turns self-assertion into an affirmation of order. If the condition of progress for him is continuing revolution, the condition of continuity is control of the revolutionary impulse. The social norms, as he conceives them, encourage revolution, but his definition of revolution reinforces authority.

Bancroft's differences from Whig history on the one hand and Romantic Prometheanism on the other carry broad social implications. The Whig metaphor of organic evolution, we know, reflected the needs of early-nineteenth-century England, a society deeply at odds with itself, trying uneasily to accommodate to middle-class forms the outmoded but still-potent traditions of aristocracy, church, and crown. We know further that Romantic Prometheanism represented a dangerous extreme of self-reliance, a concept of individuality that assumed the superiority of the autonomous heroic self to the law, whether civic or moral; and in Protestant European countries this form of extremism fed upon liberal ideology, even as it threatened the structures of middle-class society. Bancroft's continuing revolution precludes both social complexity and radical individuality. It is the expression of a modern culture, rather than of a modernizing nation—a New World society relatively unencumbered by competing traditions, as in Germany or England, without a towering feudal structure to be overthrown, as in France or Spain—a nation-culture so committed (as "Yankee America") to middle-class forms, or to forms so adaptable to liberal free enterprise, that the revolution could assume a conservative spirit.

Bancroft's rhetoric conveys the power and confidence of a capitalist economy in the process of what seemed unlimited expansion. It also conveys the deep insecurities that accompanied expansion, including not only those which might be inferred from the "open future," but, concretely, those which derived from contradictions or inconsistencies within the system itself: the regional differences that threatened the unity of the states; the anti- (or a-) social tendencies unleashed by the very norms of free enterprise—open competition, upward mobility, self-interest— and the conflicted dynamics of liberal ideology (national interest in a world of free trade, private versus corporate enterprise, national identity in a culture built on imperial expansion). These internal conflicts were never more dangerously in evidence than in the 1830s, and Bancroft addresses himself to them directly in his use of revolution as a *controlling* metaphor for national identity. In doing so, he was relying on strategies developed long before. In 1794, the Revolutionary David Austin, drawing on Edwardsean millennialism, explained that America had in fact experienced "TWO GREAT REVOLUTIONS . . . the *first* outward and political; the *second* inward and spiritual"; and these, he continued, linking the seal of the United States to the emblems of Revelation, are the wings of the eagle that is to carry mankind into the new age of the spirit. Half a century later, the Transcendentalist Bronson Alcott, drawing on the Puritan rhetoric of America as sacred place, argued that the Revolution proved that Americans possessed "the best of time and space . . . on a vantage ground to which no people have ever ascended before."[6] Bancroft elaborates these images and concepts into a full-scale myth of American process.

I mean myth in its traditional sense: the storyteller as the omniscient, impersonal voice of community. Bancroft's modernity lies in his self-consciousness about his task. He tells us that he intended his *History* to transcend polemic. As national epic it was to bridge Boston and the West, demonstrate the unity of Brahmin and Jacksonian values, establish the common middle ground of high and low culture, and so educate generations to come in the American Way. Predictably, the education entails standard liberal theories of conflict resolution: John Locke on voluntary submission, in order to safeguard rights of property, including the property of the self; Adam Smith on the mutuality of independence and interdependence, self-interest and national wealth. These and similar ideological directives are brought to life, as it were, in Bancroft's corporate bildungsroman: his story of a people forever in the course of becoming—"emerging," "rising," "infinitely expanding." He brings to bear upon that plot the various specialized influences he absorbed (Hegelian, scientific, Unitarian); but what makes it flower into a coherent *national* epic is his persistent identification of spiritual and economic development: the growth of capitalism, the unfolding meaning of "America," and the formation of the United States. In Bancroft's account the exodus of the middle classes from feudal and mercantile "bondage" begins with their discovery of the New World; their rise to power parallels that of the Anglo–American colonies; and their struggle for liberty and property culminates in the Revolutionary War.[7]

Culmination, meaning *continuity*—the commitment to an always-grander process of exodus, growth, and struggle—but, in Bancroft's account, it is now continuity anchored in a revealed plan. The Revolution links origins and telos: at one end, the Great Migration; at the other end, the millennium in process. Bancroft's description of the Puritans echoes the commonplaces of Jacksonian discourse: the "designs of Almighty Providence" intended their theocracy to lead upward toward liberal democracy; their "branches were destined to shoot forth and spread out, and extend, and blossom [throughout the] . . . vast continent." To make clear those designs, Bancroft presents the immigrants by contrast with the English Puritans of the Great Rebellion. There, defiance led to violence and violence to tyranny, as it was later to do in France. Here, exodus issued in the creation of a prosperous state, one in which the saint's *revolutio* toward God was socialized into a programmatic "morphology of conversion," and in which the federal covenant fused material, moral, and religious progress. In their insulated "wilderness-condition" they succeeded, as no European Puritan society could have hoped to do, in disciplining revolution into the service of social order—and specifically, of "social order amenable to the middle classes." Their city on a hill was a model of controlled progressivism; a "primitive form of representative democracy"; a closely regulated church-state which never lost sight, Bancroft exults, of its role as John the Baptist to "the revolution that would bring 'heaven to earth' in a New World republic."[8]

This is the language of figural prophecy: the shadow of the American Revolution falls simultaneously back across the past and forward across the future. But the figuralism is that of embattled, open-ended process. "[Our] soil was the fit *battleground* for independence," "the gift of Heaven . . . decreed by Divine counsels from all eternity" for a "momentous *combat*," signalling "the dawning *strife* of the new system against the old"[9]—through such phrases (formulaically repeated) Bancroft enshrines the anxieties of Seventy-Six as the model of identity for an expanding nation. The cultural plot that emerges was to become the official story of America. It provides the context for the "dawning strife" celebrated in "The Star-Spangled Banner," the "momentous combat" recorded in "The Battle Hymn of the Republic." And in doing so, it provides an index to the major strategies of social cohesion from the Revolution through the Civil War. I have in mind the various internal sources of conflict I noted earlier. In the 1830s virtually all of these economic, political, and regional contradictions came to focus in the opposition between gradualism and radical change. The opposition is of course embedded in the very concept of a national revolution. It also has a long history in Europe—characteristically, in the clash between reformers, who worked within the system, and utopians or millennarians who challenged the system in basic ways. During the Jacksonian period the impact in the United States of European radicalism made the differences particularly acute. And Bancroft's myth of continuing revolution, accordingly—his vision of a nation conceived in exodus and dedicated to progress—served a crucial mediative function. It posited an organically conflicted but intrinsically utopian status quo, a millennialism nourished on the persistence through struggle of established social norms.

It would be hard to overestimate the significance of this concept of revolutionary mediation. In defining America as the battleground for the future, Bancroft also defines the terms of battle as "American" versus "un-American," where "American" means *revolution* as progress through consensus, and "un-American" means *rebellion* as regression to cataclysm. It amounts to a sweeping co-optation of the radical impulse, in all its destructive, iconoclastic, *oppositional* potential, on behalf of *the* order established by *the* Revolution. Indeed, it transforms oppositionalism itself into a variety of symbolic oppositions, rooted in the prophetic meaning of America. For traditionally we recall, oppositionalism involves a dialectic confrontation between mutually exclusive or substantively different ways of seeing and being. It means revolution in its secular sense: overturning, undoing, doing away with. Symbolic oppositions, on the contrary, are symbiotic. They are mutually bound to the system that generated them. They may lead in unexpected directions, or suggest new possibilities, or find surprising forms of reconciliation, but only within a fixed, self-generating, bipolar system of meaning. Since every symbol unites opposites, or represents them as the same thing, we can understand what is being represented only by measuring it against its opposite, or by placing it within a series of comparable and related oppositions. The search for meaning is therefore at once endless and self-enclosed. Any possibility we propose invites a host of different possibilities, and any resolution of differences is implicit in the dualisms with which we began.

I treat this strategy in close detail in my discussion of *The Scarlet Letter*. Here I invoke it principally in its bearing upon Bancroft's view of history, and specifically in its relation to the symbology of errand that Bancroft inherited. The colonial Puritans, we have seen, joined sacred and secular history, sacred and secular place. They attached the concept of the profane not to the things of this world, as Christian tradition dictated, but to whatever opposed their progress into a sacred-secular New World. By Bancroft's time, that symbolic opposition provided the terms of national self-understanding. Sacred and profane stood for the opposition between the spirit of America and the realities that distorted the spirit, or hindered the process of its fulfillment. A priori, anything blessed by the adjective "American" was a positive good; but necessarily, by the logic of the symbolic mode, not everything in the United States was so blessed. Natty Bumppo represents the *American* spirit to us insofar as we deny that spirit to the no less representative Yankee woodchoppers. Both Huck Finn and Ragged Dick are self-made, in the American way, but each has to reject the values of the other in order to make it; they are bound together, as it were, in a heroics of symbolic antagonism.

The state of tension that ensued proved an inexhaustible (because self-generating) source of exultation through lament. It is no accident that Thoreau describes his life at Walden through a series of oppositions: Concord's *American* Puritan settlers versus its current profane inhabitants; America's pioneer economy versus Franklin's profane Way to Wealth; the true American, Henry David Thoreau, versus John Field, the emigrant bog-hoer living in the Old World style (Thoreau writes scornfully) in this new country. Nor is it an accident that Melville's White-Jacket praises the messianic American ship of state by contrast with actual violations of the Constitution, or that Whitman defines the American poet by contrast with poetry in America. In his history, Bancroft uses this mode of symbolic antithesis to launch a jeremiad against a broad range of national evils, from Boston snobbism to ethnic discrimination to Southern slavery. Explicitly and implicitly, he speaks of the constraints of specialization and class, the power of inherited wealth, the psychic strains of what we would now call anomie and alienation, the heavy moral costs of economic individualism. All such evils he designates in various ways as "un-American"; and having done so, he invokes the imperative of continuing revolution—the *American* paradigm consecrated in the struggles of '76—to bridge the gap between fact and ideal.

I do not mean to obscure the fact that this cultural symbology also lent itself through the century to some of the most sinister forms of Americanism: progressivist arguments for eradicating the Indians; benevolent societies for deporting the blacks; the obsession with so-called foreign conspiracies, like the Catholic migration of 1834 which (according to American Evangelicals) Satan had organized for the overthrow of America. On the contrary, I wish to suggest that the symbol of America could accommodate an endless diversity of interpretations. More than that, it encouraged controversy—provided only that the disputants kept within the terms of the symbol. They were free to criticize from virtually any standpoint, from Walden to Washington, provided that they conceived their criticism as part of a continuing investigation of un-American activities. So conceived, and so circumscribed, the very intensity of their opposition confirmed the norms of the culture. What higher defense could one offer for middle-class society than an American Way that sui generis evoked this free competition of ideas?—and what could make this freedom safer for society than to define "strife" and "conflict" (in its *truly* radical sense) within a self-enclosed American Way? The special efficacy of Bancroft's epic, considered both in its own right and as a connective between Puritan, Enlightened, and Romantic America, is that its myth of continuing revolution provides a narrative framework within which all sorts of quests for social alternatives, from the mundane to the quixotic, could be reformulated as a call for social revitalization.

I am not arguing that Bancroft was aware of all this. Let us say that by the 1830s the strategies he used were something of a cultural reflex, that on some level he understood their significance for a society in crisis, and that they provided a vehicle uniquely suited to his subject: the history of American revolution as an indefinitely prolonged rite of passage into nationhood. That ritualization of process is the most remarkable feature of Bancroft's epic. We may see behind it, as Bancroft did, a distinctive colonial tradition, reaching from the Puritans' "federal" covenant-renewals through the revivalists' proto-nationalist "concerts of prayer."* But in Bancroft that tradition matures in a story that incorporates the ritual process itself as the structure of community. All ritual is of course a function of social continuity. In "traditionalist societies," however, the rite of passage involves a limited, extra-ordinary time of trial and probation, a "suspended period" in which the initiate temporarily breaks free of history and communal norms. In Bancroft the passage *is* history; the trials, an enactment of communal norms. The ritual he sets out is not a transition into American society. It *is* America. The expanding consensus it represents is revolutionary because it is progressive, and the condition of progress is conformity through generational rededication to an America in transition.

This contrast warrants further elaboration. Anthropologists have observed (with regard to both modern and traditional communities) that the rite of passage, despite its socializing intent, may pose enormous dangers to society. By freeing initiates, however briefly, from hereditary structures, it directs them toward a state of *communitas*, a sort of cultural no-man's-land, like the heath in *King Lear*, whose values negate all social forms whatever. Communitarian values appeal to humanity at large rather than to

---

*I think here of the special use of the conversion ritual, on the part of both the Puritans and the Revivalists, as an instrument of acculturation—in effect, as a ritual passage (in fear and trembling) into the typology of America's mission. The Christian conversion rite instills fear and trembling in order to direct the initiate toward a new vision, and to re-train him in a vocabulary (regarding selfhood, community, time, and place) that inverts the meanings of secular discourse. The Puritans and Revivalists developed this into a *social* conversion rite, designed to direct the rising generation toward a special "federal" identity.

particular communities: they speak of one-ness as opposed to political or even sexual division; equality, as opposed to hierarchy; universality as opposed to tribal or national exclusiveness. Many societies have paid homage to such values, and as a rule ideology seeks to justify social structures by integrating them, through symbol and myth, with the deeper human structures of ritual *communitas*. Nonetheless, the experience itself of *communitas* has led individuals and groups to challenge their societies in basic ways. European novels like Dickens's *Great Expectations* and Balzac's *Lost Illusions* show how the rite of passage may issue in a profound criticism of middle-class dreams, not only in their deviance from the facts but in their own right, as cultural ideals. Or to choose another example pertinent to Jacksonian America: Christianity, which has been used to support many kinds of social ideology, has also led (through the conversion ritual) to many forms of social conflict, involving the dual meaning of selfhood, civic versus spiritual, or the contradictions between patriotism and community of souls, or again, especially in Protestant countries, the incompatible claims of secular place and sacred time.

The symbol of America reflects a vast cultural effort to obviate these conflicts, in any form. And it finds a consummate expression in the ritual of American process. The ritual tends to perpetuate the anxieties of passage and transition. One need only think of the peculiarly adolescent concerns of American writers, their emphasis on freedom from prescribed roles, on confrontations with the absolute, on the disparity between social and "ultimate" values, even while they return insistently to the meaning of America. But their insistence upon America suggests that, in this case, to increase tension is to further the process of acculturation. In European literature, even those works that espouse middle class society tend to expose the limitations of middle class ideals. America's major writers have often followed Bancroft in upholding those ideals even when they most bitterly assail the middle class.

I think now not only of the jeremiad form they adopted—denouncing the nation in order to reaffirm the national dream—but of its bipolar opposite, what we might call the jeremiad against jeremiads, to which some of them were equally attracted, and which equally foreclosed the prospect of radical change: the denunciation of all ideals, sacred and secular, on the grounds that the failure of American revolution proved the failure of history itself. My point is that both approaches reversed the oppositional potential of *communitas*—the one, by absorbing communitarian ideals into the process of national self-fulfillment; the other, by reading into that process the futility and fraud of all communitarian ideals. Both Emerson's "American Scholar" and Melville's *Pierre* assume an American teleology; they differ only about whether it means progress toward millennium or regress toward doomsday. And predictably enough, the sheer extremity of the choice, the utter bleakness of the doomsday view, has worked in favor of socialization. No doubt this anti-jeremiad is a minor variation on the theme of American revolution. By and large, the tradition was perpetuated by optimists like Emerson. Still, it seems a telling sign of cultural hegemony that even America's prophets of doom have played a part. In spite of themselves, they too helped transform what might have been a revolutionary threat—the experience of *communitas* issuing in genuinely alternative models of society—into a model of consensus.

From this perspective, writing wholly in the optative mood, Bancroft described the Revolution as a crusade to clear God's Country of the profane once and for all. From this perspective, he and his compatriots hailed the continuing revolution in nineteenth-century American life: for example, the continuing march Westward across Indian territories (a "march of revolution," Lyman Beecher explained in 1835, to prepare "the way of the Lord"); or the continuing pleas for revival and reform (in America, thundered Albert Barnes in 1834, "Every drunkard opposes the millennium"); or the continuing migrations of settlers, like the Mormons ("the whole of America," wrote Joseph Smith, shortly before his murder, "is Zion itself from north to south"); or for that matter, the continuing migrations of maverick explorers, like the bearded old visionary whom Timothy Flint met, "descending the Mississippi," as he said, "to the real Jerusalem"; or again, the continuing summons for a revolutionary art that would convey, as Frederick Church hoped to do in painting Niagara, the millennial effusions of the American landscape; or once more, the developing battle for women's rights—for "American women," Catharine Beecher stressed, "more than any others on earth," since they in particular must shape the "moral and intellectual character" of the people now leading the "irresistible," universal "social revolution."

"[T]his is the Country," she explained, "which the Disposer of events designs shall go forth as the cynosure of nations," and therefore "to American women . . . is committed the exalted privilege of extending over the world those blessed influences, which are to renovate degraded man."[10]

In every form revolution meant, interchangeably, to make things sacred, to make them transitional, and to make them American. Whether the rite of passage pertained to the national errand or to individual self-fulfillment, its significance as revolution lay in the unfolding telos of the New World. Thus Horatio Alger makes his heroes representative of the American spirit of independence. Thus the various nineteenth-century American imitations of *Pilgrim's Progress* center not on some generalized Tender Conscience or Good Intent (as in England), but on an imperial destiny, as in Joseph Benton's *California Pilgrim*, the story of a Western "Glad-land" that surpasses Solomon's Jerusalem in holiness and wealth. And thus Thoreau seeks to radicalize Concord through a conversion narrative that represents, in his words, "the only true America."[11] The common assumptions are all the more telling for the enormous differences in mind and imagination. In its own way, each one of these instances confirms Bancroft's myth. Whether its implications are personal or collective, spiritual or social, whether it reveals the individual as self-made or self-transcendent, the purpose of the process it celebrates feeds into the ritual of American revolution.

For the July Fourth orators of the 1830s that ritual was the key to domestication of revolt. For the leaders of the Second Great Awakening, it was a means of linking religion with American institutions and social values. For antebellum politicians, it was proof that any fundamental change could only "be for the worse": by the "immutable law" of "progress . . . Nature and . . . God," the national government already stood for "the nearest approach to . . . human perfection allotted to . . . the children of Adam."[12] For America's classic writers, the ritual functioned as an initiation into ancestral taboos, barring the revolutionary imagination from paths that led beyond the limits of liberal ideals. It was not that these writers lacked courage or radical commitment. It was that they had invested radicalism itself in a vision dedicated to the containment of revolution.

I mean "containment" in its double sense, as sustenance and as restriction. The vision set free titanic creative energies in America's classic writers, and it confined their assertion to the terms of the American myth. The dream that inspired them to defy the profane compelled them to speak their defiance as keepers of the dream. It is true that the assumed unity of sacred place and sacred time allowed them to arrogate America to themselves—to transplant the entire national enterprise, en masse, into what Thoreau calls the *sancte terre* of the American soul. But the same assumption enlisted individuality itself, rhetorically and mythically, into the service of a national ideology. Except for Emerson, no American made larger claims for the individual than Whitman did, none more vividly denounced corruption in America, and none more passionately upheld the metaphysics of the American system. This "extreme business energy," Whitman wrote, inheres in our "vast revolutionary" potential; our "almost maniacal appetite for wealth" is "part of amelioration and progress, indispensably needed to prepare the . . . results I demand. My theory includes riches, and the getting of riches, and the amplest products. . . . Upon them, as upon substrata, I raise the edifice [of revolution] . . . the new and orbic traits waiting to be launched forth in firmament that is, and is to be, America."[13]

At the risk of stating the obvious, let me add that these writers were not middle-class apologists. All of them (to varying degrees) labored against the myth as well as within it. All of them felt, privately at least, as oppressed by Americanism as liberated by it. And all of them, however captivated by the national symbol, also *used* the symbol, as Bancroft could not, to reach beyond the categories of their culture. What critics have called the limitations of time and place may also constitute the source of creative empowerment and trans-historical expression. And conversely, what critics have designated as the transcendent "spirit of America" has its source in a specific time, a concrete place. It is a spirit grounded in the culture's mythic association of America with revolution—which is to say, in Americans' tendency in times of crisis to reach back to national origins, as Bancroft did, in order to conjure up the figures of universal progress.

That strategy, be it noted, applies both to personal and to communal progress. Considered as a naturalist's conversion story, Thoreau's *Walden* may be said to repudiate Bancroft's ritual of historic process. And yet, as revolutionary *and* American works, there are basic affinities between the two. Effectually, *Walden* summons us toward the same "star of freedom" that Bancroft celebrates, heralding "the morning of a new civilization." I think here not only of their use of such terms as freedom but of the way that they apply those abstractions to a concrete way of life. *Walden* announces itself as a protest against Jacksonian economics, but the counter-model it offers is tailor-made to the Homo Economicus described by James Richardson, William Legget, Francis Lieber, Thomas Nichols, Francis Grund, Robert Rantoul, and other Jacksonian liberals: a simple and simplifying man, mobile, self-employed, living by "seasonal rhythm" and the "order of nature," his "independence disciplined by virtue" and sustained by antipathy to government controls. Like that pattern self-made man, *Walden*'s Thoreau denounces the "wicked spending," "soap-bubble business," and "wasteful acquisition," the "appalling" and "giddy passion of money-getting," the "grasping monopolizing spirit of rapacious capitalists," the "great scramble, in which all are troubled and none are satisfied"—the "tugging, trying, and scheming to advance," that characterizes *un-American* life. He, too, finally, exemplifies the *American* method for self-perfection set out in Jacksonian manuals for success: a "true value of riches," usually learned in a "purifying" state of poverty; "free exercise of confidence between man and man," based on a "natural system in ... politics"; and self-reliance geared toward "the greatest moral and intellectual reformation that ever took place in the same time in the world."[14]

This is not the hero of *Walden*, but it is enough like him to indicate Thoreau's debt to his culture. The parallels further remind us that, like Bancroft, Thoreau does not consider the evils around him to be a defect of the American Way. He sees them rather as an aberration, like the backsliding of a de facto saint or the stiff-necked recalcitrance of a chosen people. That is why his outrage is so vehement, his rejections so absolute, and so resonant with biblical allusion. Thoreau speaks as Bancroft does, under the aspect of continuing revolution. He denounces Concord not to advocate a different social order, but to awaken his neighbors to what seemed to him the governing fact of modern progress, that America "is the Great Western Pioneer whom the nations follow." A decade and a half before *Walden*, Cooper personified the American middle class as Aristabulus Bragg, the "regular mover" who supports democracy because, for all its failings, it obviates history, along with every impediment to industry, enterprise, and self-fulfillment. "A nation is much to be pitied that is weighed down by the past," Bragg explains to a visitor from the Old World. "America may, indeed, be termed a happy and a free country . . . in this, as well as in all other things. . . . I am for the end of the road at least," and for all "onward impulses."[15]

Certainly, this is not Thoreau speaking; but again, the obvious contrasts make the rhetoric they share all the more remarkable. Thoreau marches to a different drummer, but he too is a pilgrim on a national journey. The faults he perceives in America, far from proving the failure of the system, form part of his appeal to a special people to comply with the terms of its covenant. And I believe we may say much the same about *Moby-Dick*. The revolution that never surfaces on the *Pequod* obliquely affirms the values that Bancroft endorsed; its center is an unmistakably American hero, Ishmael, a "regular mover" who becomes the exemplum of liberal democracy. To be sure, Melville makes it clear that Nantucket is something other than the Great Society. Yet he focusses his criticism on an individual extremist, an antinomian romantic turned "tyrant," "mogul," "czar," "sultan"; and insofar as he identifies with Ahab's fiery quest, Melville shifts the conflict from the social to the metaphysical realm. Ahab's quarrel is not with shipowners and shareholders, nor with any middle-class frustrations to self-fulfillment (as in contemporaneous French, English, German, and Russian literature), but with God. Thus the novel tends to divide our sympathies between two modes of individualism, two forms of progress—American and un-American. And in Ishmael's revolutionary gestures toward fulfilling the federal covenant, it offers us a cultural rite of passage, a beautifully ambiguous American ritual for exorcising the rebellious Ahab in our souls. Blasphemy may enchant when it takes the form of monomania. As a *social* alternative it can only argue the need for the containment of rebellion.

Perhaps the fullest description of the radical act so contained appears in Hawthorne's fiction—in *The House of the Seven Gables*, for instance, where an incipient revolutionary, Holgrave, learns from a daughter of the Puritans to redirect his social outrage into suburban self-improvement; or more strikingly, in *The Scarlet Letter*. I discuss this novel in the next chapter; here let me simply remark that Hester's return to Boston is her radical substitute for revolt. *The Scarlet Letter* opens with a long, acerbic, and very troubled preface about Jacksonian America, and it closes with Hester's anticipation of the New World Eden to be. Linking present, past, and future, shaping the course of progress from theocracy to democracy, and yet left virtually unmentioned, is the American Revolution. The near-omission, in this greatest of America's historical romances, speaks eloquently to the paradox with which I began this chapter. It may serve summarily as a mute symbol, like Beckett's Godot, for the power of Bancroft's myth, and in general for the ritual of process which recast revolution as the American Way.

7
The Return of Hester Prynne

"The scarlet letter had not done its office": Hawthorne's stern, evasive one-line paragraph, midway through the novel, deserves the emphasis he gives it.[1] The sentence links our various views of Hester Prynne—on the pillory and in the forest, in relation to the townspeople, her husband, her lover, her daughter, herself. It seems to confirm what we are often told, that Hawthorne's meanings are endless and open-ended. To speak of an office not done, especially without specifying the office, implies a commitment to process, a principled indefiniteness. But in fact Hawthorne is saying just the opposite. His very emphasis on the negative, the "not done," invests the letter with a discreet function, an office whose fulfillment (in due time) will be the mark of narrative closure. It reminds us, as does everything else about the novel, from title to plot, that the letter has a purpose and a goal. And to speak of an unfulfilled office when fulfillment is underway, not *yet* done, is to imply teleology. Hawthorne's meanings may be endless, but they are not open-ended. On the contrary, they are designed to create a specific set of anticipations, to shape our understanding of what follows in some definite way.

"The scarlet letter had not done its office": on one hand, process; on the other hand, purpose and telos. The coherence of the symbol lies in its capacity to combine both. It has a certain end, we might say, in the double sense of *certain*, as certainty and as something still to be ascertained. The office of the letter is to identify one with the other: to make certainty a form of process, and the prospect of certain meanings a form of closure and control.

With that double prospect in view, Hester returns to New England. "Here had been her sin," Hawthorne writes; "here, her sorrow; and here was yet to be her penitence" (p. 344). Again, process and closure combined, only now with a *certain* end in view, penitence; as earlier Dimmesdale has an end in view when he prophesies a certain "glorious destiny" for "this newly chosen

194

people of the Lord" (pp. 332–333), and as later Hester does when she foresees an age of love to come. Once, long before, she transformed the A into a symbol of Able, Admirable. Now she transforms herself, able and admirable as she is, into an agent of socialization. Her cottage becomes a meeting ground for dissidents—particularly, unhappy young women chafing (as Hester had) under Puritan restrictions—and she takes the opportunity to make it a counselling center for patience and faith. In effect, she urges upon them a morphology of penitence (not unlike the official Puritan "preparation for salvation")—self-control, self-doubt, self-denial, a true sight of sin, and hope in the future, involving some apodictic revelation to come. Hester's "badge of shame" becomes the "mystic" token of integration (pp. 257, 146).

This is not some formulaic Victorian happy ending. In the first place, the ending is *not* happy. What brings Hester home, the necessity that serves in some measure (as Hawthorne promises at the start) to "relieve the darkening close" of his tale (p. 159), is no deus ex machina. It is the narrative mechanism itself, in all its "sad" and "sombre" implications (p. 345). Hawthorne sums these up through the emblem on the lovers' tombstone—the "engraved escutcheon . . . relieved by one ever-glowing point of light gloomier than the shadow" (p. 345)—an emblem that enforces our sense of closure precisely by sustaining narrative tension; for like Hester's *final* penitence *to be*, the gloom that finally is to provide relief also returns us to the ambiguities of Hester's ordeal.

In these and other ways, Hawthorne's fusion of process and telos transmutes opposition into complementarity. Hester's return effectually reconciles the various antinomies that surround her throughout the novel: nature and culture, sacred and profane, light and shadow, memory and hope, repression and desire, angel and adulteress, her dream of love and the demands of history and community. It also draws together author and subject. For as the letter's unfulfilled office, midway through the story, anticipates Hester's return, so the return of Hester anticipates Hawthorne's recovery of Puritan New England. Here had been her penitence, and here was yet to be *The Scarlet Letter; A Romance*. At the start Hawthorne reverses the disruptive effects of political office—the Democratic Party defeat that cost him his tenure at the Salem Customs House—by reaching back through the A to national origins. At the end, reversing the alienating effects of her symbol, Hester looks forward to a "brighter period" (p. 344) that relates her most intimate hopes to moral and social progress. In each case, the gesture enacts the symbolic method I noted, process and telos combined. In each case, that method in some sense parallels the techniques of Bancroft's epic *History*. And in each case those parallels reflect the strategies of what I have called the American symbology.

The Scarlet Letter gathers its extraordinary aesthetic power—its imaginative richness, complexity, and depth—from its relation to the culture. To understand the novel in its own terms is to see the ideological dimensions of its art. More than that: it is to bring into view the aesthetic power—the richness, complexity, and depth—of the mid-nineteenth-century American liberal imagination. Indeed, it may be said that *The Scarlet Letter* is precisely about that sort of reciprocity between text and context. This is a story of socialization, where the point of socialization is not to conform, but to consent. Anyone can submit; the socialized believe. It is not enough to have the letter imposed; you have to do it yourself, and that involves the total self, past, present, and future, private and public, thought and passion and action, or if necessary inaction. This is essentially the office of the A as the Puritan magistrates intended it, and as Hester finally adopts it, from her own far more tolerant but not altogether different outlook. And we may assume that the letter's "deeper meanings" correspond. *Allegoria*, as Augustine taught, is a function of *littera-historia*. By that time-honored principle of exegesis, the A is first and last a cultural artifact, a symbol that expresses the needs of the society within and for which it was produced. I refer to Hawthorne's society, of course; but I would also include Puritan New England, insofar as it contributed to the development of antebellum America, and our period as well, insofar as it may be said to build on ideological, rhetorical, and intellectual continuities from Hawthorne's time.* In this long view, the

---

*It may be well to reiterate, with reference to "Hawthorne's society" and "antebellum ideology," that here as elsewhere I am concerned with the set of social practices and cultural values we associate with the liberal Northern United States from 1820 to the Civil War. As I emphasized in earlier chapters, I am aware of the many differences within that society, and in these terms of the problem in applying such generalities as "Jacksonian" to the Northern states and to Hawthorne's Massachusetts in particular. But the same generalities, however problematic, direct attention to another crucial aspect of the story: the broad patterns of life and thought which bound together those diverse interests, groups, and regions, and within which, moreover, diversity itself was celebrated as part of a strategy of cultural cohesion.

letter's office pertains both to the symbol in the text and to the symbol as the text; and in order to highlight the relation between these, I focus on the point at which the office seems to have been fulfilled at last, the dramatic moment when Hester Prynne comes home to America.

The drama of Hester's return has gone unappreciated, no doubt because it is absent from the novel. At a certain missing point in the narrative, through an unrecorded process of introspection, Hester abandons the high, sustained self-reliance by which we have come to identify her—from her opening gesture of defiance, when she repels the beadle and walks proudly "into the open air" (p. 162), to the forest scene seven years later, when she casts off her A and urges Dimmesdale to a new life—chooses for no clear reason to abandon her heroic independence, and acquiesces to the A after all. Voluntarily she returns to the colony that had tried to make her (she once believed) a "life-long bond-slave," although Hawthorne pointedly records the rumors that Pearl "would most joyfully have entertained [her]. . .mother at her fireside" (pp. 313–314, 344). And voluntarily Hester resumes the letter as a "woman stained with sin, bowed down with shame," although, he adds, "not the sternest magistrate of that iron period would have imposed it" (p. 344). As in a camera obscura, isolation and schism are inverted into vehicles of moral, political, and historical continuity.

The reversal is perplexing because, among other reasons, it so clearly defies tradition. Had Hester returned for love alone (the A for Arthur), or under the cloud of disaster abroad (the A for adversity), we could follow her reasoning readily enough. But Hawthorne forces us instead to consider the disparity between these familiar endings and Hester's choice. The familiar endings, from *Antigone* and *Medea* through *Antony and Cleopatra*, *Tristran and Isolde*, and *Anna Karenina*, are variations on the theme of love against the world. Hester's choice self-consciously merges love *and* the world—the personal with the social, and the social with the historical. In effect, her return calls attention to the political implications of process as closure. This political emphasis is appropriate for the same reason that it is problematic: Hawthorne's portrait of Hester is a study of the lover as social rebel. Not as antinomian or witch, as he explicitly tells us, and certainly not as adulteress—if anything Hester errs at the opposite extreme, by her utter repression of eros.

Hawthorne remarks, with a note of disgust, that she had lost her "womanly" qualities, had become almost manlike in her harshness of manner and feature:

> Even the attractiveness of her person had undergone a . . . sad transformation . . . [so that] there seemed to be no longer any thing in Hester's face for Love to dwell upon; nothing in Hester's form, though majestic and statue-like, that Passion could ever dream of clasping in its embrace; nothing in Hester's bosom, to make it ever again the pillow of Affection. Some attribute had departed from her, the permanence of which had been essential to keep her a woman. (pp. 258–259)

Hester errs, then, not in her sexual transgression, but in her "stern development" (p. 259) as an individualist of increasingly revolutionary commitment. At the novel's center is a subtle and devastating critique of radicalism that might be titled "The 'Martyrdom' of Hester Prynne." It leads from her bitter sense of herself as victim to her self-conscious manipulation of the townspeople; and it reveals an ego nourished by antagonism; self-protected from guilt by a refusal to look inward; using penance as a refuge from penitence; feeding on shame, self-pity, and hatred; and motivated by the conviction that society is the enemy of the self.

Let me recall the scene I began with, in the chapter midway through the novel. Seven years have passed and the townspeople have come to regard Hester with affection, admiration, even reverence. On her part, Hester has masked her pride as humility, has repeatedly reminded them, by gesture and look, of her "*saint-like* suffering," and in general has played upon their guilt and generosity until "society was inclined to show its *former* victim a more benign countenance than she cared to be favored with, or, perchance, than she deserved" (pp. 187, 257; my italics). And like other hypocrites in Hawthorne's work, Hester pays a heavy price for success. "All the light and graceful foliage of her character had been withered up," he tells us, "leaving a bare and harsh outline, which might have been repulsive, had she possessed friends or companions to be repelled by it" (p. 258). She has none because she wants none. The "links that united her to the rest of human kind had all been broken," save for "the iron link of mutual crime" (p. 255). She considers Pearl, whom she loves, an instrument of "retribution" (p. 273). Concerning those to whom she ministers—

not only "her enemies," but those for whom "the scarlet letter had the effect of a cross on a nun's bosom"—Hawthorne points out that Hester "forebore to pray for [them], lest, in spite of her forgiving aspirations, the words of the blessing should stubbornly twist themselves into a curse" (pp. 258, 191).

It is worth stressing the severity of Hawthorne's critique. After seven years, Hester has become an avenging angel, a figure of penance unrepentant, a so-called "Sister of Mercy" who not only scorns those who call her so, but who has developed contempt for all "human institutions," "whatever priests or legislators had established" (pp. 257, 290). Despairing, therefore, of any improvement short of tearing down "the whole system of society," and doubtful even of that "remedy," she turns her energies first against "the world's law" (pp. 260, 259) and then against her daughter and herself. Her heart, Hawthorne tells us,

> had lost its regular and healthy throb, [and she] wandered without a clew in the dark labyrinth of mind; now turned aside by an insurmountable precipice; now starting back from a deep chasm. There was wild and ghastly scenery all around her, and a home and comfort nowhere. At times, a fearful doubt strove to possess her soul, whether it were not better to send Pearl at once to heaven, and go herself to such futurity as Eternal Justice should provide. (p. 261)

This is the allegorical landscape of misguided rebellion: a wild, self-vaunting independence leading by a ghastly logic of its own to the brink of murder and suicide. No wonder Hawthorne remarks at this point that "The scarlet letter had not done its office."

I do not mean by this to deny the obvious. Hester is a romantic heroine. She is endowed with all the attributes this implies of natural dignity, generosity of instinct, and what Hawthorne calls "a woman's strength" (p. 257). Although she persistently abuses or represses these qualities, nonetheless they remain potential in her—dormant but felt in her every thought and action—and Hawthorne clearly means them to move us all the more forcefully for the contrast. As he remarks after detailing her "sad transformation": "She who has once been a woman, and ceased to be so, might at any moment become a woman again, if there were only the magic touch to effect the transfiguration. We shall see whether Hester Prynne were ever afterwards so touched, and so transfigured" (p. 260). While we wait to see, Hester persistently invites our pity and praise, and by and large she succeeds, as she did with the Puritans. But to take her point of view is to prevent the scarlet letter from doing its office. It leads us, as it did Hester, into conflict—compels us to choose between the reasons of the heart and the claims of institutions—and *that sort of* conflict is precisely what the letter is designed to eliminate.

I have in mind the distinction I made in the last chapter between oppositionalism and symbolic oppositions. Both are forms of process, and both may be identified as conflict; but oppositional process—the sort of conflict which I just said the letter seeks to eliminate—assumes a dialectic form. It derives from historical contradictions; it expresses a partiality we associate with ideological partisanship; the oppositions it makes visible reflect fundamental differences that force us to take positions, rather than to mediate (in Bancroft's sense) between them. Oppositional conflict issues in disruptions and discontinuities: feudal hierarchy against liberal democracy; monotheism against polytheism; one set of credal certainties or economic interests against another. Symbolic oppositions, as we have seen, are the agents of continuity. For Hawthorne they become a form of process designed to avoid or circumvent conflict. We might see it as a partiality that recognizes its own limitations, acknowledges its own incompleteness, seeks to grow by accommodating the partial interests of others, and so tends toward tolerance, pluralism, acquiescence, inaction.

The contrary tendency toward oppositionalism is the dark side of Hawthorne's chiaroscuro portrait of Hester. Her black eyes and hair—always a danger signal in Hawthorne's (culture's) symbolic system—are complemented, so to speak, by his relentless critical commentary on her every misstep into independence. We feel it the moment she crosses the prison threshold to his gently mocking "*as if* by her own *free-will*" (p. 162; my italics). We see it detailed in her radical speculations, when her mind wanders

> without rule or guidance, in a moral wilderness as vast, as intricate and shadowy, as the untamed forest. . . . Her intellect and heart had their home, as it were, in desert places, where she roamed as *freely* as the wild Indian in his woods. . . . Shame, Despair, Solitude! These had been her teachers,—stern and wild ones,—and they had made her strong, but taught her much amiss. (p. 290; my italics)

This running gloss on the ways that the letter has not done its office reaches its nadir in her forest meeting with Dimmesdale. Amidst the fallen autumn leaves, Hester discards the A in a gesture of defiance for which (Hawthorne reminds us) her entire seven years had been the preparation. "The past is gone!" she exclaims. "With this symbol, I undo it all, and make it as it had never been!" (p. 292). And the narrator adds, with characteristic irony (characteristic among other things in that the irony borders on moralism):

> O exquisite relief! She had not known the weight, until she felt the *freedom*!. . . All at once, *as with* a sudden smile of heaven, Such was the sympathy of Nature—that wild, heathen Nature of the forest never subjugated by human law, nor illumined by higher truth— with the bliss of these two spirits! (pp. 292–293; my italics)

The radicalization of Hester Prynne builds on the politics of either/or. Hawthorne's symbolic method requires the politics of both/and. To that end, in the forest scene, Pearl keeps Hester from disavowing the office of the A, as earlier she had kept her from becoming another antinomian Anne or Witch Hibbins. Indeed, it is worth digressing for a moment to point out how closely for these purposes Pearl is bound to the A—with what painstaking care this *almost* purely anarchic figure is molded into a force for integration. Hawthorne details Pearl's restraining role with a consistency that verges on the allegorical. He sustains it through virtually all of her dialogues, with their notoriously emblematic "messages." And he reinforces this didactic-symbolic mode with his every definition of Pearl: as "imp" of the "perverse" *and* "pearl of great price," as "demon offspring," "Red Rose," "elf-child" and "mother's child" (Hester's "blessing" and "retribution" all in one); as the image simultaneously of "untamed nature" and the "angel of judgment," and, at the climactic election-day ritual, as (successively) "sin-born child," "witch-baby," the quintessential outsider who engages with and so weaves together all sections of the diverse holiday crowd—"even as a bright bird of plummage illuminates a whole tree of dusky foliage"— and finally the fully "human" daughter who breaks once and for all the "spell" of mutual isolation (pp. 208, 211, 210, 215, 202–203, 205, 330, 336, 339). Throughout this *development*—in effect our developing sense of Pearl as "the scarlet letter endowed with life"—Pearl serves increasingly to underscore what is wrong with Hester's radicalism, what remains "womanly" about Hester despite her manlike "freedom of speculation," and what sort of politics Hester must adopt if she is to help effect the changes that history calls for (pp. 204, 210, 259).

No other character in the novel, not even Hester, is potentially closer than Pearl is to representing utter discontinuity: the *broken* links between child and parent, between one generation and another, between the New World and the Old, between colonial and antebellum American history. And no other character in the novel, not even the shadowy Roger Chillingworth, is more carefully orchestrated into the narrative design, or more single-mindedly rendered a means of orchestration. Midway through the story, at the midnight scaffold, Hawthorne pointedly presents us with a *figura* of things to come: "there stood the minister, with his hand over his heart; and Hester Prynne, with the embroidered letter glimmering on her bosom; and little Pearl, herself a symbol, and the connecting link between these two" (p. 251). At the last scaffold scene Pearl kisses the minister, now openly her father at last, and Hawthorne remarks: "Towards her mother, too, Pearl's errand as a messenger of anguish was all fulfilled" (p. 339). And that office accomplished—by the one character, it will bear repeating, who might be imagined to offer an alternative vision in the novel—Hester can choose, in due time, to become the agent of her own domestication.

There is a certain irony here, to be sure, but it functions to *support* Hester's choice by reminding us of the burden of free will, when freedom is properly willed. Hawthorne writes of the fully humanized Pearl, the former "wild child" who has finally "developed all her sympathies," that she would no longer need to "do battle with the world, but [could] be a woman in it" (p. 339). It might be said of Hester upon her return that she can leave Pearl behind because she has taught herself to play Pearl to her own former Hester. She no longer needs restrictions because, after her long battle with the world, she has learned how to restrict herself—how to obviate the conflict between self and society, between the certainty of love and certain prospects of social change, between prophetic hope and things as they are; has learned, as a woman in the world, to deflect, defuse, or at least defer that inherently explosive conflict, and at best to transmute it, freely, into a faith that identifies continuity with progress.

This political level of meaning is closely connected to the moral. What I just called Hawthorne's politics of both/and is directly based upon his concept of truth. Critics often remark on the moral he draws from Dimmesdale's experience: "Be true! Be true! Be true!" (p. 341). But as usual with Hawthorne, this is hinged to the narrative by ambiguities. He tells us that he has culled the moral ("among many" others) from "a manuscript of old date" which he has "*chiefly* followed" (p. 341; my italics). And he prefaces the moral with a dazzling variety of reports about the scarlet letter (or the absence of it) on the minister's breast. For Hawthorne, partiality is to process what multiplicity is to truth—a series of limited perspectives whose effectiveness depends on their being partial without becoming exclusive, and partisan in such a way as gradually, by complementarity rather than conflict, to represent the whole.

Hawthorne's political meaning here points us toward the premises of liberal society; his historiographical meaning, toward the myth of continuing revolution. His moral meaning is grounded in the premises of Puritan thought. Behind the ambiguities of "Be true!" stands the complex Hobbist-Calvinist-Whig psychology of the Fall. *The Scarlet Letter* is a story of concealment and revelation, where the point of revelation is not to know the truth but to embrace many truths, and where concealment is not a crime, but a sin. Not crime, but sin: Hawthorne adopts this fine theological distinction for his own liberal purposes. A crime pertains to externals, and as a rule it involves others, as in the case of murder or adultery. A sin pertains to the spiritual and internal, to an act of will. It may or may not involve crime, just as a crime (murder, for example, or adultery) *may* not involve sin. It depends on the inner cause, the motive. The issue, that is, is guilt, not shame: not the deceiving of others, but the skewing of one's own point of view. The political office of the A is to make oppositionalism an agent of reciprocity. Its moral office is to lead from the willful self-blinding of a truth—paradigmatically, a truth of one's own—to the redemptive vision of many possible truths.

In the novel's next to last chapter, that office is rendered (as the chapter title tells us] through "The Revelation of the Scarlet Letter" (p. 332). The action centers on the scaffold, as it does twice previously. The first time is at Hester's midday "public exposure" (p. 172), where the A denotes various kinds of division (within the community, within Dimmesdale, and most dramatically between Hester and the community). The second scaffold scene comes midway through the novel, in the midnight meeting which draws the main characters together, and by implication the townspeople as well, for the A that flashes across the night sky lights up the entire town "with the distinctness of mid-day . . . [lending] another moral interpretation to the things of this world than they had ever borne before . . . as if [this] . . . were the light that is to reveal all secrets, and the daybreak that shall unite all who belong to one another" (p. 251). In short, the novel tends increasingly toward reconciliation through a series of ambiguous unveilings, each of which might be titled "The Revelation of the Scarlet Letter." In that penultimate chapter, Dimmesdale reconciles himself with his guilt, with Pearl, with Hester, with Chillingworth, and, in "words of flame," with the destiny of New Israel (p. 332). Now it only remains for Hester to join the telos in process. When she does so, in the Conclusion, her moral reinterpretation of things past and future may be seen to reverse her first misstep across the prison threshold. Indeed, the scene deliberately echoes that initiation into concealment so as emphatically to invert it. When Hester returns, she pauses "on the threshold" of her old home— as many years before she had paused "on the threshold of the prison door"—long enough to display to the onlookers a scarlet letter on her breast (pp. 162, 343). It is a nice instance of liminality serving its proper conservative function at last. Then, at the start of her trials, Hester had repelled the beadle, representative of "the Puritanic code of law" (p. 162), so as to assert "her own free-will." Now she returns as representative of the need for law and the limits of free will. Having abandoned the hope of erasing the past, Hester internalizes the past in all its shame and sorrow. Kafka's Penal Colony requires the fatal mechanism of authority in order to make the prisoner accept his guilt; Hester preempts the colonial mechanism by authorizing her own punishment and inscribing her guilt upon herself. In a gesture which *both* declares her independence *and* honors her superiors, she re-forms herself, voluntarily, as the exemplar of social order.

This moral design parallels the political process I outlined, but with an important difference. Hester's radicalism sets her apart, and sustains her marginality to the end. The sin she commits (her double act of concealment, first of her lover, then of her husband) links her to everyone else. She is unique as a rebel, but typical as a liar. Indeed, telling lies is the donnée of the novel as for the Puritans the prison is the donnée of their venture in utopia. It establishes the terms of human possibility in an adulterated world. Directly or indirectly—as deception, concealment, or hypocrisy, through silence (in Hester's case), cunning (in Chillingworth's), eloquence (in Dimmesdale's), or perversity (in Pearl's)—lies constitute the very ground and texture of community in *The Scarlet Letter*. This is not *simply* evil. All of Hawthorne's main characters are good people trapped by circumstance, all are helping others in spite of themselves, and all are doing harm for what might justifiably be considered the best of reasons: Hester for love, Dimmesdale for duty, the Puritan magistrates for moral order. Even Chillingworth, that least ambiguous of villains, is essentially a good man who has been wronged, who lies in order to find the truth, who prods his victim to confess (partly, Hawthorne suggests, through love), and who, in leaving his wealth to Pearl (gratuitously), provides the basis for whatever there is of a happy ending to the story.

Hawthorne owes this *complex* view of evil, good and evil entwined—the "power of blackness" heightened by the pervasive if sometimes oblique power of light—to Puritan theology. As the *New England Primer* put it, Adam's Fall did much more than fell us all. It also brought the promise of grace through Christ, the Second Adam. Justice *and* mercy, law *and* love: from these twin perspectives, the Puritans built the scaffold and imposed the A. Restrictions were necessary because the Fall had sundered the affections from the intellect, set the truths of the heart at odds with the truths of the mind. Now only faith could reconcile the two kinds of truth. They who bound themselves to a single view, *either* justice *or* mercy, were entering into a Devil's pact. They were committing themselves to a lie by concealing a part of reality from themselves, including the reality of the self in all its ambiguity, both human and divine. Hence the degeneration of Chillingworth, "demon of the intellect" (p. 321), and of Dimmesdale, until he manages to harmonize the minister's gospel of love with the lover's self-punishment. Hence, too, Pearl's fragmented identity: she is a shifting collage of retribution and love, seeking integration. And hence the reciprocal movement of Hester and the community, from opposition to mutuality. As she acts the sister of mercy toward those who merely judged her, and so judged too harshly, Hester increasingly touches the people's "great and warm heart" (p. 226). At the end, after she has passed judgment on herself, Hester gains a fuller, more generous vision of reality than she dreamed possible in the forest. Then, it was love with a consecration of its own. Now her love has the consecration of justice, morality, and community.

I rehearse this familiar pattern in order to point out that nothing in it is random or arbitrary. Not a single aspect of all this apparent multiplicity (reversals, revisions, diverse points of view) permits free choice. Hawthorne's celebrated evasiveness comes accompanied with a stern imperative. Penitence, he would urge us, has more substance than the absolutism of either/or. Drab though it seems, the morality of both/and augments personal vision by grounding it in the facts of experience. It takes more *courage* to compromise. It is a greater act of *self-assertion* to recognize our limits—to "be true" to what we most deeply are while admitting the fragmentary quality of our truth—to keep faith in our boldest convictions, while acknowledging the incompleteness of those convictions—and so to discipline ourselves, of our "own free-will," to the pluralist forms of progress.

It amounts to a code of liberal heroics. Hawthorne's focus is first and last upon the individual; his emphasis on perspective assumes faith in ambiguity; and his ambiguities compel resolution through the higher laws of both/and. Through those higher laws we learn how to sustain certain ideals *and* to deny the immediate claims of their certainty upon us; how to possess the self by being self-possessed—which is to say, how to hold the self intact by holding it in check—and from both these perspectives, how voluntarily to embrace gradualism and consensus, in the expectation that gradually, "when the world should have grown ripe for it," consensus will yield proximate justice for the community, and for the individual the prospect of unadulterated love.

The prospect leads from the moral to the aesthetic level of the novel. Again, Hawthorne himself provides the link—in this case through the parallel he assumes between moral bivalence and symbolic ambiguity. Consider the title he gives to that chapter midway through the novel. "Another View of Hester" means an inside view of her secret radicalism; it also means a public view of Hester, through her acts of charity, which in turn involves a distinction between the view of the many, who consider her "angelic," and the view of the few, "the wise and learned men" who were reluctant to give up earlier "prejudices" (p. 257). "Another view" means a true sight of Hester, as she really is (rather than as she appears), *and* it means a glimpse of Hester in medias res, in the process of development. Above all, it means another view in the sense of differences of interpretation: interpretation in the form of rumor and legend (the A that magically protects Hester "amid all peril"); interpretation as a mode of sacralization (the A as a nun's cross); interpretation as agent of social change; interpretation as vehicle of manipulation (Hester "never raised her head to receive their greeting. If they were resolute to accost her, she laid her finger on the scarlet letter, and passed on. This might be pride, but was so like humility that it produced all the softening effects of the latter quality on the public mind"); and of course interpretation as the avenue to multiple meanings—the A as sign of infamy, pillow for the sick, shield against Indian arrows, "glittering" and "fantastic" work of art (pp. 257–258, 255).

All this and more. No critical term is more firmly associated with *The Scarlet Letter* than ambiguity. What has not been adequately remarked, and questioned, is the persistent, almost pedantic pointedness of Hawthorne's technique. F. O. Matthiessen defined Hawthorne's ambiguity as "the device of multiple-choice,"[2] And so it is, if we recognize this as a device for enclosure and control. That strategy may be traced on every page of the novel, from start to finish, in Hawthorne's innumerable directives for interpretation: from the wild rose he presents to his readers in Chapter One—in a virtuoso performance of multiple choice that is meant to preclude choice (for it instructs us *not* to choose between the local flower, the figural passion flower, and the legacy of the ambiguously "sainted Anne Hutchinson")—from that symbolic rose to the heraldic device with which the novel ends: the "engraved escutecheon" whose endlessly interpretable design (one "ever-glowing point of light *gloomier* than the shadow" but a source of relief nonetheless) "*might* serve for a motto *or* brief description of our now concluded tale" (p. 345; my italics). Concluded *then* but, by authorial direction, *now* in process, a prod to our continuing speculations. The "curious investigator may still discern [it]," Hawthorne remarks, "and perplex himself with the purport" (p. 345)—and the interplay between our perplexity and its purport, like that between process and telos in the description of the rose ("It *may* serve, let us hope, to symbolize *some* sweet moral blossom, that *may* be found along the track, *or* relieve the darkening close of a tale of human frailty and suffering")—tells us that meaning, while indefinite, is neither random nor arbitrary, but gradual, cumulative, and increasingly comprehensive (p. 159; my italics).

The Scarlet Letter is an interpreter's guide into perplexity. As critics have long pointed out, virtually every scene in the novel is symbolic, virtually every symbol demands interpretation, and virtually every interpretation takes the form of a question that opens out into a variety of possible answers, none of them entirely wrong, and none in itself satisfactory. But the result (to repeat) is neither random nor arbitrary. It is a strategy of pluralism—issuing, on the reader's part, in a mystifying sense of multiplicity—through which each set of questions and answers is turned toward the same solution: all meanings are partly true; hence interpreters must choose as many parts as possible of the truth, and/or as many truths as they can possibly find in the symbol.

Let me illustrate this through the single most straightforward instance of choice in the novel. Describing Hester's "sad transformation" (midway through the story) Hawthorne remarks that her "rich and luxuriant hair had either been cut off, or was . . . completely hidden by the cap" (p. 259). For once, it seems, we have a plain truth to discover. Something has been hidden, a question about it raised, we await the moment of disclosure—and that moment reveals, of course, in "a flood of sunshine" (p. 292), that Hester had *not* cut off her hair. But of course, too, Hawthorne means us to recognize that in some sense she *had*—had cut off her "essential womanhood," had cut herself off from community, had cut away her natural luxuriance of character by willfully hiding it beneath an Odysseus's cloak of conformity. These are metaphors, not facts. But in Hawthorne's ambiguous world, a main function of choice is to blur the commonsense lines between metaphor and fact; and nowhere is that blurring process better demonstrated than at the moment of revelation, during her forest meeting with Dimmesdale, when Hester discards the A:

> By another impulse, she took off the formal cap that confined her hair; and down it fell upon her shoulders, dark and rich, with at once

a shadow and a light in its abundance, and imparting the charm of softness to her features. There played around her mouth, and beamed out of her eyes, a radiant and tender smile, that *seemed* gushing from the very heart of womanhood. . . . Her sex, her youth, and the whole richness of her beauty, came back from *what men call* the irrevocable past. (pp. 292–293; my italics)

Shadow and light, seemed and was, irrevocable and renewed, womanhood cut off/hidden/lost/restored: *The Scarlet Letter* is a novel of endless points of view which together conspire to deprive us of choice. We are enticed by questions so that we can be allowed to see the polarity between seeking *the* answer, any single answer, and undertaking an interpretation. The option is never one thing or another; it is all or nothing. We are offered an alternative not between different meanings, but between finding meaning or creating distortions; and it is meaning in that processual, pluralistic, and therefore (we are asked to believe) progressivist sense which Hester opts for when she returns to New England.

In that option lies the moral-aesthetic significance of Hawthorne's re-presentation of crime as sin. Crime involves social transgression, as in a detective story, which centers on the discovery of the criminal. Or more equivocally, it may involve a conflict of rights that must be decided one way or another, as in the tradition of the novel of adultery, which opposes the claims of the heart to those of civic order. Hawthorne makes use of both kinds of plot, only to absorb these—climactically, through Hester's return—into a story about the trials and triumphs of ambiguity. Through the office of the scarlet letter, all particulars of the criminal act, together with the conflicts they entail, dissolve and spiral into a series of enlarging reciprocities. We come to see that the issue is not a breach of commandment, but (as Hawthorne signals by the conspicuous absence from the novel of the word adultery) the gradual process by which we discern the purport of the broken law for ourselves; and we do so by turning speculation against the tendency either to take sides or to view conflicting sides as irreconcilable.

To re-present crime as sin is first of all to universalize the legal problem. It forces us to read a particular transgression in terms of innate human defects and the recurrent conflict of good and evil. But more largely it is to make the universal itself a curious object of interpretation—not in order to de-mystify it, not even to analyze it (in any strict cognitive sense), but on the contrary to invest it with richer significance and a more compelling universality. The ambiguities of *The Scarlet Letter* lead us systematically forward, from the political to the moral or religious to the aesthetic levels, toward what we are meant to understand is a series of broader and ampler meanings. *Always* ampler, and therefore at any given point indefinite—a *progression* of ambiguities whose tendency to expand in scope and depth is all the more decisive for the fact that the process occurs incrementally and in unexpected ways. The result is a liberal hierarchy of meaning: a series of unfoldings from simple to complex, "superficial" to "profound," which is as schematic, as comprehensive, and as coercive as the medieval fourfold system. Hawthorne's re-presentation of crime as sin requires us to remain vague about all issues of good-versus-evil (except the evils of oppositional partiality) in order to teach us that the Puritans' final, ambiguous view of Hester is deeper than the single-minded judgment reflected in the Governor's iron breastplate, just as her final, ambiguous position toward their bigotry opens the way for both personal and historical development.

I have been using the term *option* in connection with Hester's return in order to stress the overriding distinction in Hawthorne's "device of multiple-choice" between making choices and having choice. His point is not that Hester finally makes a choice against adultery. It is that she has no choice but to resume the A. To make choices involves alternatives; it requires us to reject or exclude on the ground that certain meanings are wrong or incompatible or mutually contradictory. To have choice (in Hawthorne's fiction) is to keep open the prospects for interpretation on the grounds that reality never means either one thing or another, but rather is meaning fragmented by plural points of view. For although the fragmentation is a source of many a "tale of frailty and sorrow," such as *The Scarlet Letter*, it is also, as *The Scarlet Letter* demonstrates, the source of an enriched sense of unity, provided we attend to the principles of liberal exegesis. And by these principles, to opt for meaning in all its multifariousness—to have your adulterous love and do the work of society too—is effectually to obviate the conflicts embodied in opposing views. More than that: it is to reconcile the contradictions implicit in the very act of personal interpretation between the fact of multiple meaning and the imperative of self-assertion.

In other words, to interpret is willfully, in the interests of

some larger truth, *not to choose*. Ambiguity is a function of pre-
scriptiveness. To entertain plural possibilities is to eliminate possible divisions. We are forced to find meaning in the letter, but we
cannot choose one meaning out of many: Chillingworth's fate
cautions us against that self-destructive act of exclusion. Nor
can we choose to interpret any of the novel's uncertainties as
contradictions: the antagonism between Hester and the townspeople (or between Chillingworth and Dimmesdale, or between the
minister and his conscience) cautions us repeatedly against that
abuse of free will. What remains, then, is the alternative that
symbols are lies, that multiple choice is a mask for absence of
meaning, and the letter an arbitrary sign of transient social structures. And Hester's incipient nihilism cautions us at every turn
against that flight from responsibility: in the first scene, by her
instinctive attempt to conceal the letter; then, three years later,
by concealing its meaning from Pearl (to Hawthorne's suggestion
that "some new evil had crept into [her heart], or some old one
had never been expelled"); later, in the forest scene, by flinging
the letter "into infinite space" and drawing an (infinitely illusory)
"hour's free breath"; and finally, at the election-day ritual, by
gloating secretly at the prospect of its annihiliation, a prospect
that Hawthorne opens to her imagination so that (by absorbing it
into what the entire novel makes us think *must* be some larger,
truer interpretation) we can effectually exclude it *as an alternative* from ours (pp. 162, 274, 300).

If we refuse to do so—if we are tempted like Hester in the
forest to reject meaning, if we make Chillingworth's choice at the
scaffold against mercy, or Dimmesdale's in his "secret closet" (p.
242) for contradiction—then interpretation has not done its office.
And lest, like these characters, we find ourselves wandering in a
maze, Hawthorne points us toward the true path, midway in our
journey through the novel. In "Another View of Hester" he im-
presses upon us: (1) the need for personal interpretation; (2) the
inevitably partial nature of such interpretation; (3) the richly varied experiential bases of interpretation; (4) the tendency of these
partial and shifting interpretations to polarize into symbolic oppositions, like metaphor and fact, natural and supernatural, good
and evil, head and heart, concealment and revelation, fusion and
fragmentation; (5) the need to recognize that these polarities, because symbolic, are never an *oppositional* source of conflict, requiring alternative solutions, but instead always entwined in sym-

biotic antagonism and therefore mutually sustaining; and (6) as the key to it all, the *clavis symbolistica*, the need for faith both in the value of experience (shifting, private, and partial though it is) and in some ultimate hermeneutical complementarity, as in an ideal prospect that impels us toward an ever-larger truth.

That faith involves a *certain* activity on the reader's part. We need to make sense of the entire process for ourselves, so that the process may in turn make sense of our partial contributions. The text elicits personal response in order to allow each of us to contribute to the expanding continuum of liberal reciprocity. It is a hermeneutics designed to make subjectivity the primary agency of change while keeping the subject under control; and it accomplishes this double function by representing interpretation as multiplicity flowing naturally into consensus. For as oppositions interchange and fuse in the text, they yield a synthesis which is itself a symbol in process, an office not yet done. It is a richer symbol now than it was before, a higher office, but still veiled in the winding *perhapses, ors,* and *mights* that simultaneously open new vistas of meaning and dictate the terms of closure.

It may be helpful to distinguish this strategy from others to which it has been compared. Hawthorne does not deconstruct the A; he does not anticipate the principle of indeterminacy; he offers neither an aesthetics of relativism nor a dialectics of conflict. We might say that in some sense he is doing all of these things, but only in the sense that to do so is to dissipate the integral force of each. His purpose is to rechannel indeterminacy into pluralism, conflict into correspondence, and relativism into consensus. Insofar as terms such as "instability" and "self-reflexiveness" apply to *The Scarlet Letter,* they are agencies of a *certain* kind of interpretation, much as accident (in an older scheme) was said to be the agency of providence, or as private enterprise and self-interest were said to be agencies of the general good in antebellum America. Frank Kermode's claim for Hawthorne's modernity— "his texts . . . are meant as invitations to co-production on the part of the reader"—is accurate in a sense quite different from that which he intended. Kermode speaks of "a virtually infinite set of questions"; *The Scarlet Letter* holds out that mystifying prospect, much as Jacksonian liberals held out the prospect of infinite possibility, in order to implicate us as coproducers of meaning in a single, coherent moral-political-aesthetic design.[3]

This contrast pertains even more pointedly to Mikhail Bakhtin's concept of the dialogic imagination, which it has recently become fashionable to apply to American novels, and *The Scarlet Letter* in particular. Dialogics is the process by which a singular authorial vision unfolds as a "polphony" of distinct voices. It entails a sustained open-ended tension between fundamentally conflicting outlooks. *Conflicting* in the oppositional sense, because they are *not* partial reflections (such as good or evil) of a more complex truth, but, each of them, the expression of a separate, complex way of understanding. And *open-ended*, because tension is sustained not through incremental layers of meaning, but through the dynamics of diversity itself, which is by definition subversive of any culturally prescribed set of designs, including those of group pluralism. Bakhtin's dialogics deny telos through a "modernist" recognition of difference.[4] Hawthorne's ambiguities imply telos through the evasion of conflict. They are modernist in the sense of modern middle-class culture—which is to say, in their *use* of difference (including marginality, complexity, and displacement) for purposes of social cohesion.

We might term this the monologics of liberal ambiguity. It serves to mystify hierarchy as multiplicity, and diversity as harmony-in-process. Dialogics unsettles the link between process and closure. Hawthorne details the manifold discrepancies between process and closure in order to make discrepancy itself— incompleteness, concealment, the distance between penance and penitence—a vehicle of acculturation. He shows us that precisely by insisting on difference we can fuse an apparently (but not really) fragmented reality. Augustine's answer to Manichean dualism was to redefine evil as the absence of good. Hawthorne's answer to the threat of multiplicity is to redefine conflict as the absence of ambiguity—and ambiguity, therefore, as the absence of conflict.

Ambiguity is the absence of conflict: Hawthorne's logic is as simple in theory as it is complicated in application. Historical facts tend toward fragmentation; but ambiguity brings this tendency under control, gives it purpose and direction—makes it (in Bancroft's sense) continuous—by ordering the facts into general polarities. Fragmentation itself thus becomes a function of consensus. For, once the fragments have been ordered into polarities, the polarities can be multiplied ad infinitum, since each polarity entails or engenders other parallel, contrasting, or subsidiary sets of polarities. The process is one of endless variation upon a theme. And vice versa: it is a process of variation endlessly restricted to a single theme. In Hawthorne's world, all polarity is by definition ambiguous, all ambiguity is symbolic, and all symbols tend toward reconciliation.

Hence the distinctly narrowing effect of his technique, in spite of his persistent allusions and deliberate elusiveness. He himself wrote of *The Scarlet Letter* (to his publisher, James T. Fields, on Nov. 3, 1850) that since the novel was "all in one tone" it could have gone on "interminably."[5] We might reverse this to say that what makes the novel hermeneutically interminable also makes it formally and thematically hermetic. In that sustained counterpoint between endlessness and monotone lies the dynamic behind Hawthorne's model of pluralist containment. Process for him is a means of converting the *threat* of multiplicity (fragmentation, irreconcilability, discontinuity) into the pleasures of multiple choice, where the implied answer, "all of the above," guarantees consensus.

The process of conversion follows the symbolic logic of the scarlet letter. It is the office of the A to demonstrate that naturally, organically, pluralism tends to absorb differences into polar opposites, and that bipolarity, properly interpreted, tends of its own accord toward integration. So conceived, the monologics of ambiguity in *The Scarlet Letter* extend to structures of gender, religion, history, psychology, aesthetics, morality, epistemology. Perhaps the most basic of these pertains to the opposition between self and society. I said earlier that Hawthorne portrays Hester as an individualist of increasingly radical commitment. I might as well have said, a radical of increasingly individualist commmitment, for his aim is to counter the dangerously diverse social possibilities to which she has access, in fantasy or fact—Indian society, witch covens, Elizabethan hierarchy, Leveller and Ranter utopia (pp. 289, 313–330)—to bring all such unruly alternatives under control, rhetorically and hence morally and politically, by implicating them all under the symbol of the unrestrained self. No symbol was better calculated to rechannel dissent into the gradualism of process. And no symbol was more deeply rooted in the culture. As *The Scarlet Letter* reminds us, it served as a major Puritan strategy of socialization, through a process of inversion that typifies all such strategies. Society in this polar opposition became the symbol of unity, and the unsocialized self was designated the symbol of chaos unleashed—"sin, in all its branches," as the Reverend John Wilson details these in the first scaffold scene for "the poor culprit's" sake (p. 176). Or mutatis mutandis, the unsocialized self was a morass of "monstrous misconceptions," as John Winthrop labelled Anne Hutchinson, and society stood not just for legal order (as against antinomianism), but for Order at large—"the law of nature and the law of grace" (to quote Winthrop again) through which "we [are] knit . . . together as one man."[6]

In either case, the polarity of self and society remained central through the successive discourses of libertarianism, federalism, republicanism, and Jacksonian individualism. Its negative pressures, implicit in Hawthorne's reference to "the sainted Anne Hutchinson" (and explicit in his essay on "Mrs. Hutchinson")—as well as in recurrent charges of antinomianism against those who were said to have "sprung up under her footsteps" (p. 159), from Edwards through Emerson—are memorably conveyed in Tocqueville's contrast between "traditional" and "modern" modes of control: "The ruler no longer says: 'You must think as I do or die.' He says: 'You are free to think differently, and to retain your life, your property, and all that you possess; but from this day on you are a stranger among us'." Its positive form may be inferred from Edwin Chapin's midcentury election-day sermon, *The Relation of the Individual to the Republic*. The self, Chapin told his Boston audience, denotes "matters of *principle*," and society "matters of *compromise*," but in the American way of "self-government" (as nowhere else) this means "compromise not *of* principle but *for* principle."[7]

The Scarlet Letter is the story of a stranger who rejoins the community by compromising for principle; and her resolution has far-reaching implications about the symbolic structures of the American ideology. First, the only plausible modes of American opposition are those that center on the self: as stranger or prophet, rebel or revolutionary, lawbreaker or truth-seeker, or any other adversarial or dissenting form of individualism. Second, whatever good we imagine must emerge—and properly understood *has* emerged and is continuing to emerge—from the "country as it is, and things as they exist,"[8] conducive as those things are to independence, progress, and other norms of group pluralism. And third, radicalism has a place in society, after all, as the example of Hester demonstrates—radicalism, that is, in the American grain, defined through the ambiguities of both/and, consecrated by the tropes of theology ("heaven's time," "justice and mercy," "divine providence"), and interpreted through the polar unities at the heart of American liberalism—fusion and fragmentation, diversity as consensus, process through closure.

In that spirit of integration, Hester comes home to Puritan New England. Or rather, she comes home to the Puritan New England of antebellum America. For like the letter it imposes, Hawthorne's immigrant colony is a cultural artifact—a very sophisticated one, to be sure, and wonderfully embroidered, but woven nonetheless out of the same cultural cloth that by 1850 had produced the myth of the country's Puritan origins. Hawthorne's return to roots involves far more than a private genealogy. For all their flaws, his Hathorne forebears were part of a venture that he believed marked the first stage of American nationhood. It is no accident that Dimmesdale's sermon on the future celebrates the transition of government from John Winthrop to John Endicott. The unspoken link between the two governors is nothing less than the nationalist tradition that connects Hester to Hawthorne. It represents the unfolding process of American self-determination, from Winthrop, the *ur*-father, through Endicott, the *ur*-patriot, whose rending of "the Red Cross from New England's banner" (Hawthorne writes elsewhere) was "the first omen of that deliverance which our fathers consummated" in 1776.[9]

These are the mythic Puritans canonized by Bancroft. They had a rich and varied life before him, from Mather through Edwards, and an even more important career after him in American historiography. At midcentury, they provided a crucial contrast in process between the Old World and the New.* Basically, it was a contrast between recurrence and progress, told as a tale of two Puritan uprisings in the early sixteen hundreds. The first of these conceived the Puritan exodus to the New World: a revolution for liberty that offered a model of progress by harnessing the energies

---

*The basic terms of contrast seem to have been established by Bancroft; but they may be discerned everywhere in the literature, and particularly in the writings of Hawthorne's circle: among others, New York's cultural pundit, Evert Duyckinck, a founder of the Young America movement and Hawthorne's major advocate in the literary world; the country's leading poet, Henry Wadsworth Longfellow, Hawthorne's lifelong friend and his first important reviewer; and the manifest destinarian John Louis O'Sullivan, Hawthorne's main publisher in the 1840s and godfather to his first child, Una. (Bancroft was a friend as well, of course, and helped secure Hawthorne's appointment at the Salem Custom House.)

of radicalism to the process of settlement, consolidation, and expansion. The Old World counterpart was the Puritan rebellion (1642–1649) that failed. Hawthorne suggests the reason for failure in his essay on Cromwell, which relates a "strange accident" in Cromwell's infancy, when a "huge ape, which was kept in the family, snatched up little Noll [as Oliver was nick-named] in his forepaws and clambered with him to the roof of the house. . . . The event was afterwards considered an omen that Noll would reach a very elevated station in the world."[10]

It is a parable for the embittered young radical whose clambering "enthusiasm of thought" (p. 260) Hawthorne details in that multi-faceted midway chapter, "Another View of Hester":

> [This] was an age in which the human intellect, newly emancipated, had taken a more active and wider range than for many centuries before. Men of the sword had overthrown nobles and kings. Men bolder than these had overthrown and rearranged—not actually, but within the sphere of theory, which was their most real abode—the whole system of ancient prejudice, wherewith was linked much of ancient principle. Hester Prynne imbibed this spirit. She assumed a freedom of speculation, then common enough on the other side of the Atlantic, but which our forefathers, had they known of it, would have held to be a deadlier crime than that stigmatised by the scarlet letter. In her lonesome cottage by the sea-shore, thoughts visited her, such as dared to enter no other dwelling in New England; shadowy guests . . . perilous as demons. (p. 259)

The key word is "forefathers." It carries the entire force of the ideological contrast I discussed in the last chapter: on one hand, the English Puritan rebels and all they prefigured, including what Hawthorne calls "the terrorists of France" (p. 165); on the other hand, the Puritans who preserved "ancient principle" (along with "ancient prejudice") and whose broad reforms, therefore, fathered the New World process that eventuated in national independence. This symbolic polarity, in which the Old World figures as social, moral, and spiritual antagonist to progress, pervades Jacksonian writing. It applies as such directly to what Hawthorne recalled in 1852 as the era of "The Compromise."[11] His return to Puritan New England in The Scarlet Letter joins two historical time frames: first, the fictional time frame, 1642–1649, with its implied contrast between models of revolt (recurrent violence in the Old

World, organic progress in the New); and second, the authorial time frame, 1848–1852, with its ominous explosion of conflict at home and abroad.

The "red year Forty-Eight," as Melville recalled it in *Clarel*, brought "the portent and the fact of war, / And terror that into hate subsides." He was referring to the series of revolutions from which Europe's kings "fled like the gods" (although by 1852 "even as the gods / . . . return they made, and sate / And fortified their strong abodes"). But he might have been referring as well to what New England conservatives considered an ominous tendency toward confrontation following the victory of the Whigs. The presidency of James Polk (1845–1849) was a high point of antebellum chauvinism. Mexico had been defeated (yielding the spoils of California, Texas, and New Mexico); the Oregon Territory appropriated (along with Nevada, Arizona, Colorado, and parts of Utah); record waves of immigrants absorbed; gold discovered in the West; the entire Great Lakes region (including several million acres of "open" land, "confiscated from the Indians"); Florida, Texas, Iowa, and Wisconsin admitted to the Union; and plans devised to extend "commercial and territorial advantages beyond the continent," to Yucatán, Cuba, Hawaii, China.[12]

Then in 1848 Polk's unexpected defeat called attention to long-festering internal divisions. We can see in retrospect how both tendencies, toward expansion and toward confrontation—"unprecedented expansion," "irreconcilable conflict"—expressed the same process of ideological consolidation. But for a good many of the disempowered Democrats these tensions of process evoked the "terrors of a European conflagration." It is no accident that Hawthorne would have connected the revolutions abroad with his loss of tenure at the Salem Customs House. As recent scholarship has demonstrated, he links both sets of events in the alternative title he offers for the novel, "THE POSTHUMOUS PAPERS OF A DECAPITATED SURVEYOR" (p. 156), and the political innuendoes are expanded from "The Custom-House" Introduction to the novel at large, in the recurrent imagery of 1848–1849 revolutions, including allusions to scaffold and guillotine.[13]

The authorial time frame, then, opens with the Year of the Red Scare: Chartist agitation in England, the First Paris Commune, *The Communist Manifesto*, and widespread revolt in

France, Austria, Germany, Belgium, Prussia, Poland, Bohemia, Rumania, Denmark, Ireland, Italy, Czechoslovakia, and Hungary. Americans at first welcomed what they interpreted as "wars of independence, like ours, against the despot and royal tyrant." But after a brief period of euphoria, when it seemed that events were proving (in George Duyckinck's words) that "our country leads the world," public opinion turned decisively against the radicals. Those who did the turning expressed disillusionment in various ways, but common to all was the contrast I described earlier between American and European revolution, as between gradual progress and recurrent violence. By spring 1848, Evert Duyckinck informed his brother George that New Yorkers associated the "agitation" with "recollections of . . . Robespierre"; shortly after, Bancroft reported that it had Boston "frightened out of its wits"; by early 1849 American conservatives concluded that "Republics cannot grow on the soil of Europe." Worse still, they had already observed the incipient effect in America itself of European conflict: the "foreboding shadows" (as one journalist put it) of "Communism, Socialism, Pillage, Murder, Anarchy, and the Guillotine vs. Law and Order, Family and Property." Bancroft at first tried to calm his conservative friends—"these insurrections," he urged, were "the echo of American Democracy . . . from France, and Austria, and Prussia, and all Old Germany," and might actually "stir up the hearts of the American people to new achievements"—but he soon conceded that events were tending in just the opposite direction: geographically, from the Old World to the New, and morally from liberty to license.[14]

License took many forms, as these antebellum Jeremiahs detailed its invasion of America. A sinister "infusion of European Socialism," they charged, was corroding "the Christian republicanism of America": "speculatists who have recently attempted to turn the world upside down . . . have [now] come hither"— "ultraists [who], attempting to advance men in truth and goodness, begin by destroying what of these they already possess"; "radicals [who seek] . . . not merely to lop off diseased branches, but for the sake of getting rid of these to uproot . . . the tree itself"; "Red Republicans" who hope to institute "the principles of the Terrorists . . . on this side of the Atlantic also," and so to "overturn the laws of . . . civilization . . . the tribunal of reason, and the voice of the natural conscience."[15] Hawthorne may be said to condense these and similar charges in his overview of Hester's nihilism:

> She had wandered, without rule or guidance, in a moral wilderness
> . . . [and] looked from her estranged point of view at human institu-
> tions, and whatever priests or legislators had established; criticizing
> all with hardly more reverence than the Indian would feel for the
> clerical band, the judicial robe, the pillory, the gallows, the fireside
> or the church. The tendency of her fate and fortune had been to set
> her free. *The scarlet letter was her passport into regions where other
> women dared not tread.* Shame, Despair, Solitude! These had been
> her teachers,—stern and wild ones,—and they had made her strong,
> but taught her much amiss. (p. 290; my italics)

The taboo regions to which Hawthorne refers had an especially ominous meaning for antebellum conservatives. By virtually all accounts (from the highbrow *North American Review* to
the evangelical *Biblical Repertory*), the most pernicious heresies
of the European Forty-Eight pertained to the domestic sphere.
Striking at the very nexus of social order and spiritual values,
the radicals were advocating "the abrogation of the family, the
breaking up of the fireside circle." They were seeking nothing less
than "to *emancipate* woman, by making her independent of man,"
thus "giving her up to follow her passions" and "making a rule of
adultery." And precisely this heresy, through which "all old laws,
all ancient morals are nullified," seemed to be gathering most
force in the United States.[16] The "regions where . . . women dared
not tread" had of course long been open territory to *male* terrorists,
not only on the continent but in England, from the early-seven-
teenth-century antinomians to the Chartists of 1848. Even there,
however, women had usually restrained themselves because (in
Hawthorne's account) they intuited that to indulge the "tendency
to speculation"—to be "set free" *as women* "without rule or
guidance, in a moral wilderness" beyond "Law and Order, Family
and Property"—would be to alter their very "natures." It would
drain them of the "ethereal essence, wherein [woman] has her
truest life."

This explanation directly precedes Hawthorne's reminder
that "The scarlet letter had not done its office"; it deserves to be
quoted at length, as offering the single most detailed account
we have of Hester's secret radical thoughts (as well as the most
sustained preview of her final vision of womanhood, after the
letter has served its *proper* office as passport back into New England history):

[A] dark question often rose into her mind, with reference to the whole race of womanhood. Was existence worth accepting, even to the happiest among them? . . . A tendency to speculation, though it may keep woman quiet, as it does man, yet makes her sad. She discerns, it may be, such a hopeless task before her. As a first step, the whole system of society is to be torn down, and built up anew. Then, the very nature of the opposite sex, or its long hereditary habit, which has become like nature, is to be essentially modified, before woman can be allowed to assume what seems a fair and suitable position. Finally, all other difficulties being obviated, woman cannot take advantage of these preliminary reforms, until she herself shall have undergone a still mightier change, in which, perhaps, the ethereal essence, wherein she has her truest life, will be found to have evaporated. A woman never overcomes these problems by any exercise of thought. They are not to be solved, or only in one way. If her heart chance to come uppermost, they vanish. (pp. 260–261)

These were not problems that exercised Anne Hutchinson or Witch Hibbins. Nor did they vex the bold theorists of Cromwell's England. But for Hawthorne, we may assume, those radicals were implicated in the unnatural reforms that Hester contemplates, and her contemplations in turn reflected the "unhealthy" feminism which he had encountered in 1841 at Brook Farm (a prerevolutionary instance, so to speak, of the invasion of European radical ideas) and which he was shortly to mock in *The Blithedale Romance* (1852).*

---

*To some extent this also includes the prophetic Hester at the end. Insofar as she retains her old rebellious ways, Hester may be said to reflect the image (widely ridiculed in the midcentury press) of the radical female "angel" who would announce the coming revolution; some self-styled *"Woman-Messiah"* who would presume "to reveal the laws . . . of the future" (Anon., "Societary Theories," *American Whig Review* VII [June, 1848], 640)—or in the words of Albert Brisbane's Fourierist manifesto, "the fully developed . . . independent woman . . . noble, pure and elevated," who would settle once and for all the "most delicate and intricate question" of "the human relation" ("The American Associationists," *United States Magazine and Democratic Review*, XVIII [February, 1846], 146–147). But by the end Hester has largely overcome such "vain imaginings"—has incorporated and transmuted them in a vision of continuity. In this larger sense, her prophecy might be related to the statue of "Liberty" sculpted by Hiram Powers, upon whom Hawthorne modelled Kenyon, the artist-hero of *The Marble Faun*. Powers began work on the statue in Florence in 1848; by 1852 he was lamenting the misfortune of creating the "goddess of Liberty in this land of . . . anarchy"— "but" he added, "as she is not likely to remain here very long it is to be hoped that she will not

We may assume, further, that Hawthorne's emphasis on the "dark question . . . of womanhood" was grounded in an event of 1848 which brought all of these radical continuities into focus for him. During the summer of that year, soon after the Women's March for Bread at Versailles, the first American Women's Rights Convention opened at Seneca Falls. It was quickly designated the most alarming symptom to date of the "Red plague of European revolution" in America; and more specifically, the plague of "the Red Republicans of our own day . . . [who] have found preachers and proselytes on this side of the Atlantic also." According to social commentators, reports of "the female 'Reds' of Europe" had already "appalled the American public," and from pulpit, press, and political platform spokesmen for order and due process rushed to make the connection:

> This is the age of revolutions. To whatever part of the world the attention is directed, the political and social fabric is crumbling to pieces; and changes which far exceed the wildest dreams of the enthusiastic Utopians of the last generation, are now pursued with ardor and perseverance. The principal agent, however, that has hitherto taken part in these movements has been the rougher sex . . . [and] though it is asserted that no inconsiderable assistance was contributed by the gentler sex to the late sanguinary carnage at Paris, we are disposed to believe that such a revolting imputation proceeds from base calumniators, and is a libel upon woman.
>
> By the intelligence, however, which we have lately received, the work of revolution is no longer confined to the Old World, nor to the masculine gender. The flag of independence has been hoisted, for the second time, on this side of the Atlantic; and a solemn league and covenant [as Cromwell termed the 1642 union of Scotland, Ireland, and England] has just been entered into by a Convention of

---

carry the infection [of European revolution] . . . with her to *America, where . . . her doctrine is received as gospel.*" Powers called the statue *America*, and Hawthorne, who urged Pierce to purchase it for the Capitol, approved the title, since "it embodies the ideas of youth, freedom, progress." The sculptor himself, he noted, was not only "a great artist," but "very American," and his work reflected this: "a female figure . . . vigorous, beautiful, planting its foot lightly on a broken chain and pointing upward." (*French and Italian Notebooks*, vol. XIV of *Works*, The Centenary Edition, ed. Thomas Woodson [Columbus, Ohio, 1980], 436; Jean Fagan Yellin, "Caps and Chains: Hiram Powers' Statue of Liberty," *American Quarterly*, XXXVIII [1986], 798–826).

Women at Seneca Falls. . . . [But these women] seem to be really in earnest in their aim at revolution, and . . . evince confidence that [in the words of the *Marseillaise*] "the day of their deliverance is at hand."[17]

Surely Hawthorne means us to hear the strains of this American *Marseillaise*, this Cromwellian Feminists' Pact, in Hester's "stern and wild" irreverence (as indeed one of the novel's first reviewers pointed out, and blamed him for embodying it in so strong a character). And surely, too, Hawthorne's overall critique of Hester's radicalism—from her bitter sense of herself as "martyr" to her self-conscious manipulation of the townspeople and outright scorn for all "human institutions," "whatever priests or legislators had established" (pp. 259–260, 290)—registers the reaction against the rising European "carnage" and its "revolting" influence "on this side of the Atlantic."* That reaction included all five major writers of F. O. Matthiessen's *American Renaissance*, in spite of their common devotion to "the possibilities of . . . democracy." Indeed, of all of Hawthorne's acquaintances only one, Margaret Fuller, gave her full support to the European revolutionaries, and it has been argued persuasively that she figures not

---

*The connection noted earlier to Anne Hutchinson, or rather to Hawthorne's sketch of "Mrs. Hutchinson" [*Works*, Riverside Edition, ed. George Parsons Lathrop [Boston, 1883], XII, 217–226] is relevant here: first, in the de-feminization of Hester (when a woman follows her own bent she "should be aware that she is relinquishing a part of the loveliness of her sex"); then, in the threat it poses to society, which Hawthorne associates with the "numerous . . . fair authors of our own day":

> there are portentous indications, changes gradually taking place in the habits and feelings of the gentle sex, which seem to threaten our posterity with many of those public women, whereof one was a burden too grievous for our fathers. . . . The evil is likely to be a growing one. As yet, the great body of American women are a domestic race; but when a continuance of ill-judged incitements shall have turned their hearts away from the fireside, there are obvious circumstances which will render female pens more numerous and more prolific than those of men. . . .

Finally, and most broadly, the connection to Anne Hutchinson is relevant in the allusions to revolution through the link that Hawthorne recalls between Hutchinson and Sir Henry Vane, governor at the time the antinomian trials opened, who returned to England to become an important figure under Cromwell: "In his mysterious eyes we may read a dark enthusiasm, akin to that of the woman whose cause he has espoused, combined with a shrewd worldly foresight, which tells him that her doctrines will be productive of change and tumult, the elements of his power and delight."

only in the ill-fated Zenobia of *The Blithedale Romance*, but, together with her allegedly illegitimate child (the gossip of Brahmin New England in 1849), in his portrait of the tormented radical, Hester Prynne. If so, it might be regarded as something of a Hawthornesque irony that Fuller returned from Europe "possessed," as she put it, "of a great history"—convinced of the importance of "social struggle" as against the consolations of prophecy—and that she drowned within sight of the lifeboats grounded on the American shore.[18]

That was in 1850, which I take to be the centerpiece of the novel's authorial time frame. It was the year of the Compromise Resolutions, including the Fugitive Slave Act, and of *The Scarlet Letter*. Eighteen fifty-two marks the close of this period, with the return of Hawthorne's political fortune through the election to the presidency of his friend Franklin Pierce. Hawthorne did his share by writing the official campaign biography, where he extols Pierce as "the statesman of practical sagacity—who loves his country *as it is*, and evolves good from things *as they exist*"—and he defends Pierce's support of the Fugitive Slave Act by comparing the abolitionists, indirectly, to Europe's "Red Republicans." The indirection suggests a political balancing act, somewhat like the Compromise Bill itself: Hawthorne did not want to alienate those of Pierce's Young America supporters who persisted in identifying European insurrection with the claims of American expansionism. (Besides, Louis Kossuth was then touring the United States, and although Hawthorne himself felt "about as enthusiastic as a lump of frozen mud," he had to acknowledge the popularity of the Hungarian revolutionary leader.) Still, the comparatist implications in the Pierce biography are unmistakable. Hawthorne charges that, like the "terrorists of France," the abolitionists are hell-bent on chaos: they would tear "to pieces the Constitution" and sever "into distracted fragments that common country which Providence brought into one nation, through a continued miracle of almost two hundred years, from the first settlement of the American wilderness until the Revolution."[19]

As critics are coming increasingly to recognize, the Civil War provides the latent context of the American Renaissance. *Moby-Dick*, *The Narrative of Frederick Douglass*, and *Uncle Tom's Cabin* (as well as Cooper's apocalyptic last novel, *The Crater*) all deal more or less directly with loomings of national cataclysm.

The visions of transcendent unity in *Walden, Leaves of Grass*, and *Eureka* all depend on a utopianism—utopian nostalgia in Thoreau's case, utopian futurism in Whitman's, dystopian metaphysics in Poe's—which circumvents or submerges the actual divisions of the time. Considered together with the popular sentimental and gothic novels of the time, these works provide a multivocal narrative of American liberalism during a crucial period of its formation. The special position of *The Scarlet Letter* in this narrative may be inferred from its centrist strategy: it employs sentimental themes and gothic techniques in order to mediate between utopian and dystopian resolutions; and as we have seen, its return to cultural origins speaks to the threat of fragmentation while proposing the benefits of gradualism.

From that centrist perspective, we might well read Hester's counsel (after the letter has done its office) as a preview of Hawthorne's answer to the abolitionists. Slavery, he explains in the Pierce biography, is "one of those evils which divine Providence does not leave to be remedied by human contrivances, but which, in its own good time, by some means impossible to be anticipated, but of the simplest and easiest operation, when all its uses shall have been fulfilled, it causes to vanish like a dream."[20] Only the security of the commonplace could allow for this daring inversion in logic, whereby slavery is represented, symbolically, as part of the "continued miracle" of America's progress. Like the scarlet letter, Hawthorne's argument has the power of a long-preserved cultural artifact.

But of course the two artifacts are different in kind. The argument in the biography reflects a certain tactic of the culture; its power derives from a system of ideas connecting racism and progress. The power of the scarlet letter derives from its capacities for mediation. It reveals the variety of tactics available to the culture at a certain historical moment. And as I have noted, antebellum culture was particularly volatile—in the sense not of transition, but of consolidation: volatility redirected into channels of social growth. It was a culture feeding on change, nourished by technological innovation, urbanization, commercial growth, territorial expansion, shifts of power centers, and waves of immigration; and as a symptom of its increasing confidence, accommodating itself to new conditions by moving toward a resolution by violence of its major internal conflict. To call Hawthorne's racism a cultural tactic is not to condone it, but to distinguish the biography from the novel. Considered as part of an intracultural debate, Hawthorne's response to the Fugitive Slave Act differs dramatically from that of abolitionists like Emerson and Stowe. As Henry James pointed out,

> Hawthorne was a democrat, and apparently a zealous one; even in his later years, after the Whigs had vivified their principles by the adoption of the Republican platform, and by taking up an honest attitude on the question of slavery, his political faith never wavered. His Democratic sympathies were eminently natural, and there would have been an incongruity in his belonging to the other party.[21]

But incongruity is not contradiction; and if we step outside the boundaries of intracultural debate, the difference between Hawthorne's "natural" Democratic allegiances and the "vivified" Whig platform he opposed reflects something else entirely: a series of no-longer-avoidable conflicts within a system whose principles and prejudices (including racism and American exceptionalism) were shared by virtually all parties, and (though not equally) by Whigs and Democrats alike. *The Life of Pierce* advances what turned out to be an inadequate mode of conflict resolution. *The Scarlet Letter* expresses a particular culture's mode of resolving crisis. It is not that the novel transcends propaganda. It is that its imaginative forms incorporate the complexity of beliefs implicit in any single-minded doctrine we commonly associate with propaganda. Hawthorne's biography is based on partisan issues; it takes a certain stand within an enclosed set of options and advances a particular course of action, out of several then available to the culture. His novel explores various options available within a set of interlinked forms of thought and expression. *The Life of Pierce* presents a certain choice. *The Scarlet Letter* represents a metaphysics of choosing. It advocates not a particular course of action, but a world view within which that course of action makes sense and takes effect.

We might call the novel thick propaganda. Its range of possibilities includes most forms of resolution generated by the antebellum North. To repeat the logic of Hester's vision (insofar as it prefigures the Pierce biography), injustice is to be removed by some "divine operation," which, however, has not yet done its office. This representation of contradiction as an ambiguity, or an absence-to-be, is not substantially different from the Liberian solution endorsed by Harriet Beecher Stowe, and enacted in the happy ending to *Uncle Tom's Cabin* by her mulatto hero, George Harris. Nor is it different in substance from the expansionist argument that to repeal the Fugitive Slave Act would revitalize the errand—would inspire the "children of the Puritans," as John Greenleaf Whittier wrote (echoing Dimmesdale's prophecy) to cross "the prairie as of old / The pilgrims crossed the sea" and thereby ("Upbearing like the Ark of old, / The Bible in our van") hasten "Freedom's holy Pentecost." Nor again is Hawthorne's solution different in substance from that proposed a decade later by those who believed *they* were the divine operation, providence incarnate, moving irresistibly toward the Armageddon of the Republic. In his debates with Douglas, Lincoln effectually reversed Hawthorne's argument—it was the anti-abolitionists, he charged, who were fragmenting the Union and subverting the fathers' legacy—and in his Second Inaugural Address (1865), reviewing the causes of the Civil War, he described "American slavery" as "one of those offences which, in the providence of God, must needs come, but which, having continued through His appointed time, He now wills to remove."[22]

The difference between Lincoln's counsel for reconciliation and Hester's for patience is the turn of a certain circular symbolic logic. The Northern rhetoric of the Civil War represents negation as affirmation—the destined Union made manifest in violence. Hawthorne's rhetoric builds on affirmation by negation—manifest inaction justified by national destiny. From this perspective, it is worth recalling the enormous force of the negative imperative in *The Scarlet Letter*. Negation is far more than a form of moral, political, and aesthetic control. It is the very ground of Hawthorne's strategy of process as closure: the antidialectics of ambiguity and irony through which he absorbs and refashions the radical energies of history. "The scarlet letter had not done its office": negation leads us forward toward that deeper significance which Hawthorne promises at the start—that comprehensive "deep meaning . . . most worthy of interpretation" (pp. 145–146)— precisely by evoking the fear of process run amuck: the national past as a history of disruptions; multiple meanings dissolving into irreconcilability; ironic reversals tending toward the tragic or the absurd; pluralism fragmenting into sheer diversity.

That is the overt purpose of Hawthorne's imperative. But his strategy goes further than that. It may almost be said to take on a counter-dynamic of its own, as though in equal and opposite reaction to the fear of uncontrolled process. Negation gathers such momentum in the course of the novel that it threatens the very process it is designed to guide. *Not* doing its office nearly comes to define the function of the symbol. When after "seven miserable years" Hester at last finds the strength to discard the A, it takes all of Hawthorne's resources (providence, Pearl, Dimmesdale, nature itself) to have her restore it against her will. And even so the restoration serves at first to highlight the letter's negative effects. As she awaits her moment of flight with Dimmesdale, Hester stands alone in the marketplace with a "frozen calmness," her face a death mask, *and because of that* with all the radical vitality for which we have come to admire her:

> after sustaining the gaze of the multitude through seven miserable years as a necessity, a penance, and something which it was a stern religion to endure, she now, for one last time more, encountered it freely and voluntarily, in order to convert what had so long been agony into a kind of triumph. "Look your last on the scarlet-letter and its wearer!"—the people's victim and life-long bond-slave, as they fancied her, might say to them. "Yet a little while, and she will be beyond your reach! A few hours longer, and the deep, mysterious ocean will quench and hide forever the symbol which ye have caused to burn upon her bosom!" (pp. 313–314)

That is why Hawthorne must bring her back; and more than that, must force her to resume the A "freely and voluntarily," "of her own free will." It is as though under pressure of her resistance the letter were slipping out of his grasp, losing its efficacy as an agent of reconciliation. In terms of what I called the novel's latent context, the impending Civil War, the antinomies in this passage ("people" and "victim," "freely" and "bond-slave") assume an explosive force, an almost irrepressible tendency toward confrontation, that endangers process and closure alike. That tendency may be seen as the political aftereffect of the rhetoric of liberty, in which "slavery" served ambiguously, as Bernard Bailyn has shown, to denote all forms of bondage, private or public, civil or political—including (for Margaret Fuller and other feminists) the

"bond-slavery" of women to men. More directly, it is the rhetorical counterpart to what Edmund Morgan, describing the ironies
of antebellum politics, termed "American freedom/American
slavery."[23] It is a testament to Hawthorne's sensitivity to those
rhetorical-political tensions that he allowed the danger to surface,
that indeed he played it out almost to the point of no return. It is
a testament to the resilience of the cultural symbology it drew
upon that nonetheless he could resume process, impose closure,
and as it were rescue the symbol from the ocean's depths, by
simply, sweepingly, *assuming* an interpretive consensus.

For the silence surrounding Hester's final conversion to the
letter is clearly deliberate on Hawthorne's part. Like the silence
which precedes Dimmesdale's decision to confess, it mystifies
Hester's choice by forcing us to represent it through the act of
interpretation. Having given us ample directives about how to
understand the ambiguous ways in which the letter had not done
its office, and having set out the ironies that thread the pattern of
American consensus from 1649 to 1849, Hawthorne now depends
on us to recognize—freely and voluntarily, for his method depends
on his seeming not to impose meaning—the need for Hester's
return. In effect, he invites us to participate in a free-enterprise
democracy of symbol making. Its cultural model is the ambiguity
universalized in the Declaration of Independence: "*We* hold these
truths to be *self*-evident." The silent problematic of "we" may
be inferred from Pip's revelation of the plural meanings of the
doubloon—"I look, you look, he looks, we look, ye look, they
look"—especially if we remember, as Pip seems not to, that Ahab's
doubloon has a single-minded purpose, and that Pip's pluralist
grammatical declension masks a social hierarchy, *descending*
from the captain's "I" to the ship-stokers' "they." The silenced
problematic of "self-evident" may be inferred from the quasi-
voluntaristic terms of Ahab's covenant: "I do not order ye; ye will
it."[24]

Hawthorne, too, may be said to elicit these problematics; but
unlike Melville he does so in order to guide us toward accommodation. When, in the most carefully prepared-for reversal in classic
American literature, Hester herself imposes the symbol, she signals her recognition that what had seemed a basic problem—basic
enough to have made her want to overturn society—is really a
question of point of view; and Hawthorne so veils this epiphany

that our multiple perspectives enact the same ideal of liberal community which his novel celebrates and represents.

It is an oblique mode of celebration, and all the more persuasive for its obliquity. Pierre Macherey argues that gaps and silences in narrative structure—the sorts of indirection in which Hawthorne specializes—demarcate the limits of ideology. According to Macherey, they are symptoms of fissures in the culture, the contradictions that the system can neither absorb nor wholly exclude. His theory seems especially pertinent to classic American literature, which abounds in strategies of process through hiatus, and to Hawthorne's work in particular. It is pertinent first of all because it conspicuously does *not* apply to the narrative gap that precedes Hester's return. Hawthorne makes that silence reverberate with all the voices of cultural authority; he transforms the gap into an ideological bridge (spanning three centuries now) between character, author, and reader. When midway through the novel we accept Hawthorne's judgment that the scarlet letter had not done its office, we acquiesce to the narrative in a willing suspension of disbelief; but when at the end we ourselves require the letter to be imposed, inventing reasons (all of them necessarily indirect, ironical) or synthesizing the views of others (each of them necessarily incomplete, ambiguous), we invest our very will to suspend disbelief in a joint-stock company of pluralist interpretation. It is an ideological leap of faith for which the entire novel has been our preparation. Hawthorne's strategies allow us, like Hester, both to dissent and to do the work of culture. And when we thus interpret away her repentance—or rather (as Charles Feidelson puts it, in what remains the best New Critical reading of the novel), her penitence "yet to be" which "will always be unfinished" because it involves "a perennial conversion of the stuff of sin and sorrow into positive freedom—the creativity, individuality, and sympathetic community of men"—then *The Scarlet Letter* has done its office.[25]

What I would suggest is the ideological *power* of gaps and silences. In general, I refer to the special genius of liberal symbology in staging interpretation as a means of co-opting dissent, or else re-forming dissent, in all its adversarial potential, in the image of the culture. In particular, I refer to the strategies by which the same visionary appeal that makes "America" into an ideological battleground also restricts the battle to the ground of American ideology. "From gap to gain is very American," writes Norman Mailer in *The Armies of the Night: History as the Novel, The Novel as History* (1968). In the mid-nineteenth century, that fictive-factual quality found its main expression in the rhetoric of expansion, opportunity, speculation, and enterprise, the symbiosis between verbal and territorial appropriation inherent in the appeal to "open country," "virgin land," "empty continent," "unmapped future," the interior "white on the chart" of the self, the I that *becomes all* by *being nothing*. In 1846, the year after John O'Sullivan popularized the phrase "manifest destiny" (in an editorial entitled "Annexation"), the explorer-pioneer-politician William Gilpin elaborated that "divine task" in terms that may be said to foreshadow the prophecies of Dimmesdale and Hester. It was "the *untransacted* destiny of the American people," Gilpin told Congress, "to subdue the continent . . . [and] unite the world in one social family."[26]

These ambiguities served different offices in 1850. In *The Scarlet Letter* and as *The Scarlet Letter*, their office is the transvaluation of the conflicts of compromise into the rhetoric of consensus. From 1848 to 1852 that rhetoric had two broad ideological aims: one, pragmatic and immediate, the tactics of concession; the other, visionary or teleogical, the myth of continuing revolution. The two aims were intertwined. Continuing revolution, we have seen, posited the gradual ascent from Puritanism to the Revolution and the nation's continuing ascent thereafter, in accordance with the principles established by the Revolution. The tacticians of concession invoked that myth of progress as a providential injunction against the threat of civil war.

The injunction issued as the 1850 Compromise Resolutions, enacted under "the great triumvirate" (John C. Calhoun, Henry Clay, and Daniel Webster), in which North and South agreed to various "amicable agreements" and "mutual promises," accommodating the interests of both regions. According to Webster, the spokesman for the North, the abolitionists' "wicked & abominable" "mischiefs" subverted all "sense of fraternal affection, patriotic love, and mutual regard." Compromise meant acceding to the demands of Southern slaveholders, but such reciprocity was precisely "the great purpose" of the founders. The interests of the republic were "not only many, but various in character . . . spiritual . . . political . . . social." So, too, were the "chords that bind the States together," "the ties that have held together the two great parties . . . from the beginning of the Government." To compromise, then, was "to defend the Constitution and to MAINTAIN THE UNION." Indeed, "the Constitution [itself] is the compromise," the nation's "binding compromise . . . faithfully kept by every congress from 1789 to 1850," and supplemented by a long succession of economic, political, and territorial acts and resolutions, such as the Compromise Tariff of 1833, which both Whigs and Democrats celebrated as a vindication of American institutions.[27]

It is pertinent that in 1850 the word compromise did not carry the primarily pejorative meanings it does today: "a committal to something derogatory"; "to expose or discredit or mischief"; "to make a shameful or disreputable concession." For the legislative majority who voted in the Compromise Resolutions, the term meant above all (according to Noah Webster's *Standard American Dictionary*) "to bind by mutual agreement," where the principles of binding had the doubled force of contract and of covenant: "an amicable agreement between parties in controversy to settle their differences, by mutual concessions"; "a mutual promise"; "an engagement to refer matters in dispute to the decision of arbitrators"; "to adjust and settle"; "to pledge by some act or declaration"; "see Promise." The weak point lay in the vagueness of "promise," especially under what turned out to be the *diverse* pressures to concede: "pledge" versus "arbitration" versus "declaration" versus "agreement." By the close of the Jacksonian period, vagueness had taken the form of ambiguity. In 1848, Chauncey A. Goodrich's "Revised and Enlarged" edition of Webster's *Standard Dictionary* officially brought to the fore, what may be found in earlier definitions but only sporadically or implicitly, that to compromise *could* mean "to put to hazard." Apparently, the increasing dysfunctions of "mutual agreements" from Massachusetts to Kansas—and from the Missouri Compromise of 1820 (which established slavery in Missouri while prohibiting it in what was to become the Nebraska Territory) to the various midcentury compromises over Southwest Territories—were affecting the course of "American English." If so, it is crucial to Hawthorne's achievement that the apotheosis of compromise—rhetorically, in Webster's great orations from 1848 to 1850; politically, as the "National Platform" that swept Pierce into office in 1852—came at the moment when the term was undergoing a decisive change.[28]

Between 1848 and 1852, the unbound, open-ended ambiguity that the term "hazard" had brought into play endowed the primary meaning of "compromise" with the power of what Freud called the "antithetical sense of primal words." "Compromise: *consent* reached by *mutual concession*"—all the volatile doubleness that had been explicit in the Revolutionary key word *independent* (isolated versus mature, cut off versus self-determined), and implicit in the ubiquitous Jacksonian *self* prefix (self-made versus self-serving, self-reliant versus self-centered), exploded in antebellum America in the struggle between the party for union and the party against concession. Both parties laid claim to "consent," of course, as the touchstone of liberal consensus. They divided mainly on pragmatics—the scope of consent, the nature of consensus—but it was now a pragmatism *at hazard*, charged with apocalyptic import. Daniel Webster's concession to the South, according to Emerson, "was the darkest passage in [our] history," a "disastrous defection (on the miserable cry of Union)," from "the principles of culture and progress." For his part, Webster pointed to the spectre of European revolution, fratricide, terror, and collapse; and against all this, speaking "not as a Massachusetts man, nor as a northern man, but as an American," he invoked "the Spirit of Compromise," alternatively named "the spirit of harmony" and "the spirit of Union." All of these said Webster, were embodied from their Puritan origins in the American city on a hill. With "the eyes of all Christendom upon us," he pleaded—with the "whole world looking towards us with extreme anxiety"—"let our comprehension be as broad as our country," and "our aspirations as high": let us once and for all make visible the "certain destiny . . . that belongs to us."[29]

From the revolutions of 1848 through the election of Franklin Pierce, this rhetoric of compromise occupied the center of a debate whose extremes were proslavery constitutionalism and proconstitutional abolitionism. I refer here to the debate within the dominant culture, but it is astonishing how few voices broke the parameters of liberal discourse, in what elsewhere (to recall the phrases of *The Scarlet Letter*) was a time of "radical speculation," "an age in which the human intellect, newly emancipated, had taken a more active and wider range than for many centuries before." As for Hawthorne, he scarcely wavered in his centrist convictions. In the Pierce biography he recalled "The Compromise" as a triumphant "test" of "the reverence of the people for the Constitution, and their attachment to the Union"; and as late as 1858 he said of a statue of Webster, "symbolizing him as the preserver of the Union, . . . I never saw such . . . massive strength . . . [and] deep, pervading energy. . . . He looks really like a pillar of the state . . . very grand, very Webster . . . he is in the act of meeting a great crisis, and yet with the warmth of a great heart glowing through it."[30] But by then the crisis of industrial capitalism was calling for new sources of strength. After 1852, with Webster's death and the struggle for the Free States, the central cultural symbols shifted steadily to embrace the armies of the North, wielding God's terrible swift sword to cut the Gordian knot of "consent"/"concession."

Not the ends but the means had changed. Compromise, "to bind by mutual agreement," had failed to provide either the mechanism for binding or the metaphors for agreement, and with due alacrity the leaders of the dominant culture had moved to preserve the union against the *hazards* of ambiguity. Some four months before Hawthorne's encomium to Webster, Lincoln set out the new rhetoric of consent in a Senate campaign speech which appropriated the Southern imagery of fragmentation for the Yankee cause: "I do not expect the house to *fall*—I *do* expect it will cease to be divided. It will become *all* one thing, or *all* the other." A year later, Emerson displayed the recuperative powers of that revision in his tribute to John Brown.* Far from being a threat to consensus, "the hero of Harper's Ferry," he said, was the

---

*The parameters of revision—and more largely, the boundaries of vision—are suggested in the parallels between the strategies of consensus after the Revolution and those at the end of the Civil War. In 1788 James Madison sought to calm the antifederalists by invoking the ambiguities of consensus at the recent Constitutional Convention: "neither side would entirely yield to the other, and consequently . . . the struggle could be terminated only by compromise"—a compromise which made manifest (once again) "that Almighty hand which has been so frequently and signally extended to our relief in the critical stages of the revolution" (Federalist 37). Some eighty years later Lincoln sought to reconcile anti-Unionists by explaining the Civil War as a broken compromise, and re-union as a set of mutual agreements to be divinely restored: "To strengthen, perpetuate, and extend their interest was the object for which the [Southern] insurgents would rend the Union, even by war; while the government [in 1861] claimed no right to do more than to restrict the territorial enlargement of it. . . . The prayers of both [sides] could not be answered; that of neither has been answered fully. The Almighty has His own purposes." For Lincoln as for Madison, those purposes had been inscribed *through* conflict by an "Almighty hand . . . frequently and signally extended to our relief" ("Second Inaugural Address" [1865], in *Speeches and Writ-*

representative of the American Republic. . . . He joins that perfect
Puritan faith which brought his fifth ancestor to Plymouth Rock,
with his grandfather's ardor in the Revolution. He believes in two
articles—two instruments shall I say?—the Golden Rule and the
Declaration of Independence.

Instruments was the better word. In 1866, as though to commemorate the triumphant reincorporation of the myth, Noah Webster's
Standard American Dictionary—now "Thoroughly Revised, [and]
Greatly Enlarged and Improved" by Noah Porter and Chauncy
Goodrich—officially retired (as archaic) the once-primary meaning of "compromise": "to bind by mutual agreement . . . *obs.*"[31]
It is a nice irony of our literary history that Hawthorne's
absolutist Concord neighbors, Emerson and Thoreau, managed to
span the spectrum of response, whereas sceptical, many-faceted
Hawthorne remained ideologically fixated, like some Ahab of
compromise. I do not think we can say that his incapacity to accept
the change ruined his career, as it did Pierce's and Webster's. But
to some extent at least it drained him of crucial intellectual and
moral resources. On some level, it accounts for the increasing
tendency of his fiction to expose (rather than reconcile) ideological
contradictions. For the fact is that of all his novels it is only about
The Scarlet Letter that we can say, as Henry James did *in praise
of Hawthorne's art*, that "the reader must look for his local and
national qualities between the lines of his writing and in the
indirect testimony of his tone, his accent, his temper, of his very
omissions and suppressions." Consider the difference in this respect between Hester's return on the one hand and on the other
Holgrave's strained conversion, Coverdale's problematic confession, or most pointedly the much-disputed homecoming of Hilda,
that other wandering daughter of the Puritans.* In his European

---

ings, 1859–1865, ed. Don E. Fehrenbacher [Library of America: New York, 1989],
II, 687).

  *In the case of *The Marble Faun*, readers from the start demanded explanations for the gaps between process and closure, as Hawthorne acidly notes in the
novel's Conclusion (where he insists instead on his technique of indirections). In
the case of the earlier novels, critics have sought to convert narrative weaknesses
into authorial strengths by assuming that Hawthorne *intended* the weaknesses—
planted these as clues by which he meant us to de-mystify cultural myths. Thus
in *The House of the Seven Gables* the sudden transmutation of the curse of private
property (as by Adam Smith's invisible hand of God) into the blessings of suburban
mobility is interpreted, along with Holgrave's conversion, as a subversive strategy

236 / *Rites of Assent*

letters and journals, Hawthorne often hints at the cause of his failing strategies of omission. He is most explicit in the preface to his last book, *Our Old Home*, which appropriately he dedicated to his old friend, Franklin Pierce:

> The Present, the Immediate, the Actual, has proved too potent for me. It takes away not only my scanty faculty, but even my desire for imaginative composition, and leaves me sadly content to scatter a thousand peaceful fantasies upon the hurricane that is sweeping us all along with it, possibly, into a Limbo where our nation and its polity may be as literally the fragments of a shattered dream as my unwritten Romance.[32]

This was 1863, at the height of the war, and it is not hard to understand Hawthorne's bewilderment and dismay. Three years earlier he had returned to an America where (he professed to believe) there was "no shadow, no antiquity, no mystery, no picturesque and gloomy wrong, nor anything but a commonplace prosperity, in broad and simple daylight." Two years later he confessed in an essay "Chiefly About War-Matters": "the general heart-quake of the country long ago knocked at my cottage-door, and compelled me, reluctantly, to suspend the contemplation of certain fantasies." We might well see in this image (as in that limbo of shattered dreams) an unconscious inversion of Hester's return. But we should also keep in mind the hurricanes of the actual which a decade earlier had *not* disturbed Hawthorne's fantasies: Southern slavery; Indian genocide; the Mexican War (through which General Pierce became a national hero); expansionist demands by men like Pierce for war against Cuba and Latin America; pervasive ethnic and religious discrimination; child labor in Northern mill towns; the grievances listed by the Seneca Falls Convention; and the manifold abuses documented in the petitions circulated by New England's abolitionist sewing circles.[33]

Hawthorne was aware in 1850 of those present and pressing evils. Some of them had earlier found their way into his short stories; some are actually recorded in the Pierce biography; others

---

on Hawthorne's part, designed to undermine the narrator, so as to direct his readers to "a troublesome encounter in which our presuppositions are altered" (Brook Thomas, *"The House of the Seven Gables*: Reading the Romance of America," *PMLA*, XCIII [1978], 208).

may be said to underlie the discontents that Hester, in her sewing circle of one, embroiders into her scarlet letter; still others are implicit in her confrontation with the immigrant "bond-servant" at Governor Bellingham's mansion, "a free-born Englishman, but now a seven years' slave" (p. 206); and others again may be discerned in the "sorrows and perplexities" which the townspeople bring to Hester, after her return, "demanding why they were so wretched, and what the remedy!" No American writer felt more detached from party politics than Hawthorne did; few were more engaged in the affairs of political office; and none was so deeply learned in American political history. There is no surprise in this. Hawthorne sought to rise above politics not by escaping history, but by representing it symbolically. To that end (in "The Custom-House" introduction) he exposes the miasma of mid-nineteenth-century patronage and (in the novel proper) the excesses of partisanship. The hiatus between introduction and story is the mytho-historical link between Hawthorne and Hester. Her reconciliation at the end is the link in turn between the novel and the biography: first, in the image that Hester may be said to project of Hawthorne's return to the patronage system; then, in the biographical image of Pierce as the great reconciler; and finally in Hawthorne's implied contrast between process in the New World and upheaval in the Old. Revolutionary Europe, in this view, was political in the narrow, exclusivist, oppositional meaning of ideology. The United States transcended ideology, so defined, for the same reason that the concept of America transcended politics: because as "America" it stood for a transpartisan, pluralistic development through compromise.

That liberal ideology fills the silence between Hester's cold defiance at the election-day ceremony and her final consolation for dissidents. Far from wanting to mute sorrow and perplexity, Hawthorne emphatically gives voice to the wretched, to a degree his contemporaries sometimes considered morbid. But he does so to elicit our acquiescence to what he believed was "the remedy," working uncoerced, in its own time and ways. For Hawthorne, no less than for Bancroft, continuing revolution was a pervasive theme—most bluntly in the Pierce biography, most elaborately in his short stories, and most subtly and complexly in *The Scarlet Letter*. The central act of the national drama that underlies the novel—the event that best explains Hawthorne's prophetic gloss on the midnight revelation of the A (midway through the novel), and that most firmly connects this (at the end) both to Dimmesdale's prophecy and to Hester's—is the American Revolution. Indeed, it is not too much to say that, together with adultery, the Revolution is the novel's fundamental donnée. Adultery is pretext, and issues in the wrong kind of revolt; the Revolution is post-script, and vindicates the role of process in an adulterated world.

The vindication is prospective as well as retrospective. It applies no less to the adulterated world of the Customs House than to Puritan New England. The absence from the novel of the word "adultery" facilitates a process of interpretation through which a problem in social accountability is deepened (Hawthorne would have us believe) into a process of symbolic perspective. So, too, in the case of the conspicuously absent word "compromise": it serves by "*indirect* testimony" to recast fears of concession into faith in consensus. And so, too, with the American Revolution. Only here Hawthorne does break the silence, briefly, in the introduction. "The British army in its flight from Boston," he writes, had discarded as worthless the "packet" containing the letter; and the "ancient yellow parchment," tied up in "faded red tape," had "remained ever since unopened" (pp. 143–145). Seventeen seventy-six thus serves to confirm the letter's venerable antiquity ("Prior to the Revolution"), its rare value as a native artifact (the British had "carried off" most "earlier documents"), and its aesthetic-historical significance—from Hester to Surveyor Pue (whose given name, Jonathan, casts him on the American side, against the Royalist John Bull) to Hawthorne, and from the Puritan forefathers through their latter-day heir to us (pp. 144–145):

> I, the present writer, as their representative, hereby take their shame upon myself for their sakes, and pray that any curse incurred by them [for their acts of persecution] may be now and henceforth removed. (p. 127)

For all its irony, the anecdote is crucial to the letter's design. It transforms the accidents of conflict into a historical chain of providences in which the Revolution is the pivotal link. As an emblem of what the British left behind, the A sanctifies the Puritan legacy, foreshadows the pattern of Hester's flight, justifies the wisdom of her return, and validates the spirit, if not the letter, of her prophecy. It amounts to a figural endorsement of Hawthorne's strategy of reconciliation.

The same figural logic, however, points in another, opposite direction. I said earlier that for Hawthorne continuing revolution was the visionary side of the rhetoric of compromise. But for Bancroft, we recall, that ritual of process entailed an emphasis on conflict and strife, the iconic representation of America as battleground for the future. Consensus in his *History* means not only union through compromise, but regeneration through violence. This model of process was equally rooted in the culture. It may be traced from the Puritans' Wars of the Lord (correlative of their gradual, forever-"preparatory" errand into the wilderness) through the Revolutionary summons to independence. Thus Samuel Sherwood in a sermon of 1776: "We had been in the steady way of maturation" into nationhood, when suddenly "floods poured from the mouth of the serpent, which at length have brought on a civil war"; and thus Tom Paine several months earlier: independence is opposed to "the least inclination toward a compromise. . . . Reconciliation is *now* a fallacious dream." This appeal to continuity through confrontation is inscribed in representative works such as Timothy Dwight's epic of the Revolution, *The Conquest of Canaan*, in cultural key words such as manifest destiny, and in large-scale social actions, such as the extermination of the Indians. The "savages," went the argument, were by definition an "extinct race"—if not now, then "in Heaven's own time"; the issue was not agency but destiny, working itself out either by natural or by human means. Andrew Jackson mobilized the human means; Emerson opted for nature. It was "the great charity of God to the human race," he explained, to prepare for "new individuals and races" by "extinguishing" old ones, and charity should be allowed to take its own course.[34]

In the antebellum North, with the Indian issue fundamentally settled, the debate shifted to the issue of slavery. It is a testament to the flexibility, the volatility, and the resilience of the American symbology that it managed to incorporate both violence and gradualism—indeed, managed to make one a function of the other and each a model of regeneration through consensus. And it seems predictable under these conditions that the metaphysicians of Indian-killing should have become leading advocates of Compromise. Those who supported the Resolutions wanted nature and providence to usher in what Webster called "the certain destiny that awaits us." Like Emerson, they were awaiting the "great charity of God to the human race." Those who opposed Compromise did not deny that certain destiny; they simply wanted to take charity into their own hands. Emerson's famous attack on the Fugitive Slave Act is exemplary. Delivered in 1854, when the negative connotations of "compromise" ("derogatory," "shameful," "disreputable") were beginning to eclipse the "promise" of "mutual concession," it warrants extended quotation as the ideological counterpart to Hawthorne's ironies of reconciliation:

> Slavery is disheartening; *but* Nature is not so helpless *but* it can rid itself at last of every wrong. *But* the spasms of Nature are centuries and ages, and will tax the faith of short-lived men. Slowly, slowly the Avenger comes, *but* comes surely. The proverbs of the nations affirm these delays, *but* affirm the arrival. They say, "God may consent, *but* not forever." The delay of the Divine Justice—this was the meaning and soul of the Greek Tragedy. . . .
> These delays, you see them now in the . . . torpor [that] exists here . . . on the subject of domestic slavery. . . . Yes, that is the stern edict of Providence, that liberty shall be no hasty fruit, *but* that event on event, population on population, age on age, shall cast itself into the opposite scale, and not until liberty has slowly accumulated weight enough to countervail and preponderate against all this, can the sufficient recoil come. . . .
> *Whilst* the inconsistency of slavery with the principles on which the world is built guarantees its downfall, I own that the patience it requires is *almost* too sublime for mortals, and *seems* to demand of us more than mere hoping. And when one sees how fast the rot spreads . . . we demand of superior men that they be superior in this—that the mind and the virtue shall give their verdict in their day, and accelerate so far the progress of civilization. . . . *But* be that sooner or later, I hope we have . . . come to a belief that there is a divine Providence in the world, which will not save us *but* through our own cooperation.[35]

These winding negations and indirections (the italics are mine) invert Hawthorne's strategy of inaction, but the inversion begins with and returns to a common symbolic outlook. Hawthorne translates the dynamics of process into social integration; Emerson, into cultural renewal. His summons to avenge, like Hawthorne's to patience, mobilizes all the universals on the side of Northern ideology. "Nature," "Divine Justice," "liberty," "the mind," "virtue," "the progress of civilization"—the very "principles on which the world is built" serve to consecrate the Yankee *our*.

This sort of troping characterizes the later Emerson. I adduce it here not to deny the radicalism of his great early essays (a subject I take up in a later chapter), but to suggest the versatility of American liberal thought and rhetoric. The "divine Providence" to which Emerson appeals is essentially the "spirit as of prophecy" for which Dimmesdale remains, and to which Hester returns— Dimmesdale, "to foretell a high and glorious destiny for the newly gathered people of the Lord" (pp. 332–333); Hester, to herald "the destined prophetess . . . angel and apostle of the coming revelation." And in turn that spirit is authorized by essentially the same liberal faith in process which Julia Ward Howe endorsed when, speaking as "angel or apostle" of the Union, she announced: "Mine eyes have seen the glory of the coming of the Lord."[36]

Hawthorne could not have intended the irony this implies, one that makes Hester's vision a foreshadowing of "The Battle Hymn of the Republic." No doubt he would have abhorred that implication if he had foreseen it. The irony was intended by the symbology he inherited; and as cultural intention it finds direct expression in the novel's persistent if sporadic rhetoric of violence. Hawthorne's reference to the Revolution makes it integral to the meanings of the A that it is a trophy of war, and this particular meaning is extended through the imagery connecting the introduction to the story proper: for example, the acrimony of self-interest, "where brethren of the same household must diverge from one another," and the prospect of economic and political "warfare," waged in the "fierce and bitter spirit of malice and revenge," "poisoned with ill-will," and leaving the defeated, after "seething turmoil," at "the mercy of a hostile administration" (pp. 154–156).

These contrapuntal ambiguities add another level of complexity and control to Hawthorne's design. They give a greater density to his strategy of multiple choice, and lend a deeper resonance to the pervasive force of negation, which verges on the dialectical only to veer in the direction of incorporation. From all these angles, they find the right symbolic focus in the national eagle,

icon of the Revolution, as Hawthorne describes it in the introduction. An "enormous specimen of the American eagle," he writes,
hovered above the Customs House door,

> with outspread wings, a shield before her breast, and a bunch of
> intermingled thunderbolts and barbed arrows in each claw. With the
> customary infirmity of temper that characterizes this unhappy fowl,
> she appears, by the fierceness of her beak and eye and the general
> truculency of her attitude, to threaten mischief to the inoffensive
> community; and especially to warn all citizens, careful of their
> safety, against intruding on the premises. . . . Nevertheless, vixenly
> as she looks, many people are seeking, at this very moment, to
> shelter themselves under the wing of the federal eagle. . . . But she
> has no great tenderness, even in her best of moods, and, sooner or
> later,—oftener sooner than late,—is apt to fling off her nestlings
> with a scratch of her claw, a dab of her beak, or a rankling wound
> from her barbed arrows. (pp. 122–123)

The eagle and the A: for all the oppositions between them,
they are symbols made out of the same cultural materials. Both
are ambiguous artifacts of authority; both are social emblems
transformed by private vision in such a way as simultaneously to
assert the self and to accommodate community; and in both cases
the act of accommodation recasts the untoward events of history—
the "ulcerated wound" of Hester's penance (p. 191), the wounds that
Hawthorne received in 1849 from the claw of Whig Party function-
aries—in terms of art as cultural work. It is the myth of Philoctetes,
historicized. And it is appropriate that the two symbols, so historicized, should find common ground in the Salem Customs House—
"Uncle Sam's brick edifice" (p. 128), entry to the republic of 1849,
as the Puritans were for Hawthorne the entry to national history.
The extraordinary force and cunning of his vision attests to the symbolic resources of what by 1850 was becoming the single most cohesive culture of the modern world.

I have been arguing that text and context are reciprocal; and
my purpose, accordingly, has been to explore (rather than expose)
Hawthorne's techniques and to call into question, so as to learn
from, the culture's powers of mystification. Still, contextual analysis assumes a priori that those powers are limited by history; and

since that assumption constitutes the adversarial donnée of this essay—somewhat as the adultery prohibition serves as the novel's donnée—I would like in closing to take note of the limitations implicit in the office of the A. To that end, I return to the ground on which I began, Hawthorne's insistent directives for interpretation. Those directives, I would suggest, are a form of special pleading; their very insistence betrays an underlying cultural-authorial anxiety. Hawthorne intends his winding indirections to control interpretation, and they do. But the windings themselves make for what he privately called "a h____l-f____d story." The repressed letters may be taken as the first sign of a strain in his method. The second was Sophia's splitting headache, after he read the last chapter aloud to her. When she recovered, she wrote to her sister Mary: "I don't know what you will think of the Romance. It is most powerful and contains a moral as terrific & stunning as a thunderbolt. It shows that the Law cannot be broken."[37]

Surely, Sophia was not just thinking of the Seventh Commandment. She was reacting, I think, as Nathaniel was, to the enormous cultural pressures brought to bear upon the Conclusion. "The scarlet letter had not done its office": the entire novel asks us to interpret this teleogically, in the affirmative, and by the end *compels* us to, as a grim necessity. It is as though Hawthorne had to overcompensate for the radicalism potential in his characters and symbols; had to find some moral absolute—some equivalent in the liberal imagination for the Thou Shalt Nots delivered from Mount Sinai—powerful enough to recall all those unleashed energies of will, eros, and language back into the culture from which they arose and, in his view, to which they belonged. He found the solution in the act of mimesis that his novel simultaneously endorses and enacts. It was to represent the development of his culture—both positively, by our assent to the almost absent Revolution that connects the novel's twin time frames, and negatively, by our rejection of the radical politics that Hester disavows in absentia—to set forth the workings of American liberal ideology, so interpreted, as the iron link between culture, nature, and the self, "the Law [that] cannot be broken."

It is to Sophia's credit that she found the "moral as terrific & stunning as a thunderbolt." And it is to Hawthorne's credit that he not only made full use of the symbolic system at his disposal, but had the integrity to indicate, if not the full costs involved, then at least some signs whereby those costs might be inferred:

the coercive force, for example, of containment by consensus, including the containment of the hell-fired artist in liberal democracy, which forms an illicit bond between the secret Hawthorne and the hidden Hester. This is perhaps what he refers to when, speaking of the scarlet letter in the Conclusion, he describes his own splitting headache: "We . . . would gladly, now that it has done its office, erase its deep print out of our own brain; where long meditation has fixed in very undesirable distinctness" (p. 340). As a symbol for this and other unerased traces of contradiction in the novel—undesired silences that (again to his credit) do not quite succeed in silencing conflict—I should like to appropriate the "angry eagle" of "The Custom-House" for my own purposes, relocating it from "The Custom House" of 1849 to the "War Matters" of 1862. In the later essay, Hawthorne sought to reconcile himself with the consensus of another "iron age," and instinctively he returned once again to the myth of national origins:

> There is an historical circumstance, known to few, that connects the children of the Puritans with those Africans of Virginia in a very singular way. They are our brethren, as being lineal descendents of the Mayflower, the fated womb which in its first labor brought forth a brood of Pilgrims on Plymouth Rock, and, in a subsequent one, spawned slaves upon the Southern soil,—a monstrous birth, but one with which we have an instinctive sense of kindred, and so are stirred by an irresistible impulse to attend their rescue even at the cost of blood and ruin. The character of our sacred ship, I fear, may suffer a little by this revelation; but we must let her white progeny offset her dark one,—and two such portents never sprang from an identical source before.[38]

Hawthorne's *Mayflower* has all the major imaginative ingredients of the dominant culture: the legend of the Puritan theocracy, womb of American democracy;* the ambiguities of good and

---

*The use of this legend for socializing purposes—providing as it did a common American genealogy for disparate immigrant groups—deserves a study in its own right. Compare, for example, Mary Antin's vision of the "ghost of the Mayflower [which] pilots every immigrant ship" (*They Who Knock at Our Gates: A Complete Gospel of Immigration* [New York, 1914], p. 25) with John Boyle O'Reilly's hymn to the "light predestined" streaming from "The Mayflower's . . . chosen womb" ("The Pilgrim Fathers," in *Old Colony Memorial: Plymouth Rock, Old Colony Sentinel*, LXVII, no. 31 [Plymouth, 1889], p. 3).

evil, agency of compromise; and the myth of continuing revolution, rationale for civil war. But it is a symbol overdetermined by history. Its "deeper meanings" point insistently to the *discontinuities* of process and the *precariousness* of the hiatus that links "rescue" to "blood and ruin." The return of the *Mayflower* is a parable of social conflict following upon (as well as generating) cultural myth. It reverberates with multiple meanings at cross-purposes with each other: the recurrent American nightmare of miscegenation; the long literary procession of mutually destructive dark-white kin (from *Clotel* through *Clarel* and *Pudd'nhead Wilson* to *Absalom, Absalom!*); the biblical types of the elect and the damned (Seth and Ham, Jacob and Esau) through which the South defended its peculiar institution; the racist use of the image of Christic sacrifice through which the North sanctified first the Union Cause and then the Martyrdom of Lincoln. Considered together with the "unhappy fowl," this "sacred ship" blackened by "revelation" is itself a monstrous birth, a Frankenstein's monster of the culture: history returning in the guise of figures designed to control it—the most familiar of symbols which now streams forth disjunctions, mocks the A-politics of both/and, and guides us (with an ambiguity of its own) to the contradictions repressed by the novel's twin contexts, 1642–1649 and 1848–1852.

Let me conclude with that image, and underscore its peculiar volatility by recalling the image that Hester projects upon her return. First, then, Hawthorne's *Mayflower*-eagle, mother of nationhood and vixen of contradictions. Second, Hester come home, the dissenter as agent of socialization, a self-professed sinner self-transformed into a herald of progress. Two figures of ambiguity; two models of the relation between rhetoric and social action; two intersections between power and imagination. They are opposites and yet uncannily alike, like the object and its reflection in a camera obscura—two sides of the same ideological coin, representing the American liberal symbology.

8
Pierre, or the Ambiguities of American Literary History

ABRAZZA—. . . Babbalanja, if Lombardo had aught to tell Mardi—why choose a vehicle so crazy?. . .

BABBALANJA—. . . I will try to tell you the way in which Lombardo produced his great Kostanza. . . . When Lombardo set about his work, he knew not what it would become. He . . . got deeper and deeper into himself; and . . . at last he was rewarded for his toils. "In good time," saith he . . . "I have created the creative." . . .

MEDIA—But . . . after all, the Kostanza found no favor in the eyes of some Mardians. . . .

BABBALANJA—Then . . . Lombardo could have wept, had tears been his. But in his very grief, he ground his teeth. Muttered he, "They are fools. . . . Oh! could Mardi but see how we work it, it would marvel more at our primal chaos, than at the round world thence emerging. It would marvel at our scaffoldings, scaling heaven; marvel at the hills of earth, banked all round our fabrics ere completed.—How plain the pyramid! In this grand silence, so intense, pierced by that pointed mass,— could ten thousand slaves ever have toiled? ten thousand hammers rung? —There it stands,—part of Mardi: claiming kin with mountains. . . ."

MEDIA—And now that Lombardo is long dead and gone— and his work, hooted during life, lives after him—what think the present company of it?. . .

ABRAZZA (*tapping his sandal with his scepter*)—I never read it.[1]

It seems appropriate to the bitter *Ambiguities* of Melville's *Pierre* that this pivotal work in his career, his most ambitious and

246

most carefully planned novel, should so long have gone virtually unread. *Pierre* is a major text not only in but about American literary history. Or more accurately, it is a story about the reciprocities among all these terms: about literary history in America (the literary market at midcentury, transatlantic Romanticism, nationalist aesthetics); about the *literary* history of the "American" (the rhetoric of "self-reliance," "self-made," "independence," "representative American"); about the history of "the literary" in America (including the symbolic mode that Melville inherited, along with Emerson and Hawthorne); and about "America" as literature made history, text become context. What unifies the novel is its sustained, dramatized critique of the ambiguities of language on all these levels of meaning. *Moby-Dick* finds a focus for its multiple discourses in the hunt for the whale. Pierre's chaotic quest finds its focus in Melville's systematic exploration of discourse itself—as "literary," as "history," and (in its "American" form) as culture.

To judge from critical response, that process of exploration has proved extraordinarily difficult to follow. But then, the same was true for most of Melville's works, for at least a century after publication. I want to show that, like the fictions which immediately preceded and followed it—*Moby-Dick* (1851) and "Bartleby, the Scrivener" (1853)—*Pierre* can be made accessible to students and specialists alike, if not to the general public that Melville intended. My purpose in this respect is pedagogical as well as scholarly: it requires an explication, layer by layer, of the ambiguities that *Pierre* dramatizes and embodies. And in order to combine explication and analysis, appreciative and cognitive criticism, I select as the vehicle of my argument a single passage, the author's Dedication of the novel, "To Greylock's Most Excellent Majesty":

> In old times authors were proud of the privilege of dedicating their works to Majesty. A right noble custom, which we of Berkshire must revive. For whether we will or no, Majesty is all around us here in Berkshire, sitting as in a grand Congress of Vienna of majestical hilltops, and eternally challenging our homage.
>
> But since the majestic mountain, Greylock—my own more immediate sovereign lord and king—hath now, for innumerable ages, been the one grand dedicatee of the earliest rays of all the Berkshire

mornings, I know not how his Imperial Purple Majesty (royal-born: Porphyrogenitus) will receive the dedication of my own poor solitary ray.

Nevertheless, forasmuch as I, dwelling with my loyal neighbors, the Maples and the Beeches, in the amphitheater over which his central majesty presides, have received his most bounteous and unstinted fertilizations, it is but meet, that I here devoutly kneel, and render up my gratitude, whether, thereto, The Most Excellent Purple Majesty of Greylock benignantly incline his hoary crown or no.[2]

The passage may be said to have all the problems that readers have traditionally complained of in *Pierre*: excess, cliché, pasteboard dramatics, unexplained reversals of meaning. Its pastoral commonplaces are echoed in the novel's sentimental opening sections, which describe noble young Pierre, the natural aristocrat, on his country estate near Greylock, alias the Delectable Mountain, with his adoring mother, Mary, and Lucy, his angelic, blue-eyed, blonde-haired bride-to-be. The unlikely windings of its logic ("but," "I know not," "nevertheless," "whether or no") may be said to foreshadow the novel's gothic reversals: mysterious letters; the ambiguous portrait of Pierre's revered dead father; the appearance of dark-haired Isabel, who claims to be Pierre's illegitimate half sister; and the subsequent melodramatics when Pierre and Isabel run off together to the city, ostensibly as husband and wife. Finally, the Dedication's postured sense of foreboding—will "his Imperial Purple Majesty . . . receive the [writer's] . . . poor solitary ray"? will Greylock "incline his hoary crown"?—permeates the novel, and finds its gloomy confirmation, as it were, in Pierre's many mishaps in the city, most elaborately in his attempts to become a great writer, which result in utter failure, murder, and suicide.

Plainly, the first point to make about *Pierre*'s convoluted and purple prose is that it is deliberate on Melville's part. And the second point is just as plain: the reason for Melville's deliberateness in this regard is that he wanted the book to sell. "Very much more calculated for popularity than anything you have yet published of mine," he assured his publisher on April 16, 1852, while completing his revisions;[3] and the fact is that pastoral sentimentalism, urban sensationalism, and gothic mannerism were staples of the best-sellers of the time. So were murderer-suicides, webs of incest and secret paternity, symbolic pairings of blonde and brunette, seraph and sensualist, and ill-fated heroes yearning for virtue and truth. In this light, the Dedication is a rather crafty appeal for patronage. The audience is transparent in the rhetoric: a middle-class literary market, provincial, patriotic, eager to see its own natural virtues and the country's virtue-inspiring nature (from picturesque maples to sublime mountains) mirrored in a new democratic literature. Accordingly, Melville links art to nature, and nature to natural aristocracy, extending local pride into a hymn to the country's purple-mountained majesty. The Dedication tells us that he was trying to please.

It also tells us why the American public did *not* benignantly incline its hoary crown. Clearly, Melville is ridiculing his subject. He makes fun of Greylock, of majesty, of the very notion of a man addressing a mountain; and the ridicule extends throughout the novel, in what amounts to a savage satire of American culture, pastoral and urban. Melville had good reason (no one better) for scorning his audience, but this time he went too far. The vitriol is too close to the surface of what he called his "rural bowl of milk." The milk curdles, and reviewers were understandably outraged. "He strikes with an impious . . . hand at the very foundations of our society"; such "antagonism . . . to all the recognized laws of social morality" can only "be supposed to emanate from a lunatic hospital." "His fancy is diseased, his morality vitiated," declared the influential critic George Washington Peck in the prestigious *American Whig Review*; we must "freeze him into silence." The consensus was boldly set out in one of the novel's first notices: "HERMAN MELVILLE CRAZY"; and in one form or another that has remained a standard view.* But textual schol-

* Significantly, the early reviewers combined denunciations of *Pierre*'s "lunacy" with remarks about its conventionality, or at any rate its resemblances to "scores" of similar scenes and characters "in your book aquaintance" (*New York Albion*, n.s. [August 21, 1852], in Hugh W. Hetherington, *Melville's Reviewers: British and American, 1846–1891* [Chapel Hill, N.C., 1968], p. 120). Conversely, the same critics who over the past half-century have been charting the parody in *Pierre* have also treated it as a case study in pathology. Raymond Weaver, who effectually launched the Melville revival, called *Pierre* "a book to send a Freudian into ravishment" (*Herman Melville: Mariner and Mystic* [New York, 1921], p. 63). Some three decades later, in the first (and in certain respects still the best) full-length treatment of the novel, Henry A. Murray presented *Pierre* as a valuable resource for Jungian analysis (Introduction to the Hendricks House Edition of the novel [New York, 1949], passim). Recent critics have extended this case study approach to the terms of Laing, Chodorow, and Lacan.

arship has shown that in fact "Melville was in complete command of his materials from the start—in command of his plot, which he did not change substantially as he labored on it, and in command of his complex and ironic attitude toward Pierre, which he also did not change."[4] In this particular instance, our sense of the satire in the style is an incentive to return to a closer analysis of the text.

Thematically considered, the Dedication is made up of a number of cunningly interlinked images and ideas, which turn out to be the novel's main concerns. I refer to the Romantic correspondence of mind and nature, the sustained contrast between Europe and America, the problems of perspective, interpretation, and naming, and the troubled relation of authorship to authority. Further, the Dedication sets out the major symbolic pattern in *Pierre*, the novel's persistent reference to mountains, hills, rocks, and stones—through analogy, image, and allusion; through the names of characters and places; and through the events that drive Pierre from Saddle Meadows, his country estate named for Saddleback Mountain nearby, alias Mount Greylock—or the Delectable Mountain, as the local inhabitants have renamed it— from "the sweet purple airs of the hills round about . . . Saddle Meadows" to the "mortar and stone" city of New York, a "wilderness" of "stony roofs, and seven-fold stony skies" encircled by "stony walls all around" (pp. 316, 269, 418, 391), where Pierre settles with Isabel in the stone-carved Church of the Apostles, as though to fulfill the promise of his name (Pierre, Peter, Christ, the rock of our salvation). And then again, there are the inversions inherent in the satire itself. The Dedication is a homage to royalty that declares the author's independence, an act of defiance made in a posture of submission, a plea for patronage that celebrates isolation, and a tribute to nature's nation which, in its allusion to the Congress of Vienna—the Great Repression of 1814, comparable to the Reaction of 1848, when (in Melville's words) "all the world around, these kings, they had the casting vote, and voted for themselves"[5]—whose *grim* allusion to Old World repression effectually equates Europe with America and the present with the past.

A rich and intricate piece of rhetoric, perhaps more intricate than necessary, as some readers have complained. The problem in the Dedication is not Melville's lack of control, but, if anything, just the reverse. The language seems *too* controlled, overdeter-

mined, self-consciously elaborated to the point of impasse. It is as
though two narrators were speaking simultaneously—one, the
proud author who is dedicating the book; the other, the humble
"I" inside the Dedication—one building up the tribute, the other
tearing it down. And neither of these, be it noted, is necessarily
Melville himself. Nor is it, necessarily, the official author of
Pierre, for whom Melville wanted an anonymous or (as he told his
publisher) "an assumed name—'*By a Vermonter*,' say."[6]

So we come to the first level of explication: *Pierre* as parody.
Whatever else may be said about it, the Dedication is meant to be
funny, and it is; and so is the novel. *Pierre* is a tragicomedy of
downward mobility, a gothic tall tale about a pretentious country
boy who makes a mess of things at home, moves to the big city,
and quickly falls from riches to rags. His fall is spiritual as well
as material. Pierre's revolt against convention ends in shambles—
family destroyed, morality desecrated, hope abandoned, not even
a book published. That repeated "I know not" in the Dedication
has broad implications for the novel. Pierre seems really *not to
know*. He knows neither what he is doing nor even what he wants.
His characteristic mode is the rhetoric of self-deceit. "Ambiguity"
in 1852 signalled mental confusion as well as semantic complexity, and it is the former far more than the latter meaning that
young Pierre embodies. He pretends to marry Isabel because, he
tells us, he wants to uphold the truth, to protect his mother from
the knowledge of his father's (supposed) sins, and to redeem his
father by himself atoning for those sins. In fact, of course, he is
doing his best to cover up a lie (or what he thinks is a lie), punishing
his mother (who soon dies of grief), and not only duplicating but
compounding his father's crime (if crime there was), all because
he has been overcome by a passion that he needs to conceal from
himself. Having made plans to run off with Isabel, he confirms
what he declares to be his high resolve for truth ("Civilization,
Philosophy, Ideal Virtue!") by rushing into Lucy's bedroom at
dawn and announcing with "imperious instantaneousness . . . 'I
am married' "; then he repeats the announcement (a lie) to his
mother, again without explanation, "stare[s] about him with an
idiot eye; [and] stagger[s] to the floor below, to dumbly quit the
house" (pp. 352, 217, 219). Now, after their flight from Saddle
Meadows to New York City, he and Isabel are together in the
bedroom of their rented flat, free at last:

"Let us light a candle, my sister; the evening is deepening."

"For what light a candle, dear Pierre?—Sit close to me, my brother."

He moved nearer to her, and stole one arm around her . . . his whole frame was invisibly trembling . . . the tremor ran from him to her; both sat dumb. . . .

"Say, are not thy torments now gone, my brother?"

"Hark thee to thy furthest inland soul"—thrilled Pierre in a steeled and quivering voice. "Call me brother no more!. . ."

"Pierre . . . trust to me. . . . [But] tell me first what is Virtue. . . ."

"Look: a nothing is the substance, it casts one shadow one way, and another the other way; and these two shadows cast from one nothing; these, seems to me, are Virtue and Vice."

"Then why torment thyself so, dearest Pierre?"

"It is the law."

"What?"

"That a nothing should torment a nothing; for I am a nothing. It is all a dream—we dream that we dreamed we dream."

"Pierre, when thou just hovered on the verge, thou wert a riddle to me; but now . . . doth poor ignorant Isabel begin to comprehend thee. . . . Yes, it is all a dream!"

Swiftly he caught her in his arms:—"From nothing proceeds nothing, Isabel! How can one sin in a dream?"

"First what is sin, Pierre?"

"Another name for the other name. . . ."

"Let us sit down again, Pierre: sit close. . . ."

And so . . . when the twilight was gone, and no lamp was lit . . . Pierre and Isabel sat hushed. (pp. 317–320)

That parodic *hush*, like the parodic *dumb* that precedes it, is typical of a constant comic discrepancy in *Pierre* between rhetoric and plot, what's being said and what's going on.* One way to

---

*What is being *said* here is of course a continuation of what has been *done* in Saddle Meadows:

> He held her tremblingly; she bent over toward him; his mouth wet her ear; he whispered it. . . . [She] leaned closer to him, with an inexpressible strangeness of an intense love, new and inexplicable. Over the face of Pierre there shot a terrible self-revelation . . . they coiled together, and entangledly stood mute. (p. 228)

For pedagogic purposes, this passage might be connected not only to the scene at the Apostles, but also—in its "strangeness," its "mute" "coiling," and its ironies

read the comedy is through the numerous parallel scenes in the thrillers of the time, by men and women scribblers alike, from Henry William Herbert's *Pierre the Partisan* to Mrs. E.D.E.N. Southworth's prolific domestic novels, beginning in 1852 (providentially) with *The Discarded Daughter* and continuing through *Vivia, or the Secret of Power* and *Ishmael, or in the Depths*. There, too, the pastoral landscape is framed by "majestic hills." There too, the dark-haired "forest girl" casts her shadow between the hero and his betrothed; brother and sister discover each other, passionately, by ancestral tokens; the rural innocent leaves for The City (New York or Philadelphia) in the hope of becoming a "famous author"; and mysterious portraits and letters unveil a hidden world of secret kinship, broken taboos, and pervasive sexual innuendo.[7]

Recent critics have decoded *Pierre* in these or similar terms. It remains to say that the object of parody is not just popular fiction but high art and more largely the reciprocities between the two. *Pierre* is valuable as a critique of the inner dynamics of the best-seller—its conventions, formulas, and narrative mechanisms—at precisely the moment that the literary marketplace was emerging in antebellum America. But the critique itself extends to include the classic forms implicit in the popular. Indeed, insofar as *Pierre* "mocks" and "subverts," its primary aim is to subvert the models of aesthetic transcendence (Shakespeare, Dante, Aeschylus) which provide the standards for mockery in the first place. The result is parody turned against itself, a satire of the comic *pretensions* of the parodic mode. For example: *Pierre* unmasks the sentimental clichés about "home" ("the sweetest and loftiest religion of this earth") and denounces the maternal tyranny they represent, sexual and social, through an alternative ideal of "universal siblinghood" ("family of man," "fraternity,"

---

of naming ("inexplicable," "inexpressible")—to the novel's sustained critique of the interpretative process, including the "terrible self-revelation" of the "American Enceladus" (pp. 396–402), which I discuss later in the chapter, and leading back to Pierre's seminal reading of the Chair Portrait:

> by irresistible intuitions, all that had been inexplicably mysterious to him in the portrait, and all that had been inexplicably familiar in the face, most magically these now coincided. . . . they reciprocally identified each other, and, as it were, melted into each other, and thus interpenetratingly unit[ed]. (pp. 103–104)

"children of God")[8]—a high rhetoric derived from Goethe, Byron, and Shelley which turns out to be equally tyrannical and hypocritical, and equally cliché (pp. 42, 103–104). Or again: *Pierre* obviously makes fun of the self-made success genre in antebellum America, the stories of young men who, in making it, come (like Ben Franklin) to represent a "rising nation";* but as the plot unfolds the satire turns increasingly against the would-be antithesis to that popular mode, the spiritual pattern of self-reliant dissent provided by Emerson and Thoreau.

Hence the problematic (rather than comic) tone of the scene I just quoted between Isabel and Pierre. To read their dialogue as parody in the traditional sense is an engaging way into the text. To read it as a critique of parodic discourse (including its pretensions to *true* depth, *true* feeling or understanding) is to recognize the unsettling reverberations of the *hush* that ends the scene. I refer to the theme of the silence which pervades the novel, and which begins, appropriately, in the tribute to mute Greylock. Earlier I spoke of two narrators in the Dedication, one naive and mystifying, the other sardonic, de-mystifying (as in the mocking narrator behind the dialogue between Pierre and Isabel). This is the place to draw attention to a third narrative level in the Dedication. I have in mind the author who hears the stony silence that elicits the tribute in the first place: the sophisticated, self-aware author who recognizes that ambiguity but cannot resolve it—who devises the harsh pun on "no" / "know" ("whether we will or no," whether Greylock approve "or no") but cannot make sense of its implications (the *disjunctions* this points to between action and knowledge)—and so insists on the process itself of rhetoric, whether the rhetoric has meaning or not. In the scene between Pierre and Isabel, this narrative voice takes the form of an author who is unable to reconcile duty and desire, virtue and truth, and

---

*This also extended to feminine models, of course. Partly, the parody in *Pierre* is directed against the popular image of the virtuous young woman cast out on her own, who becomes either the perfect wife (unlike Isabel), or the single independent woman of achievement (unlike Lucy), or who at least dies repentant and hopeful (unlike Delly). Melville turns this mode of parody against the great dramas of domesticity, especially in Greek tragedy and Shakespeare; so that *Pierre* sometimes reads esoterically like a Shakespearian problem play whose characters are stock figures of sentimental fiction: Abandoned Woman (servant class), Immigrant Orphan (upwardly mobile), Benevolent Distant Relative (unmarried, model of thrift and genteel poverty), Guardian Protector (mirror of virtue, guide to socialization, potential husband), and so on.

unable to acknowledge that failing in himself, and so keeps talking on and on, until he finds refuge in silence.

The question of parody thus opens into a problem of agency and intention. The narrative voice I am describing speaks for an author who admires Pierre's resolve to find answers, whether the world responds or not, but who recognizes, too, that what one "does" in this regard *compounds* the problem. To "*act* for Truth," as Pierre does, is to enact the *discrepancy* between a deliberating agency and the result of its intentional activity (p. 240). It is to draw out the *contradictions* inherent in subjectivity and choice (choosing good *and* acting badly; action understood as an expression of "character" *versus* action as an event in the "objective world"). The author who recognizes these ironies is closest to the source of narrative control in the novel. But he is also, ambiguously, the author who repeatedly seeks comfort in the "knowledge," which Pierre himself never gains, that "Silence is the only Voice of our God."*

---

*These phrases are taken from two parallel passages which open (respectively) the first and the second part of the novel (Books I and XIV). I quote them below to suggest how the very inversions and reversals of language become his source of narrative control:

> There are some strange summer mornings in the country when he who is but a sojourner from the city shall early walk forth into the fields, and be wonder-smitten with the trance-like aspect of the green and golden world. Not a flower stirs; the trees forget to wave; the grass itself seems to have ceased to grow; and all Nature, as if suddenly become conscious of her own profound mystery, and feeling no refuge from it but silence, sinks into this wonderful and indescribable repose. (p. 7)

* * *

> All profound things, the emotions of things, are preceded and attended by Silence. What a silence is that with which the pale bride precedes the responsive *I will*, to the priest's solemn question, *Wilt thou have this man for thy husband?* . . . Yea, in silence the child Christ is born into the world. Silence is the general consecration of the universe. . . . Silence is at once the most harmless and the most awful thing in all nature. It speaks of the Reserved Forces of Fate. Silence is the only Voice of our God. (p. 240)

What I called the first and second narrative voices correspond to (1) the naive young Pierre and (2) the embittered Pierre who sees through the facades of Saddle Meadows. The first speaks in commonplaces, the second is aggressively counter-dependent. He may be identified by his intrusive, defiant "I" ("I write precisely as I please"; "I contribute my mite" to the "infinite nonsense in this world"); by his mocking puns ("Pierre neighed out his lyrical thoughts"); and by his subverting metaphors and analogies throughout (pp. 286, 302, 191).

So we come to the second step in explication, the psychological aspect of the Dedication. And here as before we are presented with a plethora of possibilities. Those three narrative voices I spoke of—praising, ridiculing, unresolved—constitute an endlessly interpretable commentary on a primal Oedipal confrontation. Think of the varieties of emotions implicit in the eight-times-repeated "majesty," "majestic," and of how that image of overbearing authority turns into a measure of distance, a figure of alienation, and finally (since we *know* that "his Imperial Purple Majesty" will *not* respond) a trope for mere absence. Or think of the parallels between Greylock and Pierre's father as objects of contemplation, including the dizzying turns of perspective ("but," "forasmuch," "nevertheless," "or"). Or again, think of the principle of symbolic inversion inherent in the dualisms that shape the Dedication (aggression-humility, deference-contempt), particularly as that principle informs the novel's events and characters. Isabel and Lucy, for example, oppose each other as dark versus light, then as substance (dark truth) versus appearance ("light" as in "superficial"), then as eros versus *caritas*—spectre of incest (who nonetheless stands for truth) versus sister of mercy (who is then represented as the "double-hooded" murderess, Beatrice Cenci [p. 407])—and so on in endless reversals of meaning, until the two women, considered separately or together, come to seem a figure of ambivalence incarnate, like hoary Greylock.

Pierre is a story about the rhetoric of self-discovery. Significantly, the subject of the Dedication is not Greylock, but the complex authorial "I." Starting with externals, the Not-Me—nature, history, and society ("Pines and Maples," ancient customs, "we of Berkshire")—the narrator moves gradually inward, toward subjectivity and the sole self. That movement underlies the process of Pierre's development. He is first the "docile" son of Mary, queen of provincial society; then the professed husband of Isabel, "most pure" sister of "a glorious ideal" (and of his "own hidden heart"); and finally the self-absorbed author, the would-be Great Writer who spins out of his own bowels the book that he believes "will gospelize the world anew" (pp. 27, 227–228, 319).

> Live no longer to the expectation of those deceived and deceiving people with whom we converse. Say to them, O father, O mother, O wife, I have lived with you after appearances hitherto. Henceforward, I am the truth's. . . . No law can be sacred to me but that of

my own nature . . . the only right is what is after my constitution, the only wrong is what is against it. . . . I must be myself . . . [for] God is here within.[9]

This passage comes from Emerson's "Self-Reliance," of which Melville's novel is the reductio ad absurdum. Pierre moves toward God in a steady regression from society to culture to introspection; from social conformity to conformity to cultural ideals to the search for *self*-fulfillment—which is to say, for unmediated self-expression through an original relation to himself. The result is imaged through a sweeping reversal of the tribute to Greylock. The narrator describes the self as a man-made mountain, a pyramid with a secret buried at its center; in that secret lies the meaning of identity. Hence our obsessive self-involvement: "By vast pains we mine into the pyramid; by horrible gropings we come to the central room; with joy we espy the sarcophagus; but we lift the lid—and no body is there!— appallingly vacant as vast is the soul of a man!" (p. 332).

Since critics tend to read that vacancy as existential nothingness, it is worth remarking that something is discovered here by somebody. The descent into the pyramid is a metaphor not of absolute futility, but of the futility of absolute independence. The disciples who drew back the stone from Christ's sepulchre to see no body there found their faith confirmed. Melville's archeologist of the soul discovers the vast and vacant promise of the God within. In this sense his inquiry into the processes of mind devolves upon the theme of narcissism, which he repeatedly connects to the theme of incest. Indeed, the connection between narcissism and incest is central to the novel's narrative structure; each of the three stages of Pierre's descent into self-discovery may be summarized in these terms:

1) *The Saddle Meadows Idyll* (Books I–IX): The implicit sexuality between Mary Glendinning and her son—which critics have identified as the first extended treatment in modern literature of Oedipal desire—is nourished by an admiration of those qualities in themselves that each sees reflected in the other.

2) *The Flight to Isabel* (Books X–XVIII): Pierre's sexual attraction to his "sister" is based on what he can read into her about himself: she functions above all as his anima, guide to the creative dark night of his soul.

3) *The Creation of the Book* (Books XIX–XXVI): Vivia is

Pierre's fullest self-reflection, his Pygmalion's model on whom he projects what he desires for himself. In Saddle Meadows he had conceived of Isabel as an Athena to his Zeus: a woman who "never knew a mortal mother," who "seemed not of woman born," whose "lips . . . never touched a woman's breast," and whom he fancies he has conjured up as an enigmatic face, like Greylock's, "encircled by bandlets of light" (pp. 137, 54). But like her dark double, "Sister Mary," Isabel proves to be resiliently *herself*, a self-reflection who is ambiguously other. Pierre moves to resolve the conflict by creating "himself in himself, and not by reflectings in others" (pp. 20, 304). Vivia is his consummate self-made object of love.

I mean "self-made" here as a scatological pun,* and I have in mind the climax of Pierre's literary career: the author alone in his room, creating Vivia, the author-hero of his novel. Having discovered in himself "his own Alpha and Omega," Pierre puts "his soul to labor" in order to produce an imaginary "child born solely from one parent"—to father upon himself, as "Vivia," the author of a "book of sacred truth" that will reveal "deeper secrets than the Apocalypse" (pp. 304, 302, 130, 319). In effect, it is Narcissus mating with himself in the hope of begetting the New World Messiah. That the hope is ludicrous as well as spurious makes this climactic coupling a fit image of the tribute to Greylock: the last in a series of doubles (mother/son, brother/sister, author/fiction) that may be said to begin even before the novel does, with the Dedication. For in some sense, clearly, the mountain out there is a projection of the writer's inmost anxieties and aspirations; and in that sense the great stone face of Greylock, which we know will finally *not* respond, is his own, the self-made word that never materializes.

This pattern of inversions finds its narcissistic-incestuous epitome in Pierre's dream-vision of Enceladus (pp. 396–402). At the nadir of his descent into the self Pierre falls into a trance, and

*As several critics have noted, scatology is a major motif in *Pierre*. It begins in the opening overview of the family history, as in the images of Mary Glendinning "fondling" the "Major General's baton"; it continues in Pierre's musings about Lucy's "airy zone" and "peepings" into the mysterious "interior" of Isabel's guitar; and it becomes part of the texture of Melville's scenes of Pierre in New York, and indeed of the city itself, as in his description of the wharves where "the crotch of the twin-rivers pressed the great wedged city almost out of sight" (pp. 26, 80, 176, 494).

imagines that he is ascending Greylock, the Delectable Mountain, now termed the Mount of Titans. First, there is the majestic broad view, dominated by the mountain's "purple precipice"; then a closer view, which the author describes as "disordered rows of broken Sphinxes leading to the Cheopian pyramid itself." Then, climbing higher through "vapors and mists," his view narrows to a cluster of rocks resembling a group of Titans, and finally it comes to rest on the mightiest of these, Enceladus, whom he identifies with Ephialtes, the Titan who fought a furious and futile battle of mountains against the gods—misidentifies Enceladus as Ephialtes, meaning Nightmare, perhaps because in his dream Enceladus is armless, whereas the mythic Enceladus was said to have been "conspicuous for the beauty of his arms." The narrator describes the dismemberment as an "amputation"—leaving the "impotent Titan ... without one serviceable ball-and-socket above the thigh"—by which he means to suggest not castration but, in a daring variation on Ovid's *Metamorphoses*, a giant impotent phallus in the act of masturbation. "This American Enceladus," explains the narrator, "wrought by the vigorous hand of Nature's self," had "turned his vast trunk into a battering ram," and "with his whole striving trunk . . . hurled [himself] . . . again and yet again against the invulnerable steep."

What makes the Titan "impotent," then, is not sexual incapacity, but its grotesque inversion: eroticism perpetuated into the ordeal of Sisyphus; sexuality incapable of fulfillment because turned entirely in upon itself. And it is intensely turned inward because it has discovered there, after many frustrations, its one true object of desire. Earlier in the novel, the narrator wonders why it was that in Pierre, "the sole object of her love," Mary Glendinning "saw her own graces strangely transplanted into the opposite sex" (p. 9). " 'See I lakes or eyes?'," says Lucy to Pierre, lovingly—"her own" eyes (the narrator adds) "gazing down into his soul, as two stars gaze down into a tarn" (p. 42). " 'From nothing proceeds nothing'," says Pierre passionately to Isabel; " 'how can one sin in a dream?' " The answer to these rhetorical questions comes in the classic moment of recognition that ends Pierre's nightmare:

> "Enceladus! It is Enceladus!"—Pierre cried out in his sleep. That moment the phantom faced him; and Pierre saw Enceladus no more; but on the Titan's armless trunk, his own duplicate face and features

magnifiedly gleamed upon him. . . . With trembling frame he . . . woke from that ideal horror to all his actual grief.

So much for the dream of self-discovery. The rest is commentary. For although Pierre's "random knowledge of the ancient fables," the narrator continues, did not "fail still further to elucidate the vision," nonetheless "that elucidation was most repulsively fateful and foreboding; possibly because Pierre did not . . . wrest some final comfort from the fable; did not flog this stubborn rock as Moses his." This phrase may not have been intended as a double entendre, but it is an odd image of comfort, since Moses' flogging of the rock was the sin that barred him from Canaan, a familiar type of the piercing of Christ's side. Now, the narrator often hints that Pierre is a type (or would-be type) of Christ, which may be why Pierre does not flog *his* stubborn rock. The narrator performs that Mosaic service for him. "Thus smitten," he continues,

> the Mount of Titans seems to yield this following stream: Old Titan's self was the son of incestuous Coelus and Terra, the son of incestuous Heaven and Earth. And Titan married his mother Terra, another and accumulatively incestuous match. And thereof Enceladus was one issue. So Enceladus was both the son and the grandson of an incest.

And Enceladus, we might add, out of his own "bounteous and unstinted fertilizations," begat Vivia.

Ideal horror, actual grief: the doubling process in Pierre's vision extends from the mockery of the self to the scatology of naming. At the moment of self-discovery, Pierre cries out "It is Enceladus!" and sees the duplicate of his own face, magnified, on the impotent battering ram: that terrible double entendre is set within an intricate pattern of symbolic naming, doubling back from uncreated Vivia (Pierre's "Alpha and Omega") to ancient Enceladus ("American") through Moses (*typus Christi*) to Old Titan (alias Tartarus), and Coelus (or Caelum), and Terra (alias Gaea)—in sum, from Pierre's myth ("another name for the other name") back to the myth of creation. And the scatology implicit in that series of interwoven couplings is framed by still another, "contextual" series of doubles: Pierre sleeping and waking; the author and Pierre; dream and interpretation; incestuous heaven and earth, parents of life ("Vivia"); and the "coilings" of ideal and actual to which Pierre awakens, returning to Vivia ("life"). He awakens, we might say, from the "titan" of his nightmare to the "phantom" of his literary dreams. And that ambiguous awakening turns out to be still "another and accumulatively incestuous match," for Pierre's literary dreams are engendered by doublings of many prior texts. One of these is Wordsworth's concluding vision to *The Prelude* (which Melville read in galley proof in 1850). In that *ultimum* of Romantic self-discovery, the poet ascends Mount Snowdon through "hoary mist" and "vapours," and as the sky clears, he sees in nature "the type of a majestic intellect," "the emblem of a mind / That feeds upon infinity. . . / . . . intent to hear / Its voices issuing forth to silent light / In one continuous stream." The other text is the *Inferno*, canto 31, heavily marked by Melville, where the poet descends into a circle of Titans, among whom he sees Ephialtes, mired in a pit up to his waist, bound and fettered, but shaking violently in his pride. Dante tells us that he might have died from terror, had he "not seen the cords / That held [the Titan] fast."[10]

Melville's illicit marriage of Titanic pride and what Keats (thinking of Wordsworth) termed "the egotistical sublime" is very rich in implication—for the novel, for the daemonic strain in Melville's writing, and for the repressed relations between English and American Romanticism. To suggest the complexity of Melville's representation of transatlantic incest (Old World and New, as in the name of Pierre), let me note two further interlinked texts inscribed in the American Enceladus. The first comes from Melville's marginalia to *Paradise Lost*. In 1849 he glossed the scene where the rebel angels (of whom Ephialtes is a figure or type) are crushed by mountains, and commended Milton for his "profound atheistical" insights. "He always teaches under a mask," Melville noted; "and makes the Devil himself a Teacher and a Messiah." That same year he scored the scene which was to be the single most prominent source for Pierre's nightmare-vision, Keats's transformation in *Hyperion* of Milton's Hell into the dungeons of the elder gods, imprisoned by Jove. Prominent among these is Saturn ("whose hoar locks / Shone") and the Titans, lying "vast and edgeways; like a dismal cirque / Of Druid stones," until aroused by "the overwhelming voice / Of huge Enceladus," crying for revenge. Consider the contrast, from this Romantic–Miltonic perspective, between Melville's American Titan and the other titans of the American Renaissance: Walt Whitman, for one, creating *his* "Biblia Americana" (the New World version of the Romantic project of self-consecration, from Blake through Nietzsche) through the most grandiose visions of phallic narcissism in Western literature; or the natural supernaturalist Henry David Thoreau, who in 1852 "took a ramble over [Greylock's] summit at midnight by moonlight" to hear "the moaning of the wind on the rocks," and several years earlier (in *A Week on the Concord and Merrimack River*, which Melville read in 1849), recorded how he climbed Greylock through an "ocean of mist" and then watched "the day break from the top":

> As the light in the east steadily increased, it revealed to me more clearly the new world into which I had risen in the night, the new *terra firma* perchance of my future life. . . . All around beneath me was spread for a hundred miles on every side, as far as the eye could reach, an undulating country of clouds, answering in the varied swell of its surface to the terrestial world it veiled. It was such a country as we might see in dreams, with all the delights of paradise.[11]

The Emerson who brought Whitman and Thoreau to a boil brings Job's boils to poor Pierre.

But Melville is concerned here not so much with his protagonist's quarrel with God, as with the ambiguities of mind which that quarrel entails. Pierre is not Ahab. He is (among other things) the process of becoming Ahab laid bare; and the process, we have seen, leads from the parody of self-assertion to the problematics of intertextuality. It is essential to the psychodrama of *Pierre*—fundamental to Melville's revision of the bildungsroman as a tale of the ambiguities of mind—that this is a book about books, and more broadly, a book about art. The novel's structure is a surrealist regression of narrators: Melville writing about an author (or authors), writing about Pierre, writing about Vivia, writing about himself, the "apparent author-hero" (p. 352) of Pierre's fictional autobiography. The main characters are artists: Pierre a writer, Isabel a musician, and Lucy a painter. The central problem is the interpretation of a portrait, or rather a series of portraits: first, a pair of conflicting family portraits, ostensibly of Pierre's father; last, what Pierre thinks is a portrait of himself, "in the skeleton" (p. 415), by Lucy; and between these, like the centerpiece of a triptych, a fraudulent copy of Guido Reni's portrait of Beatrice Cenci (which we now know, and Melville would have been pleased to learn, is neither by Guido nor of the Cenci) paired with the portrait of a young man resembling Pierre's father, apparently, or perhaps Isabel (as she herself claims),* though the painting seems like all the others around it an avowed counterfeit—an "imported daub," numbered 99 (the number of the canto where Dante sees "the visage most resembling Christ"):[12] *"No. 99. A stranger's head, by an unknown hand"* (pp. 405–406).

Most striking of all in this respect is Pierre himself. If Vivia is the self made word, Pierre is the word made self, a sort of literary *tableau vivant*, a collage of bookish references, citations, and misquotations come to life. The narrator describes him as a mountain climber trying to scale Parnassus with "a pile of folios on his back" (p. 330). And though Pierre claims to shed his burden as he mines into himself, the allusions keep piling up—Bulwer-Lytton's Glenn and Scott's Glendinning; Milton's Christ (as well as Satan), and the New Testament Christ, alongside Job and Ishmael; Spenser's Red Cross Knight juxtaposed with Keats's Melancholy, Browne's *Anatomy*, and William Gilmore Simms's Beauchamp; Goethe's Werther, and Goethe himself in his autobiography, *Poetry and Truth*; the author-protagonist of *Sartor Resartus*; Aeschylus's Orestes and Prometheus, and Shelley's Prometheus too, as well as Mary Shelley's Frankenstein; a pantheon of mythic figures, from Apollo and Orpheus to Sisyphus and Zeus; a company of Byronic heroes (Childe Harold, Cain, Manfred); legends from Petronius and hagiographies of medieval saints; Dante the Poet, accompanied by his creations (Paolo, Agnello); a variety of Shakespearean heroes, most notably (and self-consciously) Hamlet, but also Macbeth, Romeo, Coriolanus, and even for a moment (in the dialogue with Isabel) King Lear and his Fool; and many others, including characters from Cooper, De Quincey, Mme. de Stael, Dickens, Disraeli, Godwin, Lamartine, Longfellow, Jean Paul Richter, Eugène Sue, and several forgotten heroes of popular fiction.[13] Fittingly, the authorial Vivia that Pierre creates—"directly plagiariz[ing] from his own experiences"—cannot write a sentence without "filching from Lucan and Voltaire," or alluding to the

---

*Isabel's epiphany at the gallery is one more double of the American Enceladus. Standing amidst "the empty and impotent scapes of pictures"—"mutilated torsoes of the imperfections of antiquity"—she looks intently at the portrait of the "foreign young man" and calls out to Pierre: " 'My God! see! see! . . . only my mirror has ever shown me that look before!' " (pp. 487–488)

Bible, or paraphrasing Carlyle, or evoking Novalis and other German Romantic aphorists, or referring (with a "frenzied," "reeking," "melancholy" anxiety) to various Old World thinkers, from Plato through Spinoza (pp. 352–353).

So we come to the third step in explication, the literary view of the Dedication: Saddleback, with his Keatsian "hoar locks" shining "delectably" (as Bunyan's Pilgrim might put it, alluding to the fabled Land of Beulah) in a Thoreauvian sunrise, counterpart to Wordsworth's moonlit Snowdon—Mount Greylock as intertextuality personified. So considered, the Dedication is a discourse on language. It presents a mountain-*scape*, a de-centered, self-reflective verbal portrait of Greylock in the process of being interpreted. Words about words: in retrospect, the outrage of the 1852 reviews was predictable. Equally predictable has been the endorsement of our time, and it may be well to point out that Melville was not modernist, much less postmodernist, except insofar as he was the most probing critical mind among the American Romantics. Indeed, the Dedication offers a rather direct commentary on Romantic aesthetics, as in the image of the sun through which the author claims his autonomy. Greylock, the "grand dedicatee" of Berkshire's "earliest rays," is now to receive light, whether the mountain likes it or not, from the sun (or lamp) of the creative imagination. It seems the quintessential Romantic gesture of self-authorizing—as in Whitman's "Song of Myself": "Dazzling and tremendous how quick the sun-rise would kill me, / If I could not now and always send sun-rise out of me."[14] The difference in Melville's Dedication is that the conflict turns inward, splinters into ambiguities about the self, and these inner civil wars reveal, among other things, that *this* creative sun draws its light, un-Romantically, from many other sources.

In fact, the Dedication is a pastiche of Romantic assertions about an original relation to nature: for instance, Coleridge's "magnificent hymn of Mont Blanc" (as *The Democratic Review* of 1848 described it); Shelley's poem to "inaccessible" Mont Blanc, surrounded by its "subject mountains"; Sylvester Judd's ode to Mons Christi (and "the Delectable Way" that leads to it) in his best-selling novel of 1845 (revised and enlarged for republication in 1852); perhaps Poe's "Haunted Palace," where "Wanderers in [a] happy valley" see from afar, "sitting / (Porphyrogene!) / In state his glory well befitting, / The ruler of the realm"; and perhaps even Poe's then well-known "Letter to B___," which images an Andes of the mind leading "ascendingly, to a few gifted individuals who kneel around the summit, beholding, face to face, the master spirit." Probably this pastiche extends as well to various tributes by Berkshire literati, such as Oliver Wendell Holmes and Catharine Maria Sedgwick, to "Greylock, cloud-girdled on his mountain throne." Certainly it includes reference to the poem that Sedgwick was here imitating, Thomas Gray's tribute to the bard Mordred, "whose magic song / Made huge Plinlimmon"—the highest mountain in Wales after Mount Snowdon, which Wordsworth celebrated in *The Prelude* as "a mind sustained / By recognitions of transcendent power" and "more than mortal privilege"—

> . . . whose magic song
> Made huge Plinlimmon bow his cloud-cap't head.[15]

In short, interpretation directs us not to an authorial self, but into a pyramid, "surface stratified upon surface" (p. 332), of literary reference. The empty sarcophagus has its double in a Pandora's box of intertextuality.

Still, there is a certain logic to the flow of allusions. They are not random but layered, and layered, moreover, in a broad archeological sequence. I have hinted at this pattern in outlining the sources of the Dedication; and the same pattern or structure applies to the scene at the Mount of Titans, whose meaning leads back, layer upon layer, from the exoteric to the esoteric, and from current fiction to the fables of antiquity: Sylvester Judd, Wordsworth, Milton, Dante, the Bible, Greek myth. But to indicate the richness of the novel, I offer still another example. Young Pierre in Saddle Meadows is approaching Balance Rock or the Terror Stone—so named because, like Greylock, it is "the wonder of the simple country round" (p. 159)—which Pierre has renamed for the Egyptian hero Memnon, perhaps because, like Melville, he once read Pliny's *Natural History*, where Memnon is associated with porphyrite, the purple-tinted royal stone of Egypt. According to Pliny, the porphyrite statue of Memnon, son of Aurora, rang a musical note each morning at the touch of the sun's first rays.*

---

*Prophyrite has further associations with Porphyrion, one of the leaders in the Titans' revolt, as well as with Porphyry, the chief disciple of Plotinus. It might

Byron in *Don Juan* compares this to "a strange, unearthly sound," "Sad, but serene"; and Keats compares "that Memnon's harp" to the sighs of Hyperion, when challenged by Enceladus to defy the tyranny of Olympus. Francis Bacon, a more austere reader, interprets this as a lament for

> the unfortunate deaths of young men of high promise. For such are as it were the sons of the morning, and it commonly happens that, being puffed up with empty and outward advantage, they venture upon enterprises beyond their strength . . . and falling in the unequal conflict are extinguished. But . . . [our] feeling of pity lasts long after; and more especially upon all fresh accidents and new movements and beginnings of great events, as by the touch of sunrise, the regret for them is stirred up again and renewed.[16]

At the base of the Memnon Stone, then, young Pierre (fresh from his accidental encounter with Isabel) sets out on what he imagines are the beginnings of great events. There, in a secular conversion experience, he tests the meaning of his identity, dies to his old self, and is reborn, porphyrogenitus, as—the American Hamlet, since Hamlet, the narrator explains, "is but Egyptian Memnon, Montaignized [pun intended] and modernized" (p. 162). So the process of identification leads back from the Modern to the Renaissance to Egyptian antiquities, from Pierre through Shakespeare to mythic Memnon. And so also Pierre's vision of Enceladus may be said to lead back from Judd's Mons Christi, or from Mount Calm, (the "majestic presence" overlooking the "delectable" setting of Emma Southworth's *The Discarded Daughter*) to Shelley's Mont Blanc—the Wordsworthian–Byronic personification of "The secret strength of things / which governs thought, and to the infinite dome / Of heaven is as law." Southworth noted the mountain's Shelleyan grandeur, without, however, remarking, as Melville surely did, the doubt which Shelley added: "And what were thou, and earth, and stars, and sea, / If to the human mind's

---

also be noted, in view of the persistent play in *Pierre* on the contrast between Old World and New, that Porpheero is the name Melville gives for Europe in *Mardi*, and that "porphyrogenitus" was a familiar term in the nineteenth-century political oratory as a pejorative description of European governments vis-à-vis America's. As late as 1893, the *Atheneum* (XI, 184) could speak of the "fun to be got by bringing the porphyrogenitus of the English aristocracy face to face with all that is most modern in the American democracy."

imaginings / Silence and solitude were vacancy?" The entire process leads back ambiguously from Judd and Southworth to Shelley, Wordsworth, and Byron, and also to Emerson (our American "Plotinus–Montaigne," his friend James Russell Lowell termed him), bard of New England's mountains and herald of the American "poet-priest," a "native Titan" who would one day, Emerson prophesied, "with a mountainous aspiring say, *I am God*"—leads back, that is, from popular fiction to the great English and American Romantics to Enceladus and Ephialtes and thence, by "cumulative incest," still further back to the story of creation itself.[17] In all cases, interpretation means regression. Paradigmatically, this takes the form of a spiral of interpretive associations descending (*as though* to deeper levels of meaning) from current literature to the classics, and thence through "innumerable ages" (as the narrator says of Greylock) to legend and myth. And in all cases, the process of regression reflects the parodic process I traced earlier: the incest of low and high literature, leading from social identity to cultural ideals to the primal self. It also parallels the process of Pierre's literary career: from writer of popular fiction (in Saddle Meadows) to an enthusiast of the classics (after he meets Isabel), and finally to the autonomous author of Vivia. "Oh hitherto I have piled up words," he declares, in deciding to leave for the city; "now I sit down and read" (p. 10). When later he begins to write again, Pierre finds himself "transplanted into a new and wonderful element," where "books no more are needed." Standing there upon the Mount Blanc of the mind, overlooking the "full awfulness" of the Alps within, and beyond these, across "the invisible Atlantic," the awfulness of our interior Berkshires and Rocky Mountains, he realizes that "all the great books in the world are but the mutilated showings-forth of invisible and eternally unembodied images of the soul; so that they are but mirrors, distortedly reflecting to us our own things; and never mind what the mirror may be"—Emerson's Natural Aristocrat, Byron's Don Juan, Shakespeare's Hamlet, Aeschylus's Orestes— "if we would see the object, we must look at the object itself, and not at its reflection" (p. 331).

The object itself: it is not intertextuality that undermines Pierre; nor is it the confusion of subject and object (who he is and what he reads); nor is it the recurrent conflict in his reading between the different meanings of the text. It is his inability to distinguish in these terms between mirror and reflection, and

more largely the inadequacy of that distinction in establishing
substantive differences between the perceived multiplicity of
meanings. We might call it a problem of depth. *Pierre* is a search for
origins that leads through a series of interpretations, or interpreted
personae, each of them incomplete—"amputated," "distorted,"
"fragmented"—but by their very incompleteness pointing toward
some potentially holistic identity: some inner mirror of wholeness
by which we judge the reflection to be incomplete. So understood,
ambiguity is not a threat but a spur to selfhood. It is a challenge
to make visible the primal inwardness that authorizes interpretation. What drives Pierre forward is the faith that partiality, in its
pluralist application, is the guide simultaneously to self-fulfillment and to truth in process. That faith was the rock of exegesis
for Hawthorne, and for Melville in turn as he absorbed it from
Hawthorne in particular and the culture at large. Ambiguity in
that liberal context attests both to the meaningfulness of the
reflection (the object out there) and to the primacy of the mirror
(subjectivity, or the object itself). Or to put this in *Pierre*'s terms:
Interpretation, offspring of the Ambiguities, attests to the unity
behind *and in* multiplicity. That unity involves continuity, continuity means progress (more Self, more Truth), and progress implies *hierarchy*: a series of increasingly deeper and broader "levels
of meaning," grounded in the correspondence between the One
and the Many, the object and its reflections.

I emphasize the term "hierarchy" in order to recall the extraordinary coherence of that outlook—a coherence (we have seen)
that extends to historiographical, political, and moral as well as
aesthetic process. "Hierarchy" also points to the hermeneutic
tradition that lies behind the liberal-symbolic mode. As Melville
inherited this tradition (along with Bancroft and Hawthorne), it
goes back to the origins of figural exegesis. According to Christ
himself (Matt. 12:21,40), the meaning of the crucifixion lies in a
configuration of Old Testament passages, linking Jonah's whale
to Isaiah's suffering servant. So, too (as *Pierre* reminds us), the
stone which is Christ (Eph. 2:20) *means* Jacob's pillow, the foundation stone which the Jews rejected, and the long-prophesied "stone
cut out of a mountain" which signals the millennium (Gen. 28:28,
Acts 4:11, Dan. 2:34, Rev. 2:17). For Christian interpreters, the
ambiguity of these intertextual links was the vehicle of the spirit
behind the letter of the text. Properly contextualized, the partial
and veiled revelations of particular scripture passages became

"proof-texts" of a general design. Their ambiguities, duly explicated, provided the key both to universal progress (toward the Parousia) and to the universality (in Christ) of the interpreter's inmost self. For their Romantic heirs, the source of proof shifted from the Bible to works of art (including the Bible); but the affirmation of universality—which is to say, of historical ascent and spiritual depth—remained essentially the same. In both cases, the process of interpretation devolved upon the hierarchical spirit encoded in the ambiguities of the word.

There were several routes to the spirit available to the American Romantic at midcentury. One of these Melville outlines in his review of Hawthorne's *Mosses*:

> spite of all the Indian-summer sunlight on the hither side of Hawthorne's soul, the other side—like the dark half of the physical sphere—is shrouded in a blackness, ten times black. . . . [I]t is that blackness that so fixes and fascinates me . . . this blackness it is that furnishes the . . . background, against which Shakespeare plays his grandest conceits. . . . For in this world of lies, Truth is forced to fly like a scared white doe in the woodlands; and only by cunning glimpses will she reveal herself, as in Shakespeare and other masters of the great Art of Telling the Truth.

This theory of interpretation draws on esoteric strains in theological exegesis (kabala, apocalyptica). It was termed the Satanic side of Romantic aesthetics, by those who were shocked by Blake's interpretation of Satan as the secret hero of *Paradise Lost*; but as both Blake and Melville (in his 1850 *magnalia* to Milton's epic) testify, it is a Satanism that consecrates the self. As in perspectival drawing, the "blackness, *ten times* black," provides depth. It reveals the complex wholeness of Truth, the profundity of selfhood, in mirror and reflection alike: in Milton's Satan as in his latter-day interpreters; in Hawthorne's "Young Goodman Brown" as in the "eagle-eyed" "Virginian" who recognized in that "simple little tale" a genius "deep as Dante."[18]

The enormous optimism (historical and spiritual) implicit in such discoveries of depth may be traced throughout Blake's work. For Melville they carried a unique *American* meaning. Hawthorne's achievement, he writes, is a forecast of cultural independence, a promise of Shakespeares to be born on the banks of the Ohio—or perhaps, indeed, already growing up (like Pierre in Saddle

Meadows) somewhere in the bosom of nature's nation, with "the smell of beeches and hemlocks . . . upon him; broad prairies . . . in his soul . . . [and in] his deep and noble nature . . . the far roar of Niagara":

> whilst we are rapidly preparing for that political supremacy among the nations, which prophetically awaits us at the close of the present century; in a literary point of view, we are deplorably unprepared for it; and we seem studious to remain so. . . . [But] all that is requisite to amendment in this matter, is simply this: that, while freely acknowledging all excellence . . . we should . . . duly recognize . . . those writers, who breathe that unshackled, democratic spirit of Christianity in all things, which now takes the practical lead in this world, though at the same time led by ourselves—us Americans.[19]

This nationalist and democratic spirit does not quite meet the demands of esoteric Truth, as Pierre learns to his grief. I discuss this American aspect of the novel later in the chapter. Here I invoke it to suggest the enormous value which antebellum Americans placed on the Romantic correspondence between the object and its reflection—which is to say, on the imperial claims implicit in the concentricity of self, text, and interpretation. The central tenet of that faith, as Melville had come to understand it by 1852, was Emerson's doctrine of the individual, and particularly (for present purposes) the Emersonian doctrine of right reading:

> What can we see, read, acquire, but ourselves? Cousin is a thousand books to a thousand persons. Take the book, my friend, & read your eyes out; you will never find there what I find. . . . It occurred last night in groping after the elements of that pleasure we derive from literary compositions, that it is like the pleasure which the prince LeBoo received from seeing himself for the first time in a mirror,— a mysterious & delightful surprise. A poem, a sentence causes us to see ourselves. I be & I see my being, at the same time.

These fragments from the Journals could be elaborated with excerpts from Emerson's entire corpus. They constitute what remains the boldest claim of American individualism: that all history is not only at but for one's disposal; that the independent self, as the heir of the ages (like "America" at large), must freely use the great works of the past—extracting what is relevant, discarding the outmoded, improving the imperfect—as a standing advertisement of an unbounded originality:

> The great poet makes us feel our own wealth, and then we think less of his compositions. His best communication to our mind is to teach us to despise all he has done. Shak[e]speare carries us to such a lofty strain of intelligent activity, as to suggest a wealth which beggars his own. . . . Why, then, should I make account of Hamlet and Lear, as if we had not the soul from which they fell as syllables from the tongue?

So ingested and improved, all texts and quotations from texts, all authors and authorizing agencies, become natural signs of the individual's mastery of culture, rather than of his indebtedness to it. More than that, they become the means by which he can center his thought where it transcendentally belongs, in his own being:

> Entire self-reliance belongs to the intellect. . . . It must treat things, and books, and sovereign genius, as itself also a sovereign. If AEschylus be that man he is taken for, he has not yet done his office, when he has educated the learned of Europe for a thousand years. He is now to approve himself a master of delight to me also. If he cannot do that, all his fame shall avail him nothing with me. I were a fool not to sacrifice a thousand AEschyluses to my intellectual integrity. . . . The Bacon, the Spinoza, the Hume, Schelling, Kant, or whosoever propounds to you a philosophy of the mind, is only a more or less awkward translator of things in your consciousness, which you have also your way of seeing, perhaps of denominating. Say, then, instead of too timidly poring into his obscure sense, that he has not succeeded in rendering back to you your consciousness. He has not succeeded; now let another try. If Plato cannot, perhaps Spinoza will. If Spinoza cannot, then perhaps Kant. Anyhow, when at last it is done, you will find it is no recondite, but [your own] simple, natural, common state.[20]

I quote these passages at length because they so clearly show the centrality of interpretation as a conceptual framework—a theory of subjectivity, process, and the "natural, common state"— in the construction of American identity. *Entire self-reliance!* Reading, for Emerson, enables the self to project itself ad infinitum by providing an endless array of mirrors in which the individual, like Prince LeBoo, sees himself revealed with "a mysterious & delightful surprise" in all his multifarious integrity. "Every book is a quotation," according to Emerson's headnote to "Quotation and Originality" (quoted without reference from his own earlier work); "and every house is a quotation out of all forests and mines and stone-quarries; and every man is a quotation from all his ancestors"—and therefore, as Whitman put it, quoting Emerson without acknowledgment, "there was never any more inception than there is now." And indeed there was no need to seek authorization, for quotation as inception was the core of transcendental aesthetics. It was not just that (to quote a recent Emersonian) the "relation of reader and text is . . . like Narcissus and his reflection."[21] It is that that relation between Narcissus and reflection is the incestuous begetting of a deeper, *more* entire self.

"The Bacon, the Spinoza, the Hume, Schelling, Kant, or whosoever propounds to you a philosophy of the mind, is only a more or less awkward translator of things in your consciousness": properly construed, the endless links between texts, backwards and forwards, latent and manifest, deliberate, repressed, and accidental, obviate external authority by their very endlessness—which is to say, by their inherent protean malleability. Because, finally, the source out there cannot be specified, the center of authority shifts to the "I" as authorizing agency. It is not the (indefinable) point of origin that matters, but the "present eternity" of the original and originating self:

> People forget that it is the eye which makes the horizon, and the rounding mind's eye which makes this or that man a type or representative of humanity with the name of hero or saint. Jesus, the "providential man," is a good man on whom many people are agreed that these optical laws shall take effect.
>
> * * *
>
> When I came at last to Rome, and saw with eyes the pictures, I found that genius . . . pierced directly to the simple and true; that it was familiar and sincere; that it was the old, eternal fact I had met already in so many forms,—unto which I lived; that it was the plain *you and me* I knew so well.[22]

Thus history dissolves into intertextuality as the vehicle of identity; or to put it in positive terms, intertextuality recomposes history into mirrors for my self-regard, texts for my utterance, wealth for my increase. Bancroft argues that history is teleological because its processes culminate in the American Revolution and then unfold, as continuing revolution, toward human perfection. Hawthorne makes us feel that the scarlet letter has not done its aesthetic office until it includes *us* in a ritual of interpretation whose continuity is at once communally progressive (from the Puritans) and individually self-generating. Emerson tells us that the individual expands into the One Man by returning to origins and advancing toward the infinite—and that returning and advancing are radii of the same circumference, just as origins and the infinite are already present in the act of self-reliance.

"If AEschylus be that man he is taken for, he has not yet done his office": thus the genius of the past inspires us to leave the past behind. Emerson says of "the poet" that "he delineates . . . the mountain. . . . In the strength of his constancy, the Pyramids seem to him recent and transitory." And he says much the same of *us* as readers: "when we adhere to the ideal of the poet, we have our difficulties even with Milton and Homer," and that sight of their shortcomings, when measured by our prospects, brings them into *our* orbit, as two more stars "shining serenely in [our] heaven and blending [their] light with all [our] day." In particular, Emerson calls attention in this regard to the spiritual uses of geology, the modern science that was then most effectively eroding the authority of scripture. "In the economy of the world," he declares, quoting Charles Lyell, whose revolutionary *Principles of Geology* (1836) had just opened out a "new world of the mind"—or, rather, misquoting Lyell (and misidentifying him with another geologist, James Hutton) and then using the phrase to fuse secular and scriptural authority on behalf of transcendent selfhood—"In the economy of the world . . . there are no traces of a beginning, no prospect of an end." Hence this most advanced of sciences at once probes furthest into our past and most clearly reveals our immanent powers:

> Language is fossil poetry. As the limestone of the continent consists of infinite masses of shells of animalcules, so language is made up of images, or tropes, which now, in their secondary use, have long ceased to remind us of their poetic origin. But the poet names the thing because he sees it.[23]

Within this context, and against it, Melville weaves the intricate knot-work of quotations and allusions. In the face of "the old eternal fact," the historicity in *Pierre* of "plain *you and me*" *mocks* the "optical laws" by which "the eye makes the horizon," just as the mountain or pyramid mocks the strength of constancy in the poet's delineation; and just as every gesture toward originality, each step in the descent to origins, subverts its own multiple pre-texts. The geologist, says Emerson, systematically uncovers "secondary" truths. "But the poet names the thing because he sees it." And as for the poet's interpreter: "in every work of genius we recognize our own rejected thoughts. They come back to us with a certain alienated majesty." For Melville, that return of the repressed takes the mutilated, nightmare form of Enceladus ("fateful and foreboding"): author, text, and interpretation "repulsively" made one. Against the Emersonian imperative to transcend, the pervasive parallels in *Pierre* between excavation and introspection systematically undermine both the object perceived and its perceiver. "Far as we blind moles can see," writes Melville, concerning his hero's quest to "find himself,"

> man's life seems but an acting upon mysterious hints; it is somehow hinted to us, to do thus or thus. For surely no mere mortal who has at all gone down into himself will ever pretend that his slightest thought or act solely originates in his own defined identity. . . . Pierre began to see through the first superficiality of the world, [and so] he fondly weens he has come to the unlayered substance. But, far as any geologist has yet gone down into the world, it is found to consist of nothing but surface stratified on surface. To its axis, the world being nothing but superinduced superficies. (pp. 209, 332)

In *Moby-Dick*, cetology bridges the realms of rhetoric and of fact: it steadies, sustains, and (despite the narrative catastrophe) justifies the voyage into interpretation. In *Pierre*, geology functions in just the opposite way. The excavation undertaken here of art and the self—as though in response to Greylock's imperious muteness, "*challenging* our homage"—leads back with a pitiless logic from one layered unsubstantiality to another. We might think of this as a journey that begins upon the "endless sea" of the uncharted self that Melville first describes in *Mardi*:

It is because we ourselves are in ourselves, that we know ourselves
not. . . . Do you believe that you lived three thousand years ago? That
you were at the taking of Tyre, were overwhelmed in Gomorrah? No.
But for me, I was at the subsiding of the Deluge, and helped swab
the ground, and build the first house. With the Israelites, I fainted
in the wilderness; was in court, when Solomon outdid all the judges
before him . . . I touched Isabella's heart, that she hearkened to
Columbus . . . I am the leader of the Mohawk masks, who in the Old
Commonwealth's harbor, overboard threw the East India Company's
Souchong; I am the Veiled Persian Prophet; I, the man in the iron
mask; I, Junius.

The journey proceeds in *Pierre*, or recedes, from that "wide Atlantic" of "our defined identity," the source of "greatest marvels"
and "first truths,"[24] to the global "axis" that turns out to be the
epitome of all "superinduced superficies."

Pierre; or The Ambiguities is a story about the illusions of
art, in which the illusions assume such elaborately artful forms
they might be taught as allegory. The scenes are heavily emblematic; the characters, rhetorical abstractions; and the names,
charged with portentous meaning: Reverend Fals/grave, "Bell"*
(Baal/Jezebel) Ban/ford, angelic Lucy, philosopher Plotinus,
mother Mary (styled "Queen," "saint," "immaculate," "conquer-
ing virgin" [pp. 125, 108, 22]). Its plot is a variation on the Morality
Play, a sort of Pilgrim's Regress from New Eden to Gehennom—
as, indeed, the tribute to majestic Greylock is a variation on the
Puritans' habit of dedicating their books, as Bunyan dedicated
Pilgrim's Progress, "To the . . . Incomprehensible Majesty of Jeho-
vah," "Him that is Higher than the 'Highest'."[25] And in the midst
of all these pasteboard signs is Pierre, the only begotten son of
Mary and a "perfect father" "in heaven" (pp. 26, 84)—trapped in
a self-styled imitation of Christ. We are told that Pierre's major
task is to add luster to the family name. His first act is one of
naming—"Lucy!"—as he looks up toward her window casement
(p. 7). It is the first word spoken in the novel (following the naming
of Greylock); it is accompanied by the appropriate explication ("by

*Isabel's nickname; it is pertinent to the Bunyanesque allegory I outline
below that "Isabel" itself means "Dedicated to God," and that it is her "call to
Truth" (p. 139) which inspires Pierre to leave family and home.

Heaven, thou belong'st to the regions of an infinite day!"), and it conjures up still other names: Romeo, and his abundant progeny in fiction (pp. 7–8). By the end of the novel, all explications have been dissolved and Pierre's family has been wiped out, its name erased. The last words seem to be Isabel's, after she drinks from a vial of poison, almost like Juliet:

> "all's o'er, and ye know him not!" came gasping from the wall; and from the fingers of Isabel dropped an empty vial. (p. 420)

And it is a tribute to the novel's sustained brilliance that Isabel (if it *is* she speaking) is right. Pierre is first a would-be allegorist in a world of multiple meaning; then a would-be symbolist in a world that yields no interpretations; then a would-be interpreter of the empty world of the self; then a would-be metaphor (stone) become dead fact.

The process is framed by two quasi-allegorical locales, representing the historic shift I spoke of from Christian to Romantic hermeneutics. The first locale is the Church of the Apostles where Pierre settles. According to the narrator, it is a "once sacred place" which has become a center of commerce and the law. So successful was the transformation that "the church-yard was invaded for a supplemental edifice," an "ambitious erection" of "Titanic bricks" which houses a "visionary company"—a group of "efflorescent," "crack-crowned" bohemians whose spiritual leader is the avant-garde philosopher Plotinus Plinlimmon:

> They are mostly artists of various sorts; painters, or sculptors, or indigent students, or teachers of languages, or poets, or fugitive French politicians, or German philosophers . . . glorious paupers, from whom I learn the profoundest mysteries of things . . . well-known Teleological Theorists, and Social Reformers, and political propagandists . . . suspected to have some mysterious ulterior object, vaguely connected with the . . . hasty and premature advance of some unknown great political and religious Millennium. . . . A mysterious professor of the flute was perched in one of the upper stories of the tower; and often, of silent, moonlight nights, his lofty, melodious notes would be warbled forth over the roofs of the ten thousand warehouses around him—as of yore, the bell had pealed over the domestic gables of a long-departed generation. (pp. 310–314)

As befits his spiritual position, Plinlimmon looks out from "one of the loftiest windows" of the tower, directly across from Pierre's chamber; so that it is under the philosopher's silent gaze, like the bard Mordred under the "cloud-cap't head" of "huge Plinlimmon," or like the author of the Dedication under the gaze of Greylock, that Pierre creates Vivia.*

The parallel to Greylock is worth elaborating. According to the narrator, an "inscrutable atmosphere eddied and eddied round-about this Plotinus Plinlimmon"; eventually, the "mystic-mild face in the upper window of the old grey tower began to domineer in a very remarkable manner upon Pierre. . . . But when he mentally interrogated the face . . . there was no response" (pp. 339, 341). No response, but ambiguity compounded: where Greylock challenged the author's "poor solitary" powers of creation—and where Isabel's "inscrutable," "mystic" face challenged Pierre to redeem the past by repudiating it—now Plinlimmon's face challenges him to "stand independent," "entirely alone," "solitary as at the Pole," even while it mocks his efforts to beget the fiction

---

*In view of the apparent parallels between Emerson and Plotinus Plinlimmon on the one hand (see Merton M. Sealts, "Melville and Emerson's Rainbow," *ESQ*, XXVI [1980], pp. 71–72 ff.), and , on the other hand, Melville's repeated parallels between Pierre and Prometheus, it may be worth noting Emerson's attitude to Bronson Alcott—"this modern Prometheus . . . in the heat of his quarrel with the gods":

> Very sad indeed . . . to see this halfgod driven to the wall, reproaching men, & hesitating whether he should not reproach the gods. The world was not, on trial, a possible element for him to live in. A lover of law had tried whether law could be kept in this world, & all things answered, NO. . . . I feel his statement to be partial & to have fatal omissions, but I think I shall never attempt to set him right any more. It is not for me to answer him: though I feel the limitations & exaggeration of his picture, and the wearisome personalities. His statement proves much: it is a *reductio ad absurdum*. (Journal U ([1844], in vol. IX of *Journals*, ed. Ralph H. Orth and Alfred R. Ferguson [Cambridge, Mass., 1971], p. 86)

Compare further Emerson's even-handed Plotinus-like interpretation (at once horological and chronometrical) of the Prometheus myth, in his poem on "The Adirondacs" (*Works*, ed. James Elliot Cabot [Boston, 1883], IX, 159–170), with Melville's portrait of Pierre at work on Vivia—Pierre the No-sayer, "driven to the wall" of the self; identified (through images of stone and fire) with Prometheus; virtually imprisoned at his desk ("squared to his plank" and reaching beyond "his solitude" with the help of a "crook-ended stick"); and described summarily as a mountain "ringed in with the grief of Eternity . . . a peak inflexible in the heart of Time, as the isle-peak, Piko, stands unassailable in the midst of waves" (pp. 351, 354).

that alone can certify his independence (pp. 345, 393). It is a remarkable Romantic prevision of the *deus absconditus*. And as its focal point, Plinlimmon's domineering "non-benevolent" countenance—"steady, observant . . . and most miraculously self-possessed" (p. 338)—serves as a sort of gargoyle-icon of a momentous transition in Western history, from theology to art. Melville's Janus-faced image of the moonlit church tower is memorable in this regard: on one side, the phantom church bells; on the other, the solitary flutist, warbling his "melodious notes . . . over the roofs of . . . ten thousand warehouses." And again (as in the Dedication), Melville's language takes on special resonance by contrast with Whitman's:

> There will soon be no more priests. Their work is done. . . . A superior breed shall take their place. . . . A new order shall arise and they shall be the priests of man, and every man shall be his own priest. . . . Through the divinity of themselves shall the kosmos and the new breed of poets be interpreters of men and women and of all events and things.
>
> I sound my barbaric yawp over the roofs of the world.[26]

The advent of this "new order" is the implied context of Pierre's aesthetic education. His first attempts to interpret the Chair Portrait undermine the rhetoric of authority; the closing impasse of meaning at the Counterfeit-Art Gallery dissolves the authority of rhetoric. Midway between these emblem-scenes, precisely at the novel's center, the narrator describes the "fateful" journey from Saddle Meadows to New York (p. 240). It is a dazzlingly multi-layered representation of the moment of transition: literally and culturally, from country to city; personally, from dependence to independence; socially, from traditional family to voluntary or contractual relations; philosophically and spiritually, from established pieties to a transcendental newness. And framing all of these (failed) passages—each a parodic variation on American myths of process (Bancroft, Hawthorne, Emerson)—is the transition to ontological doubt. Pierre's state of mind, Melville writes, recalls "a story once told" about a medieval priest tempted by the Devil:

> In the midst of a solemn cathedral, upon a cloudy Sunday afternoon, this priest was in the act of publicly administering the bread at

the Holy Sacrament of the Supper, when the Evil One suddenly propounded to him the possibility of the mere moonshine of the Christian Religion. . . . But by instant and earnest prayer—closing his two eyes, with his two hands still holding the sacramental bread—the devout priest had vanquished the impious Devil. Not so with Pierre. The imperishable monument of his holy Catholic Church; the imperishable record of his Holy Bible; the imperishable intuition of the innate truth of Christianity;—these were the indestructible anchors which still held the priest to his firm Faith's rock. . . . But Pierre—where could *he* find the Church, the monument, the Bible, which unequivocally said to him—"Go on; thou art in the Right; I endorse thee all over; go on." (p. 241)

The hearsay anecdote may be read as a parable of the hermeneutic tradition I have been sketching. In Melville's terms, it leads from Christian faith to Romantic doubt to doubt's post-Romantic harvest: a world of fictive surfaces, images and tropes without depth, interpretations whose levels of meaning seem to multiply in direct proportion to their absence of substance. One such interpretation is the portrait of the author(s) at work:

> Let us peep over the shoulder of Pierre, and see what it is he is writing there . . . to fill out the mood of . . . Vivia, who thus soliloquizes: "A deep-down, unutterable mournfulness is in me. Now I drop all humorous or indifferent disguises. . . ."
> Here is a slip from the floor. . . .
> "Cast thy eye in there on Vivia; tell me why those four limbs should be clapt in a dismal jail . . . and himself the voluntary jailer!" (pp. 352–353)

The windings here from reader and author ("us") to author and subject (Pierre, Vivia, "a slip from the floor") entail a regression of selves, circling " 'deep down' " and then around again, to Vivia's " 'me'," peeping over the reader's shoulder to see " 'himself'," alias Pierre.* And at the same time they circle forward, toward

---

*These deconstructing doubling-effects are grounded in a culture-specific symbology. I take up its broadly "American" meaning in the next section; but to emphasize the historical grounding, let me note at this point that the doubling of Pierre and Vivia—in which the symbol-making author confronts himself as man-made symbol—is richly suggestive of the Jacksonian representation of the self as commodity. It is intrinsic to *Pierre*'s critique of "Young America in Literature" (p. 286) that the Dedication is an advertisement and that its Mount Greylock is a

the meaning of self-consciousness, although the very process of going forward effectually dissolves the Emersonian dream of self-reliance.

The significance of that dissolution cannot be overemphasized. Emerson's dream is ambiguity triumphant in self-reliance. "I be & I see my being at the same time," he declares, and proceeds to apply this "monistic dualism, or dualistic monism," to experience at large:

> A subject and an object,—it takes so much to make the galvanic circuit complete, but magnitude adds nothing. What imports it whether it is Kepler and the sphere; Columbus and America; a reader and his book; or puss with her tail? . . . And yet is the God the native of these bleak rocks. That need makes in morals the capital virtue of self-trust. We must . . . possess our axis more firmly.

The axis, so possessed, is the solitary self, but the "capital" produced by investing in self-trust is both universal and teleological:

---

figure of the democratic marketplace which has replaced (yet somehow duplicated) the unnatural "privilege" of "old times." Melville extends this parodic perspective to his commentaries on the mechanisms of publishing—including elaborate digressions (carrying forward the themes of Dedication) on the importance of the "title page" and on the doubling processes of the photography by which the author becomes instant "public property" (pp. 291, 297). So considered, Melville's portrait of Vivia as the commodified self may be seen as a satire of the long tradition of self-marketing, beginning (say) with Ben Franklin. But here as elsewhere Melville's parody turns the satire against its own norms. Like the "I" in the Dedication, Pierre/Vivia is *also* an image of an ideal inner self, a variation on the doubleness of Emerson's Central Man ("I be & I see my being, at the same time"). In this sense, Pierre/Vivia reminds us that the transcendental "I" is the daemonic double of the liberal marketplace: double both in its indebtedness to the cultural norms it reflects and in the antithesis it offers to cultural restraints. In Emerson's great essays, the antithesis is developed into the most exhilarating *American* form of *literary* oppositionalism. In *Pierre* that literariness turns both against the culture which nourished it and against the oppositional self it was meant to serve. Franklin's contemporary Samuel Johnson argued against the Revolutionaries that, unless they were "the naked sons of Nature," living in a pure "state of nature," logic demanded that these self-proclaimed "lords of themselves, these kings of *Me*, these demigods of independence, sink down to colonists, governed by a charter" (*Taxation No Tyranny*, in *Political Writings*, ed. Donald J. Greene [New Haven, 1977], pp. 428–429). Emerson makes Nature the governing charter of the New World Kingdom of Me. *Pierre* substitutes for Johnson's colonial charter the *bonds* of Jacksonian independence.

A subtle chain of countless rings
The next unto the farthest brings;
. . . .
And, striving to be man, the worm
Mounts through all the spires of form.

And these spires of form, though "striving" upward, provide a
natural/supernatural geology of "entire self-reliance":

What was . . . solid continent, now yawns apart and discloses its
composition and genesis. I learn geology the morning after an earth-
quake [metaphor here for the 1837 Depression]. I learn fast on the
ghastly diagrams of the cloven mountain & upheaved plain and the
dry bottom of the Sea. . . . I see the natural fracture of the stone. I
see the tearing of the tree & learn its fibre & rooting. The Artificial
is rent from the eternal.[27]

Pierre embodies the ambiguities of that vision as they turn
against process and telos alike, rendering eternity a function of
"The Artificial." The novel's action is the descent of self-trust, as
in a geological excavation, toward a non-existent center—non-
existent (to repeat) in the hermeneutical, not the existential,
sense: absence of either "axis" or "genesis," "fibre" without
"rooting."

That profound silence which is the only voice of our Lord, *which I
before spoke of* [my italics]; from that divine thing without a name,
those imposter philosophers pretend somehow to have got an answer; which is as absurd as though they should say they had got
water out of a stone; for how can a man get a Voice out of Silence? . . .
   Deep, deep, and deeper we must go if we would find out the heart
of a man; descending into which is as descending a spiral stair in a
shaft, without any end, and where that endlessness is only concealed
by the spiralness of the stair, and the blackness of the shaft. (pp. 290,
336)

These depth-mocking images of *profundity, names,* and *ends* are
the Melvillean counterpart to transcendental being, seeing, and
striving ("Yet is God the native of these bleak rocks"; "I see the
eternal"; "The next unto the farthest brings"). In one perspective,
Vivia's "jail" is the terminus ad quem in the novel's search for

author and authority. In another perspective, it is just one more turn (or "slip") of a downward spiral, of which "us" is another turn, directly behind the author (or authors) who is directly behind Pierre, who brings Vivia to "life" by giving a voice to silence.

Within the novel at large, the last turn of the spiral staircase is the city jail, where Pierre, now a self-confessed failure as author and savior, is imprisoned after he murders Glendinning Stanly, the last surviving member of his family:

> That sundown, Pierre stood solitary in a low dungeon of the city prison. The cumbersome stone ceiling almost rested on his brow; so that the long tiers of massive cell-galleries above seemed partly piled on him. His immortal, immovable, bleached cheek was dry; but the stone cheeks of the walls were trickling. The pent twilight of the contracted yard, coming through the barred arrow-slit, fell in dim bars upon the granite floor. (pp. 417–418)

A barred arrow-slit, fixed upon the pent twilight of a petrified world: it makes for a fit conclusion to the great shift in symbolic authority which the novel traces, from theology to aesthetics to self-consciousness. And the pseudo-mythic weeping wall (Pierre's "cheek was dry" but "the stone cheeks of the wall were trickling") serves as a final sundown commentary on the Berk- shire-morning emblem of the Dedication. There, in the Dedica- tion, author and mountain reciprocally reflect the ambiguous rela- tion of art and life. Here, in his granite dungeon, with the stone cell-galleries mountainously piled upon him, like Pelion upon Ossa, the Titan-dreamer—"immortal, immovable, bleached"— fuses with the metaphoric mountain in the imprisoning ambigu- ities of rhetoric.

In the first case, ambiguity depends on the distance between author and mountain, a distance defined through the playful and self-affirming metamorphoses of the authorial "I": as mock-sup- plicant, as lamp or sun of the imagination, and as the variously indifferent, defiant, and willfully ironic observer of his own perso- nae. In the second case, Pierre imaged as the stone dungeon— "the native of these bleak rocks" petrified into a "cold truth" beyond "tears, contritions, and perturbations"—the ambiguities break down all distinctions, including the distinctions between subject and object, consciousness and reality. They reveal what we may see as having been implicit all along in the Dedication, that symbolically speaking there is no distance between mountain and author. Greylock is a name that issues from the silence out there; the self is born out of the silence within, in a series of impersonations ("constantly building, modifying, rebuilding") designed to mask the felt absence of identity. They are inventions ex nihilo, "two shadows cast from one nothing"—the appropriately *flat* representations of the made-up become the made-real. The mute massiveness of the one finds its true reflection, mirror imaging mirror, in the vacant vastness of the other.

It has been said that *Pierre* foreshadows the work of Heidegger and Beckett. It would be more accurate to say that it sounds a prophetic No-in-thunder to the new aesthetics it explores. The discoveries it makes are delivered in outrage. They amount to a relentless, self-lacerating unfolding of what Melville intimated in his letters to Hawthorne. In the "Being of the matter lies the knot with which we choke ourselves. As soon as you say *Me*, a *God*, a *Nature*, so soon you jump off from your stool and hang from the beam": this in the summer of 1851, while completing *Moby-Dick*; and several months later, as he began work on *Pierre*: "Leviathan is not the biggest fish;—I have heard of Krakens." Melville found the knotted term "Being"—"the Being of the matter with which we choke ourselves"—in Coleridge's *Biographia Literaria* (which he read and discussed in 1848), and in a climactic passage of *The Theory of Life*, where Coleridge rhapsodizes about the individual as the "revelation of nature," "apex of the living pyramid." "*Porphyrogeniti sumus!*" he exclaims. "We begin with the I KNOW MYSELF, in order to end with the absolute I AM." The American version, overreaching Europe's "egotistical sublime," may be found in Emerson's transparent eyeball, which, *being* nothing, sees *all*, or in Whitman's deific "Me in the centre," whose "quality of BEING, in the object's self, according to its own central idea, and of growing therefrom and thereto . . . is the lesson of nature." The Kraken is described in manuals of the time as "the mythic monster of the deep," "known to poetry and legend as the largest creature in the world," the "monstrous" product of "the deluded fancy," a creation of "optical illusions," "species Titan," "non-existent."[28]

Pierre registers the *shock* of modernism. That shock is itself not distinctive to Melville (we find it in other writers of the time, on both sides of the Atlantic); nor is modernism, in its literary sense, distinctive to the modern era. Nevertheless, *Pierre* has a special force in this regard. I think, first, of the tradition of religious symbolism that Melville inherited, and from which (although he questioned the tradition itself more rigorously than any other American of his time) he never entirely broke loose. "When the substance is gone, men cling to the shadow," writes Melville in describing the transition from the old Church of the Apostles to the new Apostles of bohemia and the avant-garde. "It would seem, as if forced by imperative Fate to renounce the reality of the romantic and the lofty, the people of the present would fain make a compromise by retaining some purely imaginative remainder" (p. 312). The cunning, sophisticated, and savage mockery here of figural exegesis ("substance," "shadow") expresses Melville's own historical double bind. It was not so much that (as Hawthorne famously remarked) he could neither accept the old faith nor "rest comfortable in his unbelief."[29] More importantly, he could not remake (or "make new") the tradition he inherited, as his great contemporaries did. He neither managed to supersede by transforming it, like Emerson, nor like Hawthorne could he accommodate to its secularized, psychologized, and aestheticized "compromises," those "purely imaginative remainders" of Protestant poetics.

More generally, I think of the nineteenth-century revolution in thought of which such accommodations were symptomatic. Michel Foucault describes this as the "profound historicity" (epitomized by Lyell's *Principles of Geology*) which undermined the entire synchronic structure of analogy in the West, and in effect recast language, from its "privileged position" into "a historical form coherent with the density of its own past." *Pierre* articulates that loss in all its implications. The novel is the fruition of the many experimental, exploratory, and subversive elements in Melville's first great phase of unfolding—from his historicist exposé in *Typee* of the ways that language prevents us from understanding others, through his linguistic exposé in *Mardi* of the ways that culture prevents us from understanding the self, to the relentless questioning in *Moby-Dick* of the entire order of things (historical, cultural, metaphysical, linguistic). But *Moby-Dick* affirms the questioning process itself. Its very form celebrates personal identity, especially in its liminal state, as quester (Ahab) or as inquirer (Ishmael), both challenging the "personified impersonal" and pondering the mysteries of otherness:

this tatooing had been the work of a departed prophet and seer of his island, who by those hieroglyphic marks, had written out on his body a complete theory of the heavens and the earth, and a mystical treatise on the art of attaining truth; so that Queequeg in his own proper person was a riddle to unfold; a wonderous work in one volume; but those mysteries were therefore destined in the end to moulder away with the living parchment whereon they were inscribed, and so be unsolved to the last.[30]

Pierre strikes through the masks of the processual "I." Melville was to develop the novel's involuted, multi-layered, distancing techniques throughout his later career, from Bartleby the Scrivener, obverse of Pierre, through the Confidence-Man's *masquerade* of difference, to the irrecoverably *inside* narrative of Billy Budd.

For young Melville, as for his contemporaries, faith in process, whether of history or of the self, meant faith in America. I have already quoted his review of *Mosses* in this respect, and, as I suggested, his admiration there for Hawthorne is animated by the prospects of a new "democratic spirit" in literature:

> if Shakespeare has not been equalled, give the world time, and he is sure to be surpassed. . . . Nor has Nature been all over ransacked by our progenitors. . . . Far from it. The trillionth part has not been said; and all that has been said, but multiplies the avenues to what remains to be said. . . .
>
> Let America then prize and cherish her writers; yea, let her glorify them. . . . [They] breathe that unshakled, democratic spirit . . . which now takes the practical lead in the world, though at the same time led by ourselves—us Americans.

Melville's appeal echoes the summons issued through the 1840s for national greatness in the arts. America, went the argument, had proved its political and economic superiority to other countries. Now the time had come to prove its cultural superiority. That was the call raised by Evert Duyckinck, Melville's close acquaintance, his guide into literary New York and coeditor of *The Literary World*, Young America's leading journal (in which he condemned *Pierre* for being "loathsome . . . muddy, foul, and corrupt"). Hawthorne reiterated Duyckinck's appeal, in his own ambiguous way, in sketching "the Master Genius, for whom our country is looking anxiously into the mist of time, as destined to fulfill the great mission of creating an American literature, hewing it, as it were, out of the unwrought granite of our intellectual quarries."[31]

The *Democratic Review*, in which Hawthorne's sketch appeared in 1844, repeated that promise (without ambiguity) throughout its columns. Titanism and the national eagle were the journal's staple fare, as indeed they were a main theme of the politics of the decade. As Constance Rourke put it, "orators kept the bird so continuously in flight from the peak of the Alleghanies to the top of Mt. Hood that its shadow was said to have worn a trail across the basin of the Mississippi",[32] and for America's Romantic and Luminist painters, that trail extended from the Berkshires, Catskills, and Adirondacks to the Western Rockies. There is no better way to illustrate the Dedication to *Pierre* than by a slide show of their enormous mountain-scapes: Jasper Cropsey's *Starruca Viaduct*, Asher Durand's *Progress*, Sanford Gifford's *Adirondacks*, Albert Bierstadt's *Turbulent Clouds*, *White Mountains, New Hampshire* and *Grandeur of the Rockies*. These painters had inherited the European view of mountain titanism, the Romantic Sublime, and they turned it into what they termed "titanism for democratic purposes." As Thomas Cole pointed out, "in civilized Europe the primitive features of scenery have long since been destroyed or modified"; whereas American scenery by contrast—as represented, say, in Cole's own paintings (*Mountain Sunrise, View of the White Mountains, Oxbow*, and *Catskill Mountains*)—spoke with the unmediated power of God's pristine revelation of "the Great Cosmic Plan": "He who stands on Mount Albano and looks down on ancient Rome, has his mind peopled with the gigantic associations of the storied past; but he who stands on the mounds of the West . . . [experiences] the sublimity of a shoreless ocean un-islanded by the recorded deeds of man."[33]

In the mid-nineteenth century, that experience was most forcefully conveyed by the work of Frederick Church, Cole's pupil and by national acclaim "the Michaelangelo of landscape Art." For Church, the "great personality of the New Continent" *was* America's mountains. "God-immanent," he termed them, and thereby "the archetype of [modern democratic] man"; and he sought to convey their prophetic spirit through his huge canvasses of the Catskills, the Andes, Niagara Falls, and Mount Katahdin. Titanism here is the very opposite of defiance or revolt. It declares the harmony between independence, individualism, progress, and the will of God. According to Church, Nature was "the theatre of the world's . . . resurrection"; America was chosen to be the central scene of that drama; and the American mountain, "the Most Signal of Earthly Facts," made visible this conjunction of sacred and secular history. It showed "the New World as Resurrection and Millennium. . .; it aspired to the eternal and the infinite; [and] it joined heaven and earth. Hence it was fit image for American 'demigods' and 'immortals' "—like the majestic, gray-locked Washington of Mount Rushmore.[34]

Democratic titanism was also a main theme of the American literary Renaissance. Let us no longer "rave of Parnassus," pleaded Theodore Parker; "the soul of song has a seat upon Monadnock, Wachusett, or Katahdin, quite as high." There indeed the country's classic writers found the native muse. Whitman discovered her—"brawling," "towering," "elemental," "titanic," "the law of my own poems"—"on Kenosha Summit"; Thoreau, in the wildness of Mount Katahdin: "What is this Titan," he wrote in a moment of rare ecstasy, "that has possession of me?" Emerson invoked "the soul of song" in his odes to the Adirondacks and Mount Monadnock:

> . . . Nature in these towers
> Uplifted shall condense her powers
>
> . . . .
>
> [And] Man in these crags a fastness find
> To fight pollution of the mind . . . .

and in a series of public addresses, including "The Natural Aristocrat" (or "Aristocracy"), which Melville probably attended in 1849. Now that we have "snapped asunder" "all feudal straps and bandages," Emerson told his audience, we look "that nature . . . should reimburse itself [in us] by a brood of Titans" who will tower like "mountains," an aristocracy of "royal natures" commensurate with America. Hawthorne, too, heralded the American Titan in a story called "The Great Stone Face," and for a brief time Melville believed he had actually discovered that "Master Genius" in Hawthorne and in his own new-found powers. In his review of Hawthorne he pictures himself amidst the Green Mountains of Vermont, with a copy of *Mosses* just received from a local "mountain girl," watching Hawthorne's "Assyrian dawn . . . from the summit of our Eastern Hill." "We want no American Goldsmiths," he concludes; "we want no American Miltons. Call [the writer] an American and have done; for you could not say a nobler thing of him."[35] Significantly, Pierre's literary career is first discussed in the chapter "Young America in Literature."

So I come to my fourth step in explication: the nationalist dimension; *Pierre* as *American* literary history. It is perhaps the novel's most conspicuous aspect, and surely its most comprehensive. The Dedication pointedly appeals for American patronage; the mountain is almost unambiguously a symbol of the American countryside; and its setting virtually promises a book sprung from the heart of American nature. And so it is, at least in its protagonist. The narrator tells us (twice, for emphasis) that *"it had been the choice fate of Pierre to have been born and bred in the country. For to a noble American youth this indeed—more than in any other land—this indeed is a most rare and choice lot. . . . In the country then Nature planted our Pierre; because Nature intended a rare and original development . . . [and] the country was a glorious benediction to young Pierre"* (pp. 19–20). Pierre's subsequent movement from agrarian family estate to urban society traces the main social and economic transition of Jacksonian America. And though the city seems mainly to contrast with Pierre's early surroundings, the continuities are equally pronounced: through family connections (Glen Stanly), early friendships (Charlie Milthorpe), literary ambitions, and continuing relations (Delly Ulver, Isabel, Lucy); through images, allusions, forms of moral conduct, and structures of social power; and above all through Pierre himself. In the city as in the country, he is an exemplary national figure, the *American* Enceladus, a natural aristocrat who dreams of becoming what Melville celebrated in his essay on Hawthorne as "the literary Shiloh of America."[36]

Everything about Pierre confirms this representative quality: his buoyant youthfulness, his fixation on the future, his vaunted self-reliance, his effort simultaneously to reject and redeem the past. What Tom Paine claims for the republic's "non-age" ("Youth is the seed-time"), and what Emerson says of "The Young American," might be said of young Pierre: he stands for a nation that is newborn, free, healthful, strong, the land of . . . the democrat, of the philanthropist, of the believer, of the saint . . . [the land that] should speak for the human race. America is the country of the Future. . . . It is a country of beginnings, of projects, of vast designs, and expectations. It has no past: all has an outward and prospective look. And herein is it fitted to receive more readily every generous feature which the wisdom or the fortune of man has yet to impress.

Above all Pierre is the representative American because of his incredible faith in words. He is the quintessential product of a culture founded on rhetoric: a "living proof-text" (p. 16) of the belief that declarations can produce independence; that covenants and contracts can make community; that one can fashion one's own constitution by proclaiming and publishing it; and that one can then resolve the anxieties peculiar to this open-ended process by redirecting them into a constitutional process of continuing interpretation and reinterpretation, from one generation to the next. In 1807 Washington Irving distinguished the United States from all other nations as being "a pure unadulterated *logocracy*, or government of words."* Thirty years later, in a novel explicity

*Irving is speaking here in the guise of a visiting Muslim. His description of the young republic is worth quoting more fully, for the tensions it reveals between "aristocracy," "pure democracy," and "mobocracy," all of these relevant to Pierre's career, and all of them feeding into the Pierre-like resolution of "wordy battle and paper war":

> I find that the people of this country are strangely at a loss to determine the nature of their government. Some have insisted that it savors of an aristocracy; others maintain that it is a pure democracy; and a third set of theorists declare that it is nothing more or less than a mobocracy. . . . [Yet] the simple truth of the matter is, that their government is a pure unadulterated *logocracy*, or government of words. In a logocracy, thou well knowest, every offensive or defensive measure is enforced by wordy battle and paper war; he who has the longest tongue is sure to gain the victory. . . . [Then], without mercy or remorse, . . . [he will] put men, women, and children to the point of the—pen! . . . [Or he will send] them a long message, i.e., a huge mass of words, all meaning nothing; because it only tells them what they perfectly know already; . . . [whereupon they will be] thrown into a ferment, and have a long talk. . . . Nations have each a separate characteristic trait, by which they may be distinguised from each other. . . . [For example,] the Italians fiddle upon everything; the French dance upon everything; and the windy subjects of the American logocracy talk upon everything. (*Salmagundi*, VII [April 4, 1807], in *Works*, ed. Evert A. Duyckinck [New York, 1860], VII, 135–144)

parodied in *Pierre*, Catharine Maria Sedgwick elaborated the virtues of "the representative American" by cataloguing his books: "a Bible, a Hymn-book, the Pilgrim's Progress, a Compend of Universal History, History of America, the American Revolution, a Life of Washington, and a Constitution of the United States, bound up with Washington's Farewell Address."[37]

Pierre is a kind of walking logocracy. The national qualities he embodies as an "American hero" are emphatically rhetorical. Even his Glendinning genealogy (pp. 37–38), from colonial "ancestors" through Revolutionary "founders,"—from "grand old Pierre" to Pierre Sr. to Pierre—is presented as a *myth* of continuity. The ambiguities that surround the "fathers" are not so much historical as historiographical. They direct us toward the events of history in order to entangle us in the narratives of the events— and specifically, in two kinds of narrative, one diametrically opposed to the other, and each claiming authority as *the* story of America. The more central of these, the mainstream national story told by Bancroft, is conveniently summarized by Melville in a well-known passage in *White-Jacket* (1849):

> Escaped from the house of bondage, Israel of old did not follow after the ways of the Egyptians. To her was given an express dispensation; to her were given new things under the sun. And we Americans are the peculiar, chosen people—the Israel of our time. . . . God has predestinated, mankind expects, great things from our race; and great things we feel in our souls. . . . We are the pioneers of the world; the advance-guard, sent on through the wilderness of untried things, to break a new path in the New World that is ours. . . . Long enough have we been skeptics with regard to ourselves, and doubted whether, indeed, the political Messiah had come. But he has come in *us*.[38]

This is White Jacket speaking, not Melville, but he speaks for the Young America movement which Melville partly espoused, and for the Jacksonian party, to which Melville's family was closely connected, in which his brother was a rising political star, and through whose patronage he was hoping in 1852 to secure a post. He speaks, in short, for liberal progressivism in antebellum America.

It would not be inaccurate to read the Dedication to *Pierre* in this perspective, as an icon of manifest destiny. In the background, recalling the motive for Exodus, is the Congress of Vienna, emblem of bondage, the past, and the failed rebellions of the Old World. It serves by contrast to highlight the Berkshire dawn, emblem both of continuity and of the future, and in both capacities radiating (as it were) a constellation of rising suns: the millennial "morning-star" that Increase Mather invoked in 1700 to revitalize the colonial errand; the chiliastic sun/Son that Jonathan Edwards in 1740 believed would shortly "rise from the West, contrary to the course of the world"; "the renovating morning" sunlight in which (forty years later) Edwards's grandson, Timothy Dwight, saw the "rising glory of America"; and the New World "star in the constellation Harp" that Emerson predicted (some forty years after Dwight) would be "the pole-star for a thousand years." "In the dawn of our independence," writes Bancroft, at the climactic moment of his epic history, "the stars . . . sang together for joy," and "like a young eagle in his upward soarings, [the young American] looked undazzled into the beams of morning."[39]

Of all this, by American rite of assent, Greylock is the "one grand dedicatee." Melville's first full expression of that tradition comes in *Mardi*, where America appears as Vivenza, "promising as the morning. . . . [in] the resplendent rising of [the] sun. . . . Vivenza! the star that must ere long lead up the constellations." He develops the theme in *Redburn* (the first major novel to set out the contrast between American innocence and European depravity), and further still in *White-Jacket* (where the U.S. Constitution comes to represent universal progress); until it reaches a high point in the rhetoric of democratic heroism aboard the *Pequod*, the ship whose wood, according to prophecy, "could only be American."[40]

I invoke that prophecy to recall Melville's equally persistent sense of America's *failure* as "redeemer nation." *Redburn* gives us ample reason to parallel (rather than contrast) Europe and America, and White Jacket, for all his chauvinism, describes a "sick" side of American society that is kept below deck, hidden from view: "practically speaking," he confesses, "our craft is a lie." In *Moby-Dick* the lie surfaces in Ishmael's pervasive critique of the *Pequod*'s social fabric: the false pieties of the New Bedford marketplace; the racial and class hierarchies at sea, as on land; the violence against nature and humanity that impels Ahab's errand under "the great god Democracy"; and the demagoguery, moral paralysis, and Devil's pacts to which free-enterprise liberalism is prey. Against all this the *Pequod* prophecy sounds a doomsday warning. "The ship! The hearse!—The second hearse! . . . its wood could only be American!": Ahab's epiphany reflects a grim alternative view of the apocalypse, one that was also current in 1850, in spite of Bancroft's popularity, or rather alongside it. I refer to what scholars have labelled the American School of Catastrophe: the tradition of the anti-jeremiad which I traced (in Chapter 2) back to seventeenth-century New England, but which gathered special force in the early republic through the convergence of two quite different cyclical views of history. One of these was the classical theory of *translatio studii* or *translatio imperii*, the belief that civilization moves from East to West. The other was the cyclical view embedded in civic humanism, the theory that republican virtue guarantees social and cultural success, but that success in turn brings luxury, corruption, decline, and fall.

Both these views, then, were fatalistic, or at least ambiguous: the promises of greatness they brought carried within them the seeds of mutability and collapse. The spokesmen for the republic recast fatalism and ambiguity alike into the teleological terms of "America." What had been the threat of historical recurrence became the anxiety of apocalyptic choice: millennium or doom. The millennial prospect joined the Enlightenment faith in progress to Puritan–Revivalist figuralism. The catastrophic prospect was its precise inversion. Continuity meant an errand into oblivion, as in the images of universal conflagration and end-time flood that conclude (respectively) George Lippard's *Quaker City* (1844) and Cooper's *The Crater* (1849)—and to project the vision across our century, the entropic finale predicted in *The Education of Henry Adams* and Pynchon's *Gravity's Rainbow*. *Pierre* represents this outlook, accurately, as the nightmare inversion of Bancroft's dream. The novel dramatizes the opposition between the two as the ambiguities of Destiny and Fate through which the story of America unfolds. Its plot devolves upon the incestuous relation between kindred views of history, mainstream and oppositional, twin offspring of the same cultural symbology, which together constitute the terms of action ("development," "success," "tragedy") in *Pierre*.

The mainstream view is explicit in Pierre's lineage. We are repeatedly told that "on both sides" he is the latest and hopefully the last best issue of a "mighty succession" of "heroes" (p. 27). Pierre's ambition is to have the "glory in *capping* the fame-column, whose tall shaft had been erected by his noble sires" (p.

12; my italics), as a sort of porphyrite monument to American nationhood. The story of the Glendinnings is the story of how the land was won, and the rhetoric surrounding young Pierre is resonant with anticipations of a mission nearing fulfillment. His approaching marriage to Lucy is said to foreshadow "the final rites" in "the march of universal Love" (p. 43). His "nameless and . . . inexpressible tenderness" for his mother offers "a glimpse of . . . glorious possibility"; their mutual "lover-like adoration . . . seemed almost to realize here below the sweet dreams of those religious enthusiasts, who paint to us a Paradise to come, when . . . the holiest passion of man shall unite all kindreds and climes in one circle of pure and unimpairable delight" (pp. 22–23). And the Delectable Mountain which overlooks these events, present and prospective, is by all literary convention a second Pisgah bordering New Jerusalem, capitol of that "great political and religious millennium" heralded by the new Apostles:

> Hosannahs to this world! so beautiful itself, and the vestibule to more. Out of some past Egypt, we have come to this new Canaan; and from this new Canaan, we press on to some Circassia. Though still the villains, Want and Woe, followed us out of Egypt, and now beg in Canaan's streets: yet Circassia's gate shall not admit them.* (p.41)

This is one narrative perspective, the novel's progressivist dimension. The second, cataclysmic perspective expresses the anxiety of succession that characterized the post-Revolutionary generation. We learn that Pierre is everywhere haunted by paternal memories; for as it happens he *fails* to measure up to "the proudest patriotic and family associations of the historic line of

---

*Circassia was a land celebrated by Byron and others for its beautiful women, its "invincible heroes," the "grand pyramidal peaks of its . . . mountains," and its recent war of independence, inspired by republican principles, which according to George Leighton Ditson, had "moved the world with wonder" (*Circassia: Or, A Tour to the Caucasus* [New York, 1850], pp. v, 225, 374, 381, 424). In its review of Ditson's book, *The Literary World* proudly reported (January 26, 1852, p. 80) the enormous interest in America "taken by the enlightened Russians in so distant a region," and commended their leader, Prince Kotsohobey, for having "but one picture in his room, a portrait of Washington." It is central to Melville's meaning here that by 1852 the Circassian revolution had failed, and that Circassia had become one more example of the cyclical view of history.

Glendinning" (pp. 9–10). He is lacking, it turns out, both in personal qualities and in historical opportunities. When he tries on his grandfather's military vest, "the pockets [fall] below his knees" (p. 38). When he recalls his forebears' deeds, "ten thousand mailed thoughts started up in Pierre's soul, and glared round for some insulted good cause to defend" (p. 20), but then he considers his own meager prospects. How can he hope to equal the heroics of his paternal great-grandfather, who took the land from the Indians? Although "mortally wounded," the narrator tells us, the old general had "sat unhorsed on his saddle in the grass, with his dying voice, still cheering his men in the fray" (pp. 9–10)—hence the name Saddle Meadows. What deeds can Pierre hope to accomplish to match those of his Revolutionary grandfather, "grand old Pierre Glendinning"? The portrait of that hero moves his third-generation heir to "an infinite and mournful longing":

> Pierre's grandfather [was] an *American* gentleman . . . during a fire in the old manorial mansion, with one dash of his foot, he had smitten down an oaken door, to admit the buckets of his *negro slaves*. . . . In a night-scuffle in the wilderness before the Revolutionary War, he had *annihilated two Indian savages by making reciprocal bludgeons of their heads*. And all this was done by the mildest hearted, and most blue-eyed gentleman in the world . . . a gentle, white-haired worshipper of all the household gods; the gentlest husband, and the gentlest father; the kindest of *masters to his slaves* . . . a sweet-hearted, charitable Christian; in fine, a pure, cheerful, childlike, blue-eyed, divine old man . . . *fit image of his God*. . . . The majestic sweetness of this portrait was truly wonderful . . . a glorious gospel *framed and hung* upon the wall, and declaring to all people, as from the Mount, that man is a noble, god-like being, *full of choicest juices*. (pp. 37–38; my italics)

The satire is excessive, especially considering that Melville modelled these republican demigods on his own forebears, and this portrait in particular on his maternal grandfather, Peter Gansevoort, "the hero of Fort Stanwix", after whom he and his wife had just named their second child.[41] But then, the same tone of excess characterizes all of the passages I quoted, beginning with the portrait of majestic Greylock, overflowing with "bounteous fertilizations." In all cases, it is the voice of the betrayed idealist, an excess of outrage bred in an excess of hope. On some level, I have been suggesting, this is Melville's voice, but it would be as imprecise to equate the two as it would be to equate Melville with his optimistic-naive narrator.* The bitter parodist of the "sweet dreams" of Saddle Meadows has his own, equally illusory faith in order, the nightmare vision of catastrope by design. And the relation between the optimist and the pessimist (as between Pierre and Vivia) develops through a series of dualisms that recast conflict into counter-dependence. *Moby-Dick* builds on a disjunction of separate voices and narrative modes. *Pierre* is the story of contradictory forms of narration seeking their separate voices and finding instead their common source in a dominant cultural rhetoric.

---

* Melville's own views here—insofar as they can be identified by negation, in contradistinction to the views of his narrators—tend toward the secular, the non-apocalyptic, and the cyclical. I have in mind the outlook he first sets out in *Mardi*, in the midst of his narrative of Vivenza (the United States), in the form of an anonymous scroll purporting to be "A Voice from the Gods." Vivenza's "grand error," it explains, lies in the

> "conceit that Mardi [the world] is now in the last scene of the last act of her drama and that all preceding events were ordained to bring about the catastrophe you believe to be at hand—a universal and permanent republic.
> "May it please you, those who hold to these things are fools. . . .
> "Time is made up of various ages; and each thinks its own a novelty. But imbedded in the walls of the pyramids . . . sculptured stones are found belonging to yet older fabrics. And as the mound-building period of yore, so every age thinks its erections will forever endure. But . . . while deriving their substance from the past, succeeding generations in time themselves decay. . . .
> "Throughout all eternity the parts of the past are but parts of the future reversed." (*Mardi, and a Voyage Thither*, in *Typee, Omoo, Mardi*, ed. G. Thomas Tanselle [Library of America: New York, 1982], pp. 1181, 1183)

This outlook, let me add, is implicit in the Dedication. As distinct from the mythic mountain—the Greylock who is either the figure of silence or else the figural Titan, son of Aurora and type of the Messiah—there is the geological mountain: "Greylock," the product of hoary age, and image of the cyclical process whereby "the parts of the past"—New World and Old, Memnon and Hamlet, Pierre Sr., and the Pierre before *him*—"are but parts of the future reversed." But this voice is not developed in the narrative proper (though it may be traced by indirection through the abundant imagery of New World "ruins," "torsoes," "amputations," and "antiquities"). What I termed the third authorial voice serves largely to mediate between these contrapuntal chroniclers of Pierre's destiny/fate. This relativist view functions by indirection as a distancing device from the various rhetorical constructions that make up the novel's plot and action. In a separate essay I discuss Melville's subsequent development of this distancing technique, through *The Piazza Tales* and *Clarel*.

For however we interpret the mystery of Pierre, Sr., the family taint is symbolic—the legacy of the fathers, Pierre's in particular and the country's in general. Isabel's face, the narrator remarks, first appeared to Pierre as a "shadow" from "[o]ut of the heart of mirthfulness . . . vaguely historic and prophetic; backward, hinting of some irrevocable sin; forward, pointing to some inevitable ill" (p. 54). Whatever her actual origins, she is a true daughter of the Glendinnings—the excluded immigrant sewing-girl who embodies the hidden, illegitimate side of their history. Isabel's shadow falls across all aspects of Saddle Meadows: across Indian mounds and traces of slave-quarters; across Mary Glendinning's abuse of Delly Ulver; across Falsgrave's abuse of religious principle; across the relation between master and servant, lady and tenant farmer; across the class hierarchy thriving "in the heart of a republic" (p. 17). Whether or not Isabel is literally related to Pierre, she is his sister metaphorically, and he is right to claim her as part of his patrimony, and right to want to redress her wrongs. "Believe me," says the mocking narrator, "you will pronounce Pierre a thorough-going Democrat in time: perhaps a little too Radical altogether to your fancy" (p. 18). Isabel offers Pierre precisely what he seeks—the "insulted good cause" through which he might "cap" the heroism of the fathers. And with that offering she gives him the incentive and the means to do just the reverse. Both by his unspoken sexual attraction to her and by his too-much-protested reason for action (to keep the paternal line intact and unsullied), Pierre manages not only to recapitulate the past's "irrevocable sin," but to bring this to its "inevitable ill."

Pierre has a good deal of astute social commentary, but Melville concentrates on the mode of disclosure, rather than on the facts disclosed. Even as Isabel de-mythicizes the Saddle Meadows Eden she re-mythicizes it as Babylon. She is modelled on the victimized orphans and weaver-girls of sentimental fiction, where in fact this character type often serves as a focus of social criticism. In this sense, the popular novels to which I referred earlier are epitomized by the best-seller of 1852, *Uncle Tom's Cabin; or Life Among the Lowly*. But *Pierre* hardly describes Isabel's cabin, and (apart from Lady Glendinning's emblematic visit to the Sewing Circle) it tells us very little about life among the lowly. Instead, the various kinds of corruption that Isabel brings into view (sexual, moral, and economic) make her into a kind of walking allegory of the catastrophic view of history. That is why the narrator connects her so emphatically to the "cruel, blood-shedding times" (p. 92) of the French Revolution. The Revolution and the Terror that followed provided the major modern precedent for a *failed* republic. From 1790 on, and with special force after the collapse of the Second Republic in 1852, American patriots had been describing France as America's figural antithesis: the Beast of Babylon, Antichrist incarnate. In *Pierre* that symbolic contrast becomes historiographical ambiguity. In country and city alike, Isabel's mystic song echoes the apocalyptic refrain, "MYSTERY, BABYLON THE GREAT, MOTHER OF HARLOTS, AND OF THE ABOMINATIONS OF THE EARTH" (Rev. 17:5), referring not to the Old World now, but to the New.*

The scriptural ground of reference here, the Book of Revelation, may be the single most sustained literary source in *Pierre*. The age of the family phaeton means 666, the number of Antichrist (Rev. 3:18); the name of the road to the Glendinning mansion, Locust Lane, evokes the plagues of the Latter Days (Rev. 9:3); Saddle Meadows is described as the land of toads and scorpions (Rev. 11:7, 18:4); New York City is emblemized by the Scarlet Whore (Rev. 17:1, 19:2); and so on, through the images of Gog and Magog (Rev. 20:8, 22:18) in which the narrator frames the novel's violent end. Pierre kills his cousin Glen, thus annihilating once and for all the "historic line of Glendinning," representing America, representing the course of history itself. It is a catastrophe which submerges the historical, aesthetic, and psychological

---

*Isabel does not therefore transcend history. On the contrary: it is one of Melville's central points that the origins and ends of her *rhetoric* of transcendence ("mystery," "soul," "inmost truth") are conspicuously historical. It is her purpose to enter into Glendinning history, not to oppose (or even expose) it. The proof she offers of her "true identity"—her claim to respectability—is a "complete deciphering of the talismanic word, Glendinning" on her (alleged) father's handkerchief, which has the letter "G" inscribed on it (p. 175). The deciphering process makes for a talismanic moment in its own right:

"*Glendinning*, thought I, what is that? It sounds something like *gentleman*;—Glen-din-ning;—just as many syllables as *gentleman*; and—G—it begins with the same letter; yet; it must mean *my father*. I will think of him by that word now;—I will not think of the *gentleman*, but of *Glendinning*. . . . [A]s I grew up . . . that word was ever humming in my head. I saw that it would prove the key to more." (p. 175)

It amounts to a memorable emblem-scene of interpretation: a witty parody of esoteric reading ("the key to more") that reveals the personal and political dimensions (class, gender, self-interest, upward mobility) of literary exegesis.

dimensions of the narrative under the trope of the end-time, and which from the start gives a special American meaning to the narrator's invocations of Fate:

> in the . . . vaingloriousness of his youthful soul . . . how unadmon-ished was our Pierre by that . . . prophetic lesson taught, not less by Palmyra's quarries, than by Palmyra's ruins. Among those ruins is a crumbling, uncompleted shaft . . . the proudstone that should have stood among the clouds [Rev. 21:17], Time left abased beneath the soil. Oh, what quenchless feud is this, that Time hath with the sons of Men [Rev. 14:14]! . . .
>
> Now Pierre stands on this noble pedastal; we shall see if he keeps that fine footing; we shall see if Fate hath not just a little bit of a small word or two to say in this world . . . we shall see if that blessing pass from him as did the divine blessing from the Hebrews [cf. Mal. 2:2, Rom. 15:29, Gal. 3:14, Heb. 12:17, Rev. 5:13]; we shall yet see whether this wee bit of latinity be very far out of the way—*Nemo contra Deum, nisi Deus ipse** (pp. 12–13, 17, 20)

---

*Melville found this "strange, but most striking proverb," in 1849, in Goethe's autobiography, *Poetry and Truth*. Goethe uses it to speculate about the daemonic element that takes possession of certain kind of heroic individual:

> Such persons are not always the most eminent men, either morally or intellectually . . . [but] a tremendous energy seems to be seated in them. . . . All the moral powers combined are of no avail against them; in vain does the more enlightened portion of mankind attempt to throw suspicion upon them as deceived if not deceivers . . . they are to be overcome by nothing but the universe itself.

In *Pierre*, this daemonic universal takes the form of Fate, and specifically the fatal curse (inverse of Israel's blessing) by which the father's sins are visited upon the children even unto the third or the fourth generation—or until, by the immutable laws of mutability, they are overcome by the universe itself. This reversal of Goethe's meaning is symptomatic of the contrast between European individuality and American representative individualism, where "genius" or "greatness" is transformed into a mode of democratic figuralism. Melville turns the *figura*, of course, against the concept of manifest destiny, but he does so by invoking its traditional manifestations: Old World ruins, European artifice versus American nature, prophecies of Israel's "divine blessings." Pierre embodies God's unalterable Will (*nemo contra Deum*) in its inherent self-contradiction (*nisi Deus ipse*). Thus the "prophetic lesson" which the narrator draws from his triple history (Palmyra, America, Pierre), leads simultaneously backward, from Pierre to the ruins of Palmyra, and forward, "vaingloriously," from Pierre's forefathers to Pierre, "son of Men," inversion of the apocalyptic Son of Man.

As one critic has put it, "*Pierre* is written in the mood as well as the metaphor of the biblical Apocalypse."[42]

This judgment expresses the view of *Pierre's* doomsday narrator. But his is only one view, as is that of his opposite, and beyond their competing figural interpretations the novel tells us little or nothing to suggest the end of history. Indeed, Melville indicates just the reverse. To begin with, all of *Pierre's* beginnings and endings are self-mocking, like the Dedication. Isabel enters the story as the fill-in for a blank in "the illuminated scroll of [Pierre's] life"— the "one hiatus . . . in that sweetly-writ manuscript"—and exits as a romance arbor of "ebon vines" (pp. 11, 421). Lucy enters as the American Juliet (Shakespeare's heroine as played by, say, Fanny Fern) and exits, "noiselessly" and precipitously, "shrunk up like a scroll" (p. 418). As for the protagonist, the narrator tells us in introducing him:

> we have been thus decided in asserting the great genealogical and real-estate dignity of some families in America, because in doing so we poetically establish the condition of Master Pierre Glendinning. . . . And to the observant reader the sequel will not fail to show, how important is this circumstance. . . . Nor will any man dream that the last chapter was merely intended for a foolish bravado. (p. 17)

In that "last chapter" Pierre exclaims, in his final "bravado" (a parody of Elizabethan revenge tragedy, as represented in Victorian melodrama):

> "Here, then, is the untimely, timely, end;—Life's last chapter well stitched into the middle! Nor book, nor author of the book, hath any sequel, though each hath its last lettering!—It is ambiguous still." (p. 418)

Clearly, for "the observant reader," the reference here is not so much to Pierre as it is to *Pierre*, into the middle of which the author has stitched Plinlimmon's ambiguous letterings. As though to emphasize the point, the narrator tells us near the novel's end (in an imitation of Carlyle's Teufelsdröckh that anticipates the manikin of Henry Adams's *Education*):

> years after [Pierre's death], an old Jew Clothesman rummaged over a surtout of Pierre's . . . [and] his lynx-like fingers happened to feel

something foreign between the cloth and the heavy quilted bomba-
zine lining. He ripped open the skirt, and found several old pamphlet
pages, soft and worn almost to tissue, but still legible enough to
reveal the title—"Chronometricals and Horologicals." Pierre must
have ignorantly thrust it into his pocket, in the stage, and it had
worked through a rent there, and . . . helped pad the padding. So that
all the time . . . he himself was wearing the pamphlet.* (pp. 342–
343)

Pad for the padding: Pierre's "untidy termination" is just one
more in an interminable series of doubles/inversions. The steady
development from the interwoven "I's" of the Dedication (through
parody, selfhood, and history) finds one more turn of *Pierre*'s geological spiral in the mirror images of Glen and Pierre. The two
cousins are the same age; each is an only son; each was a child
when his father died; one is described as the other's "personal
duplicate," his "other self"; each is a wooer of Lucy; each may be
said to have inherited Saddle Meadows (pp. 253–254). Glen Stanly
(Germanic variant of "stone") is the "Europeanized" city cousin,
the artificial aristocrat corrupted by Old World ways (p. 256).
These terms apply to Pierre as well: his French name, the artifice
of his aristocratic lineage, the corruption in his country estate
(and in his city dwelling, too), and the Old World legacy of Pierre,
Sr., which recurs in the son's "marriage" to Isabel.

I do not mean to deny the contrast between them: Glen is a
socialite, all fashion, whereas Pierre is an absolutist, "all Truth's"
(p. 160). I mean rather that in broad cultural terms that contrast
reveals them as two sides of the representative American—pragmatist and idealist, in the dual tradition (mainstream and oppositional) we have come to associate with Franklin and Edwards or

---

*This little history might profitably be compared to Hawthorne's introduc-
tory account of the wanderings of the scarlet letter, which reveal the Custom-
House A to be the legacy of Puritanism and the Revolution. The fact that Pierre
"wears" the "rag pamphlet" (p. 242) through the various stages of his agon—and
that in doing so he becomes an incarnation of its "lettering," a walking emblem
of the correspondence it insinuates between horologicals and chronometricals—
invites us to interpret it as a reversal of Hester's A. *Pierre* offers an exposé from
within of the dynamics of pluralist interpretation that *The Scarlet Letter* celebrates, and Plinlimmon's pamphlet is the model of the distancing, alienating, and
analytical (as opposed to synthetic) techniques this involves.

Thoreau.* And in this broad sense, it is important to Melville's meaning that it should be the idealist who kills the pragmatist, because the facts have not lived up to the dream. It is also important to Melville's meaning that we can interpret this the other way around. Glen is acting, he himself believes, on behalf of a higher morality, whereas Pierre, in spite of what he believes, has been conforming all along (as Lucy's fiancé, Pierre Sr.'s dutiful son, "American Hamlet," would-be Christ, and self-reliant author) to cultural norms and expectations. From either perspective, the pseudo-apocalyptic "fatal encounter" between Pierre and Glendinning—in whose "circumstances" Pierre sees

---

*Melville was to satirize this tradition in 1855 through the dualism of Franklin and John Paul Jones, and indeed, through the ambiguities of each. Franklin is the "man of wisdom . . . man of utility," the "Plato-like" contriver of *Poor Richard's Almanac*, famous alike for his "pastoral simplicity," "politic grace," "polished Italian tact," and "Arcadian unaffectedness" (*Israel Potter: His Fifty Years of Exile*, in *Pierre, Israel Potter, The Piazza Tales, The Confidence Man, Uncollected Prose, Billy Budd*, ed. Harrison Hayford [Library of America: New York, 1984], pp. 470, 476, 479). Jones is the "American type" of "idealism" mixed with "savage" "violence"—and also, ambiguously, with a Pierre-like affinity to horologicals:

> " 'God helps those that help themselves.' That's . . . been my experience. . . . What pamphlet is this? 'Poor Richard,' hey! . . . reads very much as Doctor Franklin speaks."
> "He wrote it," said Israel.
> "Aye? . . . I must get me a copy of this, and wear it around my neck for a charm." (p. 494)

Like Glen, Pierre fails in both guises—both as a chronometer and as a horologue—because in either guise he is so culturally made-up. Glen is the creature of the culture he conforms to; Pierre, of the culture he rebels against. For all his interminable talk about repudiating and being himself, Pierre remains the product of Saddle Meadows even, or especially, in the city, where his earlier "religion of the home" is transmuted into the effort to make the utopian vision of individuality manifest in the terms of American individualism. We are told that this would-be Titan sees the futility of his revolt when he realizes (or as the mocking narrator puts it, "seemed to see" in his "self-supposed non-understanding") that he stands "entirely alone," deserted by "even the paternal gods" (pp. 413, 343, 471)—precisely, that is, at the point when the aspiring god-like antinomian *should* feel most empowered. Throughout the novel, this narrator harps upon the contradictions between democratic progress and radical individuality ("all the world does never gregariously advance to Truth, but only here and there some of its individuals do; and by advancing, leave the rest behind." [p. 196]). His savage critique of the language of representative individualism is dramatized at every stage of Pierre's career and on every level of Pierre's claims to American Selfhood, including his claims to represent "Young America in Literature."

"indices to all immensities," and whose audience he imagines to be "the drawn-up worlds in widest space" (pp. 413–414)—belies both versions of American history, millennial and catastrophic.*

Pierre might have become a figure of social protest, like Bartleby, whom in some ways he resembles (as copiest, as prisoner, and as walled-in individualist). Or he might have become the subject of an absolutist's tragedy of mind, like Ahab, whom he also resembles, and whose language he sometimes echoes (mainly to parody). But Melville was not seeking here to advance alternative ways or outlooks. *Pierre* is a dramatization of the traps of cultural symbology: a meta-history of continuing revolution; a sustained critique of the rhetoric of alternative America's in the United States. It begins as a satire of social failings, judged by the standard of American ideals. It ends as a satiric representation of ideals enveloped in the "coilings" of the world that fostered them.

The result is a searching commentary on the relation between violence and myth in America. The acts of murder and suicide that end the novel speak to the dynamics of hope and outrage in American history, the spiral of promise and frustration, rededication and further outrage, which seems always at the edge of explosion, and which (from Melville's day to ours) has often sought

---

*The novel's climax is carefully prepared for this purpose—first, the publisher's rejection letter, confirming Pierre's professional failure; then, the letter from Lucy's "protectors," confirming his social disgrace; and finally his Ahab-like soliloquy on revenge:

> "now am I hate-shod! On these [two letters] I will skate to my acquittal! No longer do I hold terms with aught. World's bread of life [from his profession] and world's breath of [social] honor, both are snatched from me; and I defy all world's bread and breath [pun on "letter and spirit"]. Here I . . . challenge one and all . . . to do battle!. . . Now I go out to meet my fate." (pp. 413–414)

Appropriately, the confrontation with Glen Stanly is described in a series of doublings:

> clapping both hands to his two breasts, Pierre, on both sides shaking off the sudden white grasp of two rushing girls, tore out both pistols, and rushed headlong upon Glen.
> "For thy one blow, take here two deaths!. . ."
> Spatterings of his own kindred blood were upon the pavement; his own hand had extinguished his house. (p. 417)

release in dream- or nightmare-visions of the apocalypse. Here, too, the action tends toward either doomsday or millennium; but there is no telos, no release, only a procession of ambiguities that circle round each other and then seem to recede endlessly, two by two, into silence: "Cast *thy* eye in there on *Vivia*," "it is *Enceladus*," "*All*'s o'er and ye know *him* not"—"And yet it follows not from this, that God's truth is one thing and man's truth another; but . . . by their very contradictions they are made to correspond" (p. 249).

Pierre is an inside narrative of the myth-making process. It builds upon a series of questions of fact which are never resolved because the issues they pose do not matter; or rather, because they matter only in their irrelevance, as "mysteries" that open into the problematics of rhetoric. Their motif might be taken from the Dedication: "whether Greylock benignantly incline his hoary crown or no." It makes no difference whether or not Pierre, Sr., is technically Isabel's father, because she really *is* his daughter, metaphorically. It makes no difference whether or not Pierre and Isabel *did* commit incest, because the consequences either way lead into the incestuous realities of language and the mind. It makes no difference whether or not Pierre "actually" had a "thorough understanding" of Plinlimmon's pamphlet (p. 343)—as the narrator claims he may—because Pierre embodies *and enacts* its ambiguities. It makes no difference whether or not "Vivia's book" will ever be published, because in the long view it has been published as *Pierre** (and perhaps as *Pierre*'s predecessor as well, insofar as the accounts of Pierre at work constitute a "grotesque parody"[43] of Melville writing *Moby-Dick*). It makes no difference which of the conflicting narrators of *Pierre* is *the* author, because the real unity of the novel lies in its apparent dissonance, a series of divergent voices which are made to correspond by their very

---

*In this sense at least Melville had the last word not only about *Pierre* itself, but about its reception. The two last letters that Pierre receives may be said to mirror the two letters from Isabel which in effect inspire the creation of Vivia; and accordingly, the publisher's rejection of Vivia's epistolary "slips" makes *Pierre*'s catastrophe a foreshadowing of the novel's reviews:

"SIR: — You are a swindler. Upon the pretence of writing a popular novel for us, you have been . . . passing through our press the sheets of a blasphemous rhapsody. . . .

(*Signed*) STEEL, FLINT, & ASBESTOS" (p. 414)

contradictions. *Moby-Dick* is Melville's American Apocalypse. *Pierre* is a story about the rhetoric of the Apocalypse (among many other texts) which works itself out in an apocalypse of rhetoric.

I mean apocalypse now in its primal sense: "to unveil," "to reveal." In this sense, the first reviewers were right. As an inquiry into the ways that the rhetoric of "America" sustained itself through two centuries of discontinuity, violence, and change, *Pierre* really does strike with an impious hand at the very foundations of American society. It is also a self-immolating inquiry into Melville's inability to escape his culture, and the most scathing review ever written of his own ill-fated literary career. This latter aspect of *Pierre* lies outside the scope of this chapter; but I might mention in conclusion that even here the tribute to Mount Greylock provides a good vantage point for analysis. It has the right concerns for discussing Melville's development, including those of authorship and patronage. It has the right setting: the Berkshire "amphitheatre" where he composed much of his finest work. It foreshadows the books that follow directly after *Pierre*—*Israel Potter*, dedicated "To His Highness, the Bunker-Hill Monument," and *The Piazza Tales*, whose title story concerns an "inland voyage" to Mount Greylock—and it has the suggestive precedent of Melville's dedication of *Moby-Dick*, the year before *Pierre*, "To Nathaniel Hawthorne, In Token of His Genius."[44]

Ambiguous Nathaniel Hawthorne! He seems to have nodded benignantly in Melville's direction in the heady summer of 1851, when they picnicked together on Greylock's summit, and once thereafter, on November 12, 1856, when Melville visited him in Liverpool, en route to the Holy Land. We "took a pretty long walk together," Hawthorne recorded in his journal,

> and sat down in a hollow among the sand hills (sheltering ourselves from the high, cool wind). . . . Melville, as he always does, began to reason of Providence and futurity, and of everything that lies beyond the human ken, and informed me that he had "pretty much made up his mind to be annihilated.". . . It is strange how he persists . . . in wandering to and fro over these deserts, as dismal and monotonous as the sand hills amid which we were sitting. . . . [Still,] he has a very high and noble nature, and [is] better worth immortality than most of us.[45]

I take this to be a generous tribute. Hawthorne preferred to keep *within* the human ken, if only to keep faith in providence and futurity. And that faith, in turn, gave him a liberal breadth of sympathy for those who persisted in other ways, even to the brink of annihilation. The same irony that allowed him to see through the rhetoric of manifest destiny without having his belief in progress shaken, helped him to understand (if not quite to endorse) those who said No-in-thunder, and to appreciate the high and noble nature that shone through Melville's strange, dismal, and (to him) monotonous speculations.

But my subject is Melville's *Pierre*, not his relation to Hawthorne. Insofar as the novel's Dedication recalls the the ambitions of *Moby-Dick*, it evokes the process of Melville's creative unfolding, from 1846 to 1851, from popular fiction (*Typee, Omoo*) to novels of self-discovery (*Mardi, Redburn, White-Jacket*) to what he termed (thinking not only of Hawthorne and Shakespeare, but of his own epic work then in progress) "the great Art of Telling the Truth." In *Mardi*, "claiming kin with mountains," he had fixed his sights on a "Konstanza" which, however "crazy," would "create the creative." Two years later he wrote to his father-in-law, Lemuel Shaw: "it is my earnest desire to write the sort of books which are said to 'fail'—Pardon this egotism." That high egotism asserted itself later in 1850, in his moving letter to Hawthorne concerning his literary hopes ("Lord, when shall we be done growing?"), and more movingly still, in Ishmael's meditation, or perhaps (according to the judgment of recent authorities) Ahab's, on the ambiguities of self-discovery:

> There is no steady unretracing progress in this life; we do not advance through fixed gradations, and at the last one pause:—through infancy's unconscious spell, boyhood's thoughtless faith, adolescence' doubt (the common doom), then scepticism, then disbelief, resting at last in manhood's pondering repose of If. But once gone through, we trace the round again; and are infants, boys, and men, and Ifs eternally.[46]

The homage to Mount Greylock might well be read as an interpretation of the energizing tensions behind that astonishing development, connecting as it does the unfathomable otherness of Typee to the majestic, mute white whale. It is a terrible ambiguity of

American literary history that that interpretation should first have been set out in the fourfold quasi-allegory of *Pierre*: literally, a satire of popular fiction; psychologically, a critique of the rhetoric of selfhood; historically, a tale of two America's; and prophetically, a failed book (entitled "Herman Melville Crazy") about the failure of symbolic art.

9
Emerson, Individualism, and Liberal Dissent

What we may be witnessing is ... the end of history as such: that is, the end point of mankind's ideological evolution and the universalization of Western liberal democracy as the final form of human government. ... [T]he victory of liberalism has occurred primarily in the realm of ideas or consciousness and is as yet incomplete in the real or material world. But there are powerful reasons for believing that it is the ideal that will govern the material world *in the long run.*

Francis Fukuyama, "The End of History?" *National Interest,*
XVI (1989), 4

Let me assure him, in case he's worried, that there certainly are ["journals on the left"]. One of them, now entering its 36th year and going strong, is Dissent. ... We do it on our own, "grubby" or not. And perhaps ... we come closer to traditions of American individualism than the conservative journals.

Irving Howe, "Letter to the Editor," in response to
James Atlas's article on Fukuyama, *New York Times
Magazine,* CXXXIX (November 19, 1989), 14

And they stretched forth their hands,
through love of the farther shore.

Virgil, *Aeneid,* Book VI*

*Quoted in Kenneth Burke, "I, Eye, Ay—Emerson's Early Essay on 'Nature': Thoughts on the Machinery of Transcendence," *Sewanee Review,* LXXIV (1966), 894. Burke explains:

> In the early part of his trip to the underworld, Virgil encountered those of the dead who could not cross Cocytus and the Stygian swamps. Charon would not ferry them to their final abode because they had not been buried. Then comes the famous line:
>
> *Tendebantque manus ripae ulterioris amore...*
>
> That is the pattern. Whether there is or is not an ultimate shore towards which we, the unburied, would cross, transcendence involves dialectical

Pierre Glendinning and Hester Prynne are classic fictional representations, negative and positive, of the "traditions of American individualism" that link Francis Fukuyama, James Atlas, and Irving Howe. I have argued that those traditions build upon a complex symbolic-ideological system, involving a distinctive myth of history (predicated on the American Way "as the final form of human government"), a nationwide ritual of generational renewal and rededication, and a theory of pluralist interpretation that simultaneously empowers and constrains the self. In this chapter I focus on two journal passages by Ralph Waldo Emerson, the central philosopher of American individualism, whose major essays have become the locus classicus of American dissent. In part my purpose is broadly historical, to describe the confrontation between socialist and liberal ideologies in Jacksonian America. In part it is specific to Emerson, and what I take to be a decisive shift in his thought. Still another part, pertaining to the ambiguities that redeem Hester and undo Pierre, has to do with the dynamics of oppositionalism in liberal culture at large.

The first of the two journal entries, recorded in late November or early December 1842, seems to have come in response to the utopian socialist schemes which had just eventuated in the founding of Brook Farm. It marks Emerson's first use of the term with which he has been most closely identified and, more largely, the first formulation of radical individualism in the modern world:

> The young people, like [Orestes] Brownson, [William Henry] Channing, [Christopher A.] Greene, E[lizabeth]. P[almer]. P[eabody]., & possibly [George] Bancroft think that the vice of the age is to exaggerate individualism, & they adopt the word *l'humanité* from Le Roux [Pierre Leroux], and go for *"the race."* Hence the Phalanx, owenism [sic], Simonism, the Communities. The same spirit in theology has produced the Puseyism which endeavors to rear "the Church" as a balance and overpoise to Conscience.

---

processes whereby something HERE is interpreted *in terms of* something THERE, something *beyond* itself.

What follows is an effort to explore the "something *beyond*" in terms not of transcendence but of the sustained volatility between *here* and *there*. Whether or not that process should be called "dialectical" is one of the abiding problems of liberal dissent in the United States.

This brief passage may be read as an index to the development of the concept of individualism in Jacksonian America. To begin with, it reminds us that that development was not intrinsic to liberal discourse, but on the contrary grounded in the European socialist attack on free enterprise; that in fact "individualism" was coined in the 1820s by French radicals such as Pierre Leroux to signify "*the* vice of the age," by which they meant the source of the various evils that characterized the "modern bourgeois order": "ruthless exploitation," "civil anarchy," "spiritual root-lessness," "infinite fragmentation," "heartless competitive . . . attitudes," "social atomization," "confusion of interests," "mean egoism."[1]

In this exclusively negative sense, the term "individualism" was adopted by virtually all nineteenth-century critics of liberal society. Some of these were ancien régime conservatives; others were moderates, such as Alexis de Tocqueville, who in the second volume of *Democracy in America* (1840) provided the era's most famous definition of the term ("individualism," he concludes, "at first only dams the springs of public virtues, but in the long run it attacks and destroys all the others also").* By far the majority, as Emerson indicates, were the radical sectaries whom Karl Marx labelled utopian socialists—the followers of Robert Dale Owen, for example, and the advocates of Charles Fourier's Phalanx, and above all the Saint-Simonians, the widely influential disciples of Count Claude Henri de Saint-Simon, "le grand seigneur sans-culottes," who shaped the pejorative nineteenth-century definitions of individualism: "system of isolation [or "of isolated selves"], in work or in undertakings, the opposite of the spirit of association"; "power without obedience, rights without duties"; "the exclusive domination of capital, the reign of the bourgeois aristocracy"; "theory by which the rights of the individual prevail

---

*Tocqueville's critique, however, is not so much an attack as an effort at historicist evaluation. Similar views of individualism appear in Michel Chevalier's *Society, Manners, and Politics in the United States* (1836; English translation: Boston, 1839) and Albert Brisbane's Fourierist *Social Destiny of Man: or, Association and Organization of Industry* (Philadelphia, 1840). They represent a European liberal tradition that includes progressivists such as Benjamin Constant (a favorite of Emerson's), Wilhelm Von Humboldt, and Jacob Burckhardt, as well as social democrats such as Jean Jaures, who believed that socialism would be the logical completion of individualism.

over those of society"; "system of self-interest, as opposed to the public interest, or the general good." These definitions were aimed polemically, as an expression of class struggle, against the middle classes of Europe, and ethnographically, as cultural description, against the Northern United States.[2]

Emerson's reference to "the vice of the age" plainly shows that he took "individualism" from the socialists. But his own sense of the concept remains ambiguous. I called it radical because he aligns individualism with "Conscience" against the systemic forces of church and state. However, as Emerson develops his thought, it turns out that *this* radical alignment (individualism as conscience) is directed not against a system, at least not that of the American North. Rather, he directs it against European antiliberals: primarily the socialists, well represented by Pierre Leroux, inventor of the term "socialism,"* whom Emerson associates with Edward Pusey, a leader of the Oxford Neocatholics. And to compound the ambiguity, Emerson apparently does not mean by this double attack upon collectivism to justify the liberal state. To say that associationists like Channing and Brownson mistook the source of evil is not necessarily to argue the superiority of Jacksonian self-interest. What Emerson did conceive of as the good society he makes vivid in a second journal entry, several days later:

> The world is waking up to the idea of Union and already we have Communities, Phalanxes and Aesthetic Families, & Pestalozzian

---

*Leroux's position was "generally representative of other socialist, communist, and [European] romantic critiques of the period" (Paul E. Corcoran, *Before Marx: Socialism and Communism in France, 1830–1848* [New York, 1983], pp. 3–4). Emerson refers in this representative sense to Leroux's widely discussed treatise *L'humanité* (1840), but he was probably familiar with the arguments of Leroux's even more influential pamphlet of 1834, "De l'individualisme et du socialisme" (reprinted as an appendix to David Owen Evans, *Le Socialisme Romantique: Pierre Leroux et ses contemporains* [Paris, 1948]), one of seven remarkable visionary discourses, issued as *Sept Discours sur la situation actuelle de la societe et de l'esprit humain* (Paris, 1841), which might be seen as the European utopianist counterpart to Emerson's *Essays: First Series* (Boston, 1841). Significantly, Leroux addressed his appeals "To the Bourgeoisie and to the Proletarians," precisely the sort of class identity that Emersonian individualism is meant to obviate. For the impact during this decade of Leroux and his work ("one of the great men of France and the representative of an important school in philosophy and politics"), see Orestes Brownson, "Liberalism and Socialism," *Brownson's Quarterly Review*, 3rd ser., III (1855), 183.

institutions. It is & will be magic. Men will live & communicate & ride & plough & reap & govern as by lightning and galvanic & etherial power; as now by respiration & expiration exactly together they lift a heavy man from the ground by the little finger only, & without a sense of weight. But this Union is to be reached by a reverse of the methods they use. It is spiritual and must not be actualized. The Union is only perfect when all the Uniters are absolutely isolated. Each man being the Universe, if he attempts to join himself to others, he instantly is jostled, crowded, cramped, halved, quartered, or on all sides diminished of his proportion. And the stricter the union the less & more pitiful he is. But let him go alone, & recognizing the Perfect in every moment with entire obedience, he will go up & down doing the works of a true *member*, and, to the astonishment of all, the whole work will be done with concert, though no man spoke; government will be adamantine without any governor.
    union ideal,—in actual individualism, actual union

then would be the culmination of science, useful art, fine art, & culmination on culmination.[3]

This visionary company of separate cosmic Selves may be seen as Emerson's antidote to "the vice of the age." But far from resolving the meaning of individualism, it amplifies and complicates the ambiguity. It may be worth remarking that my concern here is cultural and ideological rather than semantic or philological. The question is not whether Emerson got the word right, but why he adopted it when and as he did. My interest, that is, centers on the symbology implicit in Emerson's effort to come to terms with "individualism." And so considered, the journal passage seems to be a striking (if oblique) endorsement of systemic individualism. It is as though Emerson had decided, on reconsidering the attacks on individualism, that the remedy was not to abandon it, but to draw out its potential. I refer, first, to his emphatic rejection of the European radicals—a wholesale repudiation of socialism which he expands in this second passage to include Italian, Swiss, and German (as well as English and French) examples, and the fields of philosophy, aesthetics, and education, in addition to social reform. Secondly, I refer to the religious context he provides for "the Church"-defying conscience: the tradition he inherited of New England dissent, leading from the Puritan imitation of Christ ("entire obedience" made visible in spiritual non-conformity) through the Edwardsean revivals—"concerts" of believers (each in himself an image of God) advancing in mystic unity toward some millennial "culmination on culmination." Finally, I refer to the secular ideal toward which all this points and which is all but explicit in Emerson's imagery. "The union is only perfect when all the Uniters are absolutely isolated. Each man being the Universe . . . let him go alone": it is a dream-vision of laissez-faire. To *go it alone* on these terms is to be a *member*, not a fragment, and as a member to embody the values of Jacksonian democracy: self-interest, balance of powers, and minimal government. To federate in this sense as *uniters absolutely isolated* is to enact the principles of group pluralism as set out in the very concept of a "United States," from the Constitution through the Compromise of 1850. And to progress into the end-time kingdom, so federated, is to enact the myth of continuing revolution: it makes teleology manifest in personal process.

In short, this is a vision of the liberal millennium. Logically, stylistically, and substantively, "union ideal" requires a corresponding "ideal individualism." The concept is called for not only by the structure of Emerson's language—his formulaic "balanced antagonism" of terms[4]—but by the argument itself. "Ideal individualism" would seem to be the prepared-for resolution of the basic questions he sets out, concerning means and ends, self and society, vice and its antidote. But at the verge of resolution, Emerson hesitates or recoils; and in a sudden leap of grammar and meaning, an incomplete sentence followed by a blank on the page, he leaves us instead with a fragmentary opposition: "union ideal,—in actual individualism, actual union."

That incomplete thought, together with the lacuna or hiatus that surrounds it, lies at the heart of Emersonian dissent. If, on the one hand, the imagery of the journal passage points us toward a liberal millennium, on the other hand the absent "ideal individualism" bespeaks Emerson's resistance to Jacksonian ideology, his aversion to identifying the ideal with any system, including that of the liberal North. And by 1842 Jacksonian ideologues were beginning to effect precisely such an identification. Initiated three years earlier, partly in response to Tocqueville's *Democracy*, the Jacksonian apologia for individualism issued in a direct inversion of the term. Through the 1840s, in what amounted to a full-scale American counter-attack against European critics, "individualism" was unofficially but effectually redefined as "the last order" and "highest reach of civilization," a system destined to perfect society by "correct[ing] abuses, one after another, until the nature of individual man is thoroughly emancipated." There is no need to elaborate the arguments: they have become something of a cultural metaphysics by now. But a couple of points deserve emphasis. The first pertains to the society at large. The Jacksonian apologia for individualism is perhaps the single most dramatic instance in American history of ideology in action. It would make for a model case study of the means by which the advocates of a particular way of life translate social values into moral absolutes; interpret the difference between what is ("abuses" and all) and what ought to be (naturally and universally) as the distance between practice and theory; and on that basis transform complaints about the system into a confirmation of the principles that sustain it. By midcentury, in America as nowhere else, individualism was being promulgated as "the ultimate perfection of man."[5] To borrow Fukuyama's pseudo-Hegelian phrase, it augured the end of history.

My second point pertains to the difference between Emerson and the Jacksonian ideologues. The Jacksonians defend individualism as a social, economic, and political system (as in fact the term then required). Individualism is for them the natural condition of a new nation-state which is bringing to fruition, institutionally, the "great progressive movement" ascending from the "state of savage individualism to that of an individualism more elevated, moral, and refined." For Emerson, on the contrary, individualism centers on the independent Self. Progress is a function of self-reliance working against the ubiquitous conspiracies of society:

> No love can be bound by oath or covenant to secure it against a higher love. No truth so sublime but it may be trivial tomorrow in the light of new thoughts. . . . I cast away in this new moment all my once hoarded knowledge, as vacant and vain . . . [and] make a new road to new and better goals.[6]

This is the early, radical Emerson, of course, seer of "perpetual inchoation," prophet of the new as transition set against repose in any form, set against telos itself; "Champion of the Individual," as William James commemorated him, whose writings from *Nature* (1836) through *Essays: First Series* (1841) develop a utopian vision of the self which transforms earlier concepts of autonomy

(Descartes's cogito, Locke's self-possessive individualism) into a self-emptying mode of visionary possession. This radical Emerson requires us to discard in order to incorporate. He insists on risk at any cost, especially the cost of social stability. He invokes the personal meaning of "constitution" against the political:

> Nothing interests me of all an individual says but that which I perceive to be constitutional to him. Thereby he is strong, &, if unchecked . . . would be a plague to society.

He advocates self-reliance against all norms and conventions, especially those of liberal individualism (self-help, self-made, self-interest). He recasts the very concept of progress into an attack on social progressivism:

> Society never advances. It recedes as fast as it progresses—its progress is only apparent, like the workers of a treadmill. Society undergoes to be sure continual changes. It is barbarous, it is civilized, it is christianized, it is rich, it is scientific. But this constant change is not constant amelioration. . . . Not in time is the race progressive.
> . . .
> All philosophy, all theory, all hope are defeated when applied to society. . . . Progress is not for society. Progress belongs to the Individual. . . . Society is, as men of the world have always found it, tumultuous, insecure, unprincipled. . . . Society must come again under the yoke of the base and selfish, but the individual heart faithful to itself is fenced with a sacred palisado. . . . And out of the strength and wisdom of the private heart shall go forth at another era the regeneration of society. . . . By myself, for myself, I can have faith, Ideas, Progress, God; but if I must apply all these to Society as we see it they become Philistery.[7]

The proper term for this outlook is individuality, the belief in the absolute integrity, spiritual primacy, and inviolable sanctity of the self. A number of scholars have discussed Emerson's thought from that perspective, but mainly from within the American context: the historian Yehoshua Arieli, for example, as a function of Jacksonian nationalism, and the political scientist George Kateb, as *the* theory of American liberal democracy, distinctive to the United States and embodied in its ripest intellectual form in transcendentalism. It is therefore worth stressing that individuality in its modern sense is neither American nor liberal nor democratic. It is European, radical, and antibourgeois: a transhistorical, transcultural concept which (according to the anthropologist Louis Dumont) derives first from Christianity, and then, in its modern genesis, as a post-Renaissance, post-Reformation ideal of self-realization, from Germany, France, and England, where it was developed in explicit antagonism to the perceived defects of systemic individualism. The following extracts from continental polemics of the 1830s are representative:

> Human societies are born, live, and die, upon the earth; there they accomplish their destinies. But they contain not the whole man. . . . There still remains in him the more noble part of his nature; those high faculties by which he elevates himself to God. . . . We, individuals, each with a separate and distinct existence. . . we have *a higher destiny than that of states.*
>
>   * * *
>
> In [our present] society . . . individualism is enthroned and individuality is outlawed . . . [But] God has willed individuality and not individualism; He has confirmed the former and quelled the latter. . . . All constitutions, all political institutions pose a threat to individuality . . . [and yet] individuality will bring about the social restoration which is being called for on all sides.[8]

Through the Romantic period and beyond, individuality served as a utopian rallying point against liberal ideology for virtually all groups in the political spectrum, left, right, and center, from royalists to anarchists. Its influence helps explain the antibourgeois animus behind the European Romantic vision of the individual. Its effects extend from the widespread theological attack on free enterprise (in the name of "Gospel individuality") to Marx's contrast in *The Communist Manifesto* (1848) between capitalist alienation and "the free development of each [individual]," or as he elaborates this in the *Grundrisse*—speculating on the classless third stage of history—"free individuality, based on the universal development of individuals." Its radical implications are striking even in that marrow of liberal thought, John Stuart Mill's *On Liberty* (1859). Nothing is more detrimental to progress, Mill writes in his discussion "Of Individuality," than the pressures of popular government and middle-class conformity:

The majority, being satisfied with the ways of mankind as they now are (for it is they who make them what they are), cannot comprehend why those ways should not be good enough for everybody. . . . [But] whatever crushes individuality is despotism, by whatever name it may be called. . . . [T]here are but few persons . . . whose experiments . . . would be likely to be any improvement on established practice. But these are the salt of the earth; without them, human life would become a stagnant pool. . . . At present individuals are lost in the crowd . . . in America, they are the whole white population; in England, chiefly the middle class. But they are always a mass, that is to say, collective mediocrity. . . . The progressive principle . . . is antagonistic to the sway of custom . . . and the contest between the two constitutes the chief interest of the history of mankind.[9]

By "contest" Mill does not mean revolution: he champions liberal democracy as the best of all possible "despotisms," and he warns specifically against "the sort of 'hero-worship' which applauds the strong man of genius for forcibly seizing on the government of the world and making it do his bidding." Still, the radical implications are unmistakable.* Mill's contrast between the "progressive principle" and middle-class "mediocrity" is

---

*Raymond Williams's historical summary is pertinent to this opposition: "The emergence of notions of *individuality*, in the modern sense, can be related to the break-up of the medieval social, economic, and religious order. In the general movement against feudalism there was a new stress on a man's personal existence over and above his place and function in a rigid hierarchical society" (*Keywords: A Vocabulary of Culture and Society* [Oxford, 1976], p. 163). The affinities here to the emergence of the concept of individualism allowed European liberals (as I note below) to adopt that concept of individualism *within limits*, as a necessary interim stage of human development. The same historical affinities allowed Americans later in the century to absorb the concept of individuality, conversely, as an ideal within the larger ideological framework of individualism. The process of absorption, however, has remained fraught with tension. It retains the paradoxical qualities I discuss below in Emerson's thought. As comparatists have noted: "in America, the post-structuralist critique of individuality has had only a feeble impact on the persistently individualist imagery of [American] institutions and popular culture. In the political, economic, and artistic spheres of public life, these images have remained unshaken by the theoretical trauma that has led to the subtleties of post-structuralist theory" (Thomas C. Heller and David E. Wellbury, "Introduction" to *Reconstructing Individualism: Autonomy, Individuality, and the Self in Western Thought*, ed. Heller, Martin Sosna, and Wellbury [Stanford, 1986], pp. 12–13).

symptomatic of a form of cultural relativism which applies to liberal democracy no less than to other ways of life. Individuality, he writes in *Political Economy*, is "a circle . . . which no government, be it that of one, of a few, or of the many, ought to be permitted to overstep," and he makes it plain here, as he does also in *On Liberty*, that the other side of this defense of privacy is a standing invitation to "antagonistic" "resistance." He also recognized, reluctantly, that the revolutionary threat this entailed was most palpable in the most antiliberal extremes: on the one hand, the elitism of the *Übermensch*, from Carlyle through Nietzsche; on the other hand, the left-wing egalitarianism that eventuated in the uprisings of 1848. "Beware of confounding individuality with individualism," warned the Saint-Simonian Alexandre de Saint-Cheron in 1831 (echoing a host of diverse European thinkers from Friedrich List to Henri Joncières and Max Stirner): "individualism [is] . . . mean egoism, lonely and disunited, which chokes all dignity . . . while the sentiment of individuality is the holy exaltation of man." So, too, the Swiss literary historian and theologian Alexandre Vinet, representing a Catholic–Romantic tradition that included such disparate writers as Sainte-Beuve, Victor Hugo, Balzac, and Lamartine: "individualism and individuality" are "two sworn enemies; the first an obstacle and negation of society; the latter a principle to which society owes all its savor, life, and reality. . . . The progress of individualism on the one side, and the gradual extinction of individuality on the other . . . constitute a double abyss . . . in which we are precipitated."[10]

Pierre Leroux, perhaps the leading socialist theorist of the time, offered the radical alternative to that looming liberal abyss. Individualism, he explained in 1832, serves only "for liberating the bourgeoisie": it leads to a "political economy . . . [of] everyone for himself . . . all for riches, [and] nothing for the poor." Individuality, on the contrary, opens into a "system of association which would realize . . . equality and brotherhood," a system whose premises Leroux expounds in his 1840 treatise, *L'humanité* (to which Emerson refers) as well as in his influential tract, "On Individualism and Socialism" (1834):

Every man is indeed a fruit on the tree of humanity; but being the product of the tree makes the fruit no less complete and perfect in and of itself. The fruit is also the tree, it contains the seeds of the

318 / *Rites of Assent*

tree which generated it. . . . Thus in his essence every man is a
reflection of society at large . . . every man is the law for which laws
are made and against which no law can prevail.[11]

On some basic level, this utopian vision underlies Emerson's
reluctance in the 1842 journal to invest the ideal in individualism.
It also contributes to his otherwise surprising endorsement of
socialist ideas of the future. For Emerson's polemic there (as elsewhere) against the "Communities" turns on means, not ends.
Although he insists "on a reverse of [their] *methods*," he embraces
their "*idea* of Union." It is a profoundly radical gesture: a disavowal *in potentia* of all systems, individualistic as well as collectivist, capitalism and communism alike, Adam Smith's together
with Fourier's, Owen's, and Pestalozzi's. The real point, Emerson
seems about to say, is not my plan for society against yours. It is
perfect union, a hope we both share, based on a dream of individuality—something "spiritual and . . . not [to] be actualized"—
which by definition sets the individual at odds with society as it
is, anywhere, at any time. In this perspective, the 1842 hiatus has
in it the potential of an absolute separation of the actual America
(individualism) from the ideal (individuality). We may read into
the absent "ideal individualism"—or into the blank on the page
that divides "actual individualism" from spiritual "culmination"—the most extreme positions of antebellum dissent: William Lloyd Garrison's, for example, in repudiating the Constitution, or Thoreau's in supporting the *armed* resistance of John
Brown, or once again, Margaret Fuller's in joining the Italian socialists of 1848.

The drama of the 1842 journal passage lies in the collision or
uncanny convergence of this spirit of individuality on the one
hand and, on the other, its cultural antithesis, the apologia for
liberal society implicit in the imagery of laissez-faire. In retrospect, we may safely say that Emerson's hesitation about adopting
or rejecting either extreme indicates a search for the proper paradox that would connect the two. We may say further, I believe,
that that search marks a turning point in his career—between the
radical early essays and the conservative "later Emerson"—and
that the key to the shift lies in his confrontation with the theory
and practice of socialism.

I noted earlier that Emerson's commitment to individuality
led him to embrace the socialists' visionary ends. I would now

add that Emerson's antipathy to their methods bespeaks his deeper commitment to liberal thought. He had not worked this through by 1842; or more accurately, he had deferred the conflict through the ambiguity of "America." His early essays distinguish between Jacksonian society and the "true America," as between ideology and utopia. He critizes the defects of laissez-faire in the name of "the Spirit of America" (to which he dedicated his journals in 1822, at the age of 19). He retreats from the pressures of specialization and industrialization, as well as from his private griefs, into "this new yet unapproachable America I have found in the West." "The American Scholar" opposes the prospect of "a nation of men" in America to America's actual "iron-lid[ded]" marketplace economy.[12] Upon such distinctions—grounded in an absolute that gains substance from the metaphors of the American way while yet claiming (by rhetorical inversion, opposition, and reversal) to transcend the actual America—Emerson built his radical doctrine of the individual. "America" was for him alternately the facts of liberal individualism and the ideals of individuality—a symbolic polarity which appeared sometimes as sheer antagonism, sometimes as probation or trial, and whose divergent meanings he somehow combined, in the early essays (1836–1841), in his consummate figure of dissent, the representative/adversarial American Self.

The socialist challenge forced the resolution of the conflict. I refer here neither to the theory nor to the practice of socialism per se, but to what these implied about Emerson's prior intellectual and imaginative commitments. Emerson was troubled by programs for collectivist living and principles of violent revolution; but the crux of the conflict for him—what made the opposition dialectical, a conflict that allowed neither for transcendence nor for bipolar synthesis, but demanded partisan choice—lay in socialism's categorical denial of "the Spirit of America." Socialism came in many guises in the 1830s, but all of them were quintessentially "Old World" in principle, in practice, and in expression. They presented fundamentally different myths of progress, based on different relations between process and telos, issuing in different rhetorics of identity, opening out to different roads to utopia, and offering, in sum, alternative models of culture. Socialism repudiated the language of "America." It contested not only the pragmatics of the marketplace, but the vision of the United States as "the country of the Future."[13] As method and in theory social-

ism denied the newness of the New World, as against the out-
wornness of the Old. It denied the concept of continuing revolution (all progress tending toward or issuing from the War of
American Independence), the prophetic claims of manifest destiny, and the typology of the regenerative West. And it may be
that in 1842 Emerson's belief in individuality, together with the
mounting criticism of individualism (as "the vice of the age")
brought him to the verge of a sweeping repudiation not only of
his society, but of his culture. Hovering in the hiatus between
"individualism" and "culmination" is a total, unequivocal disso-
ciation of the meaning of America from the United States, as
Augustine had severed the City of God from the city of man.

   To some significant extent, that crisis in cultural commitment and symbolic language contributes to the extraordinary volatility of *Essays: First Series*. I have in mind now Emerson's response to internal developments, rather than to the socialist
challenge: his alarm at the 1837 Depression, his contempt for
"King Andrew" Jackson (and still more for Jackson's "henchman,"
Martin Van Buren, elected in 1836 by a "cowardly majority"), his
fears concerning the growing urban "rabble," and his horror of the
self-made arrivistes who were threatening to bring down Boston's
Brahmin Whig establishment. These and similar "twinings and
tendrils of . . . evil," as he put it, contributed to his disgust with the
"depravity . . . stupidity & corruption," the "treacherous, short
memoried, suicidally selfish, all illogical world" of Jacksonian
free enterprise. Essentially, Emerson shared the radical scepticism
about institutions that Hester declares midway through *The Scarlet Letter*. Basically, he felt the same pure outrage at horologicals
that Pierre gives voice to, and had the same sense of political,
social, and economic injustice that mobilized over fifty socialist
communities in New England and other regions of the country
through the 1840s. His journals of 1836, when *Nature* was published and "The American Scholar" begun, bristle with scorn
for "this . . . era of Trade," with its "fever of Speculation . . . &
restlessness of politicians":

> [T]here is no Idea, no Principle. It is all scrambling for bread &
> Money. . . .
>   When I spoke or speak of the democratic element I do not mean
> that ill thing vain & loud which writes lying newspapers, spouts at
> caucuses, & sells its lies for gold. . . . There is nothing of the true

democratic element in what is called Democracy; it must fall, being wholly commercial.

In 1837 he elaborated his concept of true democracy through a critique of "Trades and Professions" which concludes that "Labor and not property is the source of real power." Soon after he expanded this subversive concept of power into a fundamental challenge to existing property and labor relations:

> the reliance on Property, including the reliance on governments which protect it, is the want of self-reliance. Men have . . . come to esteem . . . civil institutions as guards of property, and they deprecate assaults on these, because they feel them to be assaults on property. . . . But a cultivated man becomes ashamed of his property, out of a new respect for his nature.[14]

The radicalism potential in such statements is especially conspicuous by contrast with reformist appeals of the 1830s, ranging from William Ellery Channing's highbrow *Self-Culture* to the Locofoco exposés in William Leggett's *Plain-Dealer* and Theodore Sedgwick's *Public and Private Economy*. The difference between these attacks on Jacksonian free enterprise and Emerson's dissent, or for that matter between Emerson and the young dissenters of 1842, lies in the utopian intensity of Emerson's vision. By 1839, he had recoiled not only from the exaggerations of actual individualism but from the system itself, as from a vast commercial lie—had embraced a form of Romantic titanism that according to local Unitarians bordered on antinomian heresy, and according to Nietzsche on the doctrine of the Superman:

> The whole world [wrote Emerson during this period] travails to ripen & bear the sufficiency of one man. . . . He asks no vantage ground, no favorable circumstance. The obedient universe bends around him. . . . He needs no . . . church, for he is himself a prophet; no statute book, for he hath the Lawgiver. . . .
> What is the State?
> The Hero is the State
> The Soul should legislate.

On July 4, 1839, the journals record a personal "declaration of independence," apparently conceived during a walk that day in the woods around Walden Pond, which would become the corner-stone of "Self-Reliance":

> The doctrine of hatred must be preached as the counteraction of the doctrine of love when that pules & whines. I hate father & mother & wife & brother when my muse calls me & I say to these relatives that if they wish my love they must respect my hatred. I would write on the lintels of the door-post, Whim. Expect me not to show cause why I seek or why I shun company. Then again do not tell me of the obligation on me to put all poor men in good situations. I tell thee, thou foolish philanthropist, that I grudge the dollar, the shilling, the cent I give to such men as do not belong to me & to whom I do not belong. There is a class of persons to whom by all spiritual affinity I am bought & sold; for them I will go to prison, if need be; but your nonsense of popular charity, the suckling of fools, the building of meetinghouses, the alms to sots,—though I confess with shame I sometimes succumb & give the dollar it is a wicked dollar which by & by I shall have the manhood to withhold.

Shortly after this, Emerson endorsed Garrison's disavowal of the state, and advised Americans to "[g]ive up the Government without too solicitously inquiring" about consequences. The United States, he explained, is just another "government of force. . . . We are accustomed to speak of our National Union & our Constitution as of somewhat sacred . . . but these bands are trivial in the comparison" with "Individual character": "Character is centrality, the impossibility of being displaced or overset. . . . Society is frivolous, and shreds its day into scraps, its conversation into ceremonies and escapes."[15]

In this optative mood, Emerson decided to come to terms with the recent "sympathy for communistic experiments" at home and the "considerable interest in socialism" abroad. On August 4, 1840, he wrote to Margaret Fuller that he hoped to transform *The Dial* from a "papyrus reed" to "a fatal arrow":

> I begin to wish to see a different Dial from that which I first imagined. I would not have it too purely literary. I wish we might make a Journal so broad & great in its survey that it should lead the opinion of this generation on every great interest & read the law on property, government, education, as well as on art, letters, & religion. A great Journal people must read. And it does not seem worth our while to

work with any other than sovereign aims. So I wish we might court some of the good fanatics and publish chapters on every head in the whole Art of Living. I am just now turning my pen to scribble & copy on the subjects of 'Labor,' 'Farm,' 'Reform,' 'Domestic Life,' etc.

In the next year or two Emerson proceeded to publish "Fourierism and the Socialists," "English Reformers," and other essays in which, by implication at least, he welcomed the socialists' attack on individualism. Their methods he rejected at once, but at this point he was persuaded that "success depends on the Aim, not on the means. Look at the mark[,] not on your arrow. And herein is my hope for reform in our vicious modes of living. Let a man . . . fix his heart on magnificent life & he need not know the economical methods." What else *could* he do? "I see . . . that commerce, law, & state employments . . . are now all so perverted & corrupt that no man can right himself in them. . . . Nothing is left him but to begin the world anew." New England reformers were right to renounce a country in which "men are tools & not masters," a polity where "Things are in the saddle / And ride mankind," a region where "[t]he ways of trade are grown selfish to the borders of theft, and supple to the borders (if not beyond the borders) of fraud."[16]

What Emerson meant by beginning the world anew devolved then and always upon a vision of cosmic subjectivity, "the doctrine Judge for yourself[,] Reverence thyself." His journal entry of April 7, 1840, holds true for his entire career: "In all my lectures, I have taught one doctrine, namely the infinitude of the private man." And four months earlier, on January 1, 1840, he declared as his manifesto in "Politics" what we might consider to be a foreshadowing of his meditation three years later on "individualism": "the great antidote and corrective in nature to this abuse of Formal Government is the Influence of Private Character, the growth of the Individual." But in the years immediately preceding and following this "kernel of his message" (as William James called it), self-reverence had assumed such absolutist proportions in his thought, had brought him so close to a relativistic view of the merely social order (as against "the infinitude of the private man"), that he seems actually to have entertained the possibility of a wholesale reordering of the state, *verging on* the redistribution of property and wealth. He was becoming increasingly angry with a "selfish commerce & government [which] have got possession of the masses"; and although he found "no instant prospect of a virtuous revolution; yet I confess I should not be pained at a change which threatened a loss of some of the luxuries or conveniences of society." Accordingly, in two lectures at the start and end of 1841, "Man the Reformer" (January 25) and "Lecture on the Times" (December 2), he may be said to have come *to the edge* of class analysis; and in his journals and letters of 1840–1841 he sometimes ventures further still, *almost* beyond the bounds of liberalism:

> In every knot of laborers, the rich man does not feel himself among his friends,—and at the polls he finds them arrayed in a mass in distinct opposition to him. . . . [T]he people do not wish to be represented or ruled by the ignorant and base. They only vote for these, because they were asked with the voice and semblance of kindness. They will not vote for them long. . . . The state must consider the poor man, and all voices must speak for him. Every child that is born must have a just chance for his bread. Let the amelioration in our laws of property proceed from the concession of the rich, not from the grasping of the poor. Let us understand that the equitable rule is, that no one should take more than his share. . . .

> The revolutions that impend over society are not now from ambition and rapacity . . . but from new modes of thinking, which shall recompose from society after a new order, which shall animate labor by love and science, which shall destroy the value of many kinds of property, and replace all property within the dominion of reason and equity. . . .

> All our fanatics high & low seem to move now impelled by ideas which may one day emerge to the surface under the form of the question of Property. Every child that is born ought to have his just chance—perhaps that is the statement that will content all. . . .

> Judge [William Pitt] Preble . . . a very sensible person . . . is full of despondency on the entire failure of republican institutions in this country. . . . I amused the man with my thrum that Anarchy is the form & theocracy the fact to which we & all people are tending. . . .

> The monastery[,] the convent did not quite fail. Many & many a stricken soul found peace & home & scope in those regimens[,] in those chapels & cells. The Society of Shakers did not quite fail, but has proved an agreeable asylum to many a lonesome farmer &

matron. The College has been dear to many an old bachelor of learning. What hinders them that this age better advised should endeavor to sift out of these experiments the false & adopt & embody in a new form the advantage[?][17]

I italicize the qualifying terms—*almost, verging on, to the edge*—because we know that Emerson never really gave serious thought to social reorganization. Nor did he take seriously the "experiments" in collective living and common wealth. This is evident in the very playfulness of his language ("fanatics," "perhaps this . . . will content all," "amused . . . with my thrum," "did not quite fail"), as well as in his shortlist of exemplary radicals (monks, nuns, Shakers, and the old bachelor professor). It is evident, too, considering the course of international Romanticism, in the conspicuous absence of any reference whatever to socialism in the utopian passages of *Essays: First Series*, and relatively few (most of them pejorative) to "individuality" anywhere in his writing.* Even at the height of his heresy, Emerson's cultural roots were too deep for him to envision "a new form" in the "Art of Living" that would be anything other than a purified version of

---

*Generally, Emerson equates individuality with the particular as distinct from the universal. "The great man," he writes in 1838 (Journal C, in vol. V of *Journals*, ed. Merton M. Sealts, Jr. [Cambridge, Mass., 1965], p. 484), "is great by means of the predominance of Universal nature. . . . Nothing is more simple than greatness . . . yet always it astonishes because matter, appetite, & individuality always exist & rule from the earth upward six feet. Or hat high. The severity with which we judge other men's derelictions & pardon our own is a part of the amabilis insania of Individuality. The Universal tide rises in our cellar . . . but the little private puddle of the Blood trickles to the tongue and the finger ends." So, too, he speaks in "Demonology" (1839) of the "foolish individuality" in those who seek to assert their superiority over "the roll of common men": "What more easy and vulgar than to project this exuberant selfhood into a region where the individuality is forever bounded by generic and cosmical laws [?]" (vol. III of *Early Lectures*, ed. Robert E. Spiller and Wallace E. Williams [Cambridge, Mass., 1972], p. 165). Eventually Emerson did find a use for this vulgar self-projection, partly through a variation on the theories of self-interest and balance of powers—as in this journal entry of 1845 on "Individuality self-defended" (Journal W, in vol. IX of *Journals*, ed. Ralph H. Orth and Alfred R. Ferguson [Cambridge, Mass., 1971], p. 224; later incorporated in "Uses of Great Men," in *Essays and Lectures*, ed. Joel Porte [Library of America: New York, 1983], p. 628): "Nothing strikes me with more force than the powers by which individuals are protected from individuals in a world where every benefactor becomes so easily a malefactor only by continuation of his activity into places where it is not due; and where children seem so much at the mercy of their foolish parents and where almost all men are excessively social & interfering."

free enterprise (as in the 1842 journal) or a pastoral dream of agrarian laissez-faire. Even in his seemingly antinomian pronouncements, as in his 1840 declaration that "the very idea of Government in the world is Interference," he defined individuality through liberal presuppositions. (His own most daring venture in communalism was to invite the servants to dinner one day in 1841, an invitation which, once declined, was not renewed.)[18]

Still, he had to acknowledge the seriousness of the socialist challenge. All too many others were taking it up, including the admirable young people he names in the 1842 Journal (Channing, Brownson, Peabody, Greene, "and possibly Bancroft"); he was being solicited for support of Brook Farm; and he was "much thrust upon," he complained, by radical tracts and manifestoes, in which, astutely, he read the signs of impending revolution in Europe. The result was the social-rhetorical crisis I noted. Its issue has already been suggested. Increasingly through the 1840s, Emerson drew out the liberal underpinnings of his dissent—i.e., the premises of his commitment to America in its full bipolar implications, ideal *and* (not or) actual. And increasingly through the decade, in journals, lectures, *Dial* reviews, and transcendentalist "Conversations," he engaged in a pointed, persistent, and eventually vehement polemic against socialism.* Having discovered

---

*The Concord discussion groups of these years provide an interesting index to Emerson's confrontation with socialist doctrines. One example must suffice here, a "Convention at Alcott-House" (*Dial*, III [1842], 242–247), recorded by Emerson. The subject of discussion is the radical proposal, derived from various European socialist manifestoes, "That an integral reform will comprise . . . an amendment in our (1) Corn Laws, (2) Monetary Arrangements, (3) Penal Code, (4) Education, (5) the Church, (6) the Law of Primogeniture, (7) Divorce." The discussion itself develops in three stages. First comes the liberal response to radicalism, which begins in a sort of Weberian–Protestant reconciliation of the world and the spirit, but then moves toward conflict: in effect, toward the *contradiction* between pluralist rule by law and the spirit of universal love:

> a personal reform . . . is obviously the key to every future and wider good. By reformed individuals only can reformed laws be enacted, or reformed plans effected. By him alone, who is reformed and well regulated, can the appeal fairly be made to others, either privately or publicly. . . . Personal elevation is our credentials. . . .
>
> After this had been considered and approved, another of our friends offered the following [query:]. . . "How shall we find bread for support of our bodies?" . . . And the government's answer was immediately preferred, "We . . . shield the good from adversities, and we punish the evil-doers." Is this true? We thought. . . . No; government has not redeemed its promise.

that he "could not reconcile the socialist principle with [his] own doctrine of the individual," he proceeded to situate individuality within culture, as individualism.[19]

The 1842 lacuna marks Emerson's presentiment of that bond between ideology and utopia. The discovery itself is first recorded in "New England Reformers," an address delivered on March 3, 1844, which Emerson considered important enough to publish later that year as the concluding section to *Essays: Second Series*. It is an eloquent summary of his ruminations from 1840 on about socialist theories and schemes, and perhaps a catalytic event was the restructuring that year of Brook Farm. The community had begun in a tension between the "individualists," such as Hawthorne, and the "associationists" (Brownson et al) whom Emerson chides in the 1842 journal entry. But the leading individualists either left or else (as in the cases of Emerson and Thoreau) refused to join altogether, and the associationists gradually gained control. In January 1844, under the direction of George Ripley and Albert Brisbane, Brook Farm effactually became "the center of Fourierism in the United States." In Hawthorne's words, the motley group of

---

to us, and we would no longer care for its provisions. The first law, too, of Heaven is Love, and government is founded on force.

We, therefore ignore human governments . . . and declare our allegiance only to Universal Love.

At this critical juncture, where laissez-faire threatens the slip into antinomianism (or anarchy), "A third person" offers the following "thought," based on the text from Revelation, "Behold I make all things new": "the germs of this new generation are even now discoverable in human beings, but have been hitherto either choked by uncongenial circumstances, or . . . have attained no abiding growth." And from this utopian perspective, the discussion finds its resolution by descending from theory to "method" and means, or more precisely by investing "Universal" telos in local process:

On a survey of the present civilized world, Providence seems to have ordained the United States of America, more especially New England, as the field wherein this idea is to be realized in actual experience. . . .

An unvitiated generation and more genial habits shall restore the Eden on Earth, and men shall find that paradise is not merely a fable of the poets.

Such was the current of our thought; and most of those who were present felt delight in the conversations that followed. Said I not well, that it was a happy day? For though talk is never more than a portraiture of a fact, it may be, and ours was, the delineation of a fact based in the being of God.

idealists he had joined three years before—"Persons of marked individuality... [whose] bond was not affirmative, but negative"—had "blundered into the very emptiest mockery [of an] ... effort to establish the one true system."[20]

The blunder seems to have provoked Emerson to an unambiguous attack on the methods of socialism.* He had written pri-

---

* Several scholars have detailed the "traumatic effect" of "the almost simultaneous collapse of the [Brook Farm] community and of the national impulse toward Association"; others have described the "struggle which went on in Brook Farm between 'the individualists' and 'the associationists' " (Richard Francis, "The Ideology of Brook Farm," *Studies in the American Renaissance*, ed. Joel Myerson [Charlottesville, Va., 1977], p. 11; John L. Brown, "Life of Paradise Anew" in *France and North America: Utopia and Utopians*, ed. Mathé Allain [Lafayette, La., 1978], p. 79). By fall 1843, it seemed clear to Emerson that "The 'Community' of socialism is only the continuation of the same movement which made the joint stock companies for manufacturers, mining, insurance, banking, & the rest. It has turned out cheaper to make calico by companies, & it is proposed to bake bread & to roast mutton by companies, & it will be tried & done" (Journal U [November, 1843], in vol. IX of *Journals*, pp. 54–55). His insight reminds us that the failure of associationism was less a failure of socialism than the continuing confusion of the social-rhetorical crisis surrounding the concept of individualism during the 1830s and early 1840s. One example of that confusion is Orestes Brownson, a convert to Catholicism who inveighed with a convert's zeal against Protestant self-interested materialism ("that religion ... adapted to our earthly wants," favoring "the development of ... material resources ... commerce, manufactures, trade, industry"), but remained a militant antisocialist. And vice versa: although he was a firm believer in "the creed of every true American"—although he polemicized on behalf of property rights, the "general principles of our Federal Constitution," "freedom of Industry," and the "fundamental principles of [our] civil society"—Brownson was nonetheless a militant reformer, an admirer of Pierre Leroux, and a champion of individuality against individualism. His views in this respect are characteristic of the sort of liberal conundrum which Emerson's concept of individualism addressed. According to Brownson, "Individuality without Community is INDIVIDUALISM, the fruits of which are dissolution, isolation, selfishness, disorder ... [whereas] Community without Individuality may be termed COMMUNISM," a synonym for "TYRANNY." (Quotations are respectively from: "The Church and the Republic," *Brownson's Quarterly Review*, I [1856], 275; "Origin and Ground of Government," *United States Magazine and Democratic Review*, n.s., XIII [1843], 129, 132, 358; "Social Evils and Their Remedy," *Boston Quarterly Review*, IV [1841], 279; "Community System," *United States Magazine and Democratic Review*, n.s., XII [1842], 134.) Similar confusions appear in the Brook Farm platform, which was committed to "communatism" as the expression of "the spirit of progress," personal "*independence*," "the Right of Property," and the primacy of "individual development"— all this under the aegis of "America" and "our Puritan fathers," whose "great work" we are bound "to complete" (Albert Brisbane, "The American Associationists," *United States Magazine and Democratic Review*, n.s., XVIII [1846], 142, 145–

vately in 1842, as Brook Farm got underway, that the socialists had "skipped no fact but one, namely life." Now he recognized that he had to protect the ideal against their attempts at its realization. "New England Reformers" may be described as a more or less systematic application of that insight to the recent "progress of dissent" in Europe and America. To all varieties of "ultraists" Emerson offers a general rebuke concerning the primacy of the self:

> The criticism and attack on institutions which we have witnessed [against everything from "the system of agriculture" to "the institution of marriage"], has made one thing plain, that society gains nothing whilst a man, not himself renovated, attempts to renovate things around him.

Then he proceeds to his own visionary alternative. Lifting virtually verbatim the long journal passage of 1842, Emerson hails the current "spirit of protest" (a world "awaking to the idea of union") and repeats its many "magic" effects, from communication "by lightning" to "concert" without words. He omits only the separation of fact from ideal ("It is spiritual and must not be actualized"); and makes only one addition, as though to explain why that separation no longer obtains. What had been, amorphously, "union ideal,—in actual individualism, actual union" is rendered, apodictically, "The union must be ideal in actual individualism."[21]

Actual individualism, ideal union! The paradox is ultimately Christic, the Incarnation applied to a secular way of life. It is a rhetorical flourish adequate to the occasion, Emerson's first public use of the word individualism. He does not consciously acquiesce to ideology. By "actual" he means a version of the ideal, "individualism" as the intimation of an individuality lost and to be regained, as he makes plain in most subsequent references to individualism

---

146). It has been pointed out that Brook Farm was "a middle-class enterprise . . . a joint stock company rather that a communist society" (Francis, "Ideology of Brook Farm," pp. 4–5; Albert Fein, "Fourierism in Nineteenth-Century America: A Social and Environmental Perspective," in France and North America: Utopias and Utopians, p. 135); and Taylor Stoehr writes that it "was as middle class in ideology as it was in personnel. The problem was how to make the middle class honest, and how to bring everyone into it" (Nay-Saying in Concord: Emerson, Alcott, and Thoreau [Hamden, Conn., 1979], p. 74). The problem was also to coordinate the ideals of reform with those of individualism, and both with the dreams of "continuing revolution"—a task accomplished preeminently by Emerson.

through the 1840s—though always, tellingly, by contrast with socialism. Thus in a Notebook addendum to the journal entry of 1842 he complained that

> The *a priori* convictions are there [in individualism]. The plans of Owen and Fourier are enforced by counting & arithmetic. All the fine aperçus are for individualism. The Spartan broth, the hermit's cell, the lonely farmer's life are poetic; the phalanstery [Fourier], the self-supporting Village [Owen], are culinary & mean[.]

Thus, too, he complained in 1847, in a journal passage he was to use a year later to lecture European revolutionaries:

> Individualism has never been tried. All history[,] all poetry deal with it only & because now it was in the minds of men to go alone and now before it was tried, now, when a few began to think of the celestial Enterprise, sounds this tin trumpet of a French Phalanstery and the newsboys throw up their caps & cry, Egotism is exploded; now for Communism! But all that is valuable in the Phalanstery comes of individualism.[22]

And yet, it will bear repeating, through this decade the ideological tenets of Emersonian individualism become increasingly clear. To begin with, the invective against socialism grows sharper, more pointed. In 1846, contemplating how all "excellence is inflamed or exalted individualism," Emerson wondered if "Community" (or "communatism"), by contrast, were not simply "the dream of Bedlam." By 1847 he concluded that "Fourier, St. Simon, . . . Leroux, and the Chartist leader, [were] all crazy men," and perhaps Fourier in particular ("a French mind, destitute of course of the moral element"). More telling are his unabashed endorsements from 1842 to 1850 of what can only be called free-enterprise ideology. The contours of the paradise that were shadowed forth in 1842 are detailed through the decade in the frequent and direct examples he finds of "the concept of laissez-faire [in] the natural world." Adam Smith, he decided, was the one "great man among the economists," and his doctrine of "Laissez faire [was] the only way":

> Meddle, & I see you snap the sinews with your sumptuary laws . . . the powers that make the capitalist are metaphysical; the force of method, & the force of will makes banks, & builds towns. . . . [We

must therefore] leave the individual . . . to the rewards and penalties of his own constitution. . . . Persons and property have their just sway. They exert their power, as steadily as matter its attraction. . . . Hence the less government we have the better, —the fewer laws and the less confided power. . . . And though tender people may object to an aristocracy of wealth, if you think what that means, opportunity, free trade, & bringing all the powers to the surface,—it is what all aim at. . . .

Wealth brings with it its own checks and balances. The basis of political economy is non-interference. The only safe rule is found in the self-adjusting meter of demand and supply. . . . Give no bounties: make equal laws: secure life and property, and you need not give alms. Open the doors of opportunity to talent and virtue and they will do themselves justice, and property will not be in bad hands. In a free and just commonwealth, property rushes from the idle and imbecile, to the industrious, brave, and persevering. . . . Trade goes to make the governments insignificant, and to bring every kind of faculty of every individual that can in any manner serve any person, *on sale*.

. . . Trade was always . . . the mover of nations and the pillar wherein the fortunes of life hang. . . . Without it, men would roam the wilderness alone. . . . Society would stand still & men return howling to forests and caves which would now be the grave, as it was once the cradle of the human race. . . . The wit that elects the site of new mills & a new city, finds the path & true terminus of a new railroad, perceives well where to buy wild land in the western country, judging well where the confluence of streams, the change of soil, climate, or race, will make thoroughfares & markets. . . . We legislate against forestalling and monopoly . . . but the selfishness which hoards the corn for high prices, is the preventive of famine; and the law of self-preservation is surer policy than any legislation can be. . . . [In all this] society is threatened with actual granulation, religious as well as political. . . . but this rude stripping . . . of all support drives [the individual] inward, and he finds himself . . . face to face with the majestic Presence, reads the original of the Ten Commandments, the original of Gospels and Epistles.[23]

Emerson did not willingly enlist on the Jacksonian side of the transatlantic debate on individualism. Indeed, I quote him here at such length precisely because it was his intention to de-ideologize the entire issue—to reconceive socialism and liberalism as different roads toward the same meta-systemic ideal, culminating in "the majestic Presence" itself. That reconception, however, was now grounded in a historical distinction. Socialism had the idea, but the reverse methods; liberalism too had the idea, and in addition it had the modern means and methods to realize it. Five years before his 1844 epiphany (if I may call it so)—the revelation in "New England Reformers" that "the union must be ideal in actual individualism"—Emerson had defined the modern period as "the age of the first person singular." In a justly famous analysis of "The Present Age" (one that he would reiterate over and again, from 1848, in explaining his opposition to the French revolutionaries, to 1880, in his last appearance before the Concord Lyceum), Emerson proclaimed:

> The modern mind teaches that the nation exists for the Individual. . . . This is the Age of Severance, of Dissociation, of Freedom, of Analysis, of Detachment. It is the age of the first person singular. . . . The association [i.e., socialism] is for power merely, for means; the end is the enlargement and independency of the individual. Anciently society was in the course of things: there was a Sacred Band, a Theban Phalanx [prototype of the Fourierist community]. There can be none now. . . . But two parties endure, the party of the Past and the party of the Future.[24]

In 1839, and through 1842, the party of the Future was ambiguously American and/*or* transcendent. By the spring of 1844, it had found a local habitation, the Northern United States, and an ideological name, individualism. As an idea, individualism had been the subject of "all history, all poetry." But all history, Emerson had come to understand, was not the same. The modern period made a difference, as had Plato's Athens, the gospel of Christ, and the discovery of America. As an idea, individualism was a universal a priori, prefigured in Spartan broth and the hermit's cell. Now, in this "age of the first person singular," history was bringing those types to fulfillment. Hitherto "shining social prosperity was the beautitude of man," so that "the ancients thought the citizen existed for the government" and "former generations . . . sacrificed uniformly the citizen to the State." But those "primitive" habits of thought and behavior—together with the "warm negro ages of sentiment and vegetation—[were] all gone; another hour had struck," and a new principle of "actual union" had been set loose on the world, a moral credo comparable to Newton's

Principia: "Gravity is the Laissez faire principle, or Destiny, or Optimism, than which nothing is wiser or stronger." So perceived, history unfolded in a threefold spiral from East to West, Athens to Jerusalem and Rome, toward the New World:

1. *the Greek;* when men deified nature. . . .
2. *the Christian;* when the Soul became pronounced, and craved a heaven out of nature & above it. . . .
3. *the Modern;* when the too idealistic tendencies of the Christian period running into the diseases of cant, monarchism, and a church, demonstrating the impossibility of Christianity, have forced men to retrace their steps, & rally again on Nature; but now the tendency is to marry mind to nature, to put nature under the mind, convert the world into the instrument of Right Reason. Man goes forth to the dominion of the world by commerce, by science, & by philosophy.[25]

To appreciate the import of this movement toward synthesis and domination we should recall Emerson's 1836 essay on "The Individual":

> Not in time is the race progressive. Phocius, Socrates, Anaxagoras, Diogenes are great men, but . . . all theory, all hope are defeated when applied to society. . . . Progress belongs [only] to the Individual. . . . By myself, for myself, I can have faith, Ideas, Progress, God; but if I must apply all these to Society as we see it they become Philistery.

By 1846, a decade later, Emerson had found the *social* context for progress, faith, and the individual—and it turned out to be the story of America.* Here, in this land of "the Modern," where

---

*Emerson's use of individualism varies somewhat after the mid-1840s but its meanings always keep within the bounds established by the act of appropriation discussed above. Individualism for him implies the reciprocity between self-interest and the general good. He defines it as "the intellectual force of each . . . the pride of opinion, the security that we are right" ("this bitumen, fastest of elements," that makes all "things cohere"), which also acts as a guarantee of pluralism: "Perfect system. You cannot hear what I say until it is yours. . . . We are protected from the usurpation of individualism" (Journals Y and W [1845], in vol. IX of *Journals*, pp. 266, 225). Or again, from the lecture on "Plato, the Philosopher," in a passage first drafted in the 1845 journals:

> Plato would willingly have a Platonism, a known and accurate expression for the world. . . . It shall be the world passed through the mind of Plato— nothing less. Every atom shall have the Platonic tinge; every atom, every

"commerce . . . science, [and] philosophy" were at last keeping pace—so that "our economics in house & barn rapidly show their relation to the laws of geometry, of morals, & of natural history"— a new idea had come to light, an "idea roughly written in revolutions and national movements" of the past, but at last articulated with "precision":

> . . . the individual is the world.
> This perception is a sword such as was never drawn before.

Now, "for the first time" in history, the dream of self-reliance was organic to a certain society, in a certain place, as a tendency toward perfect union inherent in its laws, customs, assumptions, and institutions. Despite and *through* "this rude stripping" and "granulation," "actual individualism" was the "celestial Enterprise" in process:

> Everybody knows these exaggerating schemers, maniacs who go about in marts. . . . This is the madness of a few, for the gain of the world. The projectors are hurt, but the public is immensely a gainer.
> . . .
> If we could be directly rich, namely, by insight . . . by grandeur of

---

relation or quality you knew before . . . elements, planet itself, laws of planet and of men, have passed through this man as bread into his body, and become no longer bread, but body: so all this mammoth morsel has become Plato. He has clapped copyright on the world. This is the ambition of individualism. But this mouthful proves too large. *Boa constrictor* has good will to eat it, but he is foiled. He falls abroad in the attempt; and biting, gets strangled: the bitten world holds the biter fast by his own teeth. There he perishes. . . . In view of eternal nature, Plato turns out to be philosophical exercitations. He argues on this side and on that. (*Essays and Lectures*, p. 653)

The point is not, of course, that Platonism denies Plato's particular ambitions but that it fulfills his individualism, as the One Man fulfills one's self: I most fully exist when, *through* my grasping, boa constrictor ego, I allow the world to realize itself. Thus "the ambition of individualism," flows into a "swallowing universality" which turns out to benefit humanity at large and "eternal nature." See also: Journal Y (1845), in vol. IX of *Journals*, p. 290; Journal BO (1850), in vol. XI of *Journals*, ed. A. William Plumstead and William H. Gilman (Cambridge, Mass., 1975), p. 292; Journal CD (1847), in vol. X of *Journals*, ed. Merton M. Sealts, Jr. (Cambridge, Mass., 1973), p. 118; "Natural History of the Intellect," in *Works*, ed. Edward Emerson (Riverside Edition: Boston, 1893), XII, 46–49; "Uses of Great Men," in *Essays and Lectures*, pp. 627–628; and "Books," in *Works*, ed. Cabot, VII, 205.

thought; by imagination . . . of course, we should not then need to be indirectly rich by farms, mills, goods, & money. . . . But now the habit of alluding to our wealth, or the wealth of our blood-relations shows the invincible belief, betrays an inveterate persuasion[,] that wealth is the natural fruit of nobility of soul.

America is the idea of emancipation[:]

abolish kingcraft, Slavery, feudalism . . . explode priestcraft. . . . Extemporize government, California, Texas, Lynch Law. All this covers selfgovernment. All proceeds on the belief that as the people have made a gov.t they can make . . . their Union & law. . . .

The American Idea [:]

Emancipation[,] selfreliance[,] selfhelp[,] advance[.][26]

Union, self-reliance, mills and money, self-government, the nobility of soul, the gain of the world: it amounts to a breathtaking work of culture—a wholesale appropriation of utopia, all the hopes of reform and revolution nourished on both sides of the Atlantic by the turmoil of modernization, for the American Way.*

I spoke of "New England Reformers" as our first record of that act of appropriation, and strictly speaking that address rounds out Emerson's 1842 meditation on means and ends, process and telos. But to complete the record it should be supplemented in this regard by its companion piece, an address delivered a month before (on February 7, 1844) in the wake of the Brook Farm debacle. "The Young American" is a landmark in the development of American symbology, the New England jeremiad recast as a State of the Ideal Union Message. Where the Puritans spoke of a wilderness to be planted, Emerson hails the "sanative and Americanizing influence" of "the *land*"—this "bountiful continent that is ours,

---

*Emerson varied the narrative sequence for the typology of America, but the typology itself remained constant. A broad summary of his outlook from the mid-1840s onwards appears in a late essay, "The Sovereignty of Ethics," prophesying that "America shall introduce a pure religion" (since after all "Man does not live by bread alone, but by faith"):

The civil history of men might be traced by the successive meliorations as marked in higher moral generalizations;—virtue meaning physical courage, then chastity and temperance, then justice and love;—bargains of kings and peoples of certain rights to certain classes, then of rights to masses,—then at last came the day when, as the historians rightly tell, the nerves of the world were electrified by the proclamation that all men were born free and equal. (*Works*, ed. Cabot [Boston, 1883], X, 202–203, 181)

state on state, and territory on territory, to the waves of the Pacific." Where the Puritans invoked the unfolding of scripture prophecy, he points to "the new and anti-feudal power of Commerce," including the railroad, open markets, and free trade, whose "history" is the "sublime and friendly Destiny by which the human race is guided." All this was standard fare in 1844. But then, taking what appears to be a radical shift in direction, Emerson turns for his proof of national destiny to "the appearance of new moral causes which are to modify the state." "Government," he observes, "has other offices than those of banker and executioner"; "the true offices of the State" require us "to instruct the ignorant, [and] to supply the poor with work and with good guidance." Hence

> the new movements in the civilized world, the Communism of France, Germany, and Switzerland; the Trades' Unions; the English League against the Corn Laws; and the whole *Industrial Statistics*, so called. In Paris, the blouse, the badge of the operative, has begun to make its appearance in the saloons. Witness too, the spectacle of three Communities [Brook Farm, Fruitland, and Hopedale] which have within a very short time sprung up within this Commonwealth, besides several others undertaken by citizens of Massachusetts within the territory of other States.[27]

This daring integration of national mission with international socialism is a dramatic moment in the history of American dissent. Emerson might have presented us with a fundamental clash of modern ideologies, or else with a confrontation of alternative America's, liberal or collectivist, or perhaps with an Olympian assessment of socialism and individualism under the aspect of utopia. Instead, he subsumes the goals of socialism under the actualities of the developing Northern United States. The "value of the Communities," he argues, is "not what they have done, but the revolution which they indicate as on the way"; and the way, it turns out, together with the (continuing) revolution it indicates, is that of liberal individualism. On those grounds, Emerson embraces the "moral causes" of socialism in order to absorb these into the "beneficent tendenc[ies]" of the "laws and institutions" which have already made New England the country's "leader," and which are "destined" to make America the "leading nation" of the world:

> We cannot look on the freedom of this country, in connexion with its youth, without a presentiment that here shall laws and institutions exist on some scale of proportion to majesty of nature. . . . Which should be [the "leading nation" of the world, therefore,] but these States? Which should lead that movement, if not New England? Who should lead the leaders, but the Young American? . . . [Our present system] converts Government into an Intelligence-Office, where every man may find what he wishes to buy, and expose what he has to sell. . . . This is the good and this the evil of trade, that it would put every man into market. . . .
>
> By this means, however, it has done its work . . . trade was the principle of Liberty . . . trade planted America and destroyed Feudalism . . . it makes peace and keeps peace. . . . Trade is an instrument in the hands of that friendly Power which works for us in our own despite. . . . This beneficent tendency . . . exists and works. . . . One thing is plain for all men of common sense and common conscience, that here, here in America, is the home of man.[28]

"Common sense and common conscience"; "the true offices of the State"; a "beneficent tendency . . . for all men": Emerson's language has the ritual "plainness" of American consensus. In this spirit he confronted the outbreak of revolution in Europe four years later. The European Forty-Eight, we have seen, was broadly represented as a threat to national continuity. But many American intellectuals saw it, too, as a test of modern collectivist theories— a sort of preview of the utopia to be reached by Old World methods—and Emerson, among others, crossed the Atlantic to witness the results firsthand. His antipathy may be simply explained. The European radicals did not believe in individualism.* It was not so

---

*One example (of many) of Emerson's legacy in this regard is *Socialism and the American Spirit* (Boston, 1893), by Nicholas Paine Gilman, a professor of English and author of numerous studies on morality, economics, and social reform:

> Systematic socialism in America counts its great body of adherents among these foreign-born who have arrived but recently, and with whom it is the only feasible method of being "agin the government,"—their life-long habit at home, where the government was an alien power. The absurdity of such a position in a land where government is "of the people, by the people, and for the people" will but slowly penetrate the brain of the ignorant Pole.

much the violence that troubled him (though he lamented that "in France 'fraternity' [and] 'equality'. . . are names for assassination"), nor was it the burdens of political engagement (though he noted in London concerning talk of "a Chartist revolution on Monday next, and an Irish revolution the following week," that the scholar's "kingdom is at once over & under these perturbed regions"). As a utopianist, Emerson could accommodate ideas of all kinds, could even support insurrection under extreme circumstances. He demanded only that insurrection serve the cause of utopia, as he defined it. And in 1848 he discovered experientially what he had worked out half a decade before in his journals and lectures, that cause, means, and method were inseparable from actual individualism. This accounts for the generosity of his response. His sympathy for the "masses" of Paris and London, "dragged in their ignorance by furious chiefs to the Red Revolution," was grounded in his now firm belief that all hope for change, reformist or revolutionary, peaceful or violent, belonged to individualism:

> For the matter of Socialism, there are no oracles. The oracle is dumb. When we would pronounce anything truly of man, we retreat instantly on the individual. . . . We are authorized to say much on the destinies of one, nothing on those of many. . . . I honor the generous

---

Until it does so penetrate, men of American sense, who know what freedom means and what it costs, will keep that Pole in order,—for his own benefit!. . .

For such and for all, the prophet and guide of American literature, Ralph Waldo Emerson, speaks a counsel of perfection when . . . he declares the worth of the individual. . . . What Emerson said in 1844, reviewing the active reform period which had then apparently culminated, we may well repeat to-day: "I do not wonder at the interest these projects inspire. The world is awaking to the idea of union, and these experiments show what it is thinking of. It is and will be magic. Men will live and communicate, and plough and reap and govern, as by added ethereal power. . . . But this union must be . . . ideal in actual individualism."

There is no highway to Utopia, [and yet] . . . our imperfect civilization is in many respects wonderful beyond the scope of Sir Thomas More's highest imagination. So in all probability will our fondest dream be put to shame by the future reality. (pp. 32, 43–44, 366)

Gilman titled his last three chapters "The Higher Individualism," "Social Spirit," and "The Way to Utopia." They may be read as a cultural guide to the obverse implications of a cultural legacy that reaches (on the other side) from Thoreau to William James.

ideas of the socialists. . . . [They are] the *effects* of the age in which we live. They are not the creators they believe themselves; but . . . the unconscious prophets of a true state of society; one which the tendencies of nature lead unto, one which always establishes itself for the sane soul, though not in that manner in which they paint it.
. . .

In the question of socialism, which now proposes the confiscation of France[,] one has only this guidance. You shall not so arrange property as to remove the motive to industry. If you refuse rent & interest, you make all men idle & immoral. As to the poor a vast proportion have made themselves so, and in any new arrangement will only prove a burden on the state. . . .

Revolutions of violence then are scrambles merely. . . . There can be no [true] revolution until there are revolutionists [which is to say, true individualists]. . . .

To America, therefore, monarchs look with apprehension & the people with hope.[29]

Emerson tells us that just before he left England he was asked if there was "an American idea?" and that he spoke in reply of "monsters hard by the setting sun, who believed in a future such as was never a past, but if I should show it to them [his English hosts], they would think French communism solid and practicable by comparison." Soon after his return, he recalled further (in *English Traits*) that at this farewell dinner he had identified the Americans who held "the idea . . . of the right future" as "fanatics of a dream which I should hardly care to relate to . . . English ears, to which it might be only ridiculous,—and yet it is the only true." No doubt he had in mind something analogous to the "perfect union" he envisioned in 1842. He clarified its relation to actual individualism in his journals and lectures from 1848 through 1851:

a pure reverence for character, a new respect for the sacred quality of the individual man, is that antidote which must correct [the vices of the age]. . . . From the folly of . . . association we must come back to the repose of self-reverence.

. . . Now I believe in the closest affinity between moral and material power. Virtue and genius are always on the direct way to the control of society in which they are found. It is in the interest of society that good men should govern, and [in America] there is always a tendency so to place them. . . .

The tools of our time, namely steam, ships, printing, money and popular education, belong to those who can handle them; and their effect has been that advantages once confined to men of family are now open to the whole middle class.[30]

This passage comes from "Natural Aristocracy," an 1848 address which recasts Jefferson's agrarian concept in terms appropriate to the dawning age of Social Darwinism. Emerson delivered "Natural Aristocracy" on several occasions during the next decade and reprinted part of it in *English Traits* (1856)—fittingly, for *English Traits* is a sustained apologia for modern liberal culture. Indeed, its particular focus on the superiority of the Anglo–Saxon race and the Westering progress of civilization may be said to begin the last phase of Emerson's journey into ideology: his more or less outright identification of individuality with industrial-capitalist "Wealth" (1851) and "Power" (1860), with "American Civilization" (1862), and summarily with "The Fortune of the Republic" (1864):

One hundred years ago the American people attempted to carry out the bill of political rights to an almost ideal perfection. They have made great strides in that direction since. They are now proceeding, instructed by their success and by their many failures, to carry out, not the bill of rights, but the bill of human duties.

And look what revolution that attempt involves[:]. . .we are a nation of individuals. . . . Faults in the working . . . in our system . . . suggest their own remedies. . . . Here is practical democracy; here is the human race poured out over the continent to do itself justice. . . . The people are loyal and law-abiding. They . . . have no taste for misrule or uproar. . . . As the globe keeps its identity by perpetual change, so our civil system, by perpetual appeal to the people.

The revolution is the work of no man, but the external effervescence of nature. It never did not work. . . . Never country had such a fortune . . . as this, in its geography, its history, and in its majestic possibilities. . . . They [who] complain of the flatness of American life . . . have no perception of its destiny. They are not Americans. Let us realize that this country, the last found, is the great charity of God to the human race.[31]

Behind this vision lies Emerson's paradoxical credo of 1842–1844: "actual individualism"/"union ideal." But it is paradox now devoid of volatility or tension: "revolution" without conflict, personal agency identified with "civil system," America's "majestic possibilities" grounded in local "history," perfectionism reconceived as the progress of "a nation of individuals" from an "almost ideal" bill of rights to a universal "bill of human duties." The sense of *repose* this conveys is contextualized for us by Emerson during the late 1860s in a long glance backward over the revolutionary decades 1820–1840—a time, as he now saw it, when

> young men were born with knives in their brain . . . [and] a certain sharpness of criticism, an eagerness for reform. . .showed itself in every quarter. . . . I please myself with the thought that our American mind is not now eccentric or rude in its strength. . . . If I have owed much to the special influences I have indicated, I am not less aware of that excellent and increasing circle of masters in arts and . . . science, who cheer the intellect of our cities in this country to-day,— whose genius is not a lucky accident, but normal, and with broad foundation of culture, and so inspires the hope of steady strength advancing on itself, and a day without night.[32]

That millennial day clearly differs from the perfect union that Emerson envisioned in 1842. Then the process of fulfillment ("culmination of science, useful art, fine art") depended on the self. Now it has its "broad foundation" in a certain culture, "this country to-day," and in an "increasing circle of masters in arts and science . . . whose genius is not a lucky accident, but normal." But the two utopias are not discontinuous. The ideological word, "individualism," that joins them both is inscribed from the beginning. It may be said to have its first public dawnings in *Nature* (1836), in the distinctly American features of Emerson's Orphic poet, singing a "revolution in things [which] will attend the [coming] influx of the spirit," and a year later, in his first Phi Beta Kappa Address, as the promise of individuality embodied in "The *American* Scholar." At midcentury, the same "hope of steady strength advancing on itself"—fusing historical progress and inward apocalypse—finds its grounding in Emerson's overview of the modern options for radical change: "revolutions . . . in the interest of feudalism and barbarism," such as those he had just witnessed in Europe, versus "revolutions . . . in the interest of society," a procession of "triumphs of humanity" culminating in "the planting of America." "The Atlantic," he wrote in his journals, recalling his 1848 ocean crossing from the Old World back to the New, "is a sieve through which only or chiefly the liberal adventurous sensitive *America-loving* part of each city, clan, family, are brought . . . [and] the Europe of Europe is left."[33]

The journal entries of November/December 1842 may be said to have launched Emerson, fresh from his "heretical" *Essays: First Series* (1841), on a journey from utopia to ideology; but as I hope I have made clear, the relation between those two sites was dynamic rather than linear. The journey from one to the other was not so much a progression (or regression) as it was an oscillation between midpoint and boundary (or frontier). The European Forty-Eight marks the return of Emerson's utopia to its ideological home; but Emerson's *abiding* utopianism demonstrates the radical energies potential in American liberal ideology. The same convictions which led him to reject socialism also impelled him a decade earlier outward to the revolutionary concepts of European individuality. It was not then, or ever, a matter of transcending his culture but on the contrary of plumbing its depths. Emerson's role as prophet was to carry the basic premises of "America" as far as they would go, to the hither verge of what was ideologically conceivable—and thereby to challenge his society in the act of drawing out (*furthering*, in the double sense of the word) its grounds of consensus. In this sense, to universalize was to subvert. Emerson discovered in his culture's symbols, values, and beliefs the agencies of change, reform, and "the new" that expressed the utopian dimensions not only of his own society but of modern liberal culture at large. The later essays diffuse the volatility of the paradox this entails. They also indicate by contrast the enabling source of resistance.* Emer-

---

*Let me reiterate that the source of ambiguity—which underlies both the shift in outlook I have been describing and the continuum of Emerson's thought—represents a broad cultural logic. Stanley Cavell asks rhetorically: "is Emerson really so difficult to distinguish from those who may be taken as parodies of him?" ("Hope Against Hope," *American Poetry Review*, I [January/February, 1986], 11). Cavell is right, of course. But this distinction between the "true" Emerson and the "popular" facsimile (the Emerson who "sounds like" Ronald Reagan or George Bush) has to account not only for Emerson's adaptability (or distortability) but for his spectacular popular appeal. As the *Boston Globe* reported at his death, Emerson was "generally everywhere recognized as the ripest exponent of mental processes

sonian dissent reminds us that ideology in America works not by repressing radical energies but by redirecting them into a constant conflict between self and society: the self in itself, a separate, single, non-conformist individuality versus society en masse, individualism systematized. And it reminds us that that utopian im-

---

inspired by American conditions of existence" (April 28, 1882). Before we can agree, as we should, to the terms of Cavell's rhetorical question, we must explain Emerson's ambiguities in the following areas:

1. *Property*: "Great men have always played with property, & used it as though they used it not. Spirit is all" (Journal D [1839], in vol. VII of *Journals*, ed. A. William Plumstead and Harrison Hayford [Cambridge, Mass., 1969], p. 225); "It is . . . a blessed triumph in the eyes of the Christian to recognize that . . . the moral character of a community is mended or relaxed with the greater or less security of property and that on the same security of property Civilization depends" (Journal No. XV [1824], in vol. II of *Journals*, ed. William Gilman, Alfred Ferguson, and Merrell Davis [Cambridge, Mass., 1961], p. 288); "Property keeps account of the world, and always reveals a moral cause. The property will be found where the labor, where the wisdom, where the virtue have been, in nations . . . [or] in the individual" (Journal U [1843], in vol. IX of *Journals*, p. 17).

2. *The Matter of "America"*: see Leonard N. Neufeldt, "The Science of Power: Emerson's Views on Science and Technology in America," *Journal of the History of Ideas*, XXXVIII (1977), 330–342; John Q. Anderson, "Emerson and 'Manifest Destiny'," *Boston Public Library Quarterly*, VII (1955), 30–60; and Emerson on "American" superiority, black and Indian inferiority, and the uniqueness of the American Revolution (e.g., Journal E [1840], in vol. VII of *Journals*, p. 393; Journal V [1844?], in vol. IX of *Journals*, p. 104; and compare Wide World 6 [1822], in vol. I of *Journals*, ed. William Gilman, Alfred Ferguson, George Clark, and Merrell Davis [Cambridge, Mass., 1960], pp. 125–127, with "The Fortune of the Republic" [1864], in *Works*, ed. Cabot, XI, 413, 422–425).

3. *The Influence of Adam Smith*: see Emerson's praise for Smith's correlations between "Christian Principle," "Free Trade," free-enterprise economics, and "the laws of geometry, of morals, & of natural history. . . . 'The gods are to each other not unknown' " (Notebook XVIII [1821?], in vol. I of *Journals*, p. 300; Blotting Book III [1831], in vol. III of *Journals*, ed. William Gilman and Alfred Ferguson [Cambridge, Mass., 1963], pp. 280, 295; and Journals RS and BO [1849–1850], in vol. XI of *Journals*, pp. 80, 313).

Cavell's affirmation of Emerson's difference holds true in the context of this complex pattern of aversions. We can no more dismiss the "popular Emerson" as "parodic" than we can deny the radical potential of Emersonian individualism. The same vision which in "The Young American" conflated the actual and the ideal led three years later, in the journals of 1847, to this ringing No-in-thunder to the powers of the earth:

perative to conflict defines individuality within the ideological parameters of actual individualism.

So defined, the terms of conflict express the basis of liberal cohesion. Modern "civil society," writes Jürgen Habermas, is

> conceived as a principle of marketlike . . . association. For [in Hegel's words,] "the principle of modern states has prodigious strength and depth because it allows the principle of subjectivity to progress to its culmination in the extreme of self-subsistent personal particularity, and yet at the same time brings it back to the substantive unity and so maintains this unity in the principle of subjectivity itself."[34]

Habermas offers Hegel's principle as the "solution" to "the problem of the mediation of state and society." But it is a solution whose strength and depth rest on a paradoxical "and yet"; a solution, that is, which not only allows but calls for a continuing dissonance between fusion and fragmentation, unity and subjectivity. Roberto Ungar describes this as the self-generating friction between public and private spheres, which underlies the dynamics of group pluralism. Translated into the terms of Emersonian dissent, these dynamics issue in a vision of autonomy preserved, precariously but decisively, and all the more decisively for its precariousness, within the bounds of community. The result is a form of protest that is bound to challenge (subvert, defy, resist)

I read the fabulous magnificence of these Karuns & Jamschids & Kai Kans & Feriduns of Persia, all gold and talismans; then I walk by the newsboys with telegraph despatches . . . & Redding's shop with English steamer's journals . . . & take my own seat in the Fitchburg cars; & see every man dropped at his estate, as we pass it; & see what tens of thousands of powerful & armed men, science-armed society-armed men sit at large in this ample land of ours . . . and muse on the power which each of these can lay hold of at pleasure. . . . And I think how far these chains of intercourse & travel go, what levers, what pumps, what searchings are applied to nature . . . and I say, What a negrofine royalty is that of Jamschid & Solomon; what a real sovereignty of nature does the Bostonian possess! . . . Every man who has a hundred dollars to dispose of . . . is rich beyond the dreams of the Caesars. . . .

And as all this leaves the man where he was before, the individualism, the importance of a man to himself, the fact that his power of self & social entertainment is all, makes quickly these miracles cheap to him; the greater they are the less they really become. (Journal GH, in vol. X of *Journals*, pp. 139–40)

the consensus it represents—*bound* to challenge and by that act authorized to sustain the polarity of self and society upon which consensus depends. This is essentially the process that authorizes the contradictory-conciliatory symbol of America: contradictory, in that it *compels* the opposition between the actual and the ideal; conciliatory, in that it defines that oppositionalism as the gap to be bridged between individual and society.*

I am not arguing that Emersonian individualism is a form of liberal co-optation. It is a form of utopian consciousness developed within the premises of liberal culture. It carries with it the profoundly unsettling energies released by that culture in its formative phase—well designated "the era of boundlessness"[35]—and it sustains that profoundly energizing, destabilizing, centrifugal thrust by an appeal to subjectivity as the sine qua non of union, an appeal grounded (as Emerson's 1842 journal demonstrates) in the combined sacred and secular authority of Protestant nonconformity and the theory of natural rights. These liberal premises provided an effective framework for social cohesion before the Civil War and, after it, a triumphant rhetoric of regional and continental incorporation. They also generated the enormous volatility that on the one hand fuelled civil war and on the other hand allowed for the subversive infusion of individuality into the very concept of nationhood. So circumscribed and so empowered, Emersonian individualism comes down to us as a distinctive type of radical thought, at once opposed to systemic individualism and dependent on it—a radicalism as compelling (and in its way as comprehensive) as the competing, socialist types of radical consciousness then emerging in Europe.

The distinction I would make here requires a word of explanation. Recently, the subversive in literature has been raised to the status once reserved for the noble, the tragic, and the complex. The result is a familiar allegory with a new twist: a Manichean struggle between the One and the Many (as between good and evil), where the One takes the antagonist guise of Heterogeneity. Every hegemony, we are told, is hegemonic in its own way, but all forms of subversion, like all happy families, are essentially alike. My assumption is that oppositional forms, like those of

*These categories are archetypal, universal, like all other ideological categories, including those of slave and feudal societies; and here as elsewhere they gather substance from their specific historical content.

cohesion, co-optation, and incorporation, are fundamentally and variously forms of culture. "Emergent," "residual," "anti-hegemonic," "utopian"—all such definitions of the subversive are useful insofar as we de-mystify their claims to transcendence, universality, and the Real. This applies to the many anti-individualistic movements of the 1840s— collectivism in all its varieties ("the Phalanx, owenism, Simonism, the Communities") from Leroux to Marx. It applies as well to Emersonian individualism, a liberal mode of resistance which is susceptible equally to liberal strategies of socialization and to the volatility of liberal thought. What makes it independent also makes it counter-dependent and vice versa: what binds it to the culture in symbiotic antagonism also infuses it with a destabilizing, energizing, centrifugal vision of its own. The very terms that predicate continuity posit the duty of radical self-affirmation and the necessity for social change.

The difference here between Emerson and what I termed the Jacksonian ideologues recalls Victor Turner's distinction between the central and final phases of the liminal process. The ideologues, from the manifest destinarian John O'Sullivan to the Locofoco Robert Rantoul, apologist for minimal government, make process synonymous with cultural expansion and consolidation. Emerson's radical appropriation of individuality (1836–1841) expresses the antistructures of that process: it turns all the power of hope, mind, and imagination unleashed by free-enterprise capitalism in an apparently open, empty, and endlessly malleable New World *against* the tendency toward reaggregation. The result is a standing invitation to resist that has all the energy of pure utopia—of an ideal (to recall the phrase that Emerson deleted in 1844) which "must not be actualized"—but with a modern difference. According to Hans Blumenberg, utopia at its most intense is "a sum of negations"; it avoids "contamination by what currently exists" by banning all definition whatever, placing "a prohibition against saying anything positively imagined . . . about the new land as it will be."[36] That prohibition applies in this case as well, except that here it also expresses, paradoxically, something already imagined: the new land as America; ideal union potential in actual individualism.

I have called that form of radical imagining *dissent* because the term seems best to convey its distinctive emphasis on negation and transition, its resistance on principle to institutional controls, its open-ended, *self*-enclosed tropism for reform and change. It is a form of protest conceived at the interstices of free-enterprise theory, and developed within the gaps or lacunae in the principle of subjectivity itself between the actual and the ideal, selfhood and union; between substantive unity on the one hand and, on the other, a self-subsistent personal peculiarity with a consecration of its own.

That subversive mode finds its fullest expression in Emerson's early essays. And let me reiterate that it was precisely his commitment to "America"—a cultural symbol designed at once to exaggerate and to mask the gap between self and society—which allowed for that important development. We might remember in this connection his 1839 July Fourth journal meditation, as this was enlarged and improved later that year into the vision of "Self-Reliance":

> What have I to do with the sacredness of traditions if I live wholly from within? . . . No law can be sacred to me but that of my nature. Good and bad are but names very readily transferable to that or this; the only right is what is after my constitution, the only wrong what is against it. . . . If malice and vanity wear the coat of philanthropy, shall that pass? If an angry bigot assumes this bountiful cause of Abolition, and comes to me with his last news from Barbadoes, why should I not say to him, "Go love thy infant; love thy wood-chopper: be good-natured and modest: have that grace; and never varnish your hard, uncharitable ambition with this incredible tenderness for black folk a thousand miles off. Thy love afar is spite at home." Rough and graceless would be such greeting, but truth is handsomer than the affectation of love. Your goodness must have some edge to it,—else it is none. The doctrine of hatred must be preached as the counteraction of the doctrine of love when that pules and whines. I shun father and mother and wife and brother, when my genius calls me. I would write on the lintels of the door-post, *Whim*. I hope it is somewhat better than whim at last, but we cannot spend the day in explanation. Expect me not to show cause why I seek or why I exclude company. Then, again, do not tell me . . . of my obligation to put all poor men in good situations. Are they *my* poor? I tell thee, thou foolish philanthropist, that I grudge the dollar, the dime, the cent, I give to such men as do not belong to me. . . . [L]et us enter into the state of war, and wake Thor and Woden, courage and constancy, in our Saxon breasts.[37]

The rhetorical question that Emerson adds to the public version, "Are they *my* poor?," has been much disputed, as being a measure either of his faith in individuality or else of his laissez-faire pragmatics. The *reciprocity* in the 1839 journal entry between self-assertion and July Fourth indicates that finally Emerson does not require us to make that choice—that, indeed, he requires us *not* to make it. Similar indications abound in the essay itself, as in the reciprocity between the concepts that frame the passage I quoted: at the start, the inward "sacredness" of "my own nature"; at the end, the summons to war (directed only to "such men as ... belong to me") through a revival or revolution of "courage and constancy, in our Saxon breasts." No doubt that bipolarity of the universal *mine* and the Saxon *our* tends to submerge the self into a culturally exclusive, not to say racist, ideal of union. But the same paradox also works in the opposite direction. And in this sense it challenges, resists, or subverts "Saxon" union through the individuality made manifest in the first person possessive: "*my* own," "*my* constitution," "*my* poor."

Significantly that dynamic of dissent is directed against the structures not of socialism but of liberal America: Emerson sets his first person singular against bourgeois philanthropy as a solution to poverty; against the cult of domesticity ("father and mother and wife") as the source of spiritual value. "Are they *my* poor?" is the liberal-oppositional *cri de coeur* against what Tocqueville called the tyranny of the majority. It expresses the high utopian strain that John Jay Chapman had in mind when in 1898 he presented Emerson as "the cure and antidote" to "the vice of the age." "If a soul," he wrote, "be taken and crushed by democracy till it utter a cry, that cry will be Emerson"; and then the broader explanation: "While the radicals of Europe were revolting in 1848 against the abuses of a tyranny whose roots were in feudalism, Emerson, the great radical of America, the arch-radical of the world, was ... bringing back the attention of political thinkers to its starting point, the value of the human character," or individualism.[38]

The appeal of Emersonian dissent lies in an extraordinary conjunction of forces: its capacity to absorb the radical communitarian visions it renounces, and its capacity to be nourished by the liberal structures it resists. It demonstrates the capacities of culture to shape the subversive in its own image, and thereby, *within limits*, to be shaped in turn by the radicalism it seeks to contain. Theodore Adorno claims (as the summa of "negative dialectics") that to be radical is not to "bow to *any* alternatives," since "freedom means to criticize and change situations, not to conform by deciding within their coercive structure."[39] Emersonian dissent testifies against that dream of autonomy. Or to put it in positive terms, it testifies to the oppositional forms generated within the structures of society—in Emerson's terms, somewhere at the margins of culture, at some transitional moving point, perpetually inchoate because transitional on principle, between center and circumference.

This implies a somewhat different model of the liminal process from the one I just mentioned. Turner, following Van Gennep, speaks of antistructure and reaggregation as a logical sequence of phases (central and final) leading to ritual closure. The example of Emerson suggests that the expressive forms of antistructure may so influence the ritual forms of socialization as to make closure an office of antistructural process. The *radical* complementarity this entails is defined by neither harmony nor synthesis nor compromise, although Emerson's career shows how it may be reduced to (or returned to) such vehicles of reaggregation. Rather, it builds on a necessary friction between the various agents of reciprocity—necessary, because the friction sustains the *movement between* actual individualism and perfect union. In "Self-Reliance" this in-betweenness takes the form of reciprocity between a ritual of continuity (Independence Day) and an antagonist rhetoric of discarding (good and bad, father and mother, "this bountiful cause of Abolition" together with "the coat of philanthropy"). It finds an apt symbol in the A's for self-reliance which Emerson devised sometime between 1837 and 1839:

Selfreliance[:]

A greater respect for Man indicated by the movements of	
Antigovernment	their pursuits
AntiAssociation	politics
AntiMonopoly	education
AntiChurch	religion

To this he added an appropriately ambiguous motto: "The antidote to [social] abuse is the growth of the Individual. . . . We think our civilization near its meridian, but we are yet only at the cock-crowing and the morning star."[40]

In that uneasy relation between negation ("Antigovernment," "AntiAssociation") and continuity ("growth," "meridian") lies the importance of "America" in Emerson's early thought. So long as he did not have to confront ideological alternatives, he could extend the circle of self-reliance to the point where individuality was turned against individualism. From that liminal position at midcentury, circling from *"movement"* to *"pursuit"* (away from state and church, towards some ever-imminent, ever-receding political, educational, and religious telos)—a dynamic, to repeat, resistant to the brink of abandonment—all of our classic writers distinguished American dissent from the tradition which they dismissed as Old World revolution. All of them, with Emerson, repudiated the European Forty-Eight, and each of them, partly through that act of repudiation, forged a subversive mode of his own. Probably the most fortifying examples of subversion, so conceived, are *Walden* and *Leaves of Grass.** Emerson said of Thoreau that he "was in his own person a practical answer, *almost* a refutation, to the theories of the socialists" (my italics). We might say much the same of Whitman, from an opposite perspective: he offers a theory of the self en masse which is a personal answer, almost a refutation, to the abuses of industrial capitalism. The limitations of that theory appear most dramatically in the examples of political protest I mentioned earlier: Thoreau's defence of

---

*"How was it possible," asks John Diggins, contrasting *Walden* with Marx's "radical analysis" of the same period, "to find unalienated men [i.e., individuality] in an alienating society [i.e., individualism]? The answer would appear to be . . . a total and uncompromising independence" ("Thoreau, Marx, and the 'Riddle' of Alienation" *Social Research*, XXXIX [1972], 571–598). So it is; but as Thoreau makes abundantly clear, "independence" for him is also a *communal* term, extending from the abstraction "America" to his Concord neighbours. "Independence" is a volatile cultural key word that links his July Fourth experiment with the Puritan errand and with the frontier movement. According to Taylor Stoehr, the "most famous political encounter of transcendentalism was Thoreau's refusal of his tax bill in 1846, with its consequent night in jail [recorded in *Walden*], and its immortal explanation of his behavior in 'Civil Disobedience' " (*Nay-Saying in Concord: Emerson, Alcott, and Thoreau* [Hamden, Conn., 1979], p. 44). What binds the act to the explanation, and what makes Thoreau's symbolic action, so understood, doubly oppositional (directed against Jackson, Taylor, and Pierce, as well as against Leroux, Fourier, and Marx) is his ritual invocation of the principle of representative taxation, which had once inspired a Declaration of utopian community and so invests the summons to independence *now* with the potential of "unalienated man." Subversion may not be the right term for this outlook, but neither is co-optation.

John Brown (in spite of Brown's armed revolt) as a son of Puritan New England and "the most American of us all"; Garrison's allegiance (against the Constitution) to personal renovation and the Declaration of Independence; Fuller's jeremiadic invocation (as it were beyond Italian socialism) to "my America," "the land of the future," and "the spirit of our fathers." Considered from either a literary or a political angle, the major discourse on this mode of radical containment—in the double sense of the term, as confining and nurturing radicalism—comes in Melville's work. I have discussed *Pierre* in different terms, but it applies here as well. On one quasi-allegorical level, *Pierre* is the story of individuality born in the euphoria of Young America, trapped in the ideology of the self, and destroyed by an absolute faith in process and potential. And much the same applies to the story that followed it. In "Bartleby the Scrivener: A Tale of Wall Street," "actual individualism" signifies *both* resistance on principle *and* liberal society as defined by its radical critics ("a system of isolation, or isolated selves"; "the exclusive domination of capital"); its adversarial/representative protagonist, representing "Humanity," mocks both sides of the equation.[41]

To paraphrase the great July Fourth declaration of "Self-Reliance," Emerson wrote on the lintels of the doorpost to the indefinite future, *Individualism*. In doing so, he expanded the meaning of the term to accommodate the utopian powers of individuality— among these, the appeal to subjectivity as the sine qua non of union, an appeal sustained (as in the 1842 journals) by the combined sacred and secular authority of Protestant non-conformity and the theory of natural rights. And at the same time he confined the prospects of utopia, like some avenging angel, within the rhetorical magic circle of the resisting representative self. "In dealing with the State," wrote Emerson in "Politics"—an address he kept revising from 1836–1837, the volatile years of *Nature* and "The American Scholar" to the fall of 1842—"we ought to remember that its institutions are not aboriginal, though they existed before we were born. . . . [E]very one of them was once the act of a single man." William James rightly heard in such lines the "bugle blast" of a new philosophy, or as he put it in *Pragmatism* (1907), "a program for more work, and more particularly . . . an indication of the ways in which existing realities may be *changed*."[42] Our own view, almost a century later, need not be less sanguine for recognizing the limitations inherent in this concept of radicalism. Indeed, I have been arguing throughout that the radicalism is inseparable from those limitations, which function simultaneously as boundary and as frontier.

But we would do well to recognize the mixed blessings of the cultural symbology this represents. That critical imperative is also part of the Emersonian legacy. Our century has been witness to an extraordinary course of change: in Europe and the United States, a remarkable series of conflicts of all kinds (economic, racial, ethnic, ideational); and in the United States, a still more remarkable process of expansion, consolidation, and incorporation. We should remember in this regard that Emerson's recourse to the "single man," as to the summits of individuality, bespeaks the pervasive reach of the liberal state, even unto the realm of the protean imagination. Yet in dealing with the state, we should remember Emerson's utopian resistance as well. Our pluralist "traditions of individualism," linking William James to Irving Howe and both to Francis Fukuyama, are neither aboriginal nor postmillennial, neither modern reflections of Central Man nor "the end point of mankind's ideological development." They are institutional. In making this point, Emerson expressed the hope that those traditions would eventuate in somewhat more than "actual individualism" at last; and they have. The paradoxes they have spawned, concerning subversion and/or co-optation, subjectivity as agency of change and/or agent of social control, protest as counter-culture and/or as cultural counter-dependence, remain a central tension in American literary, cultural, and political dissent.

10

The Problem of Ideology in a Time of Dissensus

During the past couple of decades, consensus of all kinds in academia has broken down—left and right, political and aesthetic—broken down, worn out, or at best opened up. American literary studies is perhaps the most conspicuous instance. Consider the dual tradition behind F. O. Matthiessen's *American Renaissance* (1941): on the one hand, the literary consensus authorized by T. S. Eliot, which announced itself as the New Criticism; and on the other hand, the consensus history (as we have come to call it) through which Vernon Parrington defined the *Main Currents of American Thought*. Together, these traditions issued, in Matthiessen's classic, as the vision of five marginal men who represented not only their own age but the meaning of America.*

---

*This partnership in *American Renaissance* between the literary and the historical is reflected in Matthiessen's subtitle, *Art and Expression in the Age of Emerson and Whitman:* "art," meaning a small group of aesthetic masterpieces; and "expression," meaning representative works, reflecting and illuminating the culture at large. It was the remarkable achievement of Matthiessen that his book yokes these concepts gracefully together. Somehow, one concept seems to support the other. The historical designation "American" gains substance by association with an aesthetic "renaissance"; Emerson's and Whitman's art seems richer for its capacity to express "the age." Matthiessen himself did not feel it necessary to explain the connection. But we can see in retrospect that what made it work— what made it, indeed, unnecessary for Matthiessen to explain—was an established consensus, or rather a consensus long in the making which *American Renaissance* helped establish. I refer to a consensus about the term *literary* that involved the legitimation of a certain canon, and a consensus about the term *history* that was legitimated by a certain concept of America.

The importance of *American Renaissance* in that double process of legitimation is well known. Matthiessen's work set the terms for discussing the American literary tradition; it provided a canon of classic texts; and it inspired the growth of American literary studies in the United States and abroad. But the process itself of legitimation may be traced in America's emergence, between World War I and

353

And that meaning in turn built upon a still older, far broader consensus: the myths of nationhood and the ideals of personal freedom set out a century before by Bancroft and Emerson. "The one common denominator of my five writers," Matthiessen tells us, "was their devotion to the possibilities of democracy"; and predictably he locates those possibilities in "self-reliance, individualism, initiative," and (in the words of his original title) the freedom of "Man in the Open Air." Whitman, Emerson, Hawthorne, Thoreau, and Melville, he explains, all "felt it was incumbent on their generation to give fulfillment to the potentialities freed by the Revolution, to provide a culture commensurate with America's political opportunity." This was the basis, too, seven years later, for the synthetic standard *Literary History of the United States* by Robert Spiller et al. According to the opening "Address to the Reader,"

> Increasing power and vitality are extraordinarily characteristic of [our nation].... Never has nature been so rapidly and so extensively altered by the efforts of man in so brief a time. Never has conquest resulted in a more vigorous development of initiative, individualism, self-reliance, and demands for freedom. ... [Hence the Americanness of our major authors. Ours has been a literature] profoundly influenced by ideals and by practices developed in democratic living. It has been intensely conscious of the needs of the common man, and equally conscious of the aspirations of the individual. ... It has been humanitarian. It has been, on the whole, an optimistic literature, made virile by criticism of the actual in comparison with the ideal.[1]

The reason for the current ferment in American literary studies is that the assumptions behind that vision no longer account for the evidence. We have come to feel that the context they

World War II, as the major capitalist power, or in the Cold War terms of the late Forties, the leader of the Free World. Providentially, we have two sets of literary landmarks, European and American, to commemorate the process. At one end, in 1917, D. H. Lawrence's germinal *Studies in Classic American Literature* and *The Cambridge History of American Literature*; at the other end, framing the U.S. experience in World War II, *American Renaissance* (1941) and *The Literary History of the United States*, by Robert Spiller et al. (1948), which proceeds teleologically, from "The Colonies" through "Democracy" and "Expansion" to "A World Literature."

provide conceals as much as it reveals. To use an old-fashioned phrase, the paradigm has become inoperative. What we have instead is a Babel of contending approaches, argued with a ferocity reminiscent of the sectarian polemics that erupted in the early days of the Reformation, when Martin Luther (as the horrified scholastics charged, not inaccurately) put the Bible "into the hands of the commonalty" where it was "interpreted no longer by the well-conditioned learned, but by the faith and delusion . . . of all sorts of men," so that "a thousand demons [were] set loose to vex our Mother Church."[2] Of the thousand problems set loose by our current dissensus I select the problem of ideology as symptomatic of the rest. I mean by ideology the ground and texture of consensus—in this case, the system of ideas inwoven into the cultural symbology through which "America" continues to provide the terms of identity and cohesion in the United States. So considered, ideology is basically conservative, but it is not therefore merely repressive. As a general principle, ideology functions best through voluntary consent, when the network of ideas through which the culture justifies itself is internalized rather than imposed, and embraced by society at large as a system of belief. Under these conditions, the very terms of cultural restriction may become a source of creative release. They serve to incite the imagination, to unleash the energies of reform, to encourage diversity and accommodate change.

In earlier chapters I advanced this model as a description of what we have come to term the American ideology. Here I would like to enter two caveats. The first is that the term itself is somewhat misleading. *The* American ideology suggests something almost allegorical—some abstract corporate monolith—whereas in fact the American ideology reflects a particular set of interests, the power structures and conceptual forms of liberal society in the United States, as these evolved through three centuries of conflict, upheaval, transformation, and discontinuity. So considered, "America" is not an overarching synthesis, *e pluribus unum*, but a rhetorical battleground, a symbol that has been made to stand for diverse and sometimes mutually contradictory outlooks. My second caveat tends in the opposite direction—a qualification of the qualification. I would urge that, in spite of all that diversity and conflict, the American ideology has achieved a hegemony unequalled elsewhere in the modern world. For all its manifold contradictions, it is an example par excellence of the successful interaction between restriction and release. Ideology, we have seen, arises out of historical circumstances, and then re-presents these, rhetorically and conceptually, as though they were natural, universal, inevitable, and right; as though the ideals promulgated by a certain group or class (for example, Spiller et al's "virile" standards of individualism) were not the product of history but the expression of self-evident truth. The act of representation thus serves to consecrate a set of cultural limitations, to recast a certain society as Society, a certain way of life as utopia in process. Ideology denies limitation, conceptually, in such a way as to facilitate social continuity. But as we have also seen, these conceptual forms of continuity may be elastic, dynamic, and volatile. Ideology transmutes history into symbols that may deceive and entrap, as in *Pierre*, but that also, under different circumstances—as in "The American Scholar" or its Emersonian offspring, Thoreau's *Duty of Civil Disobedience* and Whitman's 1855 Preface to *Leaves of Grass*—may open new vistas of thought and action in history.

In this double capacity, restrictive and enabling, ideology stands at the crossroads between the terms *literary* and *history*, mediating between canon and context. When mediation succeeds, literary historians can proceed under the aspect of eternity, as though they were free of ideology, unfettered by limits of time and place. It is the sort of freedom that Augustine felt, in setting out the one correct path for exegesis; or the Anglican Thomas Hooker, expounding the divine right of kings; or Karl Marx, unveiling the scientific laws of history. In each case, freedom is a function of consensus. And lest I seem to have exempted myself from that process, I would like to declare the principles of my own ideological dependence. I hold these truths to be self-evident: that there is no escape from ideology; that so long as human beings remain political animals they will always be bounded in some degree by consensus; and that so long as they are symbol-making animals they will always seek to persuade themselves and others that in some sense, by relative measure if not absolutely, the terms of *their* symbology are objective and true.

I leave it to another generation to analyze the conundrums of this peculiar ideological dependency. For present purposes it may be seen as a commitment to partiality that allows for only two alternatives to the authority of established consensus: either to subscribe to a different consensus altogether, or else to confront ideology as a problem, in an attempt to understand its limits and to assess the nature and meaning of one's involvement. And that option depends in turn not just on qualities of mind but on the historical moment. It was largely a matter of history that both Matthiessen and Spiller assumed that American literary history transcended ideology. *American* for them stood for the universal possibilities of democracy; *history*, for a more or less impartial account of the facts; and *literary* for great art, to be judged in its own timeless terms. It is equally a matter of history, a measure of the dissensus of our times, that all those concepts—history, literary, and American—are now subjects of debate.

Let me briefly recall the sources of that quandary. One is the recognition that race and gender are formal principles of art, and therefore integral to textual analysis. Another is the recognition that political norms are inscribed in aesthetic judgment and therefore inherent in the process of interpretation. Still another is the recognition that aesthetic structures shape the way we understand history, so that tropes and narrative devices may be said to use historians to enforce certain views of the past. These perceptions stem from different approaches in contemporary critical discourse. Directly and indirectly, the controversies they have engendered have undermined the old terms of consensus, and thereby heightened a broad ideological awareness among Americanists, while at the same time arming them against one another with competing modes of analysis.

Still another source of this quandary, which might be termed the fall from transcendence into history, was the widespread attack during the 1980s on the so-called Myth and Symbol School of American Studies, not only by a new generation of critics, but by the founders themselves. Henry Nash Smith, for example, writes in a reassessment of *Virgin Land* (three decades later) that he failed there to consider the "tragic dimensions of the Westward Movement" because they were cloaked in ideas so familiar as to be "almost inaccessible to critical examination." Now, the same ideas ("civilization," "free land," "frontier," and "self-reliance") also obscured the views of the writers he treated, as well as serving, historically, to inspire the energies of settlement and to rationalize the atrocities of Westward expansion.[3] It amounts to a casebook example of ideology in action; a model instance of the relation between interpretation, imaginative expression, and social action that creates and sustains consensus.

The example here is mainly negative, a model of intellectual constriction. This, indeed, is the model commonly associated with ideology, as we have inherited the concept from the social sciences. According to this tradition, ideology is inherently suspect, and analysis naturally seeks to expose its limitations through a process of debunking, unmasking, and demystifying. In this case the process deserves special emphasis for the contrast it suggests between myth criticism and ideological analysis. Like ideology, myth is inherently suspect, and for much the same reasons: it is (among other things) a vehicle of culturally prescribed directives for thought and behavior. Literary critics, however, have tended to avoid the parallel by enforcing a sort of exegetical imperative of inversion. Since ideology pretends to truth, the task of analysis is to uncover, rationally, the sinister effects of its fictions. Since myths are fictions, the task is to display, empathetically, their "deeper truths"—the abiding values embedded in simple plots, the range and richness of formulaic metaphors. This double standard reflects the familiar Kantian distinction between the aesthetic and the cognitive faculties. To criticize a myth is to "appreciate" it from within, to explicate it "intrinsically," in its own "organic" terms. To criticize a piece of ideology is to see through it, to expose its historical functions, necessarily from an extrinsic, and usually from a hostile perspective.

Hence the corrective or accusatory import of "ideology" in American literary studies during the 1970s and 1980s. The Myth and Symbol School represented a generation of scholars who were discovering the field of American Studies. Many of them were post–World War II (often GI-Bill) immigrants into academia from ethnic and economic groups previously excluded from the literary profession. And the America they discovered—at once marginal, adversarial, aesthetic, and national—provided the conceptual grounds for their assimilation and ascent. The ideological critics, as they have been called, represented a second generation of immigrants into academia. Again, they came from groups which had largely been closed out of a genteel literary profession, and which had expanded now to include categories of race and gender. Having inherited the profession of American Studies, they proceeded to reassess the terms of assimilation through which the field had been secured.

In the long view, it seems clear that the process of reassessment constituted the terms of *their* assimilation as well. But in its direct effect, their turn to ideology marked an attempt to distance themselves from cultural preconceptions, so as to make the study of symbol and myth a mode of cognitive criticism. Their approach constituted a fresh direction in the field, and it had salutary results. But it was and remains problematic for literary purposes. For one thing, the extrinsic method seizes on negative aspects of ideology; its diagnoses feed on social disease. Significantly, the studies I referred to exclude consideration of the rhetoric of civil rights, the ideals of conservationism and self-realization, the appeal to liberty, and for that matter the sheer imaginative power of the culture as well as its enormous vitality. That may be no more than a choice of focus, but the choice itself misrepresents the very nature of ideology, which is to enact the purposes of a society in its totality. We come to feel, in reading these critics, that the American ideology is a system of ideas in the service of evil rather than (like any ideology) a system of ideas wedded for good and evil to a certain social and cultural order.

Another, more serious problem is that the extrinsic approach sets the literary critic at odds with the work of literature. I mean *work* here in its aesthetic sense, the construction of an imaginary world that compels a suspension of disbelief on the reader's part, and that requires, on the critic's part, an appreciation of the writer's power to compel us to that end. One familiar resolution of the problem, reinforced in different ways by Matthiessen and Spiller, is to separate high art from popular culture through a dogmatic distinction between intrinsic and extrinsic criticism. The classic writers are honored as keepers of the American myth; all other writers (especially the popular ones) are unmasked as representatives of American ideology. When Robert Rantoul invokes the tenets of laissez-faire to attack the abuses of capitalism, his views are said to be contradictory or ambivalent. When John O'Sullivan advances the principles of minimal government, self-reliance, and American progress, he is accused of using ideology to veil oppression. When Emerson, Thoreau, and Whitman express that ambivalence and advance those principles, they are praised for creating ambiguities, criticizing the actual under the aspect of the ideal, and enhancing the possibilities of democracy.

I am not forgetting the vast differences between these men in mind and imagination; nor do I mean to deny important differences in their relation to the dominant culture. My point is that the traditional dichotomy between art and ideology—a pillar of the old consensus—is controversial, and has properly become a subject of debate. For though in some sense, certainly, a work of art transcends its time—though it may be trans-historical or transcultural or even transcanonical—it can no more transcend ideology than an artist's mind can transcend psychology; and it may even be that writers who translate political attitudes into universal ideals are just as implicated as the others in the social order, and in the long run perhaps more useful in perpetuating it. This is not at all to denigrate their achievement. Nor is it to deny that American writers have sometimes used the symbol of America to expose ideological contradictions, and so on some level turned the cultural symbology against the dominant culture. Nor, finally, is it to forget the special capacities of language to break free of social restrictions, and through its own dynamics to undermine the power structures it seems to reflect. Of course it must continue to be a function of literary criticism to define what is extraordinary, irreducible, and uncontained about our major texts. My point is that any defense of art which requires a pejorative view of ideology is itself ideological, part of a strategy designed to enforce the separation of "spheres of influence": "high art" from "popular culture," business from family, government from religion, politics from aesthetics. Like other apologias for literature, as handmaid to theology or as servant of the state, this one has its origins neither in the laws of nature nor in the will of God, but in history and culture. And I would suggest that a heightened ideological awareness may help us not only to understand literary texts more fully in their own time but more precisely to define their trans-historical import.

I have in mind a cultural dialectic attuned to the power of language no less than to the language of power, sensitive to the emotional and imaginative appeal of myth while insisting on the cognitive dimensions of art. What makes this sort of model viable is the emergence over the last two decades or so of a sophisticated concept of ideology that is newly useful for the study of literature. My own views in this regard come closest to recent developments in anthropology. But to call attention to the problematic involved (my subject, let me stress, is the *problem* of ideology), I illustrate my point by reference to the various forms of Marxism, or neo-Marxism, that have broken from Marx's mechanistic view of base/ superstructure, much as recent forms of Freudianism have broken from Freud's simplistic view of art as wish fulfillment and child's play—not to deny the interactions between rhetoric and social biological reality, but to reinterpret these in ways that allow for consciousness as agency and for the shaping influence of rhetoric on reality. Basically, Marx saw ideology as false consciousness. He tended to define any ideology that differed from his own as a form of subjectivity that obfuscated scientific analysis. Recent forms of Marxism (influenced in part by a new, relativistic model of science) have abandoned that dream of objective knowledge. Much as the unconscious has come to be seen as a crucial aspect of consciousness, subjectivity for these neo-Marxists (mainly located now in American universities) has become a constituent of history.

This is not the place to detail the change. Let me simply list some of its major aspects: the emphasis on language as an intrinsic part of the *material* of history, and hence itself a central category of historical analysis; the sense of social reality as being at once volatile and malleable, and thus susceptible to radical transformation through the agencies of art; the redefinition of the work of imagination in terms of the structures of social knowledge; the concern with silences and ruptures in the text as constituting a vision of cultural alternatives (a vision muted, repressed, but nonetheless formally manifest in the world of the text); the development of a utopian hermeneutics which sees in the values, symbols, and ideas of a given culture—as these are represented in art—the primary structures of human needs and aspirations, so that interpretation becomes the bridge between ideology and the ideal. What is striking here for my purpose is the intense concern with expressive form. If the old "vulgar Marxism" tended to flatten works of art into political blueprints, this new Marxism, as though in overcompensation, compels an even closer reading of the text—a more rigorous attention to paradox, irony, and ambiguity—than that dreamed of by the New Critics. The text, it would seem, has been invested with all the subtleties of historical process so that history may be understood through the subtleties of literary criticism.

In the case of certain oppositional critics, this amounts to textuality raised to the status of biblical exegesis, where exegesis may flower (as it did for the New England Puritans) into obsessive apocalyptic correlations between scripture and good things to come. I tried earlier to outline my objections to this approach. I mention it here, however, for what I consider to be its positive value: the possibilities it makes available to literary historians beset by the problem of ideology. What I would suggest is that recent oppositional critics, including the Marxists among them, are exemplary for their insistence simultaneously on the historicity of the text and on the linguistic, expressive dimensions of historical experience. They have thus tended toward an intrinsic mode of ideological criticism, a form of historical diagnosis which requires an appreciation of ideology from within, in its full imaginative and emotional appeal. In all this they have shown richly provocative affinities with non-Marxist approaches to ideology. I think, for example, of Max Weber's concept of ideology as a positive, empowering force—not so much the child of history as a pervasive historical and cultural agent in its own right—and of Karl Mannheim's "sociology of knowledge," where all knowledge is by definition ideological, so that (in his words) reality is "the interplay between these distinctive attitudes in the total social process." For both Weber and Mannheim (as also, implicitly, for Kenneth Burke), ideology provides a focus for historical understanding that is grounded in the substantiality of expressive form. And much the same may be said of Clifford Geertz. Although Geertz confines his analysis in this respect to periods of cultural transition, still his analysis centers on the relation between ideological "systems of meaning" and historical "modes of knowledge."[4] In the wake of consensus, he writes, ideology directs the search for a new coherence. And I would add that, while waiting for the new coherence, dissensus directs us toward the problem of ideology.

This seems to me a particularly promising direction in the case of American literary studies. I have spoken of the symbol of America as a rhetorical battleground, but it could become so only because, from its origins, the symbol was so transparently ideological. What could be a clearer demonstration of the reciprocities between language and force than the system of beliefs which the early colonists imposed on the so-called New World? What clearer demonstration of the shaping power of ideology than the procession of declarations through which the republic was consecrated as New Israel, Nature's Nation in the Land of Futurity? "America" is a laboratory for examining the shifting connections between political (in the Aristotelian sense) and aesthetic systems of meaning. This is nowhere more evident than in the mid-nineteenth century, when the conflicts inherent in the symbol of America became most pronounced; and when, under pressure of vast economic change and impending civil war, the culture found expression, in all its contradictions and all its power of compelling allegiance, in a self-consciously *American* literary renaissance. It is no accident that our current dissensus has found a focus in the revaluation of this period, and particularly in the so-called radicalism of America's classic writers.

The issue is not the radicalism itself: that was virtually the donnée of the entire process of canon formation, from D. H. Lawrence through Matthiessen. The literary establishment that substituted "Song of Myself" for *The Song of Hiawatha* also sanctified Whitman as outsider and non-conformist. The scholars and critics who raised *Moby-Dick* from the dust of cetology catalogues to sudden epic prominence proceeded to acclaim Melville for his No-in-thunder to the powers of the earth. Directly and indirectly, the old consensus tended to privilege the subversive: duplicity in Hawthorne, protest in Thoreau, marginality in Poe, antinomianism in Emerson. All this, be it noted, in the name of a distinctly *national* tradition, a classic literature newly recovered for its quintessential "American-ness."

What I called the new focus of revaluation begins in the paradox of an antagonist literature that is somehow also culturally representative. That did not really trouble an earlier generation of critics because they had separated the America of the myth, represented by the country's classic writers, from the real America, represented by ideologues and their victims. The project now is somehow to integrate those two kinds of representation. This has meant taking the American Renaissance out of the realm of cultural schizophrenia which was the legacy of the old consensus, and relocating it firmly in history—which is to say, at the center of the antebellum movement toward industrialization, incorporation, and civil war. It has meant reconceiving America's "subversive literary tradition" as an insistent engagement with society, rather than a recurrent flight from it. It has meant contextualizing the ideal America's projected in the classic texts—rehistoricizing those fabled frontiers of the soul and romance lands of moral antinomies (Old Serpent and New Adam, Innocence and Experience) as works of culture: neither mirror reflections of the time nor lamps of the creative imagination, but examples of ideological mimesis, nourished by the culture they resist and antagonistic to the social forces that nonetheless compelled their complicity.

Ideology figures here as a problem at once of literary and of historical analysis. Let me outline two representative approaches to the problem. How can an antagonist literature be said to be culturally representative? And specifically, in what sense does this group of *American* classics, themselves so deeply concerned with an *American* utopia, constitute a radical tradition? One answer is implicit in the neo-Marxist perspective I noted earlier. All utopian visions express powerful feelings of social discontent; many are adopted by repressed or ascendant groups to challenge the status quo; and while some of them are thus incorporated into the ideology of a new social order, nonetheless, *as* utopian visions, even these remain a potential source of social unrest, a standing invitation to resistance and revolt. Every ideology, that is, breeds its own opposition, every culture its own counter-culture. The same ideals that at one point sustain the system may later become the basis of a new revolutionary consensus, one that invokes those ideals on behalf of an entirely different way of life, moral and material.

In the mid-nineteenth century the main source of dissent was an indigenous residual culture, variously identified with agrarianism, libertarianism, and civic humanism. By any name, it was the guiding ideology of the early republic. It had provided an impetus to revolution, a series of rituals of cohesion, and a rationale for the political and social structures of nationhood. As the economy expanded, those structures shifted to accommodate new commercial interests. But the cultural continuities were too strong, too basic, for the ideals themselves to be discarded. They were the foundational truths, after all, of liberal democracy. So the earlier rhetoric persisted, supported by preindustrial traditions and regional agrarian communities that increasingly contrasted with the ways of the Jacksonian marketplace. And on the ground of that opposition, America's classic writers developed a sweeping critique of the dominant culture. It was a diagnosis from within, based on the profound engagement of these writers with a society in transition from agrarian to industrial capitalism, and it issued in an imaginative rendering of that society which was at once radical and representative, an exposé of inherent contradictions that re-created the culture in its full complexity.

The result was more than exposé. It was a denunciation of the present that sanctified the *rhetoric* of an earlier America, a rhetoric that had lost its direct social function, though it remained nonetheless a staple of national self-definition. And thus freed of its practical tasks—which had included (by intent or in effect) the preservation of slavery in the South and the exclusion of large parts of the population everywhere in the country from the privileges of power—divested of these and other ideological responsibilities to the social order, the rhetoric could appeal now with still greater purity, as the vehicle of disinterested universal truth. If it could no longer serve the culture, it could serve the cause of culture at large, by conserving the myths of a bygone age. Accordingly, it aligned itself, against the actual course of events, with trans-historical dreams of human wholeness and social regeneration, and thereby invested the notion of an ideal America with a politically transformative potential. In sum, the ideology of the early republic became, in the utopian form of myth and promise, a fundamental challenge to the national republic. And in the major works of the American Renaissance the challenge found its classic literary expression. Both as cultural critique and as prophetic summons, these classics turned the ideological norms they represented—independence, liberty, enterprise, opportunity, individualism, democracy, "America" itself—against the American Way.

This view of American literary radicalism promises a fuller account than we have had of what Matthiessen termed the conflict between the real and the ideal America. But the assumption itself of radicalism remains questionable. It derives on the one hand from pronouncements of the writers themselves, who may not be reliable in this as in other matters, and on the other hand from the authority of critics, like Matthiessen, who may have had their own special interests for identifying (so as to identify with) an antagonist yet representative American literature. From either perspective, we must consider an altogether different possibility—that the country's major writers were not subversive at all, or that they were radical in a representative way that *reaffirmed* the culture, rather than undermining it. This approach also begins in a recognition of the utopian element in our classic texts, but it proceeds from that to note that characteristically, as a matter of course, the dominant culture adopts utopia for its own purposes. It does not simply endorse trans-historical ideals of harmony and regeneration; it absorbs and molds these in ways that support the social system. It redefines the dream-visions of organic community (paradise lost and to be regained) to fit its distinctive system of values. It re-creates the archetypes of the racial unconscious in its own image. It ritualizes the egalitarian energies of the liminal process in such a way as to harness discontent to the social enterprise. It allowed Martin Luther King, Jr., the grandson of slaves, to mobilize the Civil Rights movement on the grounds that racism is un-American; and Ronald Reagan to hitch the rhetoric of John Winthrop and Tom Paine to the campaign wagon for Star Wars.

So molded, ritualized, and controlled, utopianism has served here as elsewhere to diffuse or deflect dissent, or actually to transmute it into a vehicle of socialization. Indeed, it is not too much to see this as ideology's chief weapon. Ideology represses alternative or oppositional forms when these arise. But it seeks first of all to preempt them, and it does so most effectively by *drawing out* protest, by actively *encouraging* the contrast between utopia and the status quo. The method is as old as ideology itself. Any form of protest, utopian or other, threatens society most fundamentally when it calls into question the claims of that society to represent things as they ought to be (by divine right, natural law, the dictates of holy scripture, the forms of reason). Fundamental protest, that is, involves a historicist, relativistic perspective on the claims of ideology. And the immemorial response of ideology, what we might call its instinctive defense, has been to redefine protest in terms of the system, as a complaint about shortcomings from its ideals, or deviations from its myths of self and community. Thus the very act of identifying malfunction becomes an appeal for cohesion. To that end, ideology seeks to focus attention on the distance between vision and fact, theory and practice. To denounce a king through precepts derived from the divine right of kings is to define government itself as monarchical; just as to denounce immoral Christians by contrast with the sacred example of Christ is to Christianize morality. To define injustice through particular violations of free enterprise (or its constituent elements, such as equal opportunity and representative individualism) is to consecrate free enterprise as *the* just society.

Hence the enormous conservative, restraining power in the alliance between utopia and ideology. It allows the dominant culture not merely to enforce rules of conduct, but to circumscribe the bounds of perception, thought, and desire. And if that culture dominates not by coercion but by consent—if its rituals are not traditional but newly formed, *and "new" as well by cultural fiat* (new rituals of what Winthrop, Paine, and Reagan called a New

People in a New World); if the population, moreover, is broadly heterogeneous (and again, *heterogeneous as well by cultural fiat*, the self-proclaimed nation of nations, culture of pluralism, and haven of the oppressed and uprooted); if its power, therefore, depends on myths and values to which all levels of society subscribe, *especially the excluded or marginalized* (since to subscribe thus seems the ready way to power); and if, finally, it is a culture founded on the principles of contract, voluntarism, and self-interest—a culture whose primary unit is the self, and whose primary rites, accordingly, encourage the potentially anarchic doctrine of individualism (with its insidious affinities to individuality and the subversive claims of independent selfhood)—if the culture, that is, combines the conditions of modernization with the principles of liberal democracy, then the need to preclude alternatives a priori, before they can become radical fact, assumes special urgency.

We might say that the American ideology was made to fill that need. It undertakes above all, as a condition of its nurture, to absorb the spirit of protest for social ends; and according to a number of recent critics, it has accomplished this most effectively through its rhetoric of dissent. In this view, America's classic texts represent the strategies of a triumphant liberal hegemony. Far from subverting the status quo, their diagnostic and prophetic modes attest to the capacities of the dominant culture to absorb alternative forms, to the point of making basic change seem virtually unthinkable, except as apocalypse. This is not at all to minimize their protest. The point here is not that these classic writers had no quarrel with America, but that they seem to have had nothing *but* that to quarrel about. Having adopted the culture's *controlling* metaphor—"America" as synonym for human possibility—and having made this tenet of consensus the ground of radical dissent, they redefined radicalism as an affirmation of cultural values. For the metaphor, thus universalized, does not transcend ideology. It portrays the American ideology, as all ideology yearns to be portrayed, in the transcendent colors of utopia. In this sense the antebellum literary renaissance was truly, as Matthiessen said, both American and "the age of Emerson and Whitman"; the conjunction is embodied in "The American Scholar" and *Democratic Vistas*, both of which, in the very act of chastising the nation, identify the American future as utopia, and utopia, by extension, as the American *Way*.

So perceived, what Matthiessen termed the one common denominator of his classic texts lies in the possibilities of democracy
as these have been shaped into strategies of consensus. And the
same strategies apply to what he called the tragic-ironic visions
of Hawthorne and Melville. Both men perceived evil in many
forms, and both had a remarkable gift for seeing through those
forms to metaphysical issues; but their insight was attended by
an equally remarkable blindness to social limits. They could not
see that the issues themselves were culturally determined; that
the universals they invoked might obscure or disguise or reconcile
us to the very evils they attacked, as Ishmael reconciles himself
to the tyranny of Ahab: "who *ain't* a slave?" he explains. Of course
Ishmael's story is as much a repudiation as a celebration of Ahab.
But the issue here is not reconciliation or repudiation; it is ideological constriction. What our major writers could not conceive,
either in their optative or in their tragic-ironic moods, was that
the United States was neither utopia at best nor dystopia at worst,
neither "the world's fairest hope," as Melville put it, nor "man's
foulest crime," but a certain political system; that *in principle* no
less than in practice the American Way was neither providential
nor natural but one of many possible forms of society.[5]

Hence the representative, *American* radicalism of this classic
literature: it was the aesthetic flowering of an ideology adopted
from the start precisely for its ability to transmute radicalism of all
kinds, from religious protest to revolutionary war, into varieties of
ideological consensus. And since this approach implies a fundamental challenge both to the old consensus and to large parts of
the current dissensus, I want to add once more, at the risk of
seeming to protest too much, that the argument I have just outlined does not in any sense diminish the aesthetic power of the
texts themselves. It does not even require, on the critic's part, an
adversarial stance toward the culture. We need think no less of
Dante for his commitment to Christian figuralism; we may even
praise his culture for having provided him with so rich a system
of ideas, symbols, and beliefs. So too, with Whitman and Emerson:
they need not embarrass us by their failure, if such it was, to see
through the rhetoric of free-enterprise democracy. What they did
see, when they plumbed the emotional, imaginative, and conceptual ground of the rhetoric, was profound, humane, and exhilarating, a set of ideas and beliefs which may rank among the most
liberating ideas, the most vital and vitalizing beliefs, produced by

any culture, past or present. It was a rhetoric which enlisted the spirit of revolution in the cause of social continuity; which recast self-interest, as individualism, into a concept of self-fulfillment that allowed for mutuality and community; which invested the dream of progress with moral as well as material imperatives (or better, perhaps, which invested those moral imperatives with the concern for material improvement); which in either sense translated the spirit of expansion into a vision of growth, experimentation, and constant renewal; and which, summarily, created in the word "America" the most compelling cultural symbol of the modern era, nationally and internationally.

The rhetoric here is inseparable from the country's astonishing economic, political, and technological achievements in the nineteenth century. It is inseparable, too, from the intensity of racism, greed, frontier and urban violence, and sectional conflict building toward what was to be the century's most devastating war. But we need not overlook the one in order to condemn the other. Nor need we, with Spiller et al, obscure the cultural limits which the ideals express in order to appreciate their demands for freedom and initiative. Nor need we, finally, separate the spirit of an "older liberalism," as Matthiessen did, from the "rising forces of exploitation"[6] in order to praise Emerson's commitment to the possibilities of democracy. Those possibilities did not depend on nostalgia alone, or on some heroic lonely struggle of the creative imagination against society. Not one of the classic American texts supports this view; it cannot be substantiated by the life and thought of any one of the country's major writers. On the contrary: all of them testify that the historical achievements and the violence are together integral to the cultural dynamics which produced the American Renaissance. Consciously or not, these writers are implicated in both; and if we dissociate them, as we should, from the worst excesses of the time, we must recognize nonetheless that they were accomplices of the culture in its complex totality—antagonists of its worst qualities because advocates of its best. We will never properly understand their force of enterprise, speculation, and invention until we set this firmly within a history of American enterprise, speculation, and invention in the nineteenth century. We will never properly define their modernness until we appreciate the culture's capacity—*through* violence, disruption, and dissent—to unleash and control the tremendous energies of modernization that transformed antebellum America.

Let me illustrate the connection briefly by two unlikely examples, both of them bearing directly upon the current dissensus in
American literary criticism. The first is *Uncle Tom's Cabin*,
which is now having a renaissance of its own. No doubt, the
very fact of this renaissance highlights the repressive force of the
American ideology—with regard both to the canon that excluded
Stowe's novel from serious literary study, and to the consensus
history that derogated the rich and intricate worldview embodied
in sentimental fiction. But the novel itself stands as a great testament to the culture's sustained and sustaining *vitality*. To understand *Uncle Tom's Cabin* intrinsically, in its own terms—to appreciate its aesthetic strategies, and for that matter the enormous
appeal of its sentimentalism, then and now—is to recognize the
capacity of Stowe's society for absorbing change, for fusing the
disparate ideals of evangelical religion, domesticity, and manifest
destiny, and for turning social crisis into a movement toward
social reform. Lincoln is supposed to have called Stowe the little
woman who made the great war. It might be said more plausibly
that the forces which converged to make war irrepressible also
made possible the triumphant art of *Uncle Tom's Cabin*. It is no
accident, surely, that the two alternatives which Stowe offers to
slavery—and more largely to the exploitation of "the lowly,"
North and South—turn out to be a utopian affirmation of America's actual growth: at one end, the outmoded agrarian community
that shelters George Harris on his way to freedom; at the other
end, in the novel's happy resolution, the free-enterprise republic
that George projects, his American errand into the wilderness of
Liberia, in fulfillment of his (and Stowe's) dream.

My second unlikely example is *The Narrative of the Life of
Frederick Douglass*. We owe our new interest in this classic largely
to the work underway in black studies, which again speaks to the
limitations of the old consensus. And again I would urge that our
sense of limitation should not blind us to the powerful and positive
influence of cultural consensus in the *Narrative* itself. I refer to
the *liberating* appeal for Douglass of free-enterprise ideology. On
some level, certainly, he manipulated the ideology—the rhetoric
of equal opportunity, contract society, upward mobility, free trade,
and the sanctity of private property—to justify his flight to freedom. But it seems just as certain (to judge by his subsequent life
and work) that on another level he was being manipulated in turn
by those cultural key words *and energized by them*. Freedom for

Douglass means self-possessive individualism. It takes the form of a movement from absolute injustice (represented by the slave system) to absolute justice, represented by the tenets of American liberalism. To the extent that Douglass denounces American society, it is for not being true to its own principles, for failing to comply in practice with a social order that is utopia in theory: reasonable, moral, and spiritually as well as economically just. To some extent *The Narrative* interprets Frederick Douglass as an exemplum of that faith. And however *we* interpret the *Narrative*, we must acknowledge the creative force of its faith. More than that, we must acknowledge how flexibly it could embrace diverse traditions (including the African–American) in such a way as simultaneously to rechannel radical energies back into the culture and to inspire the work of art.

To rechannel, in this context, is not to diminish the creative power of those energies. Nor is it, to recall the argument I outlined earlier, necessarily to de-radicalize them. James M. Smith introduced the 1855 version of *The Narrative* (revised and enlarged as *My Bondage, My Freedom*) as "an American book, for Americans"; and went on to describe Douglass himself as "a Representative American man—a type of his countrymen."[7] His categories remind us how quickly Douglass's rebellion was absorbed into the mainstream symbology; but they also suggest the volatile terms of absorption. The image of "representative man" here was fundamentally at odds with the concept of "American" among even Smith's white Northern abolitionist readers. To make Douglass American was therefore not only to validate his acts of insurrection, but to extend the insurrection to ideological critique. Precisely by laying claim to the values, ideals, and myths (as well as the economic benefits) of the dominant culture, *The Narrative of . . . An American Slave, Written By Himself* highlights the historical, contingent realities behind the symbology at large. "[A] type of his countrymen," writes Smith; but what does "his" refer to—to what "country," and which "men"?—and what does *his* type ("Himself," the "American Slave") have to do with the figural American Self ("American book, for Americans")? Such questions are implicit in all three versions of Douglass's success story. They constitute an adversarial subtext, in which Douglass's very rhetoric of "freedom" and "bondage"—the rhetoric, he tells us, of *The Columbian Orator* (where the concept of freedom may be said to be in bondage to the myth of continuing revolution)—forces into view the "actual individualism" within and for which the American Type was made up—and through which it was occasionally made real.*

The ambiguities this entails speak directly to the problem of ideology in American literary studies. I have no intention of trying to resolve them here, and indeed I have drawn them out precisely to suggest what I take to be a main advantage of dissensus, that it may serve as a barrier to imposed and unearned solutions. I have in mind now not the solutions of the old consensus, but those implicit in the recent trend toward multi-culturalism. Or rather, the latest re-trend toward pluralism, for the ideal of heterogeneity (in its many forms) is integral to the American symbology, and a

*I refer here to the Emersonian text I discussed in the preceding chapter, "ideal union, in actual individualism" (Journal N [1842], in vol. VIII of *Journals*, ed. William Gilman and J. E. Parsons [Cambridge, Mass., 1970], p. 251). The ambiguity or disjunction I refer to may be illustrated by Douglass's description of his moment of triumph, when he may be said finally to fulfill the norms of the American success story. His arrival in the North, he writes, was "a glorious resurrection from the tomb of slavery to the heaven of freedom"—and heaven turns out to be the warehouses of Jacksonian New Bedford:

> I was walled in by granite warehouses of the widest dimensions, stowed to their utmost capacity with the necessaries and comforts of life. Added to this, almost every body seemed to be at work, but noiselessly so, compared with what I had been accustomed to. . . . There were no loud songs. . . . Every man appeared to understand his work, and went about it with a sober, yet cheerful earnestness . . . as well as with a sense of *his own* dignity as a man. . . .
> Every thing looked clean, new, and beautiful. (*Narrative* [1845; New York, 1968], pp. 115–116)

The parallels to Emerson are remarkable, both in phrasing and in concept ("Uniters absolutely isolated"; all "work done with concert, though no man spoke"). But in Douglass's case, the narrative "I" remains alien, adversarial—not because *he* is black, but because his blackness reveals the ideological limitations—the constructedness—of *their* utopia. In the stark contrast between the imagery of salvation and the scene of commerce, the "walled in" "heaven" that Douglass celebrates, "clean, new, and beautiful," becomes (like the terms of his *vita nuova*) all too actual: male, white, and individualistic: the free-labor alternative to the "organic" plantation system. Whether or not that contrast was intended, it makes for the unsettling, relativistic implications I suggest above—that while in some sense Douglass moves (like Bunyan's Pilgrim) from one absolute state to another, "Bondage" to "Freedom," in another sense each of these alternatives, North and South, represents a certain power structure whose injustices (Douglass emphasizes) are fortified by the rhetoric of religion. So interpreted, the freedom toward which *The Narrative* reaches is a utopian summons to social transformation that may be said (within limits) to transcend its immediate context.

continuing pattern of American scholarship. It was once said, in reaction against those who sought to define America "intellectually," that America was sheer pragmatism and process; the intellectuals had the American idea, "the people" had "the American experience." Now it is said, in reaction against those who speak of an American literature or a national culture, that the country is sheer multiplicity. The ruling elite has an American ideology; the people have their own patchwork-quilt (rather than melting-pot) American multifariousness: "America" is—many forms of ethnicity, many patterns of thought, many ways of life, many cultures, many American literatures. This is opposite to consensus only in the sense of symbolic bipolarity: the other, complementary side of the liberal rhetoric of union. The patchwork quilt is the reverse side of the familiar stars and stripes; multi-culturalism is the hyphenated American writ large.

I mean by this neither to belittle the multi-culturalist enterprise nor to equate earlier with recent American Studies. There are significant differences, and it may be that the issues raised by ideology will lead multi-culturalists to make use of the best insights of the new pluralism without succumbing to the ideological trap it signals. The insights are those which challenge familiar assumptions. The trap lies in the way that the challenge itself may become the means for avoiding the questions raised by dissensus. Every ideology construes its own way into this trap. The American way is to turn potential conflict into a quarrel about fusion or fragmentation. It is a fixed match, a debate with a foregone conclusion and a ready formula for reaching it: fusion *and* fragmentation; a continual oscillation between harmony-in-diversity and diversity-in-harmony. It is the hermeneutics of laissez-faire. All conflicts are obviated by the continual flow of the one into the many, and the many into the one, as in Adam Smith's theory of the general will, or the federalist doctrine of balance of power, or the anti-federalist doctrine of states' rights, or Whitman's self—en masse, or Poe's vision of cosmic alternation in *Eureka*, or (as we have seen) the ambiguities of Hawthorne's scarlet letter, the monistic dualisms of Emerson's Central Man, and the parodic doublings of *Pierre*. And with Melville's counter-model in mind, let me urge that the option need not be limited to consensus or multiplicity. We have another choice: whether to make use of the categories of culture or to be used by them.

Let me urge further in this regard that to recognize the limitations of ideology is to open up interpretation; whereas, conversely, to deny those limitations is to subject interpretation to ideology. The advantage in taking the former, problematic direction is not that it will lead us out of the wilderness of consensus into a Canaan of unmediated truth. Quite the contrary: it is the recognition that that promise is itself a function of ideology (variously mediated by religion, science, and art), and the possibility, therefore, that we may see the ways of the wilderness more clearly, or at least see certain of its ways that had not been apparent before. For example: (1) it may enable us to deal more fully with the historical dissensus that informs every stage of America's growth from colony to world power; (2) it may help us convey the dynamics of dissensus inherent in the very notion of an "American" literature—the unresolved "high-low" conflict at the heart of the Romantic-democratic concept of art; (3) it may help us convey the dissensus embedded in the reception of America's classic texts— the cultural controversies that from the start marked the response to *Moby-Dick*, *Leaves of Grass*, *Walden*, *The Scarlet Letter*, "The American Scholar," *Uncle Tom's Cabin*, and *The Narrative of the Life of Frederick Douglass*, all of which were conceived and received in a spirit of dissensus and all of which have remained controversial ever since, the subject of continual dispute, rediscovery, and polemical redefinition.

In short, the current dissensus in academic criticism may help bring alive the experiences of disruption and discontinuity that charaterize American literary history. Parrington submerged the problem of aesthetics in the myth of continuing revolution (from Jefferson through Whitman). Matthiessen felt he had to disengage himself from problems of history in order to serve as advocate for what he perceived as major works of art. The current Babel of literary approaches may help make the American Renaissance more integral to a living past, part of a volatile interaction between culture, interpretation, and imaginative expression that remains a vital legacy to American literature and criticism alike. More than that, it may lead us to a re-vision of the nationalist implications inherent in the notion of an American literary tradition. Looking back now at the golden age of consensus, it seems clear that Matthiessen's revisionism was rooted, consciously or not, in the ideals of the early- and mid-nineteenth century. *American Renaissance*, and the procession of critical syntheses that prepared the way for it and then followed in its wake (from, say, Lewis Mum-

ford's *Golden Day* through Edwin Fussell's *Frontier*), all reflect
the euphoria of the Young America movement and specifically
the vision of a uniquely American literature promulgated by Emerson and Whitman. In some basic sense, that is, it was the country's
rediscovered writers who set the terms for what was to become
the framework for recovering the country's literary past: the question of the American-ness of American literature.

To see this sort of parochialism as problematic is not at all to
belittle the critical legacy. The effort to define the American-ness
of American literature generated a vast amount of scholarship,
some of it, like Matthiessen's, of enduring value. Within that
framework, literary critics could join with scholars of very different disciplines (history, political science, linguistics, folklore, religion, art, law, sociology) in ways that helped organize a remarkable
variety of materials. The American-ness of American literature
was a paradigmatic hypothesis that provided techniques for teach-
ing, themes for anthologies and "casebooks" that supported those
techniques, and subjects for theses and monographs that accredited the teachers and anthologists. It raised what must once have
seemed a plethora of questions precisely by directing the question-
ers to a common resolution, centered on an ideological fiction,
"American-ness," and grounded in the assumption that that fiction encompassed matters of form and content, text and context.
In sum, it opened up new vistas for investigation while providing
the terms of closure that made sense of the investigations. And in
doing so, the focus on "American-ness" shaped a community of
teachers and students, scholars and critics, which rapidly reached
beyond national boundaries to include academic communities
throughout the world.

The development of American Studies abroad took the form
of an academic Marshall Plan. Its typical format was a group of
American experts bringing the latest news about American-ness
to their Old World colleagues. The effectiveness of that method
is a matter of history, but the format no longer suits the issues.
One advantage of dissensus is that it promises to break through
the confines of American parochialism; to provide a forum for
reconsidering American literature in an international perspective;
to replace the tautologies of exceptionalism with transnational
categories of analysis (both aesthetic and cultural, from genre to
gender); to extend the problematics of "art and expression" to
accommodate works produced by marginal or excluded groups;

perhaps even to put in question the centrality of the American Renaissance by attending to the transatlantic enterprises of earlier or later periods (e.g., the era of James, Du Bois, Wharton, Eliot, Pound, Stein, and the neglected emigrant "ethnic" writing of the early twentieth century); and to benefit from the dialogue now under way between native Americanists and "foreign" scholars, critics, and theorists trained in non-American forms of discourse.

On these and similar grounds, we may expect dissensus to yield a rich harvest in due time. That is mainly what I had in mind when I spoke at the start of finding a solution not to but *in* the problem of ideology. In its usual meaning ideology precludes dialogue. It implies a programmatic exclusivism, a closed system developed in opposition to alternative explanations and militantly committed to its particular set of truths. To deny the links between ideology and art is one such form of exclusivity. To see the problematic inescapability of those links may enable us to use ideological analysis to precisely the opposite ends: to turn the current barbarism of critical debate into a dialogue about common conflicts. In our ability to keep the dialogue open while specifying and exploring the conflicts lies the prospect of achieving an Americanist criticism worthy of our time.

Notes

1. Introduction: The Music of America

1. Walt Whitman, "I Hear America Singing," and Preface to *Leaves of Grass* (1855), in *Complete Poetry and Collected Prose*, ed. Justin Kaplan (Library of America: New York, 1982), pp. 174, 5; Ralph Waldo Emerson, "The Poet," in *Essays and Lectures*, ed. Joel Porte (Library of America: New York, 1983), p. 465; Franz Kafka, "Investigations of a Dog," trans. Willa and Edwin Muir, in *The Complete Stories*, ed. Nahum N. Glatzer (New York, 1971), pp. 280–81, 285–87, 294, 315, 303.

2. Douglas LePan, "A Country Without a Mythology," cited in Northrop Frye, *The Bush Garden: Essays on the Canadian Imagination* (Toronto, 1971), p. 164.

3. Frye, *Bush Garden*, p. 138; Margaret Atwood, *Survival: A Thematic Guide to Canadian Literature* (Toronto, 1972), pp. 31–33.

4. Benjamin, "Theses on the Philosophy of History," in *Illuminations*, ed. Hannah Arendt, trans. Harry Zohn (New York, 1968), p. 256.

5. Kafka, "Investigations," in *Complete Stories*, ed. Glatzer, pp. 312–14; Wheatley, "To His Excellency George Washington" (1775), in *Collected Works*, ed. John C. Shields (New York, 1988), p. 146; Emerson, *Nature*, in *Essays and Lectures*, ed. Porte, pp. 16, 17.

6. Emerson, "Experience," in *Essays and Lectures*, ed. Porte, p. 485; Benjamin, "Theses," in *Illuminations*, ed. Arendt, pp. 256–257.

7. Emerson, "The American Scholar" and "Experience," in *Essays and Lectures*, ed. Porte, pp. 53, 485.

8. Shatalin delivered the talk on October 2, 1990 (summarized in *Meeting Report* of the Kennan Institute for Advanced Russian Studies, VIII, no. 1, 1991), at the Woodrow Wilson International Center for Scholars.

2. The Ritual of Consensus

1. Timothy H. Breen and Stephen Foster, "Moving to the New World: The Character of Early Massachusetts Immigration," *William and Mary Quarterly*, XXX (1973), 189–222,. B. Catherine Brown, "The Controversy Over the Franchise in Puritan Massachusetts, 1654 to 1674," *William and Mary Quarterly*, XXXIII (1976), 212–41; Alexis de Tocqueville, *Democracy in America*, ed. J. P. Mayer, trans. G. Lawrence, (Garden City, N.Y., 1969), p. 279.

2. Robert Mandrou, "Cultures ou niveaux culturels dans les sociétés d'Ancien Régime," *Revue des études Sud-Est européennes*, X (1972), 415–22; Keith V. Thomas, *Religion and the Decline of Magic: Studies in Popular Beliefs in Sixteenth and Seventeenth Century England* (London, 1971), pp. 26 ff.; Christopher Hill, *The Century of Revolution: 1603–1714* (Edinburgh, 1961), p. 102; Eric J. Hobsbawm, *Primitive Rebels: Studies in Archaic Forms of Social Movement in the Nineteenth and Twentieth Centuries* (New York, 1959), p. 69.

3. Carl Degler, quoted in Stuart Bruchey, *The Roots of American Economic Growth: An Essay in Social Causation* (New York, 1968), p. 44; Max Weber, *The Protestant Ethic and the Spirit of Capitalism*, trans. Talcott Parsons (New York, 1958), pp. 55–56; Gabriel Kolko, "Max Weber on America: Theory and Evidence," in *Studies in the Philosophy of History*, ed. G. N. Nadel (New York, 1965), p. 181.

4. John Cotton, *God's Promise to His Plantations* (1630), in *Old South Leaflets*, III, no. 53 (Boston, [1896]), 17.

5. Emery Battis, *Saints and Sectaries: Anne Hutchinson and the Antinomian Controversy in the Massachusetts Bay Colony* (Chapel Hill, N.C., 1962), p. 255; Bruchey, *Roots of American Economic Growth*, p. 47; Richard L. Bushman, *From Puritan to Yankee: Character and Social Order in Connecticut, 1690–1765* (New York, 1967), p. 147; Kai T. Erikson, *Wayward Puritans: A Study in the Sociology of Deviance* (New York, 1966), p. 53; Hill, *Century of Revolution*, p. 97.

6. Samuel Williams, *A Discourse on the Love of Country* (Salem, 1775), p. 22; Ebenezer Baldwin, *The Duty of Rejoicing* (New York, 1776), pp. 38–40; Thomas Blockway, *America Saved* (Hartford, 1784), p. 24; Thomas Barnard, quoted in Ernest L. Tuveson, *Redeemer Nation: The Idea of America's Millennial Role* (Chicago, 1968), p. 31.

7. George Bancroft, *History of the United States from the Discovery of the American Continent* (Boston, 1856–74), IV, 3–15, and II, 449;

Benjamin Rush, *Address to the People of the United States* (Boston, 1787), p. 1; Timothy Dwight, *A Sermon Preached at Northampton* (Hartford, [1781]), p. 27.

8. John Adams to Thomas Jefferson, Oct. 9, 1787, in *The Adams-Jefferson Correspondence*, ed. Lester J. Cappon (Chapel Hill, N.C., 1959), pp. 202–203.

9. J. Hector St. John Crèvecoeur, *Letters from an American Farmer*, ed. W. Blake (New York, 1957), pp. 192–226; Camillo Querno [pseudonym], "The American Times," in *The Loyalist Poetry of the Revolution*, ed. W. Sargent (Philadelphia, 1957), pp. 1–37.

10. Abner Cohen, "Symbolic Action and the Structure of the Self," in *Symbols and Sentiments: Cross-Cultural Studies in Symbolism*, ed. Ioan Lewis (London, 1977), p. 121.

11. George Rudé, "Robespierre," in *Robespierre*, ed. Rudé (Englewood Cliffs, N.J., 1967), p. 173; Luis Villoro, "Hidalgo: Su violencia y libertad," *Cuadernas Americanos*, II (1952), 223; John J. Johnson, *Simon Bolivar and Spanish American Independence* (New York, 1968), pp. 3–8 ff; Kenneth Maxwell, "The Generation of the 1790's and the Idea of the Luso-Brazilian Empire," in *Colonial Roots of Modern Brazil*, ed. D. Alden (Berkeley, 1973), p. 120.

12. Eric Foner, *Tom Paine and Revolutionary America* (New York, 1976), pp. 242, 253, 217 (quoting Paine, *The Rights of Man*); Thomas Paine, *Common Sense*, in *Common Sense and Other Political Writings*, ed. Nelson F. Adkins (New York, 1953), pp. 23, 3.

13. Hans Kohn, "Romanticism and the Rise of German Nationalism," *Review of Politics*, XII (1950), 443; Robert M. Berdahl, "New Thoughts on German Nationalism," *American Historical Review*, LXXVII (1972), 65; Franco Venturi, *Roots of Revolution: A History of the Populist and Socialist Movements in Nineteenth Century Russia* (New York, 1966), p. 122; Francis R. Hill, "Nationalist Millenarians and Millenarian Nationalists: Conflicts and Cooperation in New Jerusalem," *American Behavioral Scientist*, XVI (1972), 269.

14. Tocqueville, *Democracy In America*, ed. Mayer, p. 56; Hartz, *The Liberal Tradition in America* (New York, 1955), p. 131 (citing General Root); James Fenimore Cooper, *Notions of the Americans* (Philadelphia, 1828), II, 143; Nathaniel Hawthorne, *The Marble Faun, or, The Romance of Monte Beni*, in *Novels*, ed. Millicent Bell (Library of America: New York, 1983), p. 854.

15. Benjamin Franklin, "Information for Those Who Would Remove to

America" (1784), in *Writings*, ed. J. A. Leo Lemay (Library of America: New York, 1987), pp. 975–983; Edward Pessen, "The Egalitarian Myth and the American Social Reality: Wealth, Mobility, and Equality in the 'Era of the Common Man,' " in *The Many-Faceted Jacksonian Era*, ed. E. Pessen (London, 1977), pp. 7–46; J. D. B. De Bow, *Statistical View of the U.S.* (Washington, 1854); U.S. Census Office, *Sixth Census* (Washington, 1841); Peter Temin, *The Jacksonian Economy* (New York, 1969).

16. Ramsay, *The History of the American Revolution*, ed. Lester H. Cohen (1789; Indianapolis, 1990), II, 630; Emerson, "Considerations By the Way," in *Essays and Lectures*, ed. Joel Porte (Library of America: New York, 1983), p. 1086; Whitman, Prefaces of 1855 and 1876, in *Complete Poetry and Collected Prose*, ed. Justin Kaplan (Library of America: New York, 1982), pp. 25, 71, 1010.

17. Catharine Beecher, quoted in Kathryn K. Sklar, *Catharine Beecher* (New Haven, 1973), p. 159; Catharine Beecher, *A Treatise on Domestic Economy* (1841; Boston, 1842) pp. 36–37; Stanton and Brown, quoted in Susan Phinney Conrad, *Perish the Thought: Intellectual Women in Romantic America, 1830–1860* (New York, 1976), pp. 123–24, 150.

18. William Lloyd Garrison, "No Union with Slave-Holders," *Liberator* (1837), in *Slavery Attacked; The Abolitionist Crusade*, ed. John L. Thomas (Englewood Cliffs, N.J., 1965), pp. 76–77; Garrison, quoted in William A. Clebsch, *From Sacred to Profane America: The Role of Religion in American History* (New York, 1968), pp. 93–94; Frederick Douglass, "Oration" (1854), in *Black Writers of America: A Comprehensive Anthology*, ed. Kenneth Kinnamon and Richard Barksdale (New York, 1972), pp. 89–93, 99–101; Rantoul, quoted in Rush Welter, *The Mind of America 1820–1860* (New York, 1975), p. 49; Lewis Perry, "Adin Ballou's Hopedale Community and the Theology of Antislavery," *Church History*, XXXIX (1970), 16–17 (quoting Ballou); O.B. Frothingham, *George Ripley* (Boston, 1882), p. 111; John Higham, *From Boundlessness to Consolidation: The Transformation of American Culture, 1848–1860* (Ann Arbor, Mich., 1969), p. 13.

19. Henry David Thoreau, "A Plea for Captain John Brown," in *Reform Papers*, ed. Wendell Glick (Princeton, 1972), p. 125.

20. Douglas G. Jones, *Butterfly on Rock* (Toronto, 1970), pp. 57, 87–88; Brian Parker, "Is There a Canadian Identity?" in *The Canadian Imagination: Dimensions of a Literary Culture*, ed. David Staines

(Cambridge, Mass., 1977), p. 154; Northrop Frye, *The Bush Garden: Essays on the Canadian Imagination* (Toronto, 1971), p. 138; Margaret Atwood, *Survival: A Thematic Guide to Canadian Literature* (Toronto, 1972), pp. 31–33; Frye, "Conclusion" to vol. II of *The Literary History of Canada*, ed. C. F. Klinck (Toronto, 1976; 2d ed.), pp. 220–21, 225–26.

21. Frye, "Conclusion," *Literary History of Canada*, ed. Klinck, II, 324; Barbara Novak, "American Landscape: The Nationalist Garden and the Holy Book," *Art in America*, LX (1972), 50, 52; Richard Slotkin, *Regeneration Through Violence: The Mythology of the American Frontier, 1600–1860* (Middletown, Conn., 1973), pp. 272–273.

22. Lyman Beecher, *A Reformation of Morals* (Andover, Mass., 1814), p. 9; Charles G. Finney, *Lectures on Revivals of Religion* (1835), ed. W. G. McLoughlin (Cambridge, Mass., 1960), pp. 87, 120; William G. McLoughlin, Introduction to *The American Evangelicals, 1800–1900: An Anthology*, ed. W. G. McLoughlin (Gloucester, Mass., 1976), p. 1; Francis Wayland, *The Duties of an American Citizen* (Boston, 1825), p. 19; Albert Barnes, *The Gospel Necessary to Our Country* (Washington, 1832), p. 22; William Sprague, *Lectures on Revivals* (New York, 1833), p. 212; Mark Hopkins, cited in Emerson Davis, *The Half-Century* (Boston, 1851), p. xvi; William C. Conant, *Narratives of Conversions and Revivals* (Boston, 1858), p. 29.

23. Perry Miller, *The Life of the Mind in America, from the Revolution to the Civil War* (New York, 1965), pp. 22, 47–48, 11; Lawrence J. Friedman, *Inventors of the Promised Land* (New York, 1975), pp. 286–287 (quoting Finney and the Oberlinites); George M. Frederickson, "A Founding Family," *New York Review of Books*, November 9, 1978, p. 40 (commenting on Lyman Beecher); Timothy L. Smith, "Righteousness and Hope; Christian Holiness and the Millennial Vision in America, 1800–1900," *American Quarterly*, XXXI (1979), 21–23, 44 (citing Nathaniel Ward Taylor, the evangelical Calvinists, and the "perfectionists").

24. Philip Schaff, *America* (1854), ed. Perry Miller (Cambridge, Mass., 1961), pp. 4, 15–16, 18, 20–24.

25. Edmund Wilson, *Patriotic Gore: Studies in the Literature of the American Civil War* (New York, 1962), pp. xxii-xxiii; Thomas V. Peterson, *Ham and Japheth: The Mythic World of Whites in the Antebellum South* (London, 1978), p. 95; William G. McLoughlin, Introduction to *American Evangelicals*, p. 21; James H. Moorhead,

382 / *Notes*

American Apocalypse: Yankee Protestants and the Civil War,
1860–1869 (New Haven, 1978), passim; John Higham, "Hanging
Together: Divergent Unities in American History," *Journal of American History*, LXI (1974), 10–18.

26. Alan Trachtenberg, *The Incorporation of America: Culture and
Society in the Gilded Age* (New York, 1981); Frye, *Bush Garden*, p.
104; Victor Turner, "Liminal to Liminoid, in Play, Flow, and Ritual:
An Essay in Comparative Symbology," *Rice University Studies*, XL
(1974), 86.

27. Donnelly, quoted in Michael Fellman, *The Unbounded Frame:
Freedom and Community in Nineteenth Century American Utopianism* (New York, 1973), pp. 124–25, 135–36, 142; Bellamy, quoted
in Kenneth M. Roemer, *The Obsolete Necessity: America in Utopian Writings, 1888–1900* (Kent, Ohio, 1976), p. 3; Walt Whitman,
"American Futurity," in *Gathering of the Forces*, ed. Cleveland
Rogers and John Black (New York, 1920), I, 27–28, and *Democratic
Vistas*, in *Complete Poetry and Collected Prose*, ed. Kaplan, p. 951;
Curtis Dahl, "The American School of Catastrophe," *American
Quarterly*, XI (1959), 380–90.

28. Melville, *White-Jacket, or, The World in a Man-of-War*, in *Redburn,
White-Jacket, Moby-Dick*, ed. G. Thomas Tanselle (Library of
America: New York, 1983), p. 506; and *Clarel: A Poem and Pilgrimage in the Holy Land*, ed. Harrison Hayford et al. (Evanson, Ill.,
1991), p. 461; Emerson, Journal, quoted in "Notes" to vol. VII of the
Centenary Edition of *Works*, ed. Edward W. Emerson (Boston, 1903),
p. 417, and "The Fortune of the Republic," in vol. XI of *Works*, ed.
James Elliot Cabot (Boston, 1883), 417, and "Resources," in *Works*,
ed. Cabot, VIII, 138.

29. Emerson, "Fortune of the Republic," *Works*, ed. Cabot, XI, 413.

30. Dorothy Ross, "The Liberal Tradition Revisited and the Republican
Tradition Addressed," in *New Directions in American Intellectual
History*, ed. John Higham and Paul K. Conkin (Baltimore, 1979), pp.
116, 131; Rush Welter, "The Idea of Progress," *Journal of the History
of Ideas*, XVI (1955), 414–15; Trachtenberg, *Incorporation of
America* (citing various labor leaders, Howells, and Douglass), pp.
219–220; Edmund S. Morgan, "Conflict and Consensus in the American Revolution," in *Essays on the American Revolution*, ed. S. G.
Kurtz and J. H. Hutson (New York, 1973), pp. 289–90; Aileen Kraditor, "American Historians on their Radical Heritage," *Past & Present*, LXVI (1972), 140–41.

31. Barthes, *Mythologies*, trans. Annette Lavers (London, 1972), p. 110.

32. Sniderman, *A Question of Loyalty* (Berkeley, 1981), pp. 104–141.

33. Warren Weaver, Jr., "Citizens Party Born in Unorthodox Way," *The New York Times*, April 13, 1980, p. 15.

3. The Ends of Puritan Rhetoric

1. Cotton Mather, *Magnalia Christi Americana; or, the Ecclesiastical History of New England, from its first planting, in the year 1620, unto the year of our Lord 1698, in seven books*, ed. Thomas Robbins (Hartford, 1853), I, 42, 43, 27, 44, 46.

2. John Foxe, quoted in William Haller, *Foxe's "Book of Martyrs" and the Elect Nation* (London, 1963), p. 110.

3. Larzer Ziff, "Upon What Pretext? The Book and Literary History," *Proceedings of the American Antiquarian Society*, XCV (1985), 308.

4. John Winthrop, "A Model of Christian Charity" (1630), in *Winthrop Papers*, ed. Stewart Mitchell (Massachusetts Historical Society, 1931), II, 295; Perry Miller, *Errand into the Wilderness* (Cambridge, Mass., 1958), p. 16.

5. Winthrop, "Model," in *Papers*, ed. Mitchell, II, 290, 294.

6. Johnson, *Wonder-Working Providence of Sion's Savior in New England, 1628–1651*, ed. J. Franklin Jameson (New York, 1910), p. 25.

7. Michael Wigglesworth, "God's Controversy," in *The Puritans, A Sourcebook of Their Writings*, ed. Perry Miller and Thomas H. Johnson (New York, 1963), II, 616; Nathaniel Hawthorne, *The Scarlet Letter; A Romance*, in *Novels*, ed. Millicent Bell (Library of America: New York, 1983), pp. 332–333.

8. Cotton Mather, *Theopolis Americana, An Essay on the Golden Street of the Holy City* (Boston, 1710), p. 9.

9. John Cotton, *God's Promise to His Plantations* (1630), in *Old South Leaflets*, III, no. 53 (Boston, [1896]), 17.

10. Mather, *Theopolis Americana*, p. 16.

11. Winthrop, "Model," in *Papers*, ed. Mitchell, p. 282; Mather, *Magnalia*, ed. Robbins, I, 118, and *Theopolis Americana*, p. 16; Jefferson, Letter to Henry Lee (May 8, 1825), in *Writings*, ed. Merrill Peterson (Library of America: New York, 1984), p. 1500.

12. Winthrop, quoted in Julius M. Pratt, "The Origins of 'Manifest Destiny'," *American Historical Review*, XXXII (1926–27), 795; Mel-

ville, *White-Jacket, or, The World in a Man-of-War*, in *Redburn, White-Jacket, Moby-Dick*, ed. G. Thomas Tanselle (Library of America: New York, 1983), p. 505; James "Americans Abroad," *The Nation*, XXVII (1878), 208–209.

13. Samuel Danforth, *A Brief Recognition of New England's Errand into the Wilderness*, in *The Wall and the Garden, Selected Massachusetts Election Sermons*, ed. A. William Plumstead (Minneapolis, 1968), pp. 57–62.

14. Herman Melville, *White-Jacket*, in *Redburn, White-Jacket, Moby-Dick*, ed. Tanselle, p. 506; John Adams to Thomas Jefferson, October 9, 1818, in *The Adams-Jefferson Correspondence*, ed. Lester J. Cappon (Chapel Hill, N.C., 1959), p. xliv; Thomas Paine, *Common Sense* (1776), in *Common Sense and Other Political Writings*, ed. Nelson F. Adkins (New York, 1953), p. 51; [John Louis O'Sullivan], "Annexation," *United States Magazine and Democratic Review*, XVII (1845), 5, and "The Great Nation of Futurity," *United States Magazine and Democratic Review*, VI (1839), 426; Ronald Reagan, "Closing Statement [to televised presidential debate]," *The New York Times*, September 22, 1980, p. B7.

15. Henry David Thoreau, *Walden; or Life in the Woods*, in *A Week, Walden, The Maine Woods, Cape Cod*, ed. Robert F. Sayre (Library of America: New York, 1985), p. 486; W. E. B. Du Bois, "Patriotism," *Crisis*, XVII no. 1 (1918), 10; Langston Hughes, quoted in Coretta Scott King, "King's Dream of Equality, Brotherhood is Really the American Dream," *Atlanta Journal and Constitution*, January 5, 1986, p. 7.

16. Mather, *Magnalia*, ed. Robbins, I, 44, 46.

4. Cotton Mather and the Vision of America

1. John Dunton, Letter of March 25, 1686, quoted in Julian H. Tuttle, "The Libraries of the Mathers," *Proceedings of the American Antiquarian Society*, n.s., XX (1910), 294; John Langdon Sibley, "Cotton Mather," in *Biographical Sketches of Graduates of Harvard University*, (Cambridge, Mass., 1885), III, 7; Cotton Mather, *Diary*, Massachusetts Historical Society Collections, Seventh Series, volumes 7 and 8 (Boston, 1911), I, 86. Here and throughout this essay, I have decided not to use ellipses to indicate omissions made in passages quoted from Mather's writings. Mather's habitual elaborations, cita-

tions in the "learned tongues," and baroque redundancies of expression would have made full quotation cumbersome. It would have been equally distracting, I believe, to record the numerous omissions by the use of ellipses. In all subsequent notes, Cotton Mather is abbreviated as CM. I use short titles throughout except for those works by CM which I discuss in detail.

2. CM, *Diary*, I, 86; CM, *Magnalia Christi Americana; or, the Ecclesiastical History of New England, from its first planting, in the year 1620, unto the year of our Lord 1698, in seven books*, ed. Thomas Robbins (Hartford, 1853) II, 277, 191; CM, *Diary* I, 87; CM, *Magnalia*, ed. Robbins, II, 7, 34, 142; CM, *Work Upon the Ark* (Boston, 1689), p. 2; CM, *Diary for the Year 1712*, ed. William R. Manierre II (Charlottesville, 1964), pp. 3, 125; CM *Diary*, II, 91; Barrett Wendell, *Cotton Mather: The Puritan Priest* (1891), ed. Alan Heimert (New York, 1963), pp. 170–171, 222 (quoting Samuel Mather); CM, *Diary*, II, 63–64.

3. CM, *The Sailours Companion* (Boston, 1709), p. 3; CM, *Diary* II, 14, 706–708.

4. Thomas Prince, *The Departure of Elijah Lamented* (Boston, 1728), p. 21.

5. Vernon Louis Parrington, *Main Currents in American Thought* (New York, 1930), I, 111; CM, *Diary*, II, 568.

6. CM, *Diary*, I, 201 and II, 712.

7. CM, *Diary*, I, 1, 200–201; *The Marrow of the Gospel* (Boston, 1727), p. 19; CM, *Diary*, I, 37, 39, 28–29, 479, 156, 479, and II, 579, 641.

8. Samuel Danforth, *A Brief Recognition of New England's Errand into the Wilderness* (Cambridge, Mass., 1671), p. 6; Increase Mather, "Morning Star," in *The Excellency of a Publick Spirit* (Boston, 1702), pp. 73–75; Increase Mather, *The Mystery of Israel's Salvation* (London, 1669), p. 102; John Higginson, *The Cause of God* (Cambridge, Mass., 1663), p. 11.

9. Higginson, *Cause of God*, p. 12; CM, *Diary*, I, 147, 6, 199–200, 548; CM, *Diary for the Year 1712*, ed. Manierre, p. 68; CM, *Diary*, I, 208, 113, 261–262, 233, 302, 207, 301, 302, 200.

10. CM, *Diary*, II, 387, 694, 69–70, 737–738, 695, 522, 577.

11. CM, "Paterna" quoted in Wendell, *Cotton Mather*, pp. 25–26.

12. CM, *Diary*, II, 522, 568, 577, 617, 655, 671, 761, 699, 731, 475–476,

705; CM, *Diary*, I, 515, 583; CM, *Diary for the Year 1712*, ed. Manierre, pp. 82–83.

13. CM, *Diary*, II, 585, 669, 699, 619–620, 706; CM, *Diary*, I, 424; CM, letter to Thomas Prince in *Diary*, II, 681; CM, *Diary*, I, 2–3, 51–52, 59, 50, 101, and II, 713, 753.

14. Norman Mailer, *Armies of the Night: History as the Novel, the Novel as History* (New York, 1968), p. 15.

15. CM, *Diary*, II, 259.

16. CM, *The Call of the Gospel* (Boston, 1686), p. 24; CM, *Diary for the Year 1712*, ed. Manierre, p. 50; CM, *The True Riches*, (Boston, 1724), p. 17; CM, *Diary*, II, 446, 264.

17. CM, *Diary*, I, 132; CM, *Une Grande Voix du Ciel a la France* (Boston, 1725), p. 1.

18. CM, *The Wonders of the Invisible World. Being an Account of the Tryals of Several Witches Lately Executed in New England* (London, 1693), pp. 3, 4, 12, 13, 14–15.

19. CM, *Wonders*, pp. 38, 80, 53, 194, 100, 80, 61, 65–66, 69–70, 75, 76, 77.

20. CM, *Wonders*, pp. 80, 92, 86–87, 83, 99, 84–85, 37, 125, 147, 37, 192, 196.

21. CM, *Wonders*, pp. 194, 38; CM, *Triumphs over Troubles* (Boston, 1701), Preface and p. 1; CM, *Diary*, I, 377.

22. CM, *Triumphs over Troubles*, Preface; CM, *Biblia Americana*, vol. IV, commentary on Isa. 62; quoted with permission of the Massachusetts Historical Society.

23. CM, *Wonders*, pp. 32–33; CM, *Decennium Luctuosum* (Boston, 1699), p. 21; CM, *Duodecennium Luctuosum* (Boston, 1714), p. 76.

24. CM, *The Call of the Gospel* (Boston, 1686), p. 24; CM, *The Declaration of the Gentlemen* (London, 1689), pp. 1, 22; CM, *The Boston Ephemeris* (Boston, 1683) p. xxiv.

25. CM, *Wonders*, p. 8; CM, *Present State*, pp. 34, 35, 36, 37, 33, 37.

26. CM, *The Serviceable Man* (Boston, 1690), p. 42; CM, *Present State*, p. 36; CM, *A Companion for Communicants* (Boston, 1690), Dedication, sigs. A^2 verso-A^3 recto.

27. CM, *Things for a Distres'd People to Think Upon* (Boston, 1696), pp. 27, 13; CM, *Things to be Look'd For* (Cambridge, Mass., 1691), pp. 25, 27, 25; CM, *Serviceable*, p. 28.

28. CM, *A Midnight Cry, An Essay For our Awakening out of that Sinful Sleep, To which we are at This Time too much disposed* (Boston, 1692), p. 42; CM, *The Wonderful Works of God Commemorated* (Boston, 1690), pp. 40–41; CM, *Companion*, p. 10; CM, *Things to be Look'd For*, p. 31; CM, *Things for a Distress'd People*, pp. 32, 34, 35–36, 38.

29. CM, *Eleutheria* (London, 1698), pp. 3, 27; CM, *Duty of Children*, pp. 49, 50.

30. CM, *Midnight Cry*, pp. 42, 54, 8, 15, 31.

31. CM, *Midnight Cry*, pp. 31, 8, 24, 62, 23, 24, 63, 23, 67, 66, 67.

32. CM, *Things to be Look'd For*, pp. 44, 45, 49; CM, *Midnight Cry*, pp. 32, 58, 23.

33. Henry James, *The American Scene*, ed. Irving Howe (New York, 1967), p. 37; Henry David Thoreau, *Walden*, in *A Week, Walden, Maine Woods, Cape Cod*, ed. Robert F. Sayre (Library of America: New York, 1985), p. 389; Walt Whitman, *Democratic Vistas*, in *Complete Poetry and Collected Prose*, ed. Justin Kaplan (Library of America: New York, 1982), pp. 990, 930.

34. Herman Melville, *White-Jacket, or, The World in a Man-of-War*, in *Redburn, White-Jacket, Moby-Dick*, ed. G. Thomas Tanselle (Library of America, 1983), p. 506; Ralph Waldo Emerson and Margaret Fuller, *The Dial*, I (1840), in Emerson, *Essays and Lectures*, ed. Joel Porte (Library of America: New York, 1983), pp. 1145–1146; CM, *Midnight Cry*, pp. 63, 59.

35. Edmund Morgan, *Visible Saints: The History of a Puritan Idea* (New York, 1963), p. 36 (quoting Increase Mather).

36. CM, *Duty of Children*, p. 69; CM, *The Way to Prosperity* (Boston, 1690), pp. 12–13; CM, *Duty of Children*, p. 52; CM, *Things for a Distres'd People*, pp. 60, 59.

37. Samuel Mather, *Life of Cotton Mather*, (Boston, 1729), p. 49.

38. John Cotton, "Christian Calling," in *The American Puritans*, ed. Perry Miller (New York, 1956), p. 176; George L. Kittredge, "Cotton Mather's Election into the Royal Society," *Publications of the Colonial Society of Massachusetts*, XIV (1913), 103; CM, *Manuductio Ad Ministerium: Directions for a Candidate of the Ministry* (Boston, 1726), pp. 4, 8,; CM, *Diary*, II, 372; CM, quoted in Phyllis Franklin, *Show Thyself a Man: A Comparison of Benjamin Franklin and Cot-*

ton *Mather* (Paris, 1969), p. 45; CM, *Bonifacius: An Essay upon the Good,* ed. David Levin (Cambridge, Mass., 1966), pp. 84, 86, 98–106.

39. CM, *Bonifacius,* ed. Levin, pp. 71, 52, 10, 75–78, 133, 8, 21, 36, 70, 113, 150, 8, 150.

40. CM, *Bonifacius,* ed. Levin, pp. 28, 29; *Durable Riches* (Boston, 1695), p. 12; CM, *Fisher-Man,* p. 22.

41. CM, *Bonifacius,* ed. Levin, pp. 7, 6, 17, 19–20, 12, 35, 101, 144, 113.

42. CM, *Bonifacius,* ed. Levin, pp. 57, 61, 66, 64, 67, 65; CM, quoted in Franklin, *Show Thyself a Man,* p. 50.

43. CM, *Bonifacius,* ed. Levin, pp. 64–65; Jonathan Edwards, "Life of Brainerd," in *The Works of President Edwards,* ed. S. Austin, (1808; reprint: New York, 1844), II, 381–83.

44. CM, letter to Sir Henry Ashurst (March, 1717), in *Diary,* II, 511; CM, quoted in Kuno Francke, *Cotton Mather and August Hermann Francke* (New York, 1897), pp. 56, 64; CM, quoted in Ernst Benz, "Ecumenical Relations Between Boston Puritanism and German Pietism: Cotton Mather and August Hermann Francke," *The Harvard Theological Review,* LIV (1961), 163–164, 166, 184; CM, *Diary* II, 413, 526, 329, 453.

45. CM, letter to Sir Henry Ashurst in *Diary,* II, 511.

46. CM, *Diary* I, 298, 301–02; CM, letter to John Winthrop Mather, August 15, 1716, quoted in Lee M. Friedman, "Cotton Mather and the Jews," *Publications of the American Jewish Historical Society,* XXVI (1918), 207.

47. CM, *Pasterium Americanum, The Book of Psalms In a Translation Exactly Conformed unto the Original; But All In Blank Verse, Fitted unto the Tunes commonly used in our Churches. Which Pure offering is accompanied with Illustrations, digging for "Hidden Treasures" in it; And Rules to Employ it upon the Glorious and Various Intentions of it* (Boston, 1718), pp. 264, xxx, vi, 92, 94, 102, 99, 196, 218, 261, 353; Eugene E. White, "Cotton Mather's *Manuductio ad Ministerium,*" *Quarterly Journal of Speech,* XLIX (1963), 308; CM, *Manuductio,* pp. 3, 6, 15, 121; *Psalterium,* pp. xxviii, xxix, xxx, xxxi, 40.

48. CM, *Psalterium,* pp. 208, 211, 213, 110, 123, 230, 239–40, 248, 295, 271, 307, 311, 313, 351–352, 354, 358, 256, 258, 260, 249.

49. CM, *Psalterium,* pp. 353, 356, 358, 360, 361–362, 363, 364, 366–67, 368, 369, 372, 374, 376, 378, 382, 385, 387, 390, 391, 393, 397, 399, 402, 405, 407, 409, 158, 42, xxxii–xxxiv.

50. CM, *Bonifacius*, ed. Levin, pp. 139, 154, 140, 157, 140, 45, 103, 132–133.

51. CM, *Bonafacius*, ed. Levin, pp. 110, 6, 33, 95, 141.

52. Ralph Waldo Emerson, *Nature*, in *Essays and Lectures*, ed. Porte, p. 21; CM, *Diary*, II, 668; CM, *Bonifacius*, ed. Levin, pp. 68, 142.

53. CM, *Bonifacius*, ed. Levin, p. 98; Theodore Hornberger, "Notes on the Christian Philosopher," quoted in Thomas James Holmes, *Cotton Mather, A Bibliography of his Works* (Cambridge, Mass., 1940), I, 134; Otho T. Beall, Jr. and Richard H. Shyrock, *Cotton Mather: First Significant Figure in American Medicine* (Baltimore, 1954), pp. 52, 20–21; CM, *Manuductio*, pp. 51, 50; *Bonifacius*, ed. Levin, p. 141; Theodore Hornberger, "The Date, the Source, and the Significance of Cotton Mather's Interest in Science," *American Literature*, VI (1935), 414; Kenneth B. Murdock, "Cotton Mather: Parson, Scholar, and Man of Letters," *Commonwealth History of Massachusetts*, ed. Albert B. Hart (New York, 1928), II, 324–326.

54. Beall and Shyrock, *Cotton Mather*, p. 125; CM, *The Christian Philosopher: A Collection of the Best Discoveries in Nature with Religious Improvements* (London, 1720), pp. 120, 30.

55. Theodore Hornberger, "The Effect of the New Science on the Thought of Jonathan Edwards," *American Literature*, IX (1937), 207; Kenneth B. Murdock, Introduction to *Cotton Mather: Selections*, ed. K.B. Murdock (New York, 1973), p. lii; CM, *Christian Philosopher*, p. 5; CM, *Diary for the Year 1712*, ed. Manierre, p. 67; CM, *Christian Philosopher*, pp. 5–6.

56. CM, *Christian Philosopher*, p. 11; Jonathan Edwards, "Images or Shadows," quoted in Mason I. Lowance, Jr., " 'Images or Shadows of Divine Things' in the Thought of Jonathan Edwards," in *Typology and Early American Literature*, ed. Sacvan Bercovitch (Amherst, Mass., 1972), p. 223; CM, *Christian Philosopher*, pp. 322, 125, 20, 149.

57. CM, *Christian Philosopher*, pp. 234, 235, 236, 16; Emerson, *Nature*, in *Essays and Lectures*, ed. Porte, p. 20; CM, *Christian Philosopher*, pp. 236, 17, 37, 85, 86.

58. CM, *Christian Philosopher*, pp. 21–22, 209–210, 148.

59. CM, *Bonifacius*, ed. Levin, pp. 161–163 ("Advertisement: Biblia Americana").

60. Sacvan Bercovitch, "Cotton Mather Against Rhyme: Milton and the *Psalterium Americanum*," *American Literature*, XXXIX (1967), 191–193.

61. CM, *Magnalia*, ed. Robbins, I, 417, 516; CM, *Manuductio*, pp. 46, 45.

62. CM, *Manuductio*, p. 45; CM, *Magnalia*, ed. Robbins, I, 255–56; CM, *Manuductio*, pp. 44–45.

63. CM, *Magnalia*, ed. Robbins, I, 31.

64. CM, *Manuductio*, p. 45; CM, *Magnalia*, ed. Robbins, II, 116; I, 30.

65. CM, *Magnalia*, ed. Robbins, I, 30; II, 635, 28; I, 65; II, 566 (for references to Homer, see for example I, 399, 482, 533, and II, 15–16, 343–44; for references to Virgil, see for example I, 34, 65, and II, 363, 535, 566); Nathaniel Hawthorne, *Grandfather's Chair*, in vol. VI of *Works*, ed. William Charvat, Roy Harvey Pearce, and Claude M. Simpson (Centenary Edition: Columbus, Ohio, 1972), p. 92.

66. CM, *Magnalia*, ed. Robbins, I, 46; CM, *Diary* I, 358; CM, *Magnalia*, ed. Robbins, I, 36, 27.

67. CM, *Magnalia*, ed. Robbins, I, 25–27.

68. CM, *Magnalia*, ed. Robbins, I, 27, 79; II, 509; I, 331; II, 57.

69. CM, *Magnalia*, ed. Robbins, II, 34, 142, 66; I, 157, 81, 163.

70. CM, *Magnalia*, ed. Robbins, I, 25, 332.

71. CM, *Magnalia*, ed. Robbins, II, 180, 207, 237, 277, 181, 313, 180.

72. CM, *Magnalia*, ed. Robbins, II, 447, 522, 470.

73. CM, *Magnalia*, ed. Robbins, I, 30, 46, 249; II, 653.

74. CM, *Magnalia*, ed. Robbins, II, 579.

75. CM, *Magnalia*, ed. Robbins, I 30; II, 653–654.

76. Whitman, *Democratic Vistas*, in *Complete Poetry and Collected Prose*, ed. Kaplan, p. 936.

77. Samuel Mather, *Life of Cotton Mather* (Boston, 1729), p. 6.

5. The Typology of Mission, from Edwards to Independence

1. Smith, "Millennarian Scholarship in America," *American Quarterly*, XVII (1965), 530, 537, 541–542 (quoting various Puritan ministers); Hubbard, *The Happiness of a People* (Boston, 1676), p. 61.

2. Adams, *The Necessity of Pouring Out the Spirit* (Boston, 1679), p. 35; James Allen, *New England's Choicest Blessing* (Boston, 1679), p. 13; Increase Mather, Preface to Samuel Torrey, *An Exhortation Unto Reformation* (Cambridge, Mass., 1674), sig. A1 recto; Cotton

Mather, *Theopolis Americana, An Essay on the Golden Street of the Holy City* (Boston, 1710), p. 3.

3. Edwards, Letter to William McCulloch, in *The Great Awakening*, vol. IV of *Works*, ed. C. C. Goen (New Haven, 1972), p. 560.

4. C. C. Goen, "Jonathan Edwards: A New Departure in Eschatology," *Church History*, XXVIII (1959), 32; Edwards, *A History of the Work of Redemption*, vol. IX of *Works*, ed. John F. Wilson (New Haven, 1989), pp. 479–480, and "An Humble Attempt," in *Apocalyptic Writings*, vol. V of *Works*, ed. Stephen J. Stein (New Haven, 1977), p. 330; Isaac Watts and John Goyse, Preface to Edwards, *A Faithful Narrative*, in *The Great Awakening*, vol. IV of *Works*, ed. C. C. Goen (New Haven, 1972), p. 133.

5. Alan Heimert, *Religion and the American Mind: From the Great Awakening to the Revolution* (Cambridge, Mass., 1966), pp. 64–66; Edwards, "An Humble Attempt to Promote Explicit Agreement and Visible Union of God's People in Extraordinary Prayer" (1747), in *Apocalyptic Writings*, vol. V of *Works*, ed. Stephen J. Stein (New Haven, 1977), p. 394; Edwards, *History of the Work of Redemption*, ed. Wilson, in *Works*, IX, 462, and *Some Thoughts Concerning the Present Revival of Religion in New England* (1740), in *The Great Awakening*, vol. IV of *Works*, ed. Goen, p. 358; Mather, *Magnalia Christi Americana*, ed. Thomas Robbins (Hartford, 1853), I, 42–43; Austin, "Advertisement" to Jonathan Edwards, *History of the Work of Redemption*, ed. Austin (New York, 1793), iv.

6. Alan Heimert, Introduction to Edwards, *Humble Inquiry*, in *The Great Awakening: Documents Illustrating the Crisis and its Consequences*, ed. Heimert and Perry Miller (Indianapolis, 1967), p. 424; "A Letter from the Ministers of Windham" (1745), in *The Great Awakening*, ed. Heimert and Miller, p. 401; Heimert, *Religion*, pp. 123–24 (citing Edwards and the Separates).

7. Miller, *Jonathan Edwards* (New York, 1949), p. 62; David Lyttle, "Jonathan Edwards on Personal Identity," *Early American Literature*, VII (1972), 165.

8. William Clebsch, *From Sacred to Profane America: The Role of Religion in American History*, (New York, 1968), p. 185; Roland Delattre, "Beauty and Politics: A Problematic Legacy of Jonathan Edwards," in *American Philosophy from Edwards to Quine*, ed. R. W. Shahan and K. R. Merrill (Norman, Okla., 1977), pp. 21–22; Clebsch, *From Sacred to Profane*, p. 144.

9. Cushing Strout, *The New Heavens and New Earth: Political Reli-*

gion in America (New York, 1975), p. 113; Edwards, *Some Thoughts Concerning the Revival,* in *The Great Awakening,* ed. C. C. Goen, *Works,* IV, 395, and *Images or Shadows of Divine Things,* ed. Perry Miller (New Haven, 1948), p. 102; Richard Bushman, *From Puritan to Yankee: Character and the Social Order in Connecticut* (Cambridge, Mass., 1967), pp. 37, 288; Edwards, *Some Thoughts Concerning the Revival,* in *The Great Awakening,* ed. Goen, *Works,* IV, 354–357; Robert Middlekauff, "The Ritualization of the American Revolution," in *The National Temper,* ed. Lawrence W. Levine and Middlekauff (New York, 1972), p. 103; Nathan O. Hatch, *The Sacred Cause of Liberty: Republican Thought and the Millennium in Revolutionary New England* (New Haven, 1977), passim.

10. William Smith, *Sermon XVI,* in *Works* (Philadelphia, 1803), II, 311–336; Edwards, *Images or Shadows,* ed. Miller, p. 92, and *Some Thoughts Concerning the Revival,* in *The Great Awakening,* ed. C. C. Goen, *Works,* IV, 357; Thomas Frink, *A Sermon Delivered at Stafford* (Boston, 1757), p. 4–5, and *A Sermon Preach'd Before His Excellency* (Boston, 1758), p. 30; Jonathan Mayhew, *A Sermon Preach'd* (Boston, 1754), p. 34; Michael McGiffert, *The Question of '76* (Williamsburg, Va., 1977), p. 10.

11. John Burt, *The Mercy of God* (Newport, R.I., 1759), p. 4; Nathaniel Appleton, *A Sermon Preach'd* (Boston, 1760), p. 36; Samuel Davies, *Sermons on Important Subjects* (Philadelphia, 1818), pp. 257–258; Nathan O. Hatch, "The Origins of Civil Millenialism in America: New England Clergymen, War with France, and the Revolution," *William and Mary Quarterly,* XXXI (1974), 417; Jonathan Mayhew, *Two Discourses* (Boston, 1759), p. 61; Charles Chauncy, *Marvellous Things* (Boston, 1745), p. 21.

12. Edwards, "Notes on the Apocalypse" and "Letter to a Correspondent in Scotland" (November 20, 1745), in *Apocalyptic Writings,* vol. V of *Works,* ed. Stein, 254–57, 267, 261, 449, 459.

13. David Hall, *Israel's Triumph* (Boston, 1761), p. 11; Paul Varg, "The Advent of Nationalism, 1758–1776," *American Quarterly,* XVI (1964), 180–81.

14. Jonathan Mayhew, *A Sermon Preach'd,* p. 23; Samuel Cooper, *A Sermon Before Thomas Pownall* (Boston, 1759), p. 48; Theodorus Frelinghuysen, *A Sermon on the Late Treaty* (New York, 1754), p. 9; Samuel Haven, *Joy and Salvation* (Portsmouth, N.H., 1763), p. 28; Matthias Harris, *A Sermon in Lewes* (Philadelphia, 1757), pp. 35–36.

15. Adams, *Adams Family Correspondence*, ed. L. H. Butterfield, (Cambridge, Mass., 1963–1973), II, 28; John and Abigail Adams, *Familiar Letters*, ed. Charles Francis Adams (New York, 1876), pp. 306, 403; Thomas Chittenden, broadside, quoted in Mason I. Lowance, Jr., Introduction to *Early Vermont Broadsides*, ed. John Duffy (Hanover, N.H., 1975), p. xvii.

16. Wood, *The Creation of the American Republic, 1776–1789* (1969; New York, 1972), pp. 107–108, 414; David Griffith, *Passive Obedience Considered* (Williamsburg, Va., 1776), p. 14; Jacob Duché, *The American Vine* (Philadelphia, 1775), p. 26; Jefferson, *Autobiography*, in *Writings*, ed. Merrill Peterson (Library of America: New York, 1984), p. 9; Paine, *Common Sense*, in *Common Sense and Other Political Writings*, ed. Nelson F. Adkins (New York, 1953), pp. 27, 23, 3.

17. Ramsay, *The History of the the American Revolution*, ed. Lester H. Cohen (1789; Indianapolis, 1990), I, 185; Austin, *The Millennium* (Elizabethtown, N.J., 1794), p. 415; Sherwood, *The Church's Flight* (New York, 1776), pp. 22–24.

18. Chandler Robbins, *A Sermon Preached at Plymouth* (Boston, 1794), pp. 16, 6–8; Samuel Cooper, *A Sermon Preached Before John Hancock* (New York, 1780), pp. 43–57; Robert Rantoul, quoted in Rush Welter, *The Mind of America, 1820–1860* (New York, 1975), p. 49; Wesley Frank Craven, *The Legend of the Founding Fathers* (New York, 1956), p. 71.

19. Emerson, "Journal 1826," in vol. III of *Journals*, ed. William H. Gilman and Alfred R. Ferguson (Cambridge, Mass., 1963), p. 14; Adams, *An Oration Delivered on July 4* (Newburyport, Mass., 1837), pp. 5–6; Dwight, *A Discourse on the National Fast* (New York, 1812), pp. 54, 55–56, and *A Discourse on Some Events of the Last Century* (New Haven, 1801), pp. 39–40, 42–43.

20. Dwight, *The Conquest of Canaan* (Hartford, 1785), I, 2–3, 755–57; X, 466, 524–30; Adams, quoted in *The American Revolution: A Search for Meaning*, ed. Richard J. Hooker (New York, 1970), pp. 11–12.

6. Continuing Revolution: George Bancroft and the Myth of Process

1. Gordon S. Wood, *The Creation of the American Republic, 1776–1787* (1969; New York, 1972), pp. 73, 299.

2. Ramsay, *History of the American Revolution*, ed. Lester H. Cohen (1789; Indianapolis, 1990), II, 638; Michael Paul Rogin, *Fathers and Children: Andrew Jackson and the Subjugation of the American Indian* (New York, 1975), p. 35; Adams, *Writings*, ed. Henry Alonzo Cushing (New York, 1908), IV, 315, 252; Dwight, *The Duty of Americans at the Present Crisis* (New Haven, 1798), p. 7; Dwight, *A Discourse in Two Parts* (New Haven, 1812), p. 45; Dwight, *A Discourse on Some Events of the Last Century* (New Haven, 1801) pp. 27, 31, 33; Bernard Bailyn, *The Ideological Origins of the American Revolution* (Cambridge, Mass., 1967), pp. 230–319.

3. Adams, *An Oration Delivered on July 4* (Newburyport, Mass., 1837), pp. 5–6.

4. Bancroft, *History of the United States from the Dicovery of the American Continent* (Boston, 1856–74), I, 358–361.

5. Quoted in Perry Miller, *The New England Mind: From Colony to Province* (1953; Boston, 1961), pp. 187–188; [O'Sullivan], "The Great Nation of Futurity," *United States Magazine and Democratic Review*, VI (1839); Herman Melville, *Pierre; Or, the Ambiguities*, in *Pierre, Israel Potter, The Confidence-Man, Piazza Tales, and Billy Budd*, ed. Harrison Hayford (Library of America: New York, 1984), p. 319 (my italics).

6. Austin, *The Millennium* (Elizabethtown, N.J., 1794), p. 394; Alcott, *Journals*, ed. Odell Shepard (Boston, 1938), pp. 40–41.

7. Bancroft, *History*, I, 117, 215; II, 144–145; III, 390; IV, 6–7, 13; V, 25, 429; VIII, 174–175, 323; X, 579.

8. Leonard Bacon, *Address* (1838), and Jonathan Prescott Hall, *Discourse* (1847), in *The New England Society Orations*, ed. Cephas Brainerd and Eveline Warner Brainerd (New York, 1901), I, 181, and II, 75–76.

9. Bancroft, *History*, V, 292; VI, 141; VII, 293; VI, 192; II, 85–86; I, 165, 174; V, 288; VII, 84; X, 37.

10. Beecher, *A Plea for the West* (Cincinnati, 1835), p. 10; Barnes, *On the Traffic in Ardent Spirits* (New York, [1834]), p. 20; Smith, quoted in Martin E. Marty, *Righteous Empire: The Protestant Experience in America* (New York, 1970), p. 123; Flint, *Recollections of the Last Ten Years* (1826), ed. C. Hartley Grattan (New York, 1932), p. 270; Catharine E. Beecher, *A Treatise on Domestic Economy* (Boston, 1842), pp. 36–37.

11. Benton, *The California Pilgrim: A Series of Lectures* (Sacramento, 1853), p. 14; Thoreau, *Walden*, in *A Week, Walden, Maine Woods, Cape Cod*, ed. Robert F. Sayre (Library of America: New York, 1985), p. 486.

12. W[illiam] E[vans] Arthur, *Oration on the Fourth of July* (Covington, Ky., 1850), pp. 6–7, 26.

13. Whitman, *Democratic Vistas* and "Poetry To-day in America—Shakspere [sic]—The Future," in *Complete Poetry and Collected Prose*, ed. Justin Kaplan (Library of America: New York, 1982), pp. 951–952, 1024.

14. Bancroft, *History*, V, 269, IV, 271, and X, 78; Leggett, Lieber, Nichols, Sedgwick, and Rantoul, quoted in Marvin Meyers, *The Jacksonian Persuasion: Politics and Belief* (1957; Stanford, 1960), pp. 24, 193, 172, 135, 127, 125, 148, 126, 170, 193, 173.

15. Thoreau, "Walking," *Excursions and Poems*, vol. V of *Writings*, ed. Bradford Torrey (New York, 1906), p. 219; Emerson, "The Fortune of the Republic," in *Works*, ed. Cabot, XI, 407–408; James Fenimore Cooper, *Home as Found* (New York, 1838), pp. 23–24; Emerson, "Fortune of the Republic," in *Works*, ed. Cabot, XI, 412.

7. The Return of Hester Prynne

1. Hawthorne, *The Scarlet Letter; A Romance*, in *Novels*, ed. Millicent Bell (Library of America: New York, 1983), p. 412; hereafter cited in text.

2. F. O. Matthiessen, *American Renaissance: Art and Expression in the Age of Emerson and Whitman* (New York, 1941), p. 276.

3. Kermode, *The Classic: Literary Images of Permanence and Change* (New York, 1975), p. 43.

4. Bakhtin, *Problems of Dostoevsky's Poetics*, ed. and trans. Caryl Emerson (Minneapolis, 1984), passim.

5. Hawthorne, vol. XVI of *Works, Letters, 1843–1853*, ed. Thomas Woodson, L. Neal Smith, and Norman Holmes Pearson, (Centenary Edition: Columbus, Ohio, 1985), p. 371.

6. Winthrop, *The History of New England*, ed. James Savage (Boston, 1825), I, 166, and "A Model of Christian Charity" (1630), in *Winthrop Papers*, ed. Stewart Mitchell (Massachusetts Historical Society, 1931), II, 283, 294.

7. Tocqueville, *Democracy in America*, ed. J. T. Mayer, trans. George Lawrence (Garden City, New York, 1969), p. 72; Chapin, *The Relation of the Individual to the Republic* (Boston, 1844), pp. 27, 31.

8. Hawthorne, *Life of Franklin Pierce* (1852), in *Works*, ed. George Parsons Lathrop (Boston, 1883), XII, 415.

9. Hawthorne, "Endicott and the Red Cross," in *Tales and Sketches*, ed. Roy Harvey Pearce (Library of America: New York, 1982), p. 548.

10. Hawthorne, "Oliver Cromwell," in vol. VI of *Works*, *True Stories from History and Biography*, ed. William Charvat et al., (Centenary Edition: Columbus, Ohio, 1980), pp. 9–10, 47–48.

11. Hawthorne, *Life of Pierce*, in *Works*, ed. Lathrop, XII, 413–428.

12. Melville, *Clarel: A Poem and Pilgrimage in the Holy Land*, ed. Harrison Hayford et al. (Evanston, Ill., 1991), pp. 267, 148; Larry J. Reynolds, *European Revolutions and the American Literary Renaissance* (New Haven, 1988), p. xii; David Morris Potter, *The Impending Crisis, 1848–1861*, ed. Don E. Fehrenbacher (New York, 1976), pp. 241–242.

13. Larry J. Reynolds, "The Scarlet Letter and Revolutions Abroad," *American Literature*, LXXVII (1985), 44–67.

14. Duyckinck letters (George to Evert, March 5, 1848, and Evert to George, April 18, 1848), in Reynolds, *European Revolutions*, pp. 10, 82; Bancroft (April 22, 1848), in Mark De Wolfe Howe, *The Life and Letters of George Bancroft* (New York, 1908), II, 91; George Ticknor to George S. Hillard (July 17, 1848), in *Life, Letters, and Journals of George Ticknor* (Boston, 1876), II, 234; Anon., "Revolutions Abroad," *New York Courier and Inquirer*, July 14, 1848, p. 1; Bancroft, in Howe, *Life and Letters*, II, 31, 33.

15. Anon., "The True Progress of Society," *The Biblical Repertory and Princeton Review*, XXIV (1852), 37, 21, 20; [Francis Bowen], "Mill's Political Economy," *North American Review*, LXVII (1848), 377, and "French Ideas of Democracy and a Community of Goods," *North American Review*, LXIX (1849), 281, 290; Anon., "Societary Theories," *The American Review: A Whig Journal*, VI, n.s. (1848), 645.

16. Anon., "Societary Theories," *American Review*, VI, 633, 640–641, 637.

17. Reynolds, *European Revolutions*, p. 55; *New York Herald*, reprinted in *History of Woman Suffrage*, ed. Elizabeth Cady Stanton, Susan B. Anthony, and Matilda Joslyn Gage, 6 vols. (New York, 1969), I, 805;

[Francis Bowen], "French Ideas of Democracy and a Community of Goods," *North American Review*, LXIX (1849), 324; Anon., "The True Progress of Society," *Biblical Repertory*, XXIV, 34, 37; *Rochester Democrat*, reprinted in *History of Woman Suffrage*, I, 804.

18. Matthiessen, *American Renaissance*, p. 13; Margaret Fuller Ossoli, *Memoirs*, ed. W. H. Channing, J. F. Clarke, and R. W. Emerson (Boston, 1850), II, 235, and *At Home and Abroad, or Things and Thoughts in America and Europe*, ed. A. B. Fuller (Boston, 1856), pp. 305–306, and *New York Tribune* Supplement (February 13, 1850) quoted in Bell Gale Chevigny, "To the Edges of Ideology: Margaret Fuller's Centrifugal Evolution," *American Quarterly*, XXXVIII (1986), 193; Ann Douglas, *The Feminization of American Culture* (New York, 1977), pp. 288–290.

19. Hawthorne, *Life of Pierce*, in *Works*, ed. Lathrop, XII, 415, and vol. XVI of *Works, Letters, 1843–1853*, ed. Thomas Woodson, L. Neal Smith, and Norman Holmes Pearson (Centenary Edition: Columbus, Ohio, 1985), p. 537.

20. Hawthorne, *Life of Pierce*, in *Works*, ed. Lathrop, p. 417.

21. James, *Hawthorne*, in *Essays on Literature: American Writers, English Writers*, ed. Leon Edel (Library of America: New York, 1984), p. 372.

22. Whittier, "The Kansas Emigrants," in *Complete Poetical Works* (Boston, 1894), p. 317; Lincoln, "Second Inaugural Address," in *Speeches and Writings, 1859–1865*, ed. Don E. Fehrenbacher (Library of America: New York, 1989), II, 687.

23. Bailyn, *The Ideological Origins of the American Revolution* (Cambridge, Mass., 1967), pp. 232–233; Morgan, *American Freedom/American Slavery: The Ordeal of Colonial Virginia* (New York, 1975), passim.

24. Melville, *Moby-Dick; or, The Whale*, in *Redburn, White-Jacket, Moby-Dick*, ed. G. Thomas Tanselle (Library of America: New York, 1983), pp. 1258, 969.

25. Macherey, *A Theory of Literary Production*, trans. Geoffrey Wall (London, 1978), passim; Fiedelson, "The Scarlet Letter," in *Hawthorne Centenary Essays*, ed. Roy Harvey Pearce (Columbus, Ohio, 1964), p. 62.

26. Mailer, *The Armies of the Night: History as the Novel, The Novel as History* (New York, 1968), p. 44; Thoreau, *Walden*, in *A Week*,

Walden, Maine Woods, Cape Cod, ed. Robert F. Sayre (Library of America: New York, 1985), p. 577; Emerson, *Nature*, in *Essays and Lectures*, ed. Joel Porte (Library of America: New York, 1983), p. 10; [O'Sullivan], "Annexation," in *United States Magazine and Democratic Review*, XVII, n.s. (1845); Gilpin (1846), quoted in Thomas L. Karnes, *William Gilpin, Western Nationalist* (Austin, Texas, 1970), p. 136.

27. Webster, Letters to Millard Fillmore (October 14, 1850), and William Kinney (November 23, 1850), in *Papers*, ed. Charles M. Wiltse and Michael J. Birkner (Hanover, N.H., 1986), VII, 160, 184; Merrill D. Peterson, *The Great Triumvirate: Webster, Clay, and Calhoun* (Oxford, 1987), pp. 103–108; John C. Calhoun, "Proposal to Restore a Sectional Equilibrium," in *Congressional Globe*, XXII, 451–455 (Part I, 1st session, 31st Congress); *Mobile Daily Register* (March 4, 1850), quoted in Avery Craven, "The Crisis," in *The Compromise of 1850*, ed. Edwin C. Rozwenc (Boston, 1957), pp. 14–15; Thomas Hart Benton, *Congressional Globe*, XXII, 21 (Part 1, 1st session, 31st Congress [1849–1850]); Rush Welter, *The Mind of America, 1820–1860* (New York, 1975), p. 361.

28. *Webster's Third New International Dictionary of the English Language*, Unabridged, ed. Philip Babcock Grove, et al., (Springfield, Mass., 1986); *An American Dictionary of the English Language*, revised and enlarged by Chauncey A. Goodrich and Noah Porter (Springfield, Mass., 1866); *An American Dictionary of the English Language*, revised and enlarged by Chauncey A. Goodrich (Springfield, Mass., 1849); Noah Webster, *An American Dictionary of the English Language*, 3rd edition, abridged from the Quarto Edition (New York, 1830).

29. Emerson, "The Fugitive Slave Law" (1854), in *Works*, ed. Cabot, XI, 216; Daniel Webster, "The Constitution and the Union" (March 7, 1850), "The Compromise Measures" (July 17, 1850), and "The Dignity and Importance of History" (February 23, 1852), in *Papers*, 4th ser., vol. II of *Speeches and Formal Writings*, ed. Charles M. Wiltse and Alan R. Berolzheimer (Hanover, N.H., 1988), pp. 515, 550, 576–577, 665.

30. Hawthorne, *Life of Pierce*, in *Works*, ed. Lathrop, XII, 414, and vol. XIV of *Works, French and Italian Notebooks*, ed. Thomas Woodson (Centenary Edition: Columbus, Ohio, 1980), p. 433 (September, 1858); Frank Preston Stearns, *The Life and Genius of Nathaniel Hawthorne* (Philadelphia, 1906), p. 261.

31. Lincoln, "A House Divided" (1858), in *Speeches and Writings, 1832–1858*, ed. Fehrenbacher, I, 426; Emerson, "John Brown," in *Works*, ed. Cabot, XI, 251–252; Noah Webster, *An American Dictionary of the English Language*. revised and enlarged by Chauncey A. Goodrich and Noah Porter (Springfield, Mass., 1866).

32. James, *Hawthorne*, in *Essays on Literature*, ed. Edel, p. 412; Hawthorne, vol. V of *Works*, *Our Old Home*, ed. William Charvat (Centenary Edition: Columbus, Ohio, 1970), p. 4.

33. Hawthorne, Preface to *The Marble Faun, or, The Romance of Monte Beni*, in *Novels*, ed. Bell, p. 854, and "Chiefly About War Matters" (1862), in *Works*, ed. Lathrop, XII, 299.

34. Sherwood, *The Church's Flight into the Wilderness* (Boston, 1776), p. 31; Paine, *Common Sense*, in *Common Sense and Other Political Writings*, ed. Nelson F. Adkins (New York, 1953), pp. 25–27; Jackson, "Second Annual Message" (December 6, 1830), in *Antebellum American Culture: An Interpretive Anthology*, ed. David Brion Davis (Lexington, Ky., 1979), p. 241; Emerson, "The Method of Nature," in *Essays and Lectures*, ed. Porte, p. 124.

35. Emerson, "The Fugitive Slave Law," in *Works*, ed. Cabot, XI, 224–230.

36. Howe, "Battle Hymn of the Republic," in *Parnassus*, ed. Ralph Waldo Emerson (Boston, 1875), p. 230.

37. Horatio Bridge, *Personal Recollections of Nathaniel Hawthorne* (New York, 1893), p. 112.

38. Hawthorne, "Chiefly About War Matters," in *Works*, ed. Lathrop, XII, 319.

8. *Pierre,* or the Ambiguities of American Literary History

1. Herman Melville, *Mardi, and a Voyage Thither*, in *Typee, Omoo, Mardi*, ed. G. Thomas Tanselle (Library of America: New York, 1982), pp. 1252–1263.

2. Melville, *Pierre; or, The Ambiguities*, in *Pierre, Israel Potter, The Piazza Tales, The Confidence-Man, Uncollected Prose, Billy Budd*, ed. Harrison Hayford (Library of America: New York, 1984), p. 3. All further references to *Pierre* are cited in the text. In quoting from

other works in this volume, I refer to the volume as *Melville*, ed. Hayford.

3. Melville to Richard Bentley, in *The Letters of Herman Melville*, ed. William H. Gilman and Merrill R. Davis (New Haven, 1960), p. 150.

4. Melville to Sophia Hawthorne, in *Letters*, ed. Gilman and Davis, p. 146; Evert and George Duyckinck, unsigned review, New York *Literary World* (August 21, 1852), reprinted in Herschel Parker, *The Recognition of Herman Melville* (Ann Arbor, Mich., 1967). pp. 51–56; anonymous review, Boston *Post* (August 4, 1852), in Brian Higgins, *Herman Melville: An Annotated Bibliography* (New York, 1979), p. 118; Peck, unsigned review (November, 1852), *American Whig Review*, reprinted in *Melville: The Critical Heritage*, ed. Watson G. Branch (London, 1974), pp. 316–317; Anon., New York *Day Book* (September 7, 1852), IV, no. 948; Robert Milder, "Melville's Intentions in *Pierre*," *Studies in the Novel*, VI (1974), pp. 192–193.

5. Melville, "The Piazza," in *Melville*, ed. Hayford, p. 623.

6. Melville to Richard Bentley, in Jay Leyda, *The Melville Log: A Documentary Life of Herman Melville, 1819–1891* (New York, 1951), I, 448.

7. See E.D.E.N. Southworth, *The Discarded Daughter* (New York, 1852), pp. 157, 168–169; Henry William Herbert, *Pierre the Partisan* (New York, 1848), pp. 16–18; Sara Payson Willis (Fanny Fern), *Rose Clark* (New York, 1856), pp. 275–77; Ann S. Stephens, *Bellehood and Bondage* (Philadelphia, 1873), p. 435; Maria Cummins, *The Lamplighter* (New York, 1850), pp. 47–49; Catharine Maria Sedgwick, *Married or Single?* (New York, 1840), p. 40.

8. David S. Reynolds, *Beneath the American Renaissance: The Subversive Imagination in the Age of Emerson and Melville* (New York, 1986), pp. 159–161, 292–294; Marc Shell, *The End of Kinship: "Measure for Measure," Incest and the Ideal of Universal Siblinghood* (Oxford, 1991), pp. 21–24, and "Those Extraordinary Twins," *Arizona Quarterly*, XLVII (1991), 44–47.

9. Ralph Waldo Emerson, "Self-Reliance," in *Essays and Lectures*, ed. Joel Porte (Library of America: New York, 1983), pp. 273, 272, 262.

10. Wordsworth, *The Prelude: or the Growth of a Poet's Mind*, XIV. 42, 45, 67, 70–74, ed. Ernest de Selincourt (Oxford, 1959), pp. 483, 485; *The Vision of Dante, Hell*, XXXI, trans. Henry F. Clay (New York, 1850), p. 206.

11. Keats, letter to Richard Woodhouse, in *Letters*, ed. Maurice B. Forman (Oxford, 1935), p. 227; Melville, marginalia to Milton's *Paradise Lost*, IX, 703 ff. and VI, 645–60; Keats, *Hyperion*, ll. 353–54, 34–35, 303–04, in *Poetical Works*, ed. H.W. Garrod (Oxford, 1939); Thoreau, *Journals*, IV, 161, in *Writings*, ed. Bradford Torrey (New York, 1906), and *A Week on the Concord and Merrimack Rivers*, in *A Week, Walden, Maine Woods, Cape Cod*, ed. Robert F. Sayre (Library of America: New York, 1985), p. 153.

12. *The Vision of Dante, Paradise*, ed. Clay, XXXII, p. 564.

13. All of these references have been documented in essays and notes listed in the standard bibliographical guides; see further the "Historical Note" by Leon Howard and Herschel Parker to the Northwestern Edition of *Pierre, or, The Ambiguities*, ed. Harrison Hayford, Herschel Parker, and G. Thomas Tanselle (Evanston, Ill., 1971) and Henry A. Murray's detailed notes to his Hendricks House edition of *Pierre* (New York, 1949).

14. Whitman, "Song of Myself," in *Complete Poetry and Collected Prose*, ed. Justin Kaplan (Library of America: New York, 1982), p. 213.

15. Shelley, "Mont Blanc: Lines Written in the Vale of Chamouni," l. 62, in *Works*, ed. Roger Ingpen and Walter E. Peck (New York, 1927), I, 230; John W. Carson, "Loiterings in Europe," *Democratic Review*, XXIII (July, 1848), 73 (on Coleridge); Judd, *Margaret: A Tale of the Real and the Ideal, Blight and Bloom; Including Sketches of a Place Not Before Described Called MONS CHRISTI* (Boston, 1845), p. 457; Poe, "The Haunted Palace," and "The Fall of the House of Usher," in *Poetry and Tales*, ed. Patrick F. Quinn (Library of America: New York, 1984), p. 326, and "Letter to B____," in *Essays and Reviews*, ed. G. R. Thompson (Library of America: New York, 1984), p. 5; Grey, "The Bard: A Pindaric Ode," in *Poetical Works*, ed. Austin A. Pool (Oxford, 1917), p. 57; Wordsworth, *Prelude*, ed. de Selincourt, XIV. 80, 74–75, 77, p. 485; Sedgwick, quoted in J. E. A. Smith, *History of Berkshire Country* (New York, 1885), I, 13.

16. *The Natural History of Pliny*, trans. John Bostock and H.T. Riley (London, 1855–57), V, 328–29; Bacon, "Memnon; or The Early-Ripe," in *Works*, ed. J. Spedding, R. L. Ellis, and D. D. Heath (New York, 1968), VI, 726–727. For further inversions in Melville's account, compare Bacon's Memnon with *Pierre*'s implicit parallels between Memnon and Enceladus (pp. 134–135, 346).

17. Southworth, *Discarded Daughter*, p. 20; Shelley, "Mont Blanc," *Works*, ed. Ingpen and Peck, ll. 139–141, 142–144, I, 233; Lowell, "A Fable for Critics," in *Poetical Works* (Boston, 1873), p. 139 (see also Lowell's indentifications of Emerson with Plotinus in "Emerson as Lecturer," in *Writings* [Cambridge, Mass., 1890], I, 349–360); Emerson, Journal C (1837), in vol. V of *Journals*, ed. Merton M. Sealts, Jr. (Cambridge, Mass., 1965), p. 336.

18. Melville, "Hawthorne and his Mosses," in *Melville*, ed. Hayford, pp. 1158–1160.

19. Melville, "Hawthorne and His Mosses," in *Melville*, ed. Hayford, pp. 1157–1161.

20. Emerson, Blotting Book III (1832), in vol. III of *Journals*, ed. William H. Gilman and Alfred R. Ferguson (Cambridge, Mass., 1963), p. 327 and Journal C (1837), *Journals*, V, 278; "The Over-Soul" and "Intellect," in *Essays and Lectures*, ed. Porte, pp. 396, 427.

21. Emerson, "Quotation and Originality," in The Centenary Edition of *Works*, ed. Edward W. Emerson (Boston, 1903), VIII, 176 (the headnote is a quotation from "Plato on the Philosopher," in *Essays and Lectures*, ed. Porte, p. 634); Whitman, "Song of Myself," in *Complete Poetry and Collected Prose*, ed. Kaplan, p. 190; Barbara Packer, *Emerson's Fall: A New Interpretation of the Major Essays* (New York, 1982), p. 117.

22. Emerson, "Experience" and "Art," in *Essays and Lectures*, ed. Porte, pp. 487, 436.

23. Emerson, *Nature*, "The Poet," and "Intellect," in *Essays and Lectures*, ed. Porte, pp. 34–35, 465–466, 427; Emerson, quoted in James R. Saucerman, "A Note on Emerson's Use of Lyell," *American Notes and Queries*, XX (1981), 50–52; Emerson, "The Poet," in *Essays and Lectures*, ed. Porte, p. 457.

24. Melville, *Mardi*, in *Typee, Omoo, Mardi*, ed. Tanselle, pp. 1316, 957–958.

25. Bunyan, *The Pilgrim's Progress*, ed. Roger Sharrock (Oxford, 1966); John Leycester [Josiah Ricraft], *The Civill Warres of England* (London, 1649), p. A2.

26. Whitman, 1855 "Preface" and "Leaves of Grass," in *Complete Poetry and Collected Prose*, ed. Kaplan, pp. 25, 87.

27. Emerson, Journal C (1837), in *Journals*, V, 278; Stephen E. Whicher, *Freedom and Fate: An Inner Life of Ralph Waldo Emerson* (Second

Edition: Philadelphia, 1971), p. 31; Emerson, Journal D (1838), in vol. VII of *Journals*, ed. A. W. Plumstead and Harrison Hayford (Cambridge, Mass., 1969), p. 77; "Self-Reliance" and *Nature*, in *Essays and Lectures*, ed. Porte, pp. 489–490, 5; Emerson, Journal C (1837), in *Journals*, V, 333.

28. Melville, *Letters*, ed. Davis and Gilman, pp. 124–125, 143; Sanford E. Marovitz, "Melville's Problematic *'Being,'* " *ESQ*, XXVIII (1982), 17–18; Coleridge, *Hints Towards the Formation of a More Comprehensive Theory of Life*, ed. Seth B. Watson (Philadelphia, 1848), pp. 86–87, and *Biographia Literaria*, in *Complete Works*, ed. W. G. T. Shedd (New York, 1853), III, 348; Whitman, *Democratic Vistas*, in *Complete Poetry and Collected Prose*, ed. Kaplan, p. 960; A. B. Packard, Jr., "Colossal Cuttlefish," *American Naturalist* (Salem, Mass., 1873), VII, 87–95; Erich Pontoppidon, *The Natural History of Norway* (London, 1755), Part II, pp. 200–210; "Kraken," *Encyclopaedia Brittanica* (Seventh Edition, 1842), XII, 763.

29. Hawthorne, quoted in Leyda, *Melville Log*, II, 529.

30. Foucault, *The Order of Things: An Archaeology of the Human Sciences* (New York, 1970), p. xxiii; Melville, *Moby-Dick, or The Whale*, in *Redburn, White-Jacket, and Moby-Dick*, ed. G. Thomas Tanselle (Library of America: New York, 1983), p. 1307.

31. Evert and George Duyckinck, review of *Pierre*, in *Melville*, ed. Branch, p. 301; Hawthorne, "A Select Party," in *Tales and Sketches*, ed. Roy H. Pearce (Library of America: New York, 1982), p. 952.

32. Rourke, *American Humor: A Study of the National Character* (New York, 1931), p. 64.

33. Barbara Novak, *Nature and Culture: American Landscape Painting, 1825–1875* (New York, 1980), p. 94; David Huntington, *The Landscapes of Frederick Edwin Church: Vision of an American Era* (New York, 1960), pp. 16, 49; Cole, "Essay on American Scenery," *American Monthly Magazine*, n.s., I (January, 1836), 1–2.

34. Huntington, *Landscapes*, pp. xi, 20, 16, 48–49; Barbara Novak, *American Painting in the Nineteenth Century: Realism, Idealism, and the American Experience* (New York, 1979), p. 47 (on "The Geological Timetable: Rocks").

35. Whitman, *Specimen Days*, in *Complete Poetry and Collected Prose*, ed. Kaplan, pp. 855–56; Thoreau, *The Maine Woods*, in *A Week, Walden, Maine Woods, Cape Cod*, ed. Robert F. Sayre (Library of America: New York, 1985), p. 646; Emerson, "Monadnoc" (1838),

and "Aristocracy" (1848), in *Works*, ed. James Elliot Cabot (Boston, 1883), IX, 61; X, 62, and "Literary Ethics" in *Essays and Lectures*, ed. Porte, pp. 95–96; Melville, "Hawthorne and His Mosses," in *Melville*, ed. Hayford, p. 1169.

36. Melville, "Hawthorne and His Mosses," in *Melville*, ed. Hayford, p. 1169.

37. Paine, *Common Sense*, in *Common Sense and Other Political Writings*, ed. Nelson F. Adkins (New York, 1953), pp. 19, 40; Emerson, "The Young American," in *Essays and Lectures*, ed. Porte, pp. 213–230; Sedgwick, *The Poor Rich Man and the Rich Poor Man* (New York, 1837), p. 105.

38. Melville, *White-Jacket*, in *Redburn, White-Jacket, Moby-Dick*, ed. Tanselle, p. 506.

39. I. Mather, "Morning Star," in *The Excellency of a Publick Spirit* (Boston, 1702), p. 73; Edwards, *Images or Shadows of Divine Things*, ed. Perry Miller (New Haven, 1948), p. 102; Dwight, "Greenwood Hill" (1794), in *Major Poems*, ed. William McTaggart and William K. Bottarf (Gainesville, Fla., 1969), pp. 511, 516; Emerson, "The American Scholar," in *Essays and Lectures*, ed. Porte, p. 53; Thoreau, *Walden*, in *A Week, Walden, Maine Woods, Cape Cod*, ed. Sayre, p. 316; Bancroft, *History of the United States from the Discovery of the American Continent* (Boston, 1856–74), III, 394 and VI, 243.

40. Melville, *Mardi*, in *Typee, Omoo, Mardi*, ed. Tanselle, p. 1166, and *Moby-Dick*, in *Redburn, White-Jacket, Moby-Dick*, ed. Tanselle, p. 1405.

41. Howard and Parker, "Historical Note," *Pierre*, ed. Hayford, Parker, Tanselle, p. 377; Michael Paul Rogin, *Subversive Genealogy: The Politics and Art of Herman Melville* (New York, 1983), p. 62.

42. Richard Chase, *Herman Melville: A Critical Study* (New York, 1949), p. 128.

43. Howard and Parker, "Historical Note," *Pierre*, ed. Hayford, Parker, Tanselle, p. 370.

44. Melville, *Israel Potter, His Fifty Years of Exile*, in *Melville*, ed. Hayford, p. 425; "The Piazza," in *Melville*, ed. Hayford, p. 621; and *Moby-Dick*, in *Redburn, White-Jacket, Moby-Dick*, ed. Tanselle, p. 772.

45. Hawthorne, quoted in Leyda, *Melville Log*, II, 529.

46. Melville, "Hawthorne and His Mosses," in *Melville*, ed. Hayford, p.

1160, and letters to Shaw and Hawthorne in *Letters*, ed. Davis and Gilman, pp. 92, 143; Harrison Hayford and Hershel Parker, notes to the Northwestern Edition of *Moby-Dick*, ed. Hayford, G. Thomas Tanselle, and Parker (Evanston, Ill., 1988), p. 901; Melville, *Moby-Dick*, in *Redburn, White-Jacket, Moby-Dick*, ed. Tanselle, p. 1318.

9. Emerson, Individualism, and Liberal Dissent

1. Emerson, Journal N (1842), in vol. VIII of *Journals*, ed. William Gilman and J. E. Parsons (Cambridge, Mass., 1970), p. 249; Koenraad W. Swart, "Individualism in the Mid-Nineteenth Century," *Journal of the History of Ideas*, XXIII (1962), 81; Steven Lukes, *Individualism* (Oxford, 1973), pp. 4, 6; Joseph de Maistre, "Extrait d'une conversation" (1820), in *Oeuvres complètes* (Lyon, 1884–1887), XIV, 286; Félicité Robert de Lamennais, *Des Progrès de la révolution et de la guerre contre l'église* (1829), in *Oeuvres complètes* (Paris, 1836–1837), IX, 17–18; Alexandre de Saint-Cheron, "Philosophie du droit," *Revue encyclopédique*, LII (1831), 600.

2. Tocqueville, *Democracy in America*, ed. J. T. Mayer, trans. George Lawrence (Garden City, NY, 1969), p. 507; Frank E. Manuel, *The Prophets of Paris: Turgot, Condorcet, Saint-Simon, Fourier, and Comte* (New York, 1962), p. 105; Pierre Claude Victoire Boiste, *Dictionnaire Universel de la Langue Française*, Huitième Édition, rev. Charles Nodier (Paris, 1834); J. B. Millière, *Ann. Ass. Nat.*, XXV, 547 (1870), quoted in Jean Dubois, *Le Vocabulaire Politique et Social en France de 1869 à 1872* (Paris, 1962), p. 322; Maxmilien Paul Émile Littré, *Dictionnaire de la Langue Française* (Paris, 1869); Étienne Cabet, *Salut par l'union* (1845), quoted in Dubois, *Vocabulaire Politique*, p. 322.

3. Emerson, Journal N (1842), in *Journals*, VIII, 251.

4. Emerson, Journal CO (1851), in vol. XI of *Journals*, ed. A. William Plumstead and William H. Gilman (Cambridge, Mass., 1975), pp. 371, 372, 374.

5. Anon., "The Course of Civilization," *The United States Magazine and Democratic Review*, VI (1839), 211, 208, 209, 214, 209.

6. Anon., "Course of Civilization," p. 209; Emerson, "Circles," in *Essays and Lectures*, ed. Joel Porte (Library of America: New York, 1983), p. 413.

7. Richard Poirier, *The Renewal of Literature: Emersonian Reflections* (New Haven, 1988), p. 172, quoting Emerson; *Boston Evening Transcript*, May 25, 1903, p. 3 (this is the reporter's summary of James's address); Emerson, Journal E (1842), in vol. VII of *Journals*, ed. A. William Plumstead and Harrison Hayford (Cambridge, Mass., 1969), p. 482; "The Individual," in vol. II of *Early Lectures*, ed. Stephen Whicher, Robert E. Spiller, and Wallace Williams (Cambridge, Mass., 1964), pp. 174–175, 176, 186; and Journal B (1836), in vol. V of *Journals*, ed. Merton M. Sealts, Jr. (Cambridge, Mass., 1965), p. 190.

8. Arieli, *Individualism and Nationalism in American Ideology* (Cambridge, Mass., 1964); Kateb, "Thinking about Human Extinction (II): Emerson and Whitman," *Raritan*, VI (1987), 1–22; Dumont, *Essays on Individualism: Modern Ideology in Anthropological Perspective* (Chicago, 1986); Pierre Paul Royer-Collard, quoted in François Pierre Guillaume Guizot, *General History of Civilization in Europe* (New York, 1840), p. 31; Alexandre Vinet, *Essais de Philosophie Morale et de Morale Religieuse* (Paris, 1837), pp. 148, 152, 155.

9. Vinet, *Essais de Philosophie Morale*, pp. 152–154; Marx, *Manifesto of the Communist Party*, in *The Marx-Engels Reader*, ed. Robert C. Tucker (New York, 1978), p. 491, and *Grundrisse: Foundations of Political Economy* (1857–1858), trans. N. Nicolous (New York, 1973), p. 158; John Stuart Mill, *On Liberty* (1859), ed. Currin V. Shields (New York, 1956), pp. 69, 77, 78, 80, 86.

10. Mill, *On Liberty*, ed. Shields, p. 81, *Principles of Political Economy with some of their Applications to Social Philosophy* (Boston, 1848), II, 514 (V, xi, 1), and *On Liberty*, ed. Shields, pp. 86, 90; Saint-Cheron, "Philosophie du droit," p. 29; Vinet, quoted in Swart, "Individualism," *Journal of the History of Ideas*, XXIII, 84–85.

11. Arieli, *Individualism and Nationalism*, p. 233; Leroux, "De la philosophie et du Christianisme," *Revue encyclopédique*, LV (1832), 303, 308–319, and "De l'individualisme et du socialisme" (1834), reprinted as appendix in David Owen Evans, *Le socialisme romantique: Pierre Leroux et ses contemporains* (Paris, 1948), pp. 223–232.

12. Emerson, Wide World 7 (1822), in vol. II of *Journals*, ed. William H. Gilman, Alfred R. Ferguson, and Merrell R. Davis (Cambridge, Mass., 1961), p. 3, and "Experience" and "The American Scholar," in *Essays and Lectures*, ed. Porte, pp. 485, 71, 53.

13. Emerson, "The Young American," in *Essays and Lectures*, ed. Porte, p. 217.

14. Emerson, "Wealth," in *Essays and Lectures*, ed. Porte, p. 1003; Journal F 2 (1840), in *Journals*, VII, 514; Journal A (1834), in vol. IV of *Journals*, ed. Alfred R. Ferguson (Cambridge, Mass., 1964), p. 332; Journal H (1841), in *Journals*, VIII, 137; Journal B (1836), in *Journals*, V, 237, 238, 260, 203; "Trades and Professions," in *Early Lectures*, ed. Spiller, Whicher, and Williams, II, 113–128, 124; and "Self-Reliance," in *Essays and Lectures*, ed. Porte, p. 281.

15. Emerson, Journal E (1839–1840) and Journal D (1839) in *Journals*, VII, 331–332, 334, 224, 281, 304, and "Character," in *Essays and Lectures*, ed. Porte, p. 500.

16. John T. Flanagan, "Emerson and Communism," *New England Quarterly*, X (1937), 243, 245; Emerson, *Letters*, ed. Ralph L. Rusk (New York, 1939), II, 322 (to Margaret Fuller, August 4, 1840); Journal E (1840–1841), in *Journals*, VII, 350, 342, 436; "Ode: Inscribed to W. H. Channing," in vol. IX of *Works*, ed. James Elliot Cabot (Boston, 1883), p. 73; and "Man the Reformer" (January 25, 1841), in *Essays and Lectures*, ed. Porte, pp. 136–137.

17. Emerson, Journal A (1834), in *Journals*, IV, 342; Journal E (1840), in *Journals*, VII, 342; "Politics," in vol. III of *Early Lectures*, ed. Robert E. Spiller and Wallace E. Williams (Cambridge, Mass., 1972), p. 242; William James, speech printed in the *Boston Evening Transcript*, May 25, 1903, p. 3; Emerson, Journal E (1839), in *Journals*, VII, 282; "Man the Reformer" (January 25, 1841) and "Lecture on the Times" (December 2, 1841) in *Essays and Lectures*, ed. Porte, pp. 139, 148–149, 167; *Letters*, ed. Rusk, II, 335 (to William Emerson, September 24, 1840), and III, 104–105 (to Margaret Fuller, December 21, 1842); and Journal E (1840), in *Journals*, VII, 394–395.

18. Emerson, "Reforms" (January 15, 1840), in *Early Lectures*, ed. Spiller and Williams, III, 260; *Letters*, ed. Rusk, II, 322 (to Margaret Fuller, August 4, 1840); "Politics," in *Early Lectures*, ed. Spiller and Williams, III, 246; and *Letters*, ed. Rusk, II, 389 (to William Emerson, March 30, 1841).

19. Emerson, *Letters*, ed. Rusk, III, 146 (to Margaret Fuller, February 12, 1843); John C. Gerber, "Emerson and the Political Economists," *New England Quarterly*, XXII (1940), 352.

20. John L. Brown, "The Life of Paradise Anew," in *France and North America: Utopias and Utopians*, ed. Mathé Allain (Lafayette, La., 1978), p. 79; Hawthorne, *The Blithedale Romance*, in *Novels*, ed. Millicent Bell (Library of America: New York, 1983), pp. 686, 830.

21. Emerson, Journal K (1842), in *Journals*, VIII, 209; and "Fourierism and the Socialists" and "New England Reformers" in *Essays and Lectures*, ed. Porte, pp. 1207, 593, 591, 596, 592, 591, 599.

22. Emerson, Notebook JK (1843–1847) and Journal GH (1847), in vol. X of *Journals*, ed. Merton M. Sealts, Jr. (Cambridge, Mass., 1973), pp. 378, 154.

23. Emerson, Journal O (1846–1847) and Journal V (1844?1845?), in vol. IX of *Journals*, ed. Ralph H. Orth and Alfred R. Ferguson (Cambridge, Mass., 1971), pp. 424, 402, 100; Gerber, "Emerson and the Political Economists," pp. 355, 338; Emerson, Journal RS (1848), in *Journals*, XI, 45, 9; "Politics," in *Essays and Lectures*, ed. Porte, pp. 569, 562, 567; Journal O (1847), in *Journals*, IX, 391; "Wealth" and "The Young American" in *Essays and Lectures*, ed. Porte, pp. 999–1000, 221; Wide World 10 (1823) in *Journals*, II, 138; Journal RS (1848), in *Journals*, XI, 41, "The Young American," in *Essays and Lectures*, ed. Porte, p. 219; and "Character" (1866), in *Works*, ed. Cabot, X, 118–119.

24. Emerson, "Introductory" to "The Present Age" (December 4, 1839), in *Early Lectures*, ed. Spiller and Williams, III, 189, and "Historic Notes of Life and Letters in New England," in *Works*, ed. Cabot, X, 308–309.

25. Emerson, Journal GH (1847), in *Journals*, X, 154; "Historic Notes," in *Works*, ed. Cabot, X, 308; Journal AB (1847), in *Journals*, X, 8 (citing the *Writings of Hugh Swinton Legaré*); "Historic Notes," in *Works*, ed. Cabot, X, 308, 311; and Journal RS (1849) and Journal AZ (1849?), in *Journals*, XI, 77, 201.

26. Emerson, "The Individual," in *Early Lectures*, ed. Spiller, Whicher, and Williams, II, 175–176; Journal B (1836), in *Journals*, V, 190; Journal BO (1850), in *Journals*, XI, 313–314; "Historic Notes," in *Works*, ed. Cabot, X, 308; "Circles," in *Essays and Lectures*, ed. Porte, p. 413; Journal GH (1847), in *Journals*, X, 154; Journal CO (1851) and Journal AZ (1850), in *Journals*, XI, 392, 267, 406, 407.

27. Emerson, "The Young American," in *Essays and Lectures*, ed. Porte, pp. 216–217, 214, 217, 219, 217, 228, 222.

28. Emerson, "The Young American," in *Essays and Lectures*, ed. Porte, pp. 224, 228, 221, 217, 226, 217–218, 226, 217, 226, 221, 228.

29. Emerson, "Ability," in *Essays and Lectures*, ed. Porte, p. 810; Journal LM (1848), in *Journals*, X, 310; "Aristocracy," in *Works*, ed. Cabot, X, 64; Journal LM (1848), in *Journals*, X, 310; "Historic Notes," in

Works, ed. Cabot, X, 327; Journal LM (1848), in *Journals*, X, 310; "Historic Notes," in *Works*, ed. Cabot, X, 336; Journal LM (1848), in *Journals*, X, 312, 318; "Politics and Socialism," Houghton Library ms. 200 (8), leaves 95, 101, quoted in Larry J. Reynolds, *European Revolutions and The American Literary Renaissance* (New Haven, 1988), p. 42; and Wide World 10 (1823), in *Journals*, II, 115.

30. Emerson, recorded in Edward W. Emerson, "Notes" to *English Traits*, in vol. V of The Centenary Edition of *Works*, ed. E. W. Emerson (Boston, 1903), pp. 397–398; "Stonehenge," in *Essays and Lectures*, ed. Porte, p. 922; "Aristocracy," in *Works*, ed. Cabot, X, 40, 66; and "Aristocracy" in *Essays and Lectures*, ed. Porte, p. 872.

31. Emerson, "The Fortune of the Republic," in *Works*, ed. Cabot, XI, 400–401, 412, 407, 408, 410, 412, 417.

32. Emerson, "Historic Notes," in *Works*, ed. Cabot, X, 311, 318, 347.

33. Emerson, *Nature*, in *Essays and Lectures*, ed. Porte, p. 48; "The Fortune of the Republic," in *Works*, ed. Cabot, XI, 398, 399; and Journal CO (1851), in *Journals*, XI, 397–398.

34. Ivy Schweitzer, "Transcendental Sacramentals: 'The Lord's Supper' and Emerson's Doctrine of Form," *New England Quarterly*, LXI (1988), 416; Habermas, *The Philosophical Discourse of Modernity: Twelve Lectures*, trans. Frederick Lawrence (Cambridge, Mass., 1987), p. 39.

35. Habermas, *Philosophical Discourse*, p. 39; John Higham, *From Boundlessness to Consolidation: The Transformation of American Culture, 1848–1860* (Ann Arbor, Mich., 1969).

36. Raymond Williams, *Marxism and Literature* (Oxford, 1977), pp. 121–128; Fredric Jameson, *The Political Unconscious: Narrative as a Socially Symbolic Act* (Ithaca, N.Y., 1981), passim; Blumenberg, *Work on Myth*, trans. Robert Wallace (Cambridge, Mass., 1985), p. 221.

37. Emerson, "Self-Reliance," in *Essays and Lectures*, ed. Porte, pp. 262, 273.

38. Chapman, *Emerson and Other Essays* (New York, 1898), pp. 29, 106, 107–108.

39. Adorno, *Negative Dialectics*, trans. E. B. Ashton (New York, 1973), p. 226.

40. Emerson, Notebook F, no. 1 (1836–1840), in vol. XII of *Journals*, ed.

Linda Allardt (Cambridge, Mass., 1976), p. 153; and "Politics," in *Essays and Lectures*, ed. Porte, pp. 567–568.

41. Emerson, "Historic Notes," in *Works*, ed. Cabot, X, 335; Henry David Thoreau, "A Plea for Captain John Brown," in *Reform Papers*, ed. Wendell Glick (Princeton, 1972), p. 125; William Lloyd Garrison, "Fourth of July Address, 1829," and "No Union with Slaveholders" (1832), in *William Lloyd Garrison*, ed. George M. Fredrickson (Englewood Cliffs, N. J., 1968), pp. 11–22, 52–56, 141–142; Margaret Fuller Ossoli, *At Home and Abroad, or Things and Thoughts in America and Europe*, ed. A. B. Fuller (1856; rpt. Port Washington, N. Y., 1971), pp. 326–327.

42. Emerson, "Politics," in *Essays and Lectures*, ed. Porte, p. 559; William James, speech printed in the *Boston Evening Transcript*, May 25, 1903, p. 3, and *Pragmatism* (1907), quoted in Poirier, *The Renewal of Literature*, p. 178.

10. The Problem of Ideology in a Time of Dissensus

1. Matthiessen, *American Renaissance: Art and Expression in the Age of Emerson and Whitman* (Oxford, 1941), p. xv; "Address" to *The Literary History of the United States*, ed. Robert Spiller et al. (fourth edition, revised, New York, 1974), pp. xx-xxi.

2. G. R. Elton, *Reformation Europe, 1517–1559* (London, 1963), p. 52.

3. Smith, "Myth and Ideology in *Virgin Land*," in *Ideology and Classic American Literature*, ed. Sacvan Bercovitch and Myra Jehlen (Cambridge, 1986), p. 21.

4. Weber, *The Protestant Ethic and the Spirit of Capitalism* (1904–05), trans. Talcott Parsons (New York, 1958); Mannheim, *Ideology and Utopia: An Introduction to the Sociology of Knowledge* (1936), trans. Louis Wirth and Edward Shils (New York, 1946); Geertz, "Ideology as a Cultural System," in *The Interpretation of Cultures: Selected Essays* (New York, 1973), pp. 193–233.

5. Melville, *Moby-Dick*, in *Redburn, White-Jacket, Moby-Dick*, ed. G. Thomas Tanselle (Library of America: New York, 1983), p. 1021, and "Misgivings," in *Battle-Pieces and Aspects of the War*, ed. Sidney Kaplan (Amherst, Mass., 1972), p. 13.

6. Matthiessen, *American Renaissance*, p. ix.

7. Smith, Preface to Frederick Douglass, *My Bondage, My Freedom* (London, 1855), ed. William L. Andrews (Chicago, 1987), pp. 23, 17.

Index

411